modern clinic design

STRATEGIES FOR AN ERA OF CHANGE

EDITED BY

Christine Guzzo Vickery, Gary Nyberg, AND Douglas Whiteaker

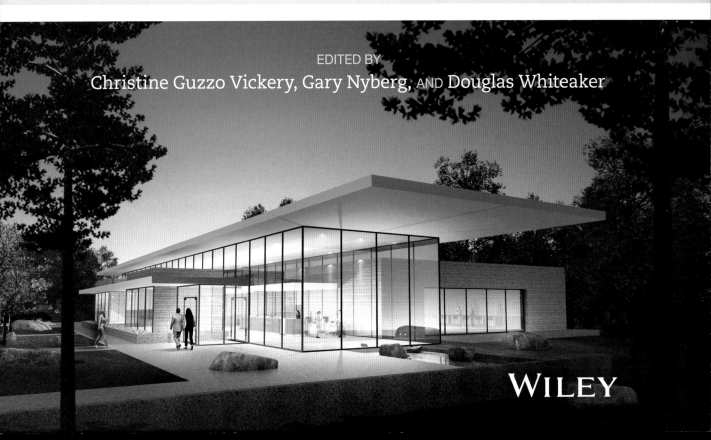

WILEY

Contents

Foreword

THIS BOOK IS ABOUT THE PRESENT, and more important, the future. Well over one billion outpatient visits occur annually in the United States, with the trend continuing to grow. These visits will occur in a variety of settings, from private physician offices to emergency departments. Although the current rate of growth has jumped, the shift from inpatient to outpatient care has been an ongoing worldwide phenomenon. A variety of factors have contributed to this shift:

- Medical advances in diagnostics, treatments, and medications that allow safe care outside the hospital environment.
- Political pressure to reduce healthcare expenditures for expensive inpatient care.
- Consumer expectations—the desire to get quick and convenient medical diagnosis and treatment.

Driven by the high costs, complexity, and safety issues, much of the research into healthcare architecture has focused on the hospital environment.. This book, in contrast, recognizes that a significant element of future healthcare will be ambulatory care. It is reasonable to assume that this building segment will become a major growth area over the next decade.

Healthcare architecture has historically combined innovation and adaptation. From the early Western medical use of temple and monastery models to the contemporary "patient-focused" care models, design philosophies have reflected the technical, functional, and cultural values of their times.

Modern Clinic Design: Strategies for an Era of Change provides an overview of current care concepts and their translation into design based on the use of analytical tools, case studies, and in-depth analysis of key planning concepts.

Clearly, the heart of ambulatory care is the exam room environment. This book provides a valuable discussion of the issues related to the design of this space, including the interplay between universality and unique care needs. Equally important is the emerging recognition that the environment can play an important role in supporting effective communications among care providers, patients, and their families. As is noted in the book, support for care of the elderly is becoming a significant issue in all areas of healthcare, presenting special patient considerations and, frequently, the need to include family in the examination experience. The integration of information technologies and mobile diagnostics will also shape the exam room environment, possibly creating divergent needs for comfort and functionality in the exam room of the future.

Over the past 50 years, since time-management techniques were first introduced to production processes, there has been the continuing desire to apply management tools to the overall healthcare delivery process and to design. The current interest in the "Lean" Toyota approach illustrates the melding of operations research tools and the participation of care providers in seeking the elimination of waste and process improvement. It is important to recognize that healthcare is not a product production process— we are not "manufacturing" healthcare in a context similar to the way in which automobiles are moved along an assembly line. Patients frequently present unique problems, both medically and culturally. The goal of standardization and reduction of variation must be seen in the context of providing effective, safe care. We can learn much from the current interest in Lean techniques, but our unique needs call for further evolution of management tools.

As an illustration, if we were focusing on the optimization of exam room resources, there would be an obvious desire to minimize scheduling, room time, and procedure variation. However, if we were focusing on a "patient-centered" experience, we might try to minimize patient travel and waiting, moving, additional diagnostics, counseling, and support tasks to the patient in the exam room, thereby introducing additional variation and lower overall room utilization.

Equally as important as inpatient care is the role that ambulatory care will play in the education of the next generation of providers. The historical use of the teaching hospital is changing. The design of "teaching clinics" will blend patient care with direct learning opportunities, group teaching, and research.

Modern Clinic Design: Strategies for an Era of Change illustrates several significant shifts in ambulatory care from traditional office environments to retail and home care models. It is reasonable to assume that advances in medical "bedside" analytics and high-speed Internet connectivity will allow components of outpatient care to be provided virtually. Current examples of these tools hold promise for a future in which patients will not have to spend time driving, parking, and waiting to get consultation and care for selected problems. This will include the impending wave of aging "boomers," who are much more computer savvy than earlier generations. We may see a new office component providing space to allow doctors and nurses to interview virtually, analyze home-transmitted data, and diagnose action. Can we adapt research from the business office experience into these settings to assure an effective work environment?

We must recognize that the design process is reflective—we gain knowledge as we proceed from planning to design, to construction. The ability to effectively manage the process requires sensitivity to the need to move quickly as well as the need to adjust and to provide time to absorb the new information emerging from the design process. Proper preparation is an important piece in supporting an effective process and minimizing restarts. *Modern Clinic Design* provides a valuable source of knowledge to planners, designers, providers, and administrators. It also serves as a valuable resource to students seeking to understand this important area of design.

The challenge for the next generation will be to use existing models as a springboard for future innovation, where needed, to respond to a healthcare world that will emphasize larger medical practice models, increased use of outpatient diagnostics and treatment, and a patient population diverse in demographics, culture, and levels of understanding

Frank Zilm, D.Arch, FAIA, FACHA
Chester Dean Lecturer on Healthcare Design
The University of Kansas School of Architecture, Planning, and Design

Preface

Opening the Dialogue on Clinic Design

THE NEED FOR A CLINIC BOOK has never been more relevant than now. The healthcare industry is undergoing major changes that are placing greater emphasis on cost-effective preventive care, wellness, and outpatient services. Healthcare organizations are reimagining their delivery methods with the constant evolution of new technology, changing reimbursements, and shifting demographics. Now more than ever, healthcare owners and designers need to collaborate to create flexible healthcare environments that support health and wellness—not just treat illness. The outpatient clinic will be a vital part of this changing healthcare landscape.

Modern Clinic Design: Strategies for an Era of Change leads healthcare owners, designers, and students through the clinic design process. Our goal is to share knowledge and expertise in the planning and design of successful clinics.

Knowledge sharing, in fact, is essential to our design approach. We have gained more than 50 years of healthcare planning and design experience since HGA Architects and Engineers was founded in 1953. During that time, our relationships with healthcare clients, design colleagues, students, and patients have evolved as we continue to learn from each other to create better and more efficient healthcare environments. *Modern Clinic Design* consolidates that collective industry-wide knowledge and reflects our commitment to both the healthcare industry and the design industry. The featured clinic plans and case studies are drawn from our research and experience, representing best approaches to different clinic modules—always with an eye on flexibility.

As with the design process, this book was a collaborative process in which we shared our individual expertise to write an informed clinic book. We pulled from our resources within HGA, but also reached out to healthcare owners, design colleagues, students, and patient user groups to research and write the book. We see *Modern Clinic Design* as an ongoing dialogue with you as we work toward a common goal to design exceptional clinics that improve the patient experience.

We are grateful to the many people who contributed to this book, from those who provided quantitative and qualitative research to those who offered insight through casual conversation. Thanks specifically to Frank Zilm, Brent Peterson, Amy Douma, Jennifer Romer, Len Kaiser, and Jennifer Klund for their contributions. We are particularly grateful to contributing author Heather Beal, whose enthusiasm and dedication as a writer and editor proved invaluable throughout the book's development.

We hope you find *Modern Clinic Design: Strategies for an Era of Change* helpful in planning a clinic. *Modern Clinic Design* simply opens the dialogue in what promises to be an exciting period in the healthcare industry.

CHRISTINE GUZZO VICKERY, CID, EDAC

GARY NYBERG, RA

DOUGLAS WHITEAKER, AIA

Understanding the Patient Experience

1

Overview

Healthcare design has been changing rapidly in recent years. In the past this movement generally focused on supporting the workflows of physicians, with patients viewed as the individuals who were receiving care rather than as active participants in their own health and wellness. The design of clinics reinforced this formal relationship in an institutional, monochromatic manner. As recently as the 1990s, white walls, rows of seating, and buzzing fluorescent light fixtures were the norm.

Since 1984, when Robert Ulrich published the landmark "View through a Window" study in *Science* magazine, interest in the relationship between design decisions and patient health outcomes has steadily grown. More than a thousand studies have now been completed in the field of evidence-based design, which the Center for Health Design defines as the "process of basing decisions about the built environment on credible research to achieve the best possible outcomes."

Five Stages of the Patient's Journey

A key strategy for approaching clinic design from the standpoint of patients is to envision what occurs at each step along the care continuum to determine how their experience can be enhanced by various aspects of the built environment. For years, design professionals have divided the patient's journey to, through, and away from a clinic into five stages: awareness, entry, assessment, treatment, and transition. These stages still provide a good basic structure for completing the research, planning, and design portions of a clinic project.

Awareness

The patient's journey begins with an awareness that he or she needs to seek care because of illness, injury, or need for routine appointments (e.g., an annual physical). Patients now have a variety of tools and resources to help them evaluate when they can address a condition through self-care and when they need to be examined by a healthcare professional in person.

Today, most clinics use the telephone, e-mail, printed postcards, letters, or text messages to remind patients that they should schedule a clinic visit to obtain preventative care services. When patients are not sure of what level and type of care they need or where this should be provided, they can use resources provided by insurance companies and healthcare organization, such as:

- **Phone triage:** patients can call a phone number anytime day or night, during the week or on weekends, to discuss symptoms and other health concerns with a healthcare professional and obtain advice. The nurse or other care provider determines how serious patients' health issues are and guides them to appropriate care.

- **Online chats and websites:** Some organizations that provide nurse-line or other phone triage services also offer the option of "chatting" with a healthcare professional online in real time. For example, in addition to calling Optum-Health's NurseLine, patients who are covered by the UPlan Medical Program can gain access via phone to Optum's library of prerecorded health messages or chat online with a nurse who can display web pages and recommend other resources as the discussion progresses.

- **E-visits and consults:** Some insurers have begun to reimburse clinics that provide certain examination and consultation services via the phone or a video connection. For example, Blue Cross and Blue Shield of Minnesota offers patients the option of interacting live with a doctor who discusses symptoms, provides a diagnosis, and, if needed, can prescribe medications for a limited range of health conditions, such as coughs, colds, flu, headaches, bronchitis, stomach aches, allergies, and sinus problems, as well as ear, eye, and urinary tract infections.

Entry

Orientation, shading, fenestration, location, and design of the reception/check-in area and wayfinding can all influence how comfortable patients feel as they approach and enter a clinic.

Orientation

Design professionals must take the climate and site conditions, natural and built environment, and connections to the community into account when determining the ideal orientation for a clinic's main public entry.

For example, the main entry to the Innovis Health Facility in Fargo, North Dakota, faces northwest in a northern climate. Although this orientation was necessary to relate the main entry to existing thoroughfares, it made keeping the cold air out of the entry atrium and adjacent areas during the winter a challenge. The architects responded by designing a long entry corridor with a side entrance that places exterior entry doors 60 feet away from the lobby.

Shading and Fenestration

Patients approaching the main entry can be set at ease when they can observe the activities that occur within a building. People who have entered the clinic can also use views through windows to identify interior and exterior landmarks that they can use to orient themselves as they plot a path to a specific destination.

■ NATALIE OFFICE BUILDING
Tulsa, Oklahoma

The grand roof forms crowning a four-story atrium of this healthcare complex clearly announce the location of the main entry while providing shade for the tall glass curtain walls. The shading helps mitigate heat gain in a warm climate, while the glazing optimizes views. A canopy extends over the vehicular arrival and departure area to provide additional shelter from the elements and highlight the specific location of the entry doors (fig. 1-1).

Reception and Check-in

Since the reception and check-in area is usually the first place where face-to-face interaction with staff occurs, it should be easy to find and be welcoming so that patients can efficiently and comfortably provide identification and insurance information, update health history data, pay required fees, and submit any diagnostic or lab test results that care providers need to review in advance of an exam. Since reception and check-in areas are highly trafficked, finishes and furnishings should also be durable and easy to maintain.

Clinic reception desks are typically located near the facility's main entry and patient drop-off area—and, ideally, have access to natural light and exterior views. Reception or check-in desks for specialized clinics can also be located near subentries or near elevator banks within a healthcare complex or medical office building.

Design professionals consider the proximity of the reception desk to seating in main lobbies or subwaiting rooms because patients generally prefer to sit where they can easily hear their name when it is called. Since patients do not like to have to cross high-traffic circulation paths, design professionals also address the relationship of the reception desk to entry and exit paths from the clinic's examination room area.

FIGURE 1-1: Natalie Office Building, Tulsa, Oklahoma. Clustered organic-shaped canopies and decorative metal support structures were designed to replicate trees. The shading from these canopies acts as a sunscreen for the glass and provides weather protection at the main entry. Additionally, the graceful canopies aid in wayfinding by clearly delineating the main building entry. Photography © by Gary Zvonkovic

■ APPLE TREE DENTAL
Minneapolis, Minnesota

This nonprofit dental healthcare organization strives to create a clinical setting that conveys a respect for the patient's time while being relaxing and calming to the senses. The patient experience begins with listening and answering questions. Patients pass through the main entry into a waiting area that has been designed with richly colored walnut veneer accents and comfortable lounge chairs and is flooded with natural light.

Those coming for an appointment are met by a greeter who is familiar with the personal preferences and health history of each patient. All check-in and checkout processes are completed in enclosed "navigation rooms." This allows a patient and dental professional to privately discuss any health concerns, customize treatment to meet the patient's specific needs, discuss insurance coverage and payment plans, and review the postclinic care plan. A toothbrushing station is also provided for patients who would like to use this before a checkup or procedure (fig. 1-2).

Assessment

Once patients decide to be examined in person by a healthcare professional, they must choose which clinic to visit. Patients with insurance typically start by checking to see if a clinic is within an approved network of providers, while those who are underinsured or uninsured often seek care at safety-net clinics that have a mission or legal mandate to provide healthcare services regardless of individuals' ability to pay.

Several qualities of the built environment also shape patients, decisions about where to seek care. These include: convenience, ease of access, visibility, and connections to the community. Medical practices consider these same factors when analyzing and selecting the ideal location for a clinic.

Convenience clinics are now located in a wide variety of places in order to provide convenience for patients. For example, primary care clinics are typically located in or near residential

STAFF / NAVIGATOR ZONE   CLINICAL ZONE   STAFF / SUPPORT ZONE   CLINICAL ZONE

FIGURE 1-2: Plan of Apple Tree Dental, Mounds View, Minnesota. Apple Tree Dental greeters meet patients as they enter the clinic and are taken to a private room, where all check-in processes are handled by the patient's navigator in private rather than at a public reception desk. The goal for Apple Tree is to make sure clients feel that they are given respect, that their needs and concerns are heard, and that they are treated as individuals. Image courtesy of Hammel, Green and Abrahamson, Inc.

neighborhoods or along regularly traveled routes so that patients can schedule appointments on their way to work or in conjunction with other activities. Locations range from office buildings and mixed-use developments to strip malls, shopping centers, and community crossroads. Major drugstore and discount retail chains are partnering with healthcare organizations to provide services on a drop-in basis. These "convenience care clinics" are expected to become even more common as demand continues to grow for the preventative care services they provide (flu shots, for example).

Specialty clinics provide a different kind of convenience. They tend to be located near major highway intersections in suburban and rural areas so that patients from across a region can easily reach them; or they are located in densely populated urban areas where multimodal forms of transportation are available. This structure has been referred to as the "hub and spoke model," with primary care delivered along the spokes and specialized care at major hubs.

Ease of Access

Since patients who visit a clinic are often ill, injured, or otherwise debilitated, the last thing they want to do is to spend time figuring out how to locate a clinic, find a parking space, use mass transit, or simply enter and exit the site. Key questions planning and design professionals ask to make sure a clinic provides convenient and efficient access include:

- How many patients will this clinic serve now and in the future? When there are major shifts predicted, it is especially valuable to review current and projected demographic data about the patient population and community a clinic will serve.

- What hours will it be open?

- How will it be staffed?

- How will most people travel to the clinic? For example, if patients and staff can reach a clinic located in an urban area by walking, biking, or using mass transit, this typically reduces the amount of parking (surface or covered) that is required.

- Is the site large enough to accommodate the required amount of parking? Ideally, free, secure, and abundant parking should be provided near the clinic's main entry because parking-related issues can amplify patients' anxiety levels before they even enter a facility.

- Can vehicular access be provided via familiar routes or major thoroughfares or highways?

- Will this facility provide primary care, serve as a satellite clinic for a larger healthcare organization, or be a regional hub that provides a diverse range of services?

■ WHITTIER CLINIC
Minneapolis, Minnesota

This satellite clinic for the Hennepin County Medical Center (HCMC) is located in a densely populated urban area just over two miles away from HCMC's downtown healthcare campus. Since it was to be constructed on a former industrial site on the gritty, underdeveloped end of one of Minneapolis' historic thoroughfares, the clinic's architecture needed to be distinctive enough to make it easy to locate and memorable. The design accomplishes these objectives by featuring a dynamic façade that mixes metal, masonry, and glass with colorful accents to reference the industrial history of the site, reflect the character of the surrounding neighborhood, and creatively incorporate the hues of HCMC's logo.

Landscape architects on the project team addressed the fact that many patients reach this clinic by walking, biking, or using mass transit by including a public plaza near the primary entry that has planters that function as both seats and walls. This area of the site provides a partially sheltered, outdoor place where patients can wait if they arrive early for a clinic appointment, and it supplies overflow seating for the transit stop adjacent to the plaza (fig. 1-3).

Visibility

Design professionals blend architecture, branding, exterior lighting, and landscaping to ensure that a clinic's visibility makes it easy for patients to find and distinct enough for them to remember it.

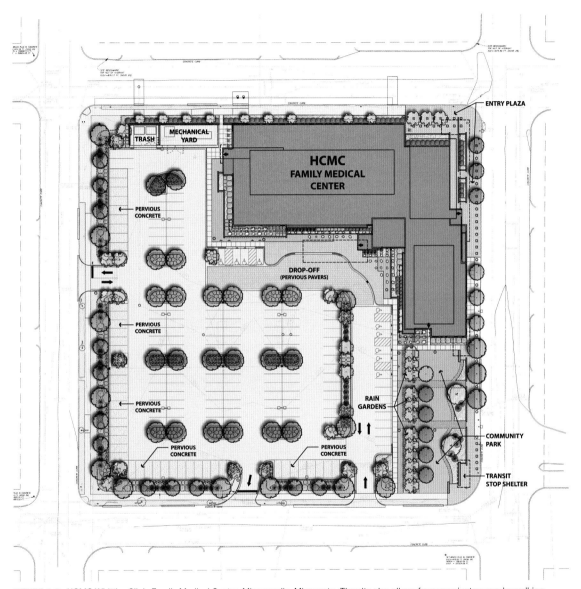

FIGURE 1-3: HCMC Whittier Clinic Family Medical Center, Minneapolis, Minnesota. The site plan allows for convenient access by walking, biking, mass transit, or automobile. Image courtesy of Hammel, Green and Abrahamson, Inc.

Architecture

Many aspects of a clinic's design provide opportunities to express how its mission, vision, values, the type of services it provides and care delivery model make it unique. Decisions about architectural forms, materials, and style; interior layout, finishes, and furnishings; and landscaping and site amenities can all help to distinguish a clinic in the marketplace, and, most importantly from the patient's perspective, to build comfort through familiarity.

■ OWATONNA HEALTHCARE CAMPUS
Owatonna, Minnesota

This healthcare campus, which was built as a collaboration of Allina Health and the Mayo Clinic Health System, is on a site located along a major highway, where it can easily be seen from a distance. Access is provided via well-marked highway exits, frontage roads, and a county road that connects the clinic and hospital directly to the town of Owatonna. Colocating their facilities made it possible for Allina and Mayo to merge some departments so that patients no longer have to go to multiple locations for lab tests or diagnostic imaging, to see a specialist, or to undergo surgery.

Branding

Applying brand standards does not mean that clinics that are part of a health system have to be identical. Context, climatic conditions, geographic location, size, the range and type of services provided, and the demographic characteristics of a clinic's patient population can strongly influence decisions about which aspects of a brand program are appropriate for a particular medical practice located in a specific community. Design professionals often develop an architectural and interior design palette

that provides the staff at individual clinics with a range of choices that all fall within a larger healthcare network's corporate identity system.

■ ALTRU HEALTH SYSTEM
Grand Forks, North Dakota

As part of the master plan for updating Altru's existing health centers, design professionals developed a series of graphic icons to create visual interest, aid with wayfinding, and convey Altru's emphasis on health, wellness, service, respect, and dignity. Designers drew their inspiration from the natural surroundings of Grand Forks, North Dakota, where the Altru Health System is headquartered, and selected images

FIGURE 1-4: Altru Health System, Devils Lake, North Dakota. The cattail icon used here indicates a department entry. Departments are labeled by icon for ease in wayfinding. Information desk personnel direct patients to department entries by giving them the name of the icon associated with the department. Photography by Paul Crosby

that are familiar and comforting for patients and their families. The final set of icons includes:

- **Water,** which is an integral part of the community and serves as a source of life, energy, and vitality.
- **Flax,** which is a primary crop in the area and is well known for its health benefits.
- **The sunflower,** which represents growth and from which oil and seeds that offer health benefits can also be produced. Its vibrant yellow color also suggests joy and sunshine.
- **Wheat,** which evokes prosperity, health, and wellness because it is a major contributor to the local economy.

- **Cattails,** which grow naturally along fertile wetlands and are reminiscent of nature in its purest sense.
- **Wildflowers,** which bloom from the spring through the fall and communicate the natural changes in the landscape.

These icons are used on both the exterior and interior of Altru facilities and served as a springboard for developing design standards, which were implemented in two clinics that were completed in 2012. For example, a canopy is used to announce the main entrance at each clinic, with signage and graphics used to distinguish various spaces within each building (figs. 1-4, 1-5).

FIGURE 1-5: Altru Health System. The Altru Devils Lake Clinic is the first clinic to be built in 10 years for a growing system in North Dakota. The goal for this owner was to develop a consistent brand, quality level of care, and common imagery across multiple campuses. The broad expanse of glass is used as a wayfinding device; the colors of the brick and precast concrete are found in the surrounding natural environment. Photography by Paul Crosby

Exterior Lighting

A clinic's visibility can be heightened and its architecture and landscaping enhanced by exterior lighting that creates smooth transitions between the site, the building, and surrounding areas. The two most common strategies design professionals employ are uplighting and downlighting.

Uplighting can make a clinic appear inviting by accentuating key architectural forms and features or certain aspects of landscaped areas (trees, for example). Design professionals often use uplighting to expand the sense of space under a canopy. If the canopy has a lighter finish than the ground covering, uplighting can further brighten the entry area by bouncing light off of the canopy's surfaces.

It can, however, be difficult to conceal light fixtures that are part of an uplighting design. Thus lighting designers not only select fixtures that blend with the architecture and landscaping, but also verify that these can be mounted in locations where they achieve the desired effect yet avoid creating glare.

In contrast, downlighting is typically used to illuminate ground, sidewalk, and street surfaces. It is better for defining and drawing attention to pathways, landscaped areas, and certain site features, such as outdoor seating areas (fig 1-6).

FIGURE 1-6: Encircle Health Ambulatory Care Center, ThedaCare Health System, Appleton, Wisconsin. Natural daylight, warm wood tones, and varied light sources create comfortable and inviting waiting spaces in this ambulatory care center (ACC). Throughout, regional architecture, artwork, and materials inform the interior and exterior detailing. From stone used on the building exterior and surrounding the elevator banks to terrazzo tile floors with aggregate from the Wisconsin River, a dialogue exists between exterior context and interior design. See figure 2-3 for interior image of Encircle Health. Photography by Michael Leschisin, Image Studios, Inc.

Landscaping

The layout, grading, plantings, hardscape areas, exterior furnishings, and other aspects of a site's design can help create a positive experience for patients, their visitors, staff, and members of the community who live and work near a clinic.

Landscape architects work with architects, civil and structural engineers, interior designers, and lighting designers to understand what the overarching design concept for a clinic is and then determine how landscaping can contribute to achieving a unified, harmonious design (fig. 1-7). They accomplish this by:

- Assessing a site's development potential by reviewing information about its topography, hydrology, flora, fauna, geology, and climate.

- Collaborating with other design team members to identify which areas of a site are optimal for development to help determine where a building should be placed and oriented.

- Sharing their knowledge about the meanings and emotions associated with various plant materials. For example, evergreens project life, deciduous trees with canopies create a sense of shelter, and indigenous plants supply comfort through familiarity.

- Considering how plantings and other landscaping materials will look during different seasons, which ones are indigenous plants, and what the scale of plants will be as they mature. Flowering plants bring joy and life during the spring and summer months. Fall colors can enliven a landscape when the

FIGURE 1-7: Froedtert Health, Milwaukee, Wisconsin. This sketch was generated as an initial concept to illustrate landscape design in relationship to adjacent architecture. In a healthcare environment, the landscape architect works to create spaces that promote a positive experience for patients, visitors, staff, and the community, while bringing nature within reach and providing a warm, welcoming, and healing environment. Image courtesy of Hammel, Green and Abrahamson, Inc.

leaves of trees or other plants are transformed by cooler weather. Evergreens not only retain their color year-round but can also be quite beautiful during the winter, when their branches hold the freshly fallen snow.

- Addressing climatic conditions. For example, in regions with extreme weather, patients and other clinic occupants should have access to views of attractive landscapes from the inside of a clinic.

- Using trees, plantings, and outdoor structures to create microclimates that provide shade during the summer or that allow the sun to supply warmth in the spring and fall, when the weather is typically cool.

ST. LUKE'S HEALTHCARE CAMPUS
The Woodlands, Texas

The vision for this campus, which is located in the hill country north of Houston, Texas, was to establish a community medical center that would carry the St Luke's brand of quality care to a rapidly growing population at a convenient and easily accessible location. The architecture evokes the vernacular forms, warm colors, and local materials used throughout this region of the state. The buildings feature metal or wood-shingle roofs, large porches, and native materials such as limestone and cedar. Loggia, landscaped terraces, and public concourses provide optimal views of the site (fig. 1-8).

Connections to the Community

Clinics can heighten patient awareness of their location and the type of services they offer by creatively connecting with their communities. Some clinics do this by including group-visit or education rooms that extend the services of a facility beyond treating patients to positively affecting the health of the community. For

example, local residents may be able to attend Alcoholics Anonymous meetings, smoking-cessation classes, yoga, prenatal care, or diabetes training sessions.

Design professionals also seek ways to use building forms, materials, and other details to express the values and aspirations of the city, suburb, town, or greater geographic region in which a clinic is located.

ORANGE CITY HOSPITAL AND CLINIC (OCHC)
Orange City, Iowa

This replacement healthcare facility serves a community in which the residents' Dutch heritage and traditional values are part of daily life. The connection of the clinic to this area's history and to the rural landscape is expressed by the use of natural materials, the introduction of sunlight throughout interior spaces, and the provision of exterior views from multiple locations (fig. 1-9).

FIGURE 1-8: St. Luke's Healthcare Campus, The Woodlands, Texas. The architectural design evokes the vernacular forms and local materials used throughout this region of Texas. The use of familiar materials gives patients and families a sense of community embrace and comfort. Photography © by Gary Zvonkovic

FIGURE 1-9: Orange City Hospital and Clinic, Orange City, Iowa. Designers used warm woods, a nature-based color palette, and stone to reinforce a sense of familiarity for patients and family visiting the facility. Lobby paintings inspired by aerial views of the surrounding landscape were created by a local artist and underline the strong sense of community in Orange City.   Photography © by Dana Wheelock

■ FAIRVIEW MEDICAL CENTER
Maple Grove, Minnesota

The goal of this facility was to effectively and efficiently provide residents of an affluent, fast-growing Twin Cities suburb with leading-edge academic- and community-based healthcare provided by the three project partners: the University of Minnesota, University of Minnesota Physicians (UMP), and Fairview Health Services. This 138,605-square-foot building is located next to the Elm Creek Park Reserve, which features wetlands and more than 20 miles of trails. Thus, a major design challenge was to create a visual balance between the facility's built and natural surroundings.

Design professionals tied the building to its surroundings by selecting local split-faced limestone for some of the exterior walls. These anchor the building to the ground, create a transition from the built environment to the natural surroundings, and recall the site's agrarian heritage. Public spaces are oriented toward the natural views (figs. 1-10, 1-11).

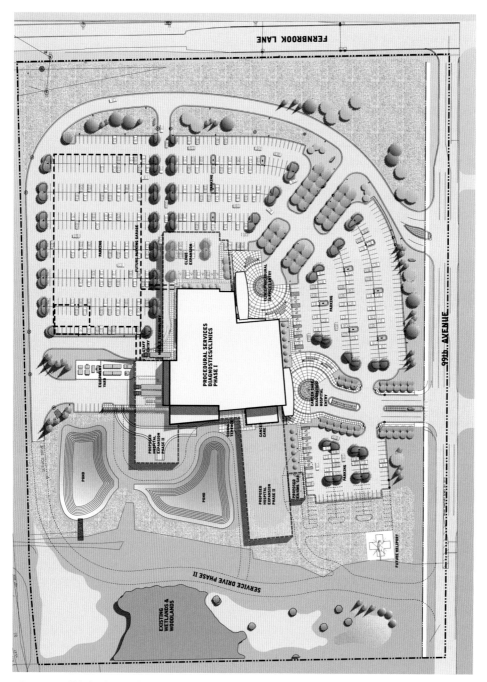

FIGURE 1-10: Fairview Medical Center, Maple Grove, Minnesota. Fairview Medical Center is strategically located on the site to overlook the wetlands and the natural habitat. Image courtesy of Hammel, Green and Abrahamson, Inc.

Treatment

Although chapter 4, "Designing for Flexibility," and chapter 6, "The Exam Room Today," address the design of clinic treatment spaces in detail, a new trend has been for healthcare services to flow toward the patient rather than having patients move from one department to another within a clinic, between buildings in a medical complex, or to and from primary care and specialized care facilities.

These "point-of-care" and consolidation strategies strive to improve patient safety by reducing the risk of injuries that can occur when a patient moves between various locations and by minimizing medical errors that are more apt to occur when information is lost or miscommunicated along the way. Offering a range of coordinated services in a single facility and bringing services to the patient typically reduces patient anxiety as well, and physically reinforces a clinic's commitment to "patient-centric" care.

The shift in focus from treating diseases and injuries to promoting wellness has also had an impact on the design of clinics because patients are expected to take an active role in caring for their health outside of the clinic. In addition to more space being allocated for consultations in

FIGURE 1-11: Fairview Medical Center, Maple Grove, Minnesota. Located within the medical center is the Children's Specialty Clinic. The pattern of floor tile was designed to create the appearance of a pond with fish and other native creatures. Grasses imbedded in glass and lighting designed to replicate bugs are a nod to the Elm Creek Watershed and County Park trail system bordering the clinic site.   Photography © by Dana Wheelock

and around treatment (exam) rooms, the demand for educational resources, space, and programs has increased.

Waiting rooms in some clinics are now being designed to serve as "information grounds" where patients and those accompanying them can informally share knowledge, experience, and emotional support. This can help to alleviate stress for patients who have chronic conditions or extended-care regimes. Design professionals consider the size of the waiting room, the seating layout, and the location and display of information resources to create information grounds that work well. If the waiting room is too large or patients are seated formally or too far away from each other, they are less likely to feel comfortable conversing.

It is also challenging to balance some patients' desire for social interaction while still providing private places for others who want to rest, read, reflect, or divert their attention from the stress of an illness or injury until they advance to the treatment areas of the clinic.

◼ HAZELDEN IN PLYMOUTH, A PART OF THE HAZELDEN BETTY FORD FOUNDATION
Plymouth, Minnesota

Three decades after opening this treatment center to help youth, young adults, and their families recover from addiction and transform their lives, Hazelden decided to renovate and expand the existing buildings to meet growing needs.

Design-team members began by observing patient and family group sessions and surveying staff, alumni, and parents to gain insight into the challenges that patients (ages 12 to 25) and their families faced. The resulting design blends richly hued colors and natural materials with thoughtful decisions about lighting, building forms, and landscaping to create a soothing, psychologically healing environment.

The remodeled main entrance and admission area now includes three individual waiting rooms to provide privacy for families during the especially emotional time when a patient is being admitted to a treatment program. A separate public waiting room overlooks the healing garden. This room can also be used for outpatient family and group therapy sessions.

Since Hazelden values the positive role that family members can play in supporting a patient's recovery and lasting wellness, the newly constructed building areas include rooms for group therapy sessions, lectures, and counseling. Landscaped exterior spaces now include a labyrinth, a healing garden, and an amphitheater with a fire pit. The former porte cochere is being converted into a dining terrace (fig. 1-12).

Transition

In the past, the transition period that followed completion of an examination was typically kept as short as possible so that clinics could maximize throughput. The more services they could provide for patients within a set period of time, the higher their compensation.

As reimbursement structures continue to shift toward compensating healthcare professionals based on patient health outcomes, doctors and nurses are taking more time to equip patients with the information they need to recover their health, maintain wellness, better manage chronic conditions, and achieve the quality of life they desire. This has led to a general increase in the amount of space needed for educational and consultation purposes while reducing or eliminating the need for checkout stations in clinics when this task is completed in an exam or consult room.

Checkout

When a checkout station is preferred, its location and design characteristics strongly influence the likelihood that patients will stop to complete crucial tasks at the end of their clinic visit. If they cannot easily determine where to check out, are concerned about privacy, or are left waiting too long, patients are likely to leave the clinic without formally checking out.

Healthcare organizations are taking it more seriously when patients skip this step because more of them are being paid for "episodes of care." Thus, they are not reimbursed for unnecessary return visits to the clinic. In short, there is new incentive to help patients fully understand how they can recover and remain healthy outside of the clinic.

These factors have amplified the importance of designing spaces where patients can promptly, efficiently, and thoroughly complete checkout tasks. General guidelines design professionals use to accomplish this goal include:

- Locate checkout areas in convenient places, such as on the path that connects exam rooms to the lobby, so that patients can easily find them as they retrace their steps and leave the clinic through a main entrance.

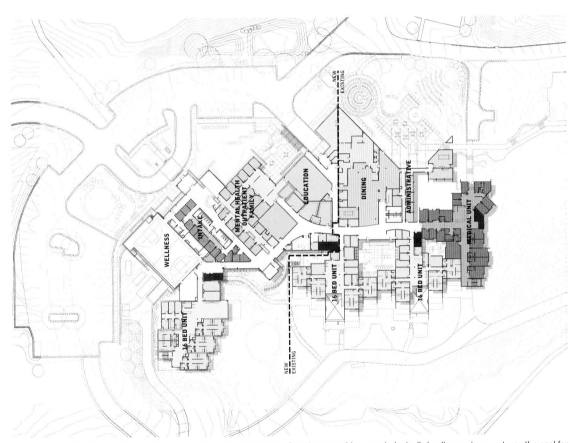

FIGURE 1-12: Hazelden Betty Ford Foundation, Plymouth, Minnesota. Creating a soothing, psychologically healing environment was the goal for the renovation and expansion of Hazelden in Plymouth. Providing ample space for privacy by dividing the main waiting space into three smaller spaces, providing views to healing gardens from within the waiting room, and giving access to the gardens on the exterior are a few of the enhancements made to improve the patient and family experience. Image courtesy of Hammel, Green and Abrahamson, Inc.

- Coordinate architectural forms, interior finishes and furnishings, and signage and lighting so that these work together to clearly communicate where checkout spaces or rooms are located. For example, a custom-designed checkout desk with pendant lights or sconces, changes in ceiling heights, floor patterns, and colors or textures of interior finishes can all be used to accentuate a checkout station.

- Select comfortable furnishings and allocate sufficient space to accommodate patients of varying sizes and physical abilities. Desks or work surfaces can allow staff and patients to remain standing or to be seated, with at least one section being wheelchair accessible.

The following examples of checkout locations illustrate the challenges of balancing convenience, privacy, operating costs, and comfort to achieve a checkout space that contributes to a positive patient experience.

The Loop

The most common location for checkout is on the exam room side of the reception desk. This requires patients to circle back toward the main reception and entrance areas. Since confidential health information is being exchanged, design professionals pay particular attention to achieving visual and acoustical privacy from the more public reception area on the opposite side of this multipurpose staff workstation.

The most private option is to provide a checkout room or space that can be visually and acoustically separated from other clinic areas when a door is closed. Printers can either be located in each checkout room or in a shared space accessible only to staff.

A checkout area can also be created by locating this function at the end of a reception desk that is farthest from public use areas and telephones so that conversations cannot be overheard. At a minimum, installing acoustic panels between the checkout area and the public and staff work areas can provide basic visual and acoustical privacy.

Designated Areas

Some clinics prefer to have a designated checkout room or alcove near an entry or exit. This option is better for people who are wearing gauze, are pale or weak after a treatment or minor procedure, or who do not want to walk back through the public waiting room for other reasons. Visual and acoustical privacy can still be achieved if the corridor connecting the exam room area to the exit has some sound absorption qualities and if an alcove is not directly adjacent to or across from staff work areas or exam rooms.

Exam Room Checkout

Many clinics complete checkout and rescheduling tasks in exam rooms to provide a high level of acoustic and visual privacy. The tradeoff is that spending more time in the exam room to accomplish these tasks can require that there be more exam rooms per physician.

Most exam rooms are equipped with work surfaces, seating, and a computer, which make it easy for clinicians to discuss care plans, review patient health records and related educational materials, issue prescriptions, and schedule follow-up appointments.

As clinics continue to stress the importance of patients adhering to visit care plans after they leave the clinic, new needs for specialized spaces have arisen, such as those used by health coaches and telehealth personnel. For example, the follow-up activities of most clinics have increased. It is now a matter of routine for clinics to determine what a patient's preferred mode of communication is for receiving appointment reminders or for checking in with a doctor, nurse, or health coach, who can help them monitor and manage their health.

In addition to receiving a phone call to remind them about an appointment, patients can sign up to receive newsletters, information about incentive programs that promote wellness, and announcements about research results or discoveries related to their specific health condition. This information can be sent via direct mail, e-mail, or text-messaging.

Patients can also obtain information from websites or blogs (or through software applications) that can help them make informed health and lifestyle choices. Social media groups are now connecting patients who have similar conditions or health concerns. Healthcare organizations and insurers can also make password-protected websites available to their patients to enable them to see test results, schedule appointments, or review the steps they need to complete before arriving at a clinic for an exam, treatment, or minor procedure. Decisions about how to use technology to save resources and staff time can have a major impact on clinic design.

■ HEALTHEAST SPINE CLINIC
Maplewood, Minnesota

The design of this clinic focuses on the patient's journey toward wellness. Members of the research and design team began with value-stream mapping, physical mock-ups, and large group integration events to draw upon all staff perspectives. Based on this preliminary research, it became clear that in order for the multidisciplinary teams to collaboratively address the unique health issues and needs of each patient, the physical therapy and consultation spaces, as well as exam and procedure rooms, needed to be in close proximity to each other. The clinic's layout is zoned into public and patient areas with a "backstage" collaborative

work space to support and enhance this care delivery model (fig. 1-13).

■ HAZELDEN BETTY FORD FOUNDATION
Center City, Minnesota

The Hazelden Betty Ford Foundation is one of the world's largest and most-respected private nonprofit alcohol and drug addiction treatment organizations. In 2013, it won the White House Behavioral Health Patient Empowerment Challenge Award for its "Mobile MORE Field Guide to Life" software application, developed to help patients manage their recovery and health once they leave a treatment center. The app is based on Hazelden's MORE website (My Ongoing Recovery Experience), which offers personalized continuing care.

Methods of Discovery and Evaluation

Initially, holding focus group sessions was the favored methodology for "hearing the voice of the patient." However, over the years there has been a shift toward healthcare and design professionals observing and surveying patients while they are still in the clinic setting. Examples of research methods used to learn which specific aspects of a clinic's design and healthcare delivery processes matter most to patients include content analysis, photo journaling, interviews and surveys, and shadowing.

Some healthcare organizations are also using research strategies that are similar to those used in the retail and hospitality industries. For example, Holy Redeemer Health System, with multiple locations in and near Philadelphia, Pennsylvania, uses "mystery shoppers," who act like patients and are then surveyed about their experience to establish a baseline for other forms of discovery and evaluation.

FIGURE 1-13: HealthEast Spine Clinic, Maplewood, Minnesota. The clinic was designed so that the physical therapy, consultation, exam, and procedure rooms were close to each other. Being close to one another allows for easier collaboration among multidisciplinary teams. Image courtesy of Hammel, Green and Abrahamson, Inc.

Content Analysis

This includes reviewing marketing and communications materials (print, broadcast, and interactive), patient educational information, and other items provided by a clinic's owner that address its mission, core values, care philosophy and processes, range of services, patient population statistics, and performance goals and achievements.

Photo Journaling

This research method combines photography and note-taking. Design professionals equip patients and clinic staff with cameras and ask them to take photos of spaces, objects, or aspects of a clinic's design and operations that enhance or detract from the patient experience. For this method to be effective:

- The photos should present insights about the functionality of the environment or symbolize the significance of a process or experience, whether good or bad.

- Once photos have been captured, patients and staff should provide written notes—journal entries—describing the significance of each image.

- The photos should represent experiences of the five senses that either work well and contribute to positive patient satisfaction levels or create frustration and inefficiencies.

- To respect patient privacy, no pictures of patients or documentation related to patient information should be taken.

This is a qualitative method that captures user perspectives in a fun and engaging manner. However, it can be challenging to draw broad conclusions because of the variety of information that might be received.

Interviews and Surveys

As the provision of care continues to shift from hospitals to clinics, a number of states and healthcare organizations are using basic parts of the Clinician and Group Consumer Assessment of Healthcare Providers and Systems (CGCAHPS) survey to develop their own research tools for collecting data about the patient experience. For example, Minnesota Community Measurement, an independent nonprofit organization, has established a survey tool, database, and related website that patients can use to search for and compare clinics by name, city or zip code—or by how often they provided care that led to the best results for a specific condition.

Patient perception and experience surveys can be conducted through the mail, over the Internet, or by researchers who interview patients (and staff) in person. The questionnaires combine open- and closed-end questions to obtain qualitative and quantitative results. Some directly address aspects of the built environment, such as cleanliness, waiting time, wayfinding, privacy, comfort, and safety.

Shadowing

Shadowing is a research tool that healthcare organizations and design professionals use to observe:

- Patients' behavior and interactions with people, products, and processes in situ rather than in a controlled environment.

- Real-time situations in order to collect both quantitative and qualitative data.

- How different users (patients, visitors, doctors, nurses, and so on) interact with each other and with clinic spaces.

- A specific process, task, or cycle time.

- An individual's behavior over a designated period of time.

It is important to develop an appropriate shadow log to record tasks performed, time spent, travel paths, and other details. Types of information that could be recorded include frequency and sources of interruptions, workflow processes, time spent in specific areas, cycle times, wayfinding challenges, travel distances and patterns, wasteful practices, and repetitive activities.

Since it can be challenging to capture all activities accurately, an important first step is to define the information that is needed to address a specific design challenge. Conducting a pilot test of the log will provide the opportunity to make any necessary adjustments prior to completing the full shadowing study.

To avoid interfering with the natural behaviors of the individuals they are shadowing, observers should remain 5 to 10 feet away from them and not speak to them.

To protect patient privacy, observers should not enter private exam rooms, consultation rooms, or procedure rooms and should not eavesdrop on conversations.

A major benefit of shadowing is that researchers often notice details that patients or staff may overlook or inadvertently omit during an interview or while completing a survey.

A Day in the Life

This method combines shadowing and interviewing. A researcher shadows a patient and takes notes based on observations. In some instances, the patient may also be asked to record answers to specific questions at different intervals throughout a clinic visit. Shortly after the "day experience," patients are interviewed. This method can reduce recall distortion and overcome ideological biases that may occur when surveys or interviews are the only tools used to collect data.

Limiting Factors

A number of factors can limit reliable access to the patient's perspective or the usefulness of information that is gathered. For example, the privacy rule of the Health Insurance Portability and Accountability Act of 1996 (HIPAA) protects the confidentiality of all "individually identifiable health information" held or transmitted by clinics in any form or media—electronic, paper, or oral.

Communications vehicles and reports that healthcare organizations provide for a content analysis are often "sanitized' before they are published and distributed or otherwise shared with people outside of the clinic.

Shadowing, interviewing, or surveying patients can make them aware that their actions and statements count. This can bias their responses and skew the research results. It can also be difficult to determine how much time needs to be spent shadowing patients to collect

enough data to accurately represent the needs and preferences of a patient population. It is not sufficient to base assumptions on a single shadowing event. To broaden the validity of the results, data should be collected from several individuals at varying times of the day on different days of the week. Thus, while shadowing is an informative and versatile tool, it can be quite time-consuming to collect and analyze the data.

■ SSM HEALTH CARE, SAINT CLARE HEALTH CENTER
Fenton, Missouri

This replacement healthcare campus was planned and designed to accommodate a patient population increase of nearly 50 percent that was occurring along the fast-growing Interstate 44 corridor outside of St. Louis. Design professionals and the owner (SSM Health Care) began the planning and design process by reimagining the care delivery process.

This entailed conducting a series of interactive workshops with SSM's leadership, healthcare professionals and support staff, and user groups to obtain their input about what constitutes an ideal patient environment. The design team then employed photo journaling, staff-patient shadowing, targeted interviews, and brainstorming techniques to map the actual patient experience, streamline work processes, eliminate waste, and increase efficiency. Through this process, the design team helped SSM determine how to achieve a high-quality built environment that promotes the provision of accessible, safe, affordable, quality healthcare services.

Trends

The major trend affecting the patient experience in recent years has been the movement from the Era of Episodic Care, which focused on treating diseases and injuries, toward the Era of

Continuous Care, which emphasizes preventing these ailments and optimizing patients' health throughout all life stages. Phased implementation of the Affordable Care Act and advances in technology have contributed to this evolution, while demographic factors have intensified the need for it to occur.

Technology

The rapid rate of technological advancement that began in the 1970s and has gained momentum over the years continues to transform the patient experience by expanding access, facilitating point-of-care delivery processes, and making it possible for patients to monitor and better manage their health outside of the clinic.

Patients can use the Internet to schedule appointments, gain access to their health history information, confirm insurance coverage, and review other basic information in advance of arriving at the clinic. They can also consult with healthcare professionals via phone, e-mail, and online chats.

Remote monitoring and management of health is quickly becoming commonplace. Patients are using software applications, mobile digital devices such as smartphones, and access to the web and other tools for everything from staying on top of preventative care and wellness regimes to managing chronic conditions. For example, vital-signs monitoring and glucose-level reporting equipment exists that can transmit information over the Internet—at regular intervals or in real time.

Healthcare Reform

As implementation of the Affordable Care Act has shifted reimbursement structures from the "pay for production" to the "pay for performance" model, healthcare organizations and design professionals have more closely examined the ways in which design of the built environment can enhance the quality of the patient experience and, by extension, contribute to the achievement of targeted health outcomes.

As healthcare organizations have expanded their definition of the "care continuum," design professionals have also paid greater attention to what patients do before and after a clinic visit. For example, if patients are able to update their health record information and register online, this can reduce the amount of space a clinic needs for registration and check-in.

■ MIDWAY INTERNAL MEDICINE CLINIC
St. Paul, Minnesota

The research for this project led the HealthEast Care System to create intake rooms that were separate from examination rooms. Information was found to be missing or to have been lost in transit between the time when nurses or medical assistants took a patient's vitals and reviewed health information and when a physician started an exam. Now, patients are first seen in an intake room, where those essential first steps are completed, before they move on to exam rooms, where they are seen by a physician. This has reduced the total number of exam rooms because the wait times are shorter within them and the turnover is more rapid. Since the majority of patients are frequent visitors, there is a small private office near the exit where discharge tasks are completed. Family members are encouraged to join the patient and staff members there so that they can understand the postclinic care plan and provide support needed by the patient (fig. 1-14).

Demographics

The population of the United States is increasing. Clinics are seeing more elderly, bariatric, and culturally diverse patients. Design professionals are tracking these demographic trends closely to make certain that patients of all ages, backgrounds, and capabilities feel welcome at clinics.

Age

Growth in the patient population is occurring at both ends of the age spectrum for a number of reasons. First, life expectancy has steadily increased in the United States. Experts predict that between the years 2000 and 2030, the elderly population in the United States will have increased by more than 100 percent. The varying levels of support and assistance required by this growing segment of the patient population must be thoughtfully addressed by clinic design. For example, high-contrast colors, proper lighting, and the inclusion of hand rails and space for walkers and canes can make clinic spaces more comfortable for older patients and easier for them to navigate.

At the same time, the Patient Bill of Rights included in the Affordable Care Act has made it

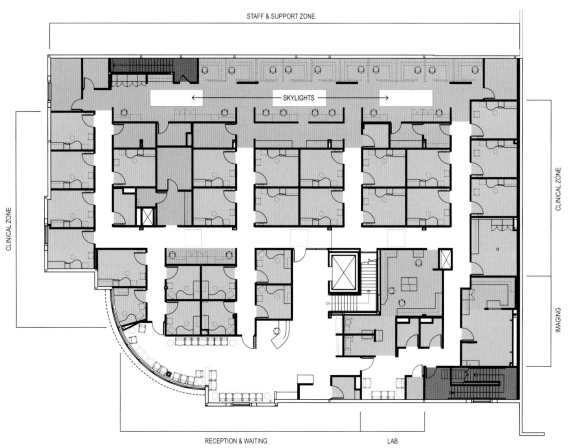

FIGURE 1-14: HealthEast Midway Clinic, St. Paul, Minnesota. Patients are first seen in an intake room, where first steps are completed, before they move on to exam rooms and are seen by a physician. This has reduced the total number of exam rooms needed because the wait times within them are shorter and turnover is more rapid. Image courtesy of Hammel, Green and Abrahamson, Inc.

possible for parents to keep their children on a family insurance policy until they are 26 years old. This has spurred an increase in the number of children, youth, and young adults who have health insurance coverage, and has resulted in greater diversification within the pediatric patient population. Thus the design of pediatric clinics where patients can be treated up to age 21 must also address how the preferences of teens and adolescents differ from those of small children.

For example, research shows that adolescents and teens prefer neutral colors and artwork with realistic images. They generally want less-juvenile surroundings, more privacy, and more age-appropriate diversions, such as computer and video games or reading materials that address topics of interest to them and their peers. Many prefer to have a curtain or other room divider included in exam rooms. This still allows a parent or guardian to remain in the room during the exam to hear the doctor's comments while the curtain is drawn.

■ ADOLESCENT TREATMENT CENTER
Winnebago, Minnesota

This freestanding treatment center was completed in August 2010. It replaced a facility that had opened in November 1981, when the care philosophy for treating all people with addictions focused on institutionalizing them in spartan settings with very little color and only the most basic of furnishings.

In contrast, the design of the new treatment center creates a comfortable, nurturing environment in the midst of a pastoral setting. Pitched roofs and the residential scale of individual building components present a familiar, home-like appearance. The soothing, earth-toned hues used throughout the facility are all in the same color family, but vary in intensity. The residential

zone has the most muted colors, the dining room includes more saturated colors, and the classroom zone has the most intense colors because this is where energy and engagement are desired. Building components were arranged to optimize window placement and provide quality views of the exterior.

Materials had to be as durable as they were attractive so that the young behavioral health patients could not vandalize or destroy them. For example, a deep sepia stain adds warmth to the polished concrete floor in the dining room. Acoustical tiles are mounted high enough to be out of reach in the classrooms because these can be easily punctured or otherwise defaced. Exposed wooden trusses add texture and beauty to corridor ceilings without being easily accessible to patients who might consider carving into them.

Although this center was initially designed as an inpatient facility, the growing need for outpatient behavioral health services and group therapy sessions has led the staff to use the classrooms and large multipurpose room for these purposes (fig. 1-15).

Diversity

According to a 2011 report by the Congressional Research Service titled *The U.S. Foreign-Born Population: Trends and Selected Characteristics,* there are 38 million people living in the United States who are "foreign born," which represents 12.5 percent of the nation's total population. This segment has been growing more rapidly than the native-born population, representing nearly one-third of the total increase in the population of the United States between 2000 and 2008 (30 percent). Design professionals are addressing this increased diversity by:

• Providing space and furnishings to accommodate members of extended families, interpreters, or other partners-in-care.

FIGURE 1-15: United Health District Winnebago Treatment Center, Winnebago, Minnesota. The pastoral setting of the Winnebago Treatment Center provides a comfortable, nurturing environment for patients and families. Pitched roofs and the residential scale of individual building components present a familiar, home-like appearance. The building interior is treated similarly through the use of exposed wooden trusses and soothing earth-toned finishes.   Photography by Red Door Creative

- Researching religious customs when the population served by a clinic includes patients of a specific faith (or with varying faiths). For example, some religions require separate spaces for women and men.
- Bringing colors that are prevalent in the art and artifacts of a particular culture into a clinic's architecture and interiors.
- Providing touch-screen technology when clinics serve a multilingual patient population.
- Including pictograms or symbols in wayfinding systems.

■ ROSELAWN CLINIC
St. Paul, Minnesota

This clinic serves a diverse ethnic population, and a vibrant color palette and culturally specific artwork were chosen to appeal to its predominantly Hispanic, Russian, Asian, and black patient population. It also houses a specialty clinic, the HealthEast Latina Clinic, where a Spanish-speaking certified nurse midwife provides special services for Latina women.

Obesity

This health condition is especially serious in the United States, where more than two-thirds (68.7 percent) of adults are either overweight or obese. Although some progress has been made toward reducing the rates of obesity among preschool children, and adult obesity rates began leveling off in 2013, addressing the needs of bariatric patients and their guests remains an important priority for design professionals.

Experts at the Facility Guidelines Institute (FGI) developed the following recommendations to ensure that bariatric patients and their guests retain their dignity and independence and feel welcome in healthcare facilities:

- The layout, dimensions, and furnishings of patient and staff interaction spaces in clinics, such as registration, billing, checkout, exam, procedure, and consultation rooms, should accommodate bariatric patients. For example, a registration work area or alcove would need to be wider and deeper to provide sufficient room for assisted devices and bariatric seating while preserving patient privacy.

- At least 10 percent of the furniture in public areas should be designed to accommodate bariatric patients and guests and, ideally, be combined and arranged with standard furnishings so that bariatric patients are not segregated and confined to specific areas.

- Exam or procedure rooms designed to provide healthcare services for bariatric patients should be a minimum of 200 square feet in size with at least 5 feet clearance around the exam table.

- Portable or built-in lift systems should accommodate at least 800 pounds.

- Extra space should be allocated for storage of lift equipment. The storage space required per patient when a portable lift is used is 35 square feet. It is 25.2 square feet per patient when a built-in mechanical lift is used.

- Furniture, plumbing fixtures (commodes and sinks, for example), and casework should be floor-mounted and/or designed to accommodate 1,000 pounds.

- Walls should have extra-strength blocking to support grab bars and handrails.

- When larger waiting rooms are needed to accommodate obese patients and partners-in-care, calculations should be based on 18 net square feet per person (versus the standard of 15 nsf/person).

- All entry doors, including those from parking garages, should be wider and provide power-assist capabilities.

- If seating is built in, handrails that will support 400 pounds should be provided so that patients can assist themselves when they rise from a seated position.

In addition to obtaining construction and testing information about the strength and durability of bariatric furnishings, fixtures, and equipment from product manufacturers, design professionals also use criteria provided by the Center for Health Design, such as:

- Frames constructed of 16-gauge steel or lower and 1.25 inches or more with box welds at the joints are sturdier than wooden frames.

- Cushions should have extra-thick, high-density, 100 percent urethane foam.

- The foundation for the chair cushion should be at least 0.75 inches of engineered wood.

- Hardware should be able to sustain heavy use.

It is important to recognize that bariatric furnishings are not just bigger and stronger. They must also blend with the overall interior design scheme so that patients and their guests feel welcome and comfortable. Major points to consider include:

- The circumferences and widths of limbs and torsos are significantly larger in the bariatric segment.

- When armrests are included, their height needs to be raised enough to offset increased body mass.

- Some bariatric seating is designed to allow people to rock their bodies as an aid to egress (standing up).

These recommendations are focused on helping bariatric patients to accomplish goals such as getting in and out of a chair independently, getting on and off of a commode without (or with minimal) assistance, and disrobing and getting dressed with minimal or no help. Design should emphasize similarities rather than draw attention to differences between the people who visit a clinic.

Design Considerations and Strategies

A key goal of clinic design is to reduce the level of anxiety most patients experience while awaiting or obtaining healthcare services. Design professionals address this challenge by considering what the health condition of patients seen at a particular clinic is likely to be and creating environments that are safe, efficient, comfortable, and easy to navigate. Patients' privacy must also be protected.

Health Condition

A patient's particular health condition influences where they will seek care. For example, those who have chronic conditions (for example, heart disease, diabetes, and cancer) or require long-term care visit clinics where specialized services such as dialysis or infusion are provided. Patients who have been injured typically go directly to urgent-care clinics.

Safety

If patients do not believe that a clinic provides a safe environment from the moment they first see it, they will not want to complete their approach. If they feel that their safety is in jeopardy during a clinic visit or as they leave the building or site, they are likely to seek care elsewhere in the future. Design professionals use a variety of strategies to address these concerns, such as lighting, views, ergonomics, and infection control.

Infection Control

According to the Centers for Disease Control and Prevention (CDC), the most important and efficient step a clinic can take toward controlling the risk of healthcare-associated infections is to institute a hand-hygiene program and install the necessary equipment in strategic locations throughout the facility. This topic is addressed in detail in chapter 5, "Clinic Planning Concepts," and chapter 6, "The Exam Room Today."

Since floor, wall, ceiling, furniture, and equipment surfaces can all pose contamination risks, materials and finishes should be evaluated with the goal of minimizing or eliminating the chance that they will become breeding grounds for bacteria and other microorganisms. Durability is also a key consideration for high-contact surfaces that need to be frequently cleaned and disinfected.

Some materials, such as copper and brass, have been shown to have germicidal and antibacterial qualities. Research indicates that copper doorknobs can kill some of the bacteria-resistant superbugs that have been found in healthcare environments. Brass doorknobs disinfect themselves in eight hours or less, but stainless steel and aluminum products never do.

In May 2011, the Center for Health Design published *The Evidence-Based Design Furniture Checklist*. Three sections of this checklist address patient safety by making the following recommendations:

- To reduce the risk of contamination, furniture surfaces should be easy to clean, without joints or seams that can complicate maintenance processes and create reservoirs for infectious organisms.
- Seating that has a space between the back and seating surface is typically easier to keep clean.
- Nonporous surfaces and materials should be used to prevent contaminated body fluids from soaking into them.

The characteristics that privacy curtains and other room dividers should have to optimize patient safety are addressed in chapter 6, "The Exam Room Today."

Views

The "prospect-refuge theory," described in the book titled *The Adapted Mind: Evolutionary Psychology and the Generation of Culture,* proposes that people feel safer when they have clear, unobstructed views of what is going on inside, outside, and around a clinic building. For example, providing direct sightlines from the main reception desk to the front entry can enhance patients' sense of security, as they can immediately see that staff is monitoring who is entering and exiting a clinic. This theory generally asserts that people prefer:

- To be in environments that allow them to "see without being seen."
- To seek refuge on the edges of open spaces.
- To have some sense that they are being sheltered overhead by a roof, a tree canopy, or a trellis, for example, rather than remain in a

space where there is only a side and back surface to protect them.

- To be in a space that at least has a back or side to protect them rather than no vertical surfaces whatsoever.
- To be in spaces that provide multiple views from most locations and multiple ways to navigate through, as well as exit from, a space (surveillance and escape).

When people are already experiencing fear or stress, the desire for refuge is heightened. Thus, people perceive an environment that contains a balance between prospect (views of others) and refuge (screening and shelter) opportunities to be safer and more pleasant.

■ WHITTIER CLINIC
Minneapolis, Minnesota

A street-level staff corridor flanked with large-scale artwork promotes a sense of safety by revealing some of the activities occurring within the building while providing exterior views to monitor what is occurring around it. The building's scale, massing, fenestration, and configuration of spaces relate to the context and characteristics of its neighborhood in order to make the clinic welcoming to patients as well as people who pass by.

Lean Design

While healthcare organizations have long recognized the value of eliminating waste from a clinic's operations, in recent years Lean design professionals have addressed, more specifically, how recommendations they make affect the patient experience. They have done this by including patients earlier, more actively, and to a greater degree in the research phases of projects and by equipping clinic owners with tools for obtaining postoccupancy feedback, with which they can make the continuous improvements that matter most to patients. For example, patients define an efficient clinic visit as one that keeps travel, wait, and treatment time to a minimum.

■ DIGNITY HEALTH MEDICAL OFFICE BUILDING
Woodland, California

This project illustrates how Lean analysis and design can improve the patient experience while improving operational efficiency and productivity. Dignity Health, owner of this medical office building, wanted to increase the number of prescriptions filled by the on-site pharmacy. Design professionals proposed a Lean process that included setting goals for improvements, defining the current state, and envisioning the ideal future state:

- **Goals:** Dignity Health wanted to increase prescription capacity by 33 percent per month, decrease patient wait time, reduce errors, improve the pharmacy's workflow and reduce conflicts, and increase patient privacy. Initially, Dignity planned to increase the size of the pharmacy to achieve these goals.

- **Current state:** The Lean design team completed a root-cause analysis that divided the constraints into four categories: prescription generation, prescription fill, inventory control, and human factors. The Lean design team made site observations, conducted interviews, and photographed existing constraints. It also created adjustable-height mock-ups to explore solutions for eliminating wasted movements at the prescription fill and collection stations and used floor plan modifications to identify workflow solutions. The research revealed that patients did not obtain their prescriptions from the on-site pharmacy because they did not want to have to wait very long for them or because it was too much trouble to return to the pharmacy later. Thus, pharmacists were wasting time filling and bagging prescriptions that were never picked up. The core team also learned that the pharmacists' tasks and physical spaces overlapped in ways that added waste to workflows.

- **Future state:** The core team presented potential solutions to pharmacy staff members, who discussed them, expanded the list, and voted to choose the recommendations they believed would provide the highest efficiency, improve patient satisfaction, and achieve the other stated project goals. The selected recommendations included:

  - Providing a new 4'-wide adjustable-height work surface and shared printer station between every two stations.

  - Installing a patient notification board in the seating area niche outside the pharmacy.

  - Providing a new prescription fill counter, with 5'-wide standardized layout.

  - Adding a door to the existing window wall to utilize the existing building core waiting area.

  - Providing a dedicated and ergonomic place for the Problem Tech to work.

  - Increasing the number of prescription fill stations by one.

By implementing these design improvements and reducing the amount of time spent repackaging prescriptions, pharmacy staff not only increased number of prescriptions filled at this location but also improved the patient experience by limiting wait time to seven minutes or less and providing a more private space in which to exchange pharmaceutical and related health information.

Comfort

A clinic's wayfinding and lighting systems, seating, indoor air quality, and temperature influence how comfortable patients and their visitors feel during a clinic visit. Providing positive distractions also helps to keep patients' minds off any pain or anxiety they are experiencing, while noise puts all clinic occupants—staff and visitors—on edge.

Wayfinding

Well-designed wayfinding can put patients and other visitors at ease by helping them to quickly and easily find their desired destination. Information about interior wayfinding systems is included in chapter 5, "Clinic Planning Concepts" (figs. 1-16, 1-17).

Directions

Patients begin to find their way to a clinic before they leave home. They receive appointment reminders via mail, e-mail, text, or phone that provide directions to a facility's location. To aid

wayfinding, printed or digital reminders should provide graphic and written directions. Ideally, the location of the clinic should be shown relative to major highways, intersections, access roads, parking areas, or mass transit stops.

Since patients frequently check a clinic's website for wayfinding information, graphic and written directions that are posted on it should be easy to understand. Patients should be able to print directions in a user-friendly format. Interior floor plans should be available online as well, with circulation paths clearly marked.

Site Signage

Guidelines for the design of signage that directs patients to, through, and away from a clinic's site include:

- Provide signage at a height between five feet and eight feet along pedestrian paths, including those that connect parking areas to public entries.

FIGURES 1-16, 1-17: The Everett Clinic Smokey Point Medical Center, Smokey Point, Washington; ZGF Architects LLP. Graphic images and numbers integrated into the interior architecture provide clear wayfinding cues. Warm woods, natural materials, clean simple lines, and varied ceiling heights create visual interest. The Smokey Point Medical Center offers a full range of primary and specialty medical services, including allergy, behavioral health, dermatology, heart and vascular, pediatrics, and vision services. Photography © by Benjamin Benschneider

- Include signs that direct drivers to the proper level and space in a parking ramp and signs to guide pedestrians to the proper entry.

- Locate signs near mass transit stops or along bike and pedestrian pathways for patients who use these modes to travel to a clinic. Signs other than the main clinic identification sign should be smaller and positioned at pedestrian eye level.

- Use large text on signage for suburban and rural clinics if it must be seen at a substantial distance or from vehicles traveling at higher speeds than in urban settings. In general, larger signage is required at vehicular entrances to a site to direct visitors to the main entry and drop-off area.

- Keep messaging to a minimum. The main goal is to help visitors reach the clinic building, where they will receive more specific directional information.

Architecture

A clinic's architecture can also help to put patients at ease by aiding wayfinding. A key strategy design professionals use is to establish a hierarchy of spaces. For example, a tiered relationship can be established between reception and check-in spaces serving clinics that have high rates of throughput, offer specialized care, or are located within commercial buildings or on healthcare campuses. Typically, receptionists are stationed at a desk near the main entry to greet patients and direct them to more specific check-in areas.

Other architectural strategies design professionals use to bolster the effectiveness of a clinic's wayfinding system include providing architectural landmarks as visual cues that help patients to orient themselves, or using wider corridors to indicate a higher level of importance in circulation corridors (fig. 1-18).

Seating

The arrangement, location, and design features of seating influence patient perceptions. In addition to making sure that clinics have adequate, comfortable, and universally accessible seating, design professionals:

- Use different types of seating to accommodate the varied health conditions of patients. For example, benches or sofas can provide extra space for orthopedic patients who have casts, splints, or slings. Recliners allow patients who need to rest or who are uncomfortable when they are seated in a fully upright position to sit at an angle.

- Avoid using seating styles or creating arrangements that look too stark, too formal, or too institutional.

- Select fabrics with natural colors and motifs as well as those that are demographically and culturally appropriate for the patient population a clinic serves.

- Configure seating and related furnishings in flexible groupings that can easily be adjusted to accommodate the varying needs of patients and their guests (fig. 1-19).

Lighting

It is no surprise that patients consistently rank lighting among the most important elements of a clinic's design, because the level and quality of illumination present in a space affect people's emotions, health, and general outlook. Fortunately, technological advances have given lighting designers more choices than ever, enabling them to determine how color, light levels, distribution of light within a space, and many other factors can be combined to enhance the patient experience.

FIGURE 1-18: New York University's Men's Health Clinic, New York, New York; Perkins + Will. Strategically placed wooden planes draw attention to the reception desk and the art wall. Varied wood tones and use of bright upholsteries creates a professional space that does not look like a clinic.   Photography © by Halkin Mason Photography

Demographic characteristics such as age and ethnicity, as well as geographic location and other factors, influence the decisions design professionals make about lighting. For example, aging eyes require higher illumination levels and more contrast between colors. People in northern climates prefer light that falls on the warm end of the color spectrum, while those in southern climates prefer cool-hued illumination.

Key guidelines design professionals use for integrating light into the design of a clinic include:

- Since people are naturally attracted to light, it can be used to call attention to key activity nodes.

- Lighting fixtures should be located and directed to avoid casting deep shadows that can make patients appear sicker than they feel.

FIGURE 1-19: New York University's Men's Health Clinic, New York; Perkins + Will. Waiting spaces accommodate the needs of clients through a variety of seating options. Natural materials and textures, diverse lighting, and warm tones are welcoming. Photography © by Halkin Mason Photography

- Using a variety of fixtures creates visual interest and more inviting interiors.
- Task-oriented lighting is needed for transaction and private work surfaces.
- Indirect lighting can make a space feel brighter, but it is not as energy-efficient as direct lighting because light from an indirect fixture must travel from the source to a surface and be reflected to a third surface.
- The sources of direct lighting fixtures should be shielded to minimize glare.

- Corridor lighting can aid wayfinding and help the emotional transition of patients to the exam rooms, where brighter task lights serve functional needs.
- The color temperature of light sources should complement or strengthen the hues used throughout a space.
- Ambient lighting levels should be high enough for patients, guests, and staff to easily find their way through a clinic, to read various forms, publications, and signage, and to use

computers, digital devices, and other equipment without creating glare on smooth work surfaces, walls, floors, ceilings, or computer monitors (figs. 1-20, 1-21).

Natural Light

Numerous research studies have found that exposure to natural light can reduce patients' feelings of depression, lessen agitation, and ease pain. When introducing natural light into interiors, design professionals address how to minimize glare, relate interior illumination to what is going on outside of a clinic, and create smooth transitions between natural and artificial light levels.

FIGURE 1-20: UMP Mill City Clinic, Minneapolis, Minnesota; Perkins + Will. The Mill City Clinic, located in the heart of Minneapolis, was designed with professionals and urban dwellers in mind. Clean uncluttered details, simple sophisticated materials, and soft lighting allowed designers to create a timeless space and a respite from the buzz of the city. Photography by Christopher Barrett

■ HAZELDEN IN PLYMOUTH
A part of the Hazelden Betty Ford Plymouth, Minnesota, Foundation

Natural light enters this 50,000-square-foot treatment center through windows, skylights, and a clerestory that runs the entire length of a "Main Street" corridor. To convey permanence, a thick stone wall starts at the new porte cochere and runs the entire length of the building. Openings in this wall introduce additional natural light into interiors and symbolize breakthrough moments in the recovery process.

Full-Spectrum Light

This phrase is often used to imply that the spectral power of a light source is uniformly distributed across the visible spectrum. Although some manufacturers, marketing materials claim full-spectrum light does everything from reduce hyperactivity to increase muscle strength and cure seasonal affective disorder, more research is

FIGURE 1-21: UMP Mill City Clinic, Minneapolis, Minnesota; Perkins + Will. Clerestory windows allow natural daylighting to filter through the public space into clinical areas. Warm wood tones and a sophisticated art program add interest and enhance the patient waiting experience. Photography by Christopher Barrett

needed in order to substantiate these assertions in a scientifically acceptable manner. Design professionals typically use two industry standards to evaluate light color:

- The Color Rendering Index (CRI) measures the color shift objects experience when illuminated by a light source. CRI scores run from 1 to 100, with 100 being a perfect match with a reference source. For warm-colored light, the reference source is usually an incandescent light, and for cool-colored light, it is typically daylight. A quality lighting installation would specify sources with a CRI of at least 80.

- The Correlated Color Temperature (CCT) is the color of the light itself as expressed in degrees Kelvin (K). The CCT of the light should complement colors used in the space.

Energy Conservation

A clinic's lighting design should provide the right amount of light in the right places at the right time. Photo sensors, motion detectors, timers, and dimming devices can be linked to lighting control systems to help achieve this goal and manage energy costs.

In recent years, design professionals have begun integrating light-emitting diodes (LEDs) into illumination systems for clinics because these sources use approximately 75 percent less electricity than comparable incandescent lamps. LEDs are small light sources that become illuminated by the movement of electrons through a semiconductor material. Criteria to review when considering the use of LEDs in a clinic setting include:

- **Cost.** LEDs are generally more expensive to purchase and replace than conventional light sources.

- **Size.** A benefit of LED technology is that it makes small light fixtures possible for some applications.

- **Light quality.** LEDs are highly directional light sources, making them ideal for accentuating design details, such as artwork or the material texture of a surface.

- **Color rendition.** A high-quality LED source can render color quite accurately.

- **Heat emission.** LEDs generate heat, and if this is not diverted or absorbed by a heat sink mechanism, which spreads the heat out in order to get rid of it, the claimed lamp life will be shortened dramatically.

- **Other qualities.** LED sources turn on instantly and do not flicker when dimmed if quality-compatible products are used. They also have a much longer life span than incandescent and fluorescent sources.

Indoor Air Quality

A critical comfort and safety issue for clinics is one that few people notice unless their eyes are itchy, they feel drowsy, or they are experiencing other effects of poor indoor air quality (IAQ). When a clinic's ventilation system does not properly "make up," circulate, and filter indoor air, the shortfall is hard to miss. This is an especially salient issue to address in the public spaces of a clinic, such as main lobbies or waiting areas, where a higher density of occupants typically means a greater amount of outside air is required to maintain quality indoor air. This goal can be achieved by:

- Increasing the size of the air handling system serving high-occupancy building zones in order to provide a higher air exchange rate.

- Carefully locating diffusers to avoid creating drafts when the air exchangers are at full-flow levels.

- Exhausting rather than recirculating air from these zones—especially if they serve potentially infectious patients.

- Equipping HVAC systems with electronic sensors and controls that enable them to automatically respond to wide variations in occupancy levels. This helps to keep comfort levels consistent while also conserving energy.

Design professionals also avoid using furniture or finishes made with materials that contain volatile organic compounds (VOC)—especially formaldehyde and benzene, which not only can trigger respiratory issues but are also carcinogenic.

Temperature

It takes a concerted effort by architects, interior designers, mechanical engineers, and other professionals to achieve and maintain comfortable interior temperatures in clinics—especially when climatic conditions on the exterior of a building change throughout the day and can vary dramatically between seasons.

Since the reception and main lobbies are high-use areas and are typically near the main connection between a clinic's interior and exterior (the front entry), mechanical engineers strive to maintain comfort by considering the orientation of a clinic's entry, the layout and qualities of its interiors, and the characteristics of the building envelope so that they can properly size, configure, and route heating, cooling, and ventilation systems.

For example, the thermostat for reception areas is often located near a return air grille by the check-in desk. Since it is good practice to exhaust the air from the reception area to the exterior of the building, the exhaust air grille is usually located on or near an exterior wall. However, the building's envelope typically only influences the temperature of a room up to 15 feet from its exterior walls. Many reception and check-in areas are located deeper into the interior than this. In those instances, a single thermostat located near the reception desk could not accurately gauge how much make-up air should

be brought in from the outside and how much existing air should be exhausted to keep the temperature, relative humidity, and air quality of the entire reception area comfortable.

Such conditions require multiple zones of temperature control to strike an ideal balance and ensure the comfort of patients, their guests, and clinic staff. These controls need to be integrated and sequenced in order to work consistently and harmoniously.

Vestibules

The design of vestibules also plays an important role in establishing and maintaining comfort. They introduce patients to a clinic and physically link its interior with what is going on outside its walls. When vestibules are well designed and function properly, patients barely notice them. When they don't work correctly, everyone notices.

Depending on their dimensions and other aspects of a clinic's design, vestibules can serve as small waiting rooms for patients who are being picked up or as a place where items such as wheelchairs, strollers, or maintenance equipment can be stored.

Basic vestibule design consists of outer and inner glass doors, inset floor mats, a zoned air conditioning unit, and, at times, a bench to provide seating. Most issues that arise with the design of vestibules relate to thermal complaints (cold air is entering the lobby and reception desk during the winter), a lack of adequate distance between doors, and the timing between automatic outer doors closing and automatic inner doors opening. Design strategies for addressing these issues include:

- Consider using a revolving outer door or staggering door positions to prevent temperature transfer from outside to inside. Wind infiltration can be reduced by orienting outside doors at a 90-degree angle to the interior doors in a vestibule.

- Although national codes require 7 feet between doors in colder climates, it may make sense to provide 10 to 15 feet to achieve a more effective buffer distance.

- Recent research indicates that the lobby configuration and mechanical-system airflow are the main factors affecting comfort—rather than the distance from front door to desk. Since a vestibule is part of an integrated design process, final decisions should be considered in relation to all space adjacencies and mechanical system layout and capacity.

- Although vestibules primarily serve a utilitarian function, they should project a welcoming presence through ample lighting, clean materials, and clear signage because they are the first and last clinic space patients and other visitors encounter.

Personal characteristics of the clinic's patient population influence designers' choice of doors. For example, elderly patients, those using wheelchairs or other access devices, and parents or caregivers using strollers to transport small children generally do not like to have to use a revolving door to enter a building.

■ ALTRU HEALTH SYSTEM VESTIBULE STUDY
Grand Forks, North Dakota

With Altru Health System located in North Dakota, two owner concerns for the comfort of patients, family, staff, and healthcare professionals are finding a way to keep the building interior warm in the winter and minimizing the impact the strong winds have on interior comfort. In order to test for the best approach to reducing the amount of cold air entering the building, a scenario looking at the following conditions was obtained from the Grand Forks International Airport (fig. 1-22):

- 7.5 mph wind from the south, 21°C outside temperature

- Desired indoor space temperature of 70°F

- Worst-case scenario of both the outer doors and lobby doors standing wide open

All plan view temperature contours represent a z-plane slice at three and a half feet from the floor.

Noise

Since loud or irritating noises can cause unwanted physiological responses, such as an increase in blood pressure, pulse rate, or respiration, design professionals first identify the potential sources and locations of noise (e.g., equipment, alarms, collaborative work areas), then they devise methods for dampening or eliminating this distraction. Typical strategies employed by design professionals include:

- Locating the sources of noise away from the clinic areas where patients spend the majority of their time, such as waiting areas, consultation spaces, and exam rooms.

- Installing high-performance sound-absorbing acoustical ceiling tiles that shorten the reverberation times and reduce sound propagation.

- Ensuring that walls in private spaces, such as consultation and exam rooms or telehealth workstations, extend to the ceiling.

- Using materials and furnishings such as carpet or rubber floors to absorb sound, when possible and appropriate. Carpets, draperies, and upholstered furniture can all help to dampen noise, but decisions about if and where to use them in a clinic should be reviewed in the context of infection-control risks associated with specific spaces.

- Installing a sound-masking system that produces white or pink noise. White noise is perceived as a constant background buzz that makes unwanted sounds less audible. Pink noise is a frequency-specific sound that is used to cancel out sound.

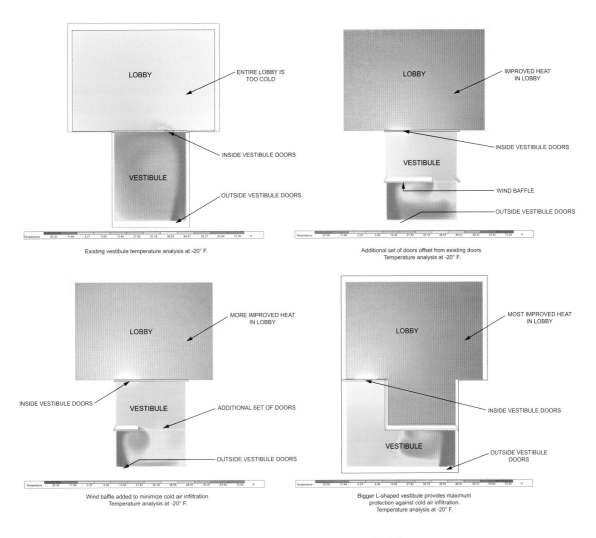

Vestibule remodel to minimize cold air infiltration from outside to lobby.

FIGURE 1-22: Altru Health System Devils Lake Clinic, Devils Lake, North Dakota. Designers had two concerns related to the comfort of patients, family, staff, and healthcare professionals: finding a way to keep the building interior warm in the winter and minimizing the impact that strong winds have on interior comfort. Moving away from a rectangular vestibule to a new L-shaped vestibule allows for the greatest temperature control, as the air is trapped in the leg closest to the entry door. Image courtesy of Hammel, Green and Abrahamson, Inc.

Positive Distractions

Few patients have ever enjoyed spending more time in a healthcare facility than is absolutely necessary, but as the U.S. population has become increasingly "time starved," design professionals have streamlined the layout of clinic spaces to support healthcare processes aimed at minimizing wait time. They have also provided positive distractions such as artwork, exterior views, music, water elements, gardens, and fireplaces to make wait time pass more enjoyably, and created places where visitors can read, watch television, play, or use computers.

Artwork

Visual art can help to alleviate stress if design professionals take care to avoid wildly abstract or surreal images, which can be confusing or create a negative distraction. Research has shown that patients respond positively to nature paintings and prints. Bold colors and clear contrast between artwork and its surroundings can create visual interest and focus attention on a specific architectural element or activity node.

Art that relates to the specialized care provided by a clinic and art created by individuals who have similar health conditions can provide positive diversion. For example, art made by children is frequently displayed in pediatric clinics, and art created by cancer survivors is often exhibited in oncology treatment centers.

Design professionals also use art in waiting rooms, corridors, and exam rooms, as well as throughout a clinic, to integrate forms, colors, and textures that are familiar to the local community.

■ DANA-FARBER CANCER INSTITUTE'S ART COLLECTION
Boston, Massachusetts

For more than a decade, the Dana-Farber Cancer Institute has integrated artwork into the design of its clinics in order to enhance the healing environment. For example, more than 500 works by regional and national artists are displayed throughout the 14-story Yawkey Center for Cancer Care that opened on this medical campus in 2011.

Dana-Farber's growing art collection conveys the institute's belief that art can enhance the patient experience by creating inspiration, moments of reflection, and healing. This healthcare organization began to incorporate original artwork throughout its facilities in 1998, when it formed an Art and Environment Committee to direct the installation of art for an interior renovation. The committee now includes patients, family members, trustees, and staff who manage the acquisition and installation of hundreds of pieces of art. Patients, visitors, and staff have all provided positive feedback acknowledging how art enhances the interior environment throughout the entire campus.

Works include contemporary, pop, abstract, and representational art in a range of forms, from sculpture to mixed-media, works on paper, and paintings. The committee avoids pieces that suggest clinical processes that might remind patients of their illnesses. The art program also serves as an educational resource that introduces art and new artists to patients and staff who ordinarily may not visit a museum. To accomplish this, Dana-Farber provides a fully accessible Acoustiguide audio and online tour of the collection.

Music

Soft, soothing music that has no accented beats, a slow tempo, and a smooth melody can reduce anxiety. Instrumental music is less distracting than music with lyrics. However, since finding music that is acceptable to all patients and those waiting with them can be a challenge, one option is to allow individuals who prefer to choose their own music to use portable audio devices while they are waiting or undergoing minor procedures, such as having a cavity filled in a dental clinic.

Many clinics have found a satellite service to be the most economical and reliable source of music. Care providers can select two or three stations to provide some variety for staff and patients. Other options include playing a loop of songs that have been recorded on a compact disc or setting up playlists on an iPod and connecting this digital device to a sound system. Some phone systems offer a music option as well that can be played over an intercom system.

Views

Research indicates that people prefer to view nature or something calming or interesting that keeps them connected with the life outside of a clinic while they are waiting to be seen by a healthcare professional. Since the majority of individuals find views of nature to be relaxing, design professionals use a variety of strategies for integrating these into a clinic's design, including:

- Strategically sizing and placing windows and doors. These can also provide access to fresh air and bring natural light into a clinic's interiors.

- Using plants, water elements, or aquariums to, literally, "bring nature indoors." Beginning in the 1980s, studies on the health effects of aquariums found that viewing activities occurring within them could help people relax—especially children suffering from hyperactivity disorders, the elderly, and others arriving at the clinic under especially stressful circumstances. Neither the size nor the shape of the aquarium appear to matter significantly: if a clinic can only afford a small countertop aquarium, this is still worth considering. Virtual aquariums are becoming popular because of their lower purchase and maintenance costs.

- Integrating nature-inspired materials, textures, patterns, and artwork into the interior design.

Interior views can have a calming effect, too. Views of artwork, exterior gardens, or other landscape elements, or simply the ability to clearly see what other people are doing, can help alleviate stress. Using too many windows can create a fishbowl effect when there is a great deal of activity going on directly outside of them.

■ HEALTHEAST'S GRAND AVENUE CLINIC
St. Paul, Minnesota

This clinic is located on a major thoroughfare in a densely populated urban neighborhood. To keep patients in the waiting room connected to the outside world while preserving their privacy, the design team used computer modeling and other techniques to establish the proper height and opacity for custom translucent films with a flowing grass pattern that were printed on acrylic and affixed to the waiting room windows. Clear glass above these films directs natural light deep into this space.

■ FAIRVIEW MEDICAL CENTER
Maple Grove, Minnesota

Design professionals for this suburban healthcare campus embraced the scenic views of its site by incorporating the natural colors, textures, and wood species of the surrounding prairie and the adjacent Elm Creek Park Reserve, which features wetlands and more than 20 miles of trails.

Designers also drew on the perspectives provided by parents of pediatric patients and the patients themselves to create the design for the Children's Specialty Clinic. It has its own double-glass door entry, reception desk, and check-in area, as well as a brightly colored waiting room. The floor tile pattern beneath a soffit creates the appearance of a pond with fish and other creatures that provide positive distractions for the children (see fig. 1-11).

Water and Fire Features

The decision to include gardens and water elements inside of medical facilities is controversial. While these design features have a soothing effect on most patients, they can also serve as a breeding ground for infection. This makes establishing a maintenance program for fountains and plants as important as the decision about whether or not to include these in a clinic's design.

Water elements and the strategic use of plantings can also be used to conceal utilitarian spaces that can be awkwardly located out of necessity on constrained sites. The sound of moving water can be used to mask noise in high-traffic areas of a clinic. Generally, design professionals:

- Avoid using water elements in clinics where patients with immune system deficiencies are being treated.
- Review manufacturing and construction information to make sure the facilities staff is comfortable with the level of maintenance that is required. Options for water treatment include the use of chlorine, copper-silver ionization, or ultraviolet light. Aerators used to prevent water stagnation must be regularly cleaned and maintained to eliminate the risk of *Legionella* contamination.
- Consider using a looped water system to minimize maintenance requirements.
- Look for self-contained water features using purified water that is continually sanitized as it circulates through the system.

Design professionals should talk to the local authorities having jurisdiction over water and fire features before including this element in the design of a healthcare facility.

Fireplaces

Since ancient times, fireplaces have been the heart of a building. They evoke feelings of contentment, warmth, and comfort. But a poorly designed fireplace fueled by natural gas can be a safety hazard. If code officials do not allow gas fireplaces, there are good electric or virtual fireplace options.

Television

Clinic waiting areas are now frequently equipped with televisions to help take patients' minds off the purpose of their visit. Strategies to consider when specifying equipment and identifying the best location for televisions in waiting rooms include:

- Selecting televisions that can be muted or whose volume can be easily lowered (ideally via a remote control)
- Making sure there is an audio privacy zone separate from the television viewing area for people who prefer to read, rest, or engage in other quiet activities.
- Placing a television on a low table or credenza with seating clustered near it, rather than hanging it from the ceiling. This can create a separate zone where those who choose to view can do so.

In recent years, healthcare organizations have begun subscribing to closed-circuit television programs or providing streaming video from the Internet. For example, clinics can display the Continuous Ambient Relaxation Environment Channel (CARE) on televisions to provide hours of nonrepetitive nature images, or use live feeds from zoos to distract children from the pain or stress they may experience during a visit to a healthcare facility.

On the other hand, some clinics have chosen not provide televisions as a distraction. This is because an increasing number of people have tablets or smartphones that they use for entertainment.

Computers

Providing wireless access to the Internet, as well as a zone in the waiting room with a work surface, chairs, and electrical outlets, can make it easier for patients to use laptop or notebook computers they have brought with them to a clinic. Design professionals research the impact that providing a designated computer area will have on electricity demand so that the related costs can be considered by the client early in the planning process.

Reading

To facilitate reading, lighting levels should be high enough to prevent eyestrain and fatigue. Task lighting and multiple lighting levels should be provided. Specialized seating can also be used to create an efficient, attractive reading area. Providing places to display and set down reading materials is also important.

Play Spaces

Most waiting rooms have a separate children's zone to make it easy to corral kids and keep them safely out of the traffic patterns of other patients and staff. There should be sufficient space for kids to move around and play, as well as for family members or other guests to sit nearby or participate in play activities. Teens also like to have a designated zone, when possible, in which they can to listen to music, play video games, read, or relax in other ways.

◼ MAYO CLINIC, T. DENNY SANFORD PEDIATRIC CENTER
Rochester, Minnesota

Positive distractions integrated into the kid-friendly design of this clinic include art, such as a floor pattern that represents the Mississippi River flowing out of Lake Itasca, and a live video feed from the Minnesota Zoo allows children to watch the activities of various animals in real time and learn about Minnesota's ecosystems. An animal-themed wayfinding system features rooms with bear tiles or a giant green frog on the floor. Making younger patients feel comfortable in a medical setting is an important aspect of the patient experience at Mayo Clinic (figs. 1-23, 1-24).

 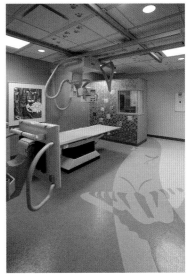

FIGURES 1-23, 1-24: Mayo Clinic, T. Denny Sanford Pediatric Center, Rochester, Minnesota. The design establishes a welcoming environment for the thousands of children and their family members who visit the center every year from around the world. In planning the space, the Mayo Clinic sought to welcome patients into its "home" by sharing the beauty and vastness of Minnesota's natural environment—from rivers and lakes to forest and prairies. The design taps into the imagination of children and their sense of wonder by recognizing their intrinsic curiosity. While some children will spend only a day at the Mayo Clinic, others may return over weeks or months to receive care. Engaging children's imaginations by bringing imagery of the outside into the pediatric center helps to ease young patients' anxiety as they begin the healing process. Photography © by Dana Wheelock

Notes

1. Roger S. Ulrich, "View through a Window May Influence Recovery from Surgery," *Science* 224 (1984): 420–22.

2. The Center for Health Design, n.d., "EDAC," http://www.healthdesign.org/edac.

3. University of Minnesota, Office of Human Resources, "24/7 Nurse Line," http://www1.umn.edu/ohr/wellness/health/nurseline/index.html.

4. Blue Cross Blue Shield of Minnesota, "OnlineCareAnywhere," http://www.onlinecareanywheremn.com/?gclid=CLSJvJ7g5LkCFc9i7AodFQ0ALQ.

5. Holy Redeemer: HealthCare. HomeCare. LifeCare, http://www.holyredeemer.com/Main/Home.aspx.

6. U.S. Department of Health and Human Services, "Survey Form," http://bphc.hrsa.gov/policiesregulations/performancemeasures/patientsurvey/surveyform.html.

7. U.S. Department of Health and Human Services, "Health Information Privacy," http://www.hhs.gov/ocr/privacy.

8. Katherine Cwiek, Jennifer Etkin, Craig Holm, George Karageorgiou, and Elisabeth Meinert, *Primary Care in an Era of Health Care Reform: Strategies for Reorienting Health Care Delivery System toward Primary Care* (Philadelphia: Health Strategies and Solutions, Inc., 2012), 15–17.

9. Tanya L. Tivorsak, Maria T. Britto, Brenda K. Klosterman, Dawn M. Nebrig, and Gail B. Slap, "Are Pediatric Practice Settings Adolescent Friendly? An Exploration of Attitudes and Preferences," *Clinical Pediatrics* 43 (2004): 1–8.

10. William H. Kandel, "The U.S. Foreign-Born Population: Trends and Selected Characteristics," Congressional Research Service, 7-5700, www.crs.gov, R41592.

11. Trust for America's Health, "F as in Fat: How Obesity Threatens America's Future 2013," http://healthyamericans.org/report/108/.

12. Robert Wood Johnson Foundation, "Signs of Progress on Childhood Obesity," http://www.rwjf.org/en/about-rwjf/newsroom/features-and-articles/signs-of-progress-in-childhood-obesity.html.

13. The Facility Guidelines Institute, *Guidelines for Design and Construction of Health Care Facilities* (Chicago: ASHE, 2010).

14. Linda Gabel and Evan Musheno, "Understanding the Special Needs of the Bariatric Population: Design, Innovation, and Respect," KI, 2010, http://www.ki.com/pdfs/Understanding_Needs_Bariactric_Population.pdf.

15. Eileen Malone, Julie R. Mann-Dooks, and Joseph Strauss, "Evidence-Based Design: Application in the MHS," HFPA Planning & Programming Division, 2007, https://facilities.health.mil/Repository/getFile/7.

16. "What Door Handles Actually Kill Bacteria?" http://articles.mercola.com/sites/articles/archive/2008/11/20/what-door-handles-actually-kill-bacteria.aspx.

17. Phyllis J. Kuhn, "Doorknobs: A Source of Nosocomial Infection?" Medical Economics Company Inc., 1983, http://members.vol.at/schmiede/MsgverSSt.html.

18. Todd Hutlock, "An Evidence-Based Design Furniture Checklist, Interview with Eileen Malone and Barbara Dellinger," *Healthcare Design* 10 (September 2010): 24–28. http://www.healthcaredesignmagazine.com/sites/healthcaredesignmagazine.com/files/Evidence_Based%20Design%20Furniture%20Checklist_2.pdf.

19. Leda Cosmides, John Tooby, and Jerome H. Barkow. "Introduction: Evolutionary Psychology and Conceptual Integration," in

The Adapted Mind: Evolutionary Psychology and the Generation of Culture, eds. Leda Cosmides, John Tooby, and Jerome H. Barkow (New York: Oxford University Press, 1992).

20. Energy Star, "Light Bulbs for Consumers," http://www.energystar.gov/index. cfm?fuseaction=find_a_product. showProductGroup&pgw_code=LB.

21. Energy Star, "Light Bulbs for Consumers," http://www.energystar.gov/index. cfm?fuseaction=find_a_product. showProductGroup&pgw_code=LB.

22. Christine Guzzo Vickery, "The Healting Power of Artwork Revisited," *Healthcare Design,* July 27, 2012.

23. Franklin Becker and Stephanie Jones Douglass, "The Ecology of the Patient Visit: Physical Attractiveness, Waiting Times, and Perceived Quality Of Care," *Healthcare Design,* November 1, 2006.

24. Historynet.com, "Florence Nightingale."

25. Roger S. Ulrich, "View through a Window," 420–22.

26. Sara O. Marberry, "A Conversation with Roger Ulrich," *Healthcare Design,* October 31, 2010.

27. Committee on Quality of Health Care in America, *To Err Is Human: Building a Safer Health System* (Washington, DC: National Academies Press, 1999), 1–5.

28. Agency for Healthcare Research and Quality, "A Decade of Evidence, Design, Implementation: Advancing Patient Safety," 2012, http://www.ahrq.gov/professionals/ quality-patient-safetly/patient-safety-resources/resources/advancing-patient-safety/index.html.

29. Institute for Health Improvement, "What Happened to Josie," 2002, www.ihi.org/ education'IHIOpenSchool/Resources/pages/ activities/whathappenedtojosieking.aspx.

30. Ted Kolota, "Why Is Health Information Exchange So Hard?" 2012, http://tedkolota .com/?s=josie+king.

31. Kaveh G. Shojania, Bradford W. Duncan, Kathryn M. McDonald, and Robert M. Wachter, *Making Health Care Safer: A Critical Analysis of Patient Safety Practices* (Rockville, MD: Agency for Healthcare Research and Quality, 2001).

32. Committee on Quality of Health Care in America, *Crossing the Quality Chasm: New Health System for the 21st Century* (Washington, DC: National Academies Press, 2001).

33. Ann Page, Keeping Patients Safe: Transforming the Work Environment of Nurses (Washington, DC: National Academies Press, 2004.

34. "Transforming Hospitals: Designing for Safety and Quality," YouTube video, 13:42, Posted by "jackjorgens," November 2, 2011, http://www.youtube.com/ watch?v=6afKavZbw7Y.

35. Gowri Betrabet Gulwadi, Anjali Joseph, and Amy Beth Keller, "Exploring the Impact of the Physical Environment on Patient Outcomes in Ambulatory Care Settings," *Health Environments Research & Design Journal* 2 (2009): 21–41.

36. Centers for Medicare and Medicaid Services, "The Center for Consumer Information & Insurance Oversight," http://www.cms.gov/ cciio/Resources/Fact-Sheets-and-FAQs/ index.html#Patient's Bill of Rights.

37. The Beryl Institute, "Defining Patient Experience," http://www.theberylinstitute. org/?page=DefiningPatientExp.

Select Bibliography

Beryl Institute. "Defining Patient Experience," http://www.theberylinstitute.org/?page=DefiningPatientExp.

Center for Health Design. "Pebble Project." https://www.healthdesign.org/pebble.

Centers for Medicare & Medicaid Services. "HCAHPS: Patients' Perspectives of Care Survey," 2013. http://www.cms.gov/Medicare/Quality-Initiatives-Patient-Assessment-Instruments/HospitalQualityInits/HospitalHCAHPS.html.

Committee on Quality of Health Care in America. *Crossing the Quality Chasm: New Health System for the 21st Century.* Washington, D.C.: National Academies Press: 2001. http://www.iom.edu/~/media/Files/Report%20Files/2001/Crossing-the-Quality-Chasm/Quality%20Chasm%202001%20%20report%20brief.pdf.

Cwiek, Katherine, Etkin, Jennifer, Holm, Craig, Karageorgiou, George, and Meinert, Elisabeth. *Primary Care in an Era of Health Care Reform: Strategies for Reorienting Health Care Delivery System toward Primary Care.* Philadelphia: Health Strategies and Solutions, Inc., 2012.

Facility Guidelines Institute. *Guidelines for Design and Construction of Health Care Facilities.* Chicago: ASHE 2010.

Liker, Jeffrey. *The Toyota Way: 14 Management Principles from the World's Greatest Manufacturer.* New York: McGraw-Hill, 2004.

Page, Ann, ed. *Keeping Patients Safe: Transforming the Work Environment of Nurses.*" Washington, DC: National Academies Press, 2004.

Shojania, Keveh G., Duncan, Bradford W., McDonald, Kathryn M., and Wachter, Robert M. *Making Health Care Safer: A Critical Analysis of Patient Safety Practices.* Rockville, MD: Agency for Healthcare Research and Quality, 2001.

Ulrich, Roger S. "View through a window may influence recovery from surgery." *Science* 224 (1984): 420–22.

Worth, Judy. *Perfecting Patient Journeys.* Cambridge, MA: Lean Enterprise Institute, 2012.

Overview

Lean is a management philosophy that focuses on eliminating wasted time, energy, and resources so that organizations can more efficiently create products or provide services. The Lean Methodology (Lean) was originally developed to eliminate waste through continuous improvements to industrial work processes.

Implementation of the Patient Protection and Affordable Care Act and major demographic, design industry, and economic trends are converging to radically reshape the way healthcare services are being delivered in the United States. By emphasizing flexibility, adaptability, and continuous improvement, Lean is an especially appropriate and useful methodology for healthcare organizations to use during this period of dynamic and far-from-fully-predictable change.

More Patients and Higher Expectations

The ACA is not the only force behind the anticipated exponential increase of the patient population in the United States. The demand for affordable, safe, and quality care is also being driven by the fact that one of the largest population segments, aging baby boomers, has higher quality-of-life expectations than earlier generations and will not only be requiring more care but will also be expecting access to the information and advice they need to live better and longer.

Importance of Human Resources

Lean experts recognize that it is a lot harder to replace staff than to manage inventory. This is especially critical at a time when the healthcare industry is experiencing shortages of nurses and primary care providers. As implementation of the ACA adds 40 million more people to the ranks of the insured, there will be increased competition between healthcare organizations to attract and retain top employees.

By investing in Lean Design, which addresses ergonomics and generally strives to eliminate wasted time and energy spent by staff on redundant or unnecessary tasks, healthcare organizations can demonstrate their commitment to providing a safe and productive work environment.

The high cost of labor in the healthcare industry also makes employing the Lean Methodology in the design and operations of a clinic a strong strategy. The largest cost for most healthcare organizations is labor, yet industry leaders know that using reductions in force (RIFs) as a broad-brush, cost-cutting strategy is typically counterproductive. Approximately 70 percent of healthcare organizations' budgets are spent on labor because the employees providing direct care are highly educated, licensed professionals or require other specialized training. In contrast, labor constitutes between 15 and 20 percent of manufacturers' budgets. Rather than simply reducing head counts, Lean focuses on how the redesign of processes and spaces can help care providers work to the top of their abilities and training without overburdening them.

The Link with Green Design

The Leanest, greenest square foot of space is the one that never has to be built. Waste in clinic processes translates into excess square footage when caregivers must take unnecessary steps to serve patients or when equipment, rooms, or other resources are underutilized.

One of the major ways that Lean principles dovetail with those of sustainable design programs, such as LEED for Healthcare and the Green Guide for Health Care, is by eliminating excess square footage during the predesign phase of a building project, when the size, features, and configuration of spaces are being defined. Reducing excess space results in a smaller building footprint. This, in turn, reduces the total cost of construction materials and related labor, as well as the energy embedded in manufacturing and transporting materials that are no longer needed.

Building less square footage also means that there is less space to heat, cool, plumb, illuminate, and serve with electricity and water, resulting in a commensurate decline in the operation and maintenance costs and the environmental impact of a right-sized clinic.

Improved Integration

During the past decade, as healthcare and building industry leaders have been trying new approaches to improve how healthcare facilities are designed and constructed, there has been a concurrent trend toward earlier collaboration in the planning process by architects, interior designers, engineers, contractors, and others. Some healthcare organizations and design firms have taken this a step further by linking "integrated project delivery" to Lean and developing the Integrated Lean Project Delivery (ILPD) model.

The contractual agreement governing ILPD typically involves the owner, contractor, and architect. Architects, engineers, contractors, subcontractors, vendors, and leaders and key staff from the owner's organization all work together from the beginning of the planning phase to clearly define how success will be measured, generate and analyze alternatives, and integrate innovative ideas contributed by all team members into a final design solution. Their common goals are to reduce waste and optimize efficiency throughout all phases of the design and construction process.

■ WEST COAST CLINIC

In 2004, this integrated nonprofit healthcare system, which serves patients throughout Northern California, adopted the Integrated Lean Project

Delivery model. It has used this methodology to complete several projects since that time.

Under the interrelated contractual agreement used for the design and construction of a medical office building, the architect and contractor combined their respective contingencies and were held jointly accountable for any design or construction errors and omissions. This encouraged them to work together to resolve problems, in contrast to creating an adversarial relationship like the ones that often arise using the traditional design-bid-build delivery process.

Core team members met regularly to discuss and jointly resolve issues based on the shared goal of finding the best solution for the project as a whole. They used Building Information Modeling (BIM) from the outset to coordinate and facilitate their efforts. They set target costs for each system and then focused their design efforts on hitting these targets.

As a result, the three-story medical office building was designed and completed in 25 months. It was finished under budget, even though exterior canopies were added during construction to connect campus buildings.

Lean Roots

To understand why architects and other professionals began applying Lean to the design of healthcare facilities, it is important to first review the series of innovations that led to the creation and use of Lean by manufacturers.

Frederick Taylor

In the late 1890s, when early industrial engineers began to study how economic efficiency and labor productivity could be improved, Frederick Taylor used his observations of individual workers and work methods to develop what became known as the theory of scientific management (or Taylorism). Taylor helped lay the groundwork for Lean by studying workflows and standardizing individual tasks in order to improve industrial productivity. Too much standardization, however, can cause boredom, alienation, and distrust.[1]

Frank and Lillian Gilbreth

Frank Gilbreth studied the separate steps in work processes and analyzed the time and motions that were needed to complete them. He invented "process mapping" (or charting), which is used to identify waste, streamline work processes, determine what can be standardized, better understand how an organization operates, and build consensus for improvements. This technique is still the one most frequently used by Lean experts because it distinguishes between activities that create waste and those that add value. Lean experts refer to their use of this technique as "value-stream mapping."

In contrast to Frank Gilbreth's focus on the technical aspects of what workers could accomplish, Lillian Gilbreth was concerned with the human aspects of time management strategies. She was among the first researchers to recognize the impact of fatigue and stress on worker productivity. She also examined psychological factors by studying what motivated workers and observing how their attitudes affected outcomes.

Eli Whitney

While Eli Whitney may be best known as the inventor of the cotton gin, his standardization of the use of interchangeable parts at the beginning of the 1800s was a major advancement for manufacturers because it reduced the number of extra parts they had to purchase and eliminated the costs of storing these parts.

One of the ways Lean Design professionals apply this concept (which evolved into the "just-in-time" inventory strategy) is by working with staff at a healthcare facility to establish which supplies and equipment they need to have immediately available, identify the best location(s) and most efficient means for storing these items, and determine how restocking can be done on demand.

In general, Lean experts try to make sure care providers and other staff members have the right equipment and supplies, in the right amount, in the right place, and at the right time.

Henry Ford

In 1913, Henry Ford was the first person to fully integrate a production process when he combined interchangeable parts with standardized work and moving conveyance to achieve what he called "flow production." This combination of business strategies later evolved into just-in-time (JIT) supply-chain management, a concept that Toyota incorporated into its Lean Manufacturing techniques.

While Ford was able to achieve large batch production and a continuous flow of products through his factory, he was not able to provide variety at the same time. For example, the Model T came in one color (black), and all Model T chassis were nearly identical until the mid-1920s.

Kiichiro Toyoda

Based on his belief that the just-in-time approach Ford used for managing inventory at his plants was key to the success of auto manufacturing, Kichiro Toyoda established the Toyota Motor Company. However, since the firms supplying parts for Toyota were still using antiquated approaches to production, they could not keep pace with demand. During and after World War II, the Toyota Motor Company knew it had to improve or it would disappear.

However, for a number of reasons, it took until the 1970s for Toyota's version of JIT supply-chain management to achieve success.

By 1990, Toyota had grown to reach half the size of General Motors, which was the largest auto manufacturer in the world at that time.

Since initially Toyota did not have the same volume of demand for its cars that U.S. automakers had, the company had to be more careful with each car it produced, and it could not have excess inventory on hand. This motivated Toyota to perfect the JIT process and combine it with customization of cars that were manufactured in small batches.

By focusing on obtaining the right quantity of raw materials to produce the right number of autos in the right place at the right time, Toyota became the largest global auto manufacturer in 2008, and it continues to compete with General Motors for this designation.[2]

Joseph Juran

Until the 1980s, factories in the United States were characterized by excessive worker supervision and product inspection. This changed in the 1990s, when management consultant and engineer Joseph Juran popularized the "artisan concept," which states that workers know what their job responsibilities are, know when the result is unacceptable, and have the knowledge to bring substandard work up to par.

Lean applies this concept by recognizing that the staff members who have experience with daily workflow are in the best position to describe and map current work processes, as well as to provide insights into how they can be improved.

Another of Juran's key theories is based on 19th-century Italian economist Vilfredo Pareto's statement that 80 percent of the wealth in his country was held by 20 percent of the population. In 1937, Juran asserted that this principle also applied to defects. By focusing on the 20 percent of defects that cause 80 percent of the problems,

organizations could maximize the impact of their quality-improvement efforts.

Lean uses Juran's "Pareto Principle" to prioritize which processes should be improved by separating the "vital few" from the "useful many."

The Machine that Changed the World

In 1990, the book *The Machine that Changed the World,* by James Womack, Daniel Jones, and Daniel Roos, was first published. It summarized and described Toyota Motor Company's strategies for streamlining its manufacturing process and eliminating waste. Although other automakers had begun to successfully apply the principles of Lean production, the Lean Methodology had not been applied outside of the auto industry. But since *The Machine that Changed the World* provided a groundbreaking analysis of the entire Lean process, from product development and supplier management to production, sales, and service, it provided information that leaders in other industries could adapt and apply.

Michael Hammer and James Champy

In the early 1990s, Michael Hammer and James Champy published *Reengineering the Corporation: A Manifesto for Business Revolution.* This book described their development of a business management strategy that focused on analyzing and redesigning workflows in order to improve customer service, cut costs, and become more competitive.

By 1998, however, healthcare industry leaders had begun to prefer the Lean Methodology because it enabled them to take small steps that would result in major changes over time. This approach also allowed for constant course corrections as organizations strove to reach an ideal state.

Since Lean and reengineering became popular in the United States around the same time, the differences between these business methodologies can be unclear. What sticks in most people's mind about "reengineering" is that major corporations used this as a basis for completing large-scale layoffs in the 1990s. In contrast, a key distinguishing characteristic of Lean is the value it puts on human resources.

Although in the United States the word "lean" to refer to business operations can connote "cutting to the bone," the proper application of Lean principles addresses challenges like understaffing and overutilization of other resources that affect how well people can work, not just how efficiently they can do their jobs.

Lean and Healthcare Design

As healthcare organizations have become increasingly aware of the importance the built environment can play in helping them to anticipate and properly adapt to dynamically changing conditions, they have hired architects and other design professionals with Lean expertise to help them streamline and update their facilities.

When Lean Design professionals are an integral part of a project team, they can ensure that recommendations for process improvements are supported—or even enhanced—by the layout and qualities of the built environment. The overarching goal of Lean healthcare design is to eliminate physical barriers that prevent medical professionals and other specially trained staff from delivering affordable, safe, high-quality care.

Although Lean is known for its systemic approach to cutting costs, it has always given the highest weight to improving quality. Thus, Lean strategies and principles are especially useful for helping healthcare organizations advance toward the Affordable Care Act's " ideal state," in which a much larger patient population will have access to safe and affordable high-quality care.

New Care Models

Lean can also be used to help test, refine, and institute new care models, such as the Accountable Care Organization (ACO), which is described in the Affordable Care Act. An ACO consists of a network of care providers and healthcare facilities that share responsibility for providing care for a specific patient population for a set period of time. All ACO members agree to collaboratively manage the health needs of this patient population. Lean can help ACOs that are assembling the different components of care for patients—primary care, specialists, in-patient and outpatient facilities, and the like —to determine how all of these parts can efficiently and effectively work together to "deliver the right care to the right people at the right time."[3]

Unique Challenges

The design of healthcare facilities presents challenges that Lean experts do not encounter in the manufacturing realm. For example, Toyota's Lean experts could identify, test, refine, and implement some process improvements within a week. It is rarely this easy to alter the built environment so quickly. Shortening walking distances for patients or care providers, reducing wait times, and otherwise improving the efficiency of clinical processes often requires that space be resized and reconfigured. Moving walls, rerouting building systems, and finishing and furnishing repurposed areas often require a phased approach to implementation.

Risks

Toyota and other Lean manufacturers can test products to the point of failure to learn as much as possible about what works and what does not. Obviously, healthcare organizations must be more cautious because their actions directly affect the welfare of staff, patients, and other people.

Lean Design professionals for healthcare facilities must constantly consider the human impact of their recommendations. However, the ability to fail with limited risk and to "reset"—to make course corrections and update a healthcare organization's vision for an "ideal future state" over time—are essential for the successful application of the Lean Methodology.

Another form of risk can arise when the recommendations Lean Design consultants have made for improvements are not initiated or not fully implemented within a set period of time. In some instances, this results when Lean Design professionals have presented options for change before clients are ready (or willing) to take the first step towards process improvement because leaders or other employees of a healthcare organization are uncomfortable with change. This can make it extremely difficult to achieve consensus for a specific plan of attack, even when the collaborative Lean project team includes key stakeholders and decision makers from the client's organization.

Personnel responsible for implementation can also change during the course of a project, as can other factors (new legislation or economic downturn, for example) that have a major influence on how effective the initial recommendations can be.

Key Concepts

The way that Lean defines the key concepts such as value, standardization, takt time, cycle time, and waste shapes how Lean principles are applied to the design of healthcare facilities.

Value

According to the Lean philosophy, value is defined by the customer. Patients are the customers of healthcare organizations. To maximize value for patients, Lean Design professionals identify all of the steps in the processes that occur within a healthcare facility, then develop schemes designed to eliminate each step, action, or characteristic of the built environment that does not enhance the quality of care patients receive. In order to be defined as value, a customer must be willing to pay for it, it must transform or change in state, and it has to be performed correctly the first time (fig. 2-1).

Standardization

Standardization, which helped early industrialists improve productivity and quality, is a key tenet of Lean Design because relating certain work tasks or processes to quantifiable metrics, such as takt time or cycle time, makes it easier to set goals for improvement and to measure progress objectively.

Standardizing tasks, equipment, supplies, and spaces in clinics and other healthcare facilities can improve their operational efficiency, help to reduce errors, and enhance the quality of care provided for all patients. For example, standardizing all of the medical supplies used in a clinic and where and how they are stored can make it easier for staff to locate and restock them. This not only reduces the amount of time wasted on "hunting and gathering" activities but also enables care providers to quickly and accurately locate the specific items they need to treat patients.

Standardization can also clarify roles and responsibilities for staff and equip them with tools such as checklists, templates, and procedural or policy guidelines that enable them to provide a consistent quality of care for all patients.

Takt Time

Takt is the German word for "beat." If takt time is the heartbeat of a process, the goal of the Lean team is to even out arrhythmia in order to achieve a steady, specified pace.

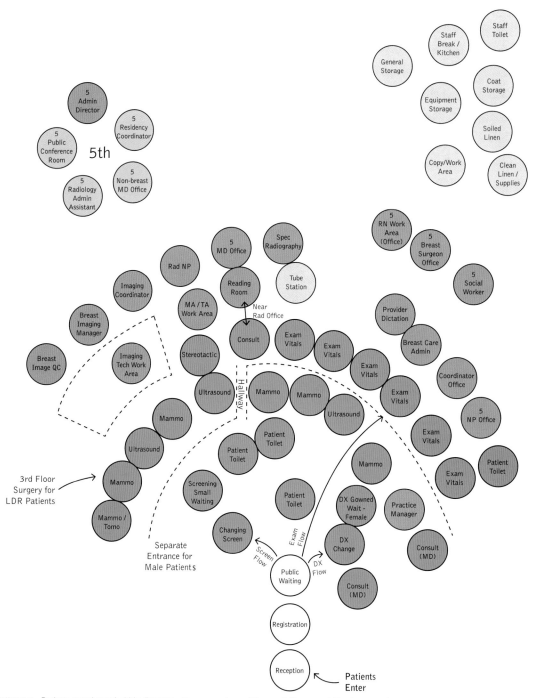

FIGURE 2-1: Patient experience bubble diagram. Image courtesy of Hammel, Green and Abrahamson, Inc.

For manufacturing processes, takt refers to how many units must be produced within a defined period of time in order to meet customer demand. When applied to the design of healthcare facilities, takt time is the longest period of time that can be spent completing each task while still meeting patients' needs and expectations.[4]

Takt time $= \dfrac{\text{Available time}}{\text{Customer demand}}$

If patients expect their clinic sessions to be completed at a rate of one per hour, for example, Lean experts analyze whether or not the current healthcare delivery process is meeting this expectation and, if not, what changes can and should be made.

Takt time is measured in minutes, hours, or days and is related to specific activities or processes, such as the registration, exam, and checkout procedures.

Cycle Time

This is the average time it takes for patients to move through a particular activity in a clinic, from the time they begin check-in, to the time they complete check-in or the time they begin the encounter with the healthcare provider to the time the provider begins with the next patient. Cycle times vary according to the culture of a clinic, the type and variety of services it provides, and the characteristics of the patient population it serves. Decreasing cycle time by eliminating waste increases the number of patients that can be examined and treated in a healthcare facility (fig. 2-2).[5]

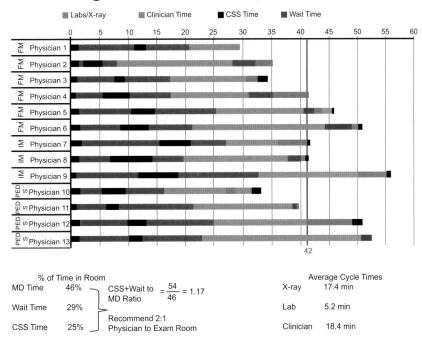

FIGURE 2-2: Average lead time per provider. Illustration of cycle time and wait time for each component of the clinic visit for a sample of family practice, internal medicine, and pediatric care providers. Image courtesy of Hammel, Green and Abrahamson, Inc.

Waste

In a healthcare setting, waste is defined as anything that does not add value for the patient. The three categories of waste specifically targeted by Lean are known by their Japanese terms, *muri, mura,* and *muda.* Muri, or "overburdening," arises when people or equipment are used beyond their natural limits. Mura, or "unevenness," results from varying periods of hyperactivity and lulls (bottlenecks or idleness, for example). Muda occurs from using more people, time, equipment, materials, and space than required (fig 2-3).[6]

Muri (Overburdening)

Staff fatigue and burnout are particularly critical issues for the healthcare industry, which is already experiencing labor shortages. In addition to patient-care suffering when staff members are pressed for time, equipment, and other resources to do their jobs well, errors and injuries are more likely to occur when clinicians and other employees are overburdened.

Mura (Unevenness)

This form of waste arises from unevenness or irregularity in the flow of people and resources along the care continuum.

FIGURE 2-3: Encircle Health Ambulatory Care Center, ThedaCare Health System, Appleton, Wisconsin. Three elements of innovation were addressed for this owner: Streamlining processes to eliminate waste while responding to patient needs; balancing costs while achieving LEED goals; and implementing the project using an Integrated Process Delivery format. An integrated project delivery team, including the owner, architect, engineer, landscape architect, contractor, and asset/property management staff, was developed early in the process. Photography by Michael Leschisin, Image Studios Inc.

■ MIDWEST CANCER CENTER

This specialized facility, which is located in the Midwest, combines two practices (hematology and oncology) into a single location. Most of the patients visiting this clinic have infusion treatments and must have blood drawn in advance to verify that their white blood-cell counts are at an appropriate level.

The project team began by interviewing patients and clinic staff members to define what the ideal patient experience should be, identify where inefficiencies were occurring, map the current state, and envision an ideal future state. This research revealed that patients for one of the practices were having their blood drawn a day in advance to make sure the test results were back before treatments were scheduled to begin.

The bottleneck for this process was traced to a centralized lab facility that also served a hospital. The clinic's test results were often delayed because precedence was given to meeting the hospital's need for lab services. Data showed that the volume of testing for the combined practices would be high enough to merit including a stat lab with two lab technicians in the clinic. Now results are available in as little as 10 minutes.

Muda

In healthcare facilities, this form of waste arises whenever an activity is completed without providing value for patients. The "eight wastes" that Joseph Juran identified in manufacturing processes are also those that Lean experts strive to remove from operational and healthcare delivery processes. These wastes include human potential that is not utilized or is underutilized, waiting, inventory, unnecessary transportation, defects, motion, overprocessing, and overproduction.

Human Potential Not Utilized or Underutilized

Waste in terms of human resources occurs when the expertise, skills, and experience of caregivers and other clinic staff are not employed to the best of their abilities or when knowledge is not shared for the benefit of patients.

■ MIDWEST CLINIC

Care providers at this Midwest clinic began examining patients before the medical assistants could obtain all of the essential health information needed to complete an accurate assessment. Patients' medical records were missing immunization histories and other key documentation components. Since keeping this type of information up to date was part of the medical assistants' role at this clinic, it was clear that the medical assistant staff needed more time with patients to meet the regulatory documentation standards. After the clinic increased intake time from 7 to 15 minutes, they saw a 50 percent increase in vaccine administration.

Waiting

In manufacturing, time and other resources are wasted when goods are not being processed or transported. In clinics and other healthcare facilities, waste arises when the delivery of the services patients need is stalled and they must wait for them to be provided or to complete the next step in the clinic visit. Staff members can also waste time and energy when they have to wait for information to be expeditiously communicated to them or for supplies and equipment to become available.

■ PREADMISSION TESTING CLINIC—NORTHEAST

This project used the remodeling of an existing clinic as a catalyst for streamlining the care delivery process and improving patients' experiences as they complete preop tests and exams. Information gathered during the research, design, and implementation phases of the clinic remodel continues to inform a larger health system's facilities planning decisions.

The preadmission testing facility was conducting 45 in-person visits and 45 telephone visits per day. The average time patients spent in the clinic was 112 minutes (40 minutes in the waiting room and 72 minutes in the exam room). Age served as the main criterion for scheduling patients, and all exam periods were the same length. Patients were seen by three care providers during their visit: a medical assistant, a registered nurse or nurse practitioner, and a physician. Registered nurses followed patients as they progressed through the visit.

Patients typically received four "touches"—interactions with staff—while in the clinic. They were left alone for 30 minutes of their total visit.

At the same time, health system administrators projected that a 20 percent increase in patient load would occur over the next 10 years. If the clinic and its processes were left in their current state, this would require the addition of two exam rooms to the eight already there.

The "fatigue factor" was also a major concern. The clinic's staff members had stopped scheduling exams after 2:30 p.m. so they could catch up with paperwork. This meant that, at times, patients who had scheduled afternoon appointments were kept waiting for an hour or more before being seen.

In addition, too many tests such as EKGs and blood tests were being completed. Since physicians did not have sufficient information in advance to determine which tests were required for specific patients, they would order all of the tests associated with various procedures. The health system's leaders wanted to reduce the percentage of tests that did not add value.

Lean Design professionals collaborated with members of this clinic's staff, representatives from the parent healthcare system's patient advisory board, and others to identify the most important features for the remodeled facility. When they had completed this exercise, the advisory group was given notes they could use to identify which of the features were game changers, and which they were for or against.

Based on the results of these interactive sessions, the architects developed six "extreme schemes," then worked with the clinic's leaders and special advisors to identify which aspects of each scheme they liked best and why they liked it. The final design combined these preferences.

The Lean project team also recommended changes to the care delivery process, which included converting to 100 percent telephone registration and developing a takt time that better related the duration of exams to individual patients' health needs and staff availability. A long-term goal was to enable patients to register online.

While reorganizing and standardizing the clinic's exam room flow, the project team discovered that an anesthesia questionnaire patients had been required to complete before being roomed was redundant. Eliminating this form reduced wait times by 20 minutes. Telephone registration will allow staff to answer questions and send educational information in advance. Patients will know what to expect when they arrive at the clinic and what they should bring with them.

The improved care model is expected to cut the average time each patient spends in the clinic in half (from 112 to 58 minutes). This, in turn, will increase patient turnover and reduce the total number of exam rooms currently needed to six. The two remaining exam rooms that already exist should be able to accommodate the projected future growth.

Inventory

Organizations that store more supplies and equipment than is needed waste the resources used to construct and maintain storage space, as well as the time expended managing this excess inventory. Additional waste can occur if items purchased in advance are not used by their expiration date or become technologically obsolete while they are awaiting use.

Generally, clinics should store just what they need on site and have an efficient process for ordering supplies and equipment. Here, a key challenge for Lean Design professionals is to determine how much storage space is required on site, where it should be located within the clinic, and how this space can be adapted for different functions in the future if the efficiency of just-in-time inventory processes is perfected and the need for storage space reduced.

◼ EAST COAST CLINIC

Several forms that presented information in different languages occupied an entire 20-foot wall of this clinic. After a simple shift in thinking, forms are now printed on demand in the appropriate language. This reduces the waste of unused, outdated forms and the space required to store them.

Unnecessary Transportation

Whenever patients, test results and other medical information, or supplies and equipment must be moved excessively or unnecessarily, time and energy are wasted. This waste can also increase the risk of errors.

◼ MIDWEST CLINIC

A fundamental process question arises when discussing where to perform lab draws in the clinic. Should the lab draw be performed in the clinic exam room or at a centralized drawing station? If the lab result will not be reviewed at this same clinic, having the patient stop by a draw station on the way out does not add steps to their process if they are easily able to walk. Patients who have difficulty walking or require an escort to a centralized lab draw location introduce a safety concern and added effort for the clinic staff in providing the escort. It might be better to complete the lab draws for these patients in the exam room to reduce risk and eliminate the additional handoff between the escort and the phlebotomist.

Defects

Major goals of Lean Design for healthcare facilities include minimizing the risk of medical errors and taking the steps necessary to ensure that the physical environment is safe for all building occupants and users.

◼ MIDWEST OUTPATIENT CLINIC

For a number of years, a major goal of a renowned Midwestern healthcare organization has been to standardize care across all of its facilities, including the care provided at its private outpatient facility. These standardization efforts have been focused on reducing errors and decreasing the learning curve for staff members who move between facilities.

To this end, the healthcare organization has its own Lean staff members who are dedicated to discovering ways to improve the care delivery process. These staff members routinely shadow care providers and examine each step for a process in question in order to determine if a step is necessary, the result of a regulatory requirement, or a work-around.

The organization also hosts focus group sessions that address issues such as the layout, location, and qualities of a particular clinic space. Participants range from designers, engineers, physicians, and nurses to patients and contractors.

A major design decision for a new ambulatory care center was informed by this ongoing

Lean process. The registration, check-in, and checkout areas for the clinic (which was part of a larger medical complex) were consolidated into a central location that serves both outpatient and inpatient facilities. This reduced the total amount of space needed for these functions.

Motion

One of the most common forms of "motion waste" found in healthcare occurs when the design of a facility requires care providers or patients to take more steps than necessary. This wastes time and energy. It can also create safety concerns for patients who arrive at clinics weakened by injury or illness, or for people with disabilities. Reducing the number of steps can not only reduce labor costs and alleviate fatigue but can also increase the amount of time care providers spend with patients, thus improving the quality of care and health outcomes.

■ MILITARY MEDICAL FACILITY

The project parameters for a Midwestern military medical facility were established using federal standards for healthcare facilities. This meant the Lean team hired to improve the preliminary design that had been submitted to secure funding had to make recommendations that could be accomplished within the established project budget and timeframe.

Most of the clinical space in the preliminary design was organized around a centralized nurse station. Designers realized that while this scheme typically minimizes travel distances for the nursing staff, in this instance it did not take full advantage of the healthcare institution's advanced adoption of communication and digital-record technology.

Designers pointed out that digital technology could facilitate in-room registration and scheduling, while decreasing the total duration of patient visits. When they examined the potential impact of locating nursing staff closer to the physicians' offices while using an electronic communications system and one-stop exam rooms, designers discovered travel times would be reduced for patients and physicians by 2 percent and 8 percent, respectively. These numbers pale, however, when compared to the 49 percent reduction in distances nurses would travel if all recommended changes are made.

Overproduction and Overprocessing

Overproduction occurs when something is produced in excess, earlier, or faster than the next process needs it. Overprocessing occurs any time more work is done (or more services are provided) than is required by the customer.

■ SPECIALTY CLINIC

The Lean Design team collaborated with key members of this care system's facilities staff to set priorities for the spaces that this new clinic would include, and to determine what the optimal sizing, sequencing, and configuration of these spaces should be. The clinic hired a nurse practitioner to be the first point of contact for patients. This staff member assesses the severity of patients' conditions and the clinical necessity of seeing the specialist, who then determines if complementary care methods that might help them avoid surgery are warranted. Wastes are eliminated in two locations: triaging patients to the specialist (overproduction) and avoiding the prospect of unnecessary surgery (overprocessing).

The Lean Design Process (3Ps)

The major phases of the Lean design process parallel the three that Lean experts have used historically to improve the efficiency and productivity of manufacturing companies: preparation, process, and production.

Members of the Lean team *prepare* by conducting research. They review background materials and data provided to them by clients, and interview, shadow, or otherwise observe patients and staff to identify where errors, bottlenecks, work-arounds, and other inefficiencies are occurring.

Lean team members summarize their key research findings about existing *processes* by sketching a "current state flow map" to show where waste can be removed and highlight where value can be added. The Lean project team then holds brainstorming and other interactive work sessions with patient and staff advisory groups to develop an "ideal future state flow map" that illustrates how improvements can be made.

Depending on the difficulty and complexity of the design challenges, team members *produce* computer models and animations, build full-scale mock-ups, or run beta tests to develop "extreme schemes" that explore strategies for improving the care environment in ways that support changes in care delivery processes. Lean Design professionals also use these tools and techniques to test and refine details of each scheme and arrive at a final, preferred design.[7]

Research

This phase entails agreeing on what processes need to be studied, how to map them, who will participate, and how logistics will be handled. Accurately defining a scope of work also includes establishing what a healthcare organization expects the impact of applying the Lean Methodology will be.

Once design professionals know where an owner is in "the Lean Journey," they can assemble the proper mix of Lean team members and determine where to begin. It is also important to define the measures of success before starting the research portion of the Lean Design process

so that strategies and schemes can be tested against these criteria as work progresses.

Lean Design professionals use a variety of tools and techniques in order to "learn to see" where waste occurs and where value can be added by strategically designing or modifying the design of a healthcare facility. Since patients are the primary customers of healthcare organizations, Lean Design professionals begin by listening to patients' voices.

The Voice of the Customer

Patients define what value is. To "hear their voices," members of the Lean team review patient surveys, interview patients and staff, and shadow them to directly observe the process from the patient and family perspective. They also use data analysis, indirect research, and direct interaction to learn what patients need and expect.

Data Analysis

Healthcare organizations often collect information from surveys and feedback forms, online questionnaires, blog comments, and other sources that Lean Design professionals review to identify key concerns and opportunities for improvement, as well as to summarize suggestions that patients, staff, and others provide.

Indirect Research

Industry publications, studies, market and financial analyses, articles about a clinic and its staff, and the materials a healthcare organization uses to communicate to its patients can collectively provide a "360-degree" perspective on how a clinic is perceived by all users and occupants, as well as by its surrounding community.

Direct Interaction

Lean Design professionals frequently plan and lead focus-group discussions, conduct phone interviews, and conduct "go-tos" to observe processes in situ by following staff and patients through the steps of the care delivery process or watching how they interact with building features and equipment at the point of use.

When necessary, members of the Lean Design team also meet one-on-one with patients, staff, and key stakeholders to hear their stories and "mine the nuggets" from this anecdotal information.

The information gathered, analyzed, and summarized by using these research strategies can then serve as a reference as healthcare organizations work toward improving their processes and facilities (fig. 2-4).[8]

Value-Stream Mapping

Lean views the healthcare delivery process as a stream of activities along which value can be added and waste eliminated. A key reason why Lean Design professionals interview and

I am ready, are you?

Narrative
When I come to the clinic for care, it is because I am in pain. Know that I may already be nervous about the treatment I will receive or discussing my treatment plan with my provider. Wait times across the board at the clinic create feelings of anxiety and stress, negatively impacting my already weakened current state. I require prompt, reliable and consistent scheduling to support my overall health and well being.

Headlines
Seem to always be behind schedule (3)

Waited for 1 hour even though 1st or 2nd appointment of the day.
Do not call people come in early when you still have to wait
The wait was unreasonably long (3)
The patient in the room next to me was very upset with his wait.

Too long of a wait before and after visit in exam room (2)
The long wait time once I was called in to the exam room (3)

When provider is running late tell us + periodically check with us so we know we have not been forgotten
The provider seem to be always busy, didn't have time for a patient and behind schedule (2)

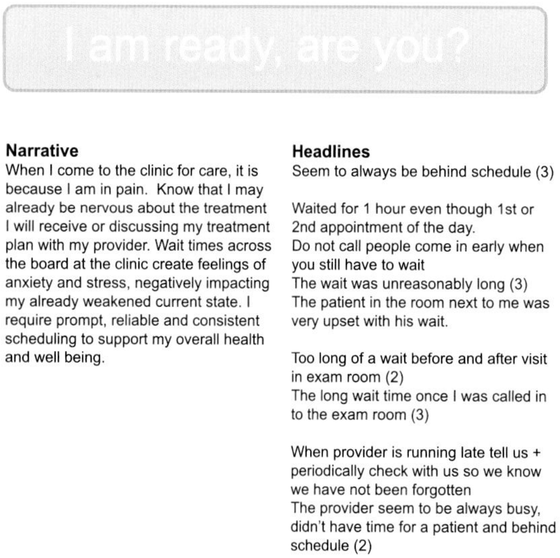

FIGURE 2-4: An example of one of 14 themes of patient headlines for a clinic. Patients were asked, "If you could change one thing, what would it be?" Image courtesy of Hammel, Green and Abrahamson, Inc.

observe the people working along these streams is that these staff members deliver care directly to patients. That means they not only know the most about what works and what does not but also have unique insight into which changes will provide the greatest value for patients (e.g., reduce wait times, reduce costs).

As part of the multidisciplinary project team, Lean Design professionals use the research information to diagram the value streams occurring within a specific facility or between related facilities. The resulting value-stream maps illustrate the sequencing of how people and resources flow along the care continuum and depict the interrelationships between these flows.

Using this technique enables Lean team members to understand how changing one step in a process or a single aspect of a design can create a ripple or domino effect.

An improvement to one part of a value stream should not negatively affect other parts (or related processes). For example, if a clinic converts to the one-stop exam room model and patients still wait an excessively long time to be seen by a care provider, the new design has only relocated where the patient's time is being wasted and has not solved the problem.

Value-stream mapping helps to ensure that recommendations made by the Lean team work together rather than conflict with each other.

Mapping the Current State

To easily visualize all of the processes occurring in a healthcare facility, the Lean team hosts a workshop to create a one-page "current state map." Participants address questions such as:

- How does the healthcare delivery process currently work?
- What are the key activities that take place at each step along the care continuum?
- Who is involved at each step?

- What is the average amount of time required to complete each step (e.g., takt time)?
- Where is waste occurring at or between steps?
- Where can value be added?

The resulting map establishes the baseline for improvements and serves as a springboard for the next step in the Lean process, which entails envisioning and mapping the Ideal Future State for a healthcare facility.

Mapping the Ideal Future State

Members of the Lean team typically kick off this phase by holding focus groups or other interactive work sessions with key stakeholders (patients and staff advisory groups, for example) in order to arrive at a collective vision of an ideal future state that would enable people, equipment, and supplies to flow smoothly through a healthcare facility with no waste, redundancies, or other inefficiencies.

Participants address questions such as:

- Which redundant or unnecessary tasks can be eliminated?
- Which steps can be condensed and/or reorganized?
- Are there better ways to allocate resources and responsibilities?
- How can the built environment be designed (or modified) to support these process improvements?
- Which attributes and strategies provide the most value for patients?

Pulling Value Through

The diagram that Lean experts create based information from the interactive work sessions should show how all steps in the healthcare delivery process can be tightly sequenced and synchronized to enable patients to efficiently "pull" the value they desire from them. Lean building design supports "pull" when a facility enables clinicians, support staff, and patients to obtain exactly what they need when they need it.

■ UROLOGY CLINIC

In the clinic environment, the most visual sense of pull is the coordination of the appointment time with the pace of the care provider. Medical assistants, who work ahead of the provider, establish this pace by taking patients to exam rooms, recording their height and weight, taking their vitals, and recording their medical history. The chief concern at this urology clinic is that overproducing could potentially lead to repetition of work that has already been completed.

Patients are essentially pushed along before providers are ready for them. This introduces waiting time for the patient and, as a result, introduces unnecessary "inventory" into a highly valued exam space.

This situation arises when patients arrive early, the scheduled appointment types and times are not synchronized with the provider's true pace, and/or there are unexpected variations in the provider's day. In a pull system, countermeasures would be implemented to room or "pull" the patient at the optimal time in order to reduce waiting by the patient while ensuring high provider productivity.

The End-to-End Value Stream

The implementation of the Affordable Care Act has put more emphasis on the provision of preventative and follow-up care, as well as on addressing community health issues. This has prompted Lean experts to examine value streams from "end to end," with the goal of providing a full context for understanding processes that occur within a healthcare facility, as well as those that occur before patients arrive and after they leave.[9]

Laying Out the Plant

In the same manner as industrial engineers develop layouts to optimize the productivity of manufacturing plants, Lean Design professionals size, sequence, and configure spaces within a healthcare facility in ways that support improvements in its operational and care delivery processes.

As the emphasis of clinic design has shifted towards enhancing the patient experience, Lean Design professionals have concentrated on devising layouts that streamline the patient's movement along the care continuum—from entry and registration through exam and consultation to checkout. Lean Design professionals address the following factors when creating layout options for healthcare clients to consider (figs. 2-5, 2-6):

- Human work factors, such as ergonomics, travel distances, and safety
- Quality control
- Inventory control
- Logistics and the flow of supplies, equipment, and people
- Immediate and long-term costs[10]

FIGURE 2-5: An example of a team identifying the key adjacency relationships within the clinic environment from the staff perspective. Image courtesy of Hammel, Green and Abrahamson, Inc.

Extreme Scheming

Lean Design professionals use a set-based approach to generating multiple "extreme schemes," testing each scheme against pre-defined project criteria and collapsing the attributes that a client prefers from the "sets" of characteristics and strategies associated with each scheme into a final design solution.

One of the strategies Lean experts use to understand and convey how different decisions relate to and can affect each other is to write all of the design attributes and improvement strategies on Post-It notes and arrange these on a wall.

All of those that are aligned and can be employed synergistically fall into the "And" category. Those that are diametrically opposed or represent an equivalent alternative fall into the "Or" category.

Mocking It Up

Depending on the difficulty and complexity of the design challenges for a particular building or a facility prototype, team members use computer modeling and visualization software, build full-scale mock-ups, or run beta tests to fully develop and refine aspects of "extreme schemes." The following projects demonstrate how mock-ups and

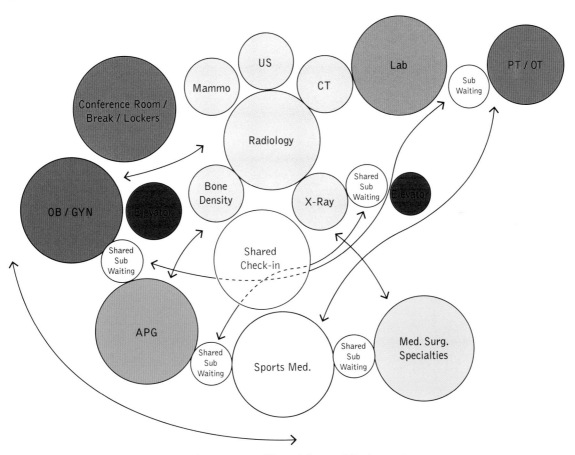

FIGURE 2-6: Key adjacencies bubble diagram. Image courtesy of Hammel, Green and Abrahamson, Inc.

"rapid prototyping" can be used to test aspects of the chosen scheme (fig. 2-7). (For in-depth examples of mock-ups, see chapter 3.)

Health System Design Standard Improvements Project

A Midwest-based health system, which was already achieving patient ratings in the top percentile for some of its departments, wanted to further improve efficiency and positive patient outcomes while also preparing for long-term growth.

To accomplish these objectives, the Lean team developed standards for new construction and renovation projects that concentrated on five core areas: ambulatory care (outpatient diagnosis and treatment), inpatient care, physician offices, administrative offices, and support services.

Developers, architects, construction managers, and key subcontractors collaborated with Lean experts from predesign to identify excess square footage and to reduce the materials, time, and labor that would have otherwise have been needed to construct wasted space.

Research

The Lean team invited former patients and members of their families, clinic administrators, caregivers, and other staff members to provide input so that decisions affecting the care environment would reinforce improvements in clinic processes. Design professionals on the Lean team also interviewed more than 3,500 people nationwide to learn more about their patient experiences. The interviews revealed that patients,

Mock-up - Exam Room

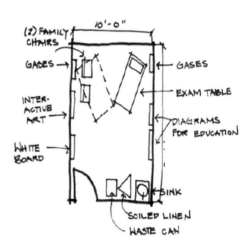

FIGURE 2-7: An example from rapid prototyping mock-ups that integrate the patient and family experience with staff workflow and the physical environment.   Image courtesy of Hammel, Green and Abrahamson, Inc.

other visitors, and clinic staff members want privacy, respect, safety, some individual control, and a pleasant healing environment.

Mock-ups and Prototypes

Based on research results, Lean Design professionals began rapid prototyping simulations. They mocked up scenarios that placed caregivers, patients, and family members in various situations, asked them to perform tasks or experience the situation, and requested feedback. Healthcare administrators were asked about nontraditional operational strategies, such as outsourcing food service and central sterile processing.

The real-time scenarios provided the critical information needed to streamline clinic processes by reorienting spaces and objects within the facilities and eliminating wasted time or effort. Concepts developed during the predesign process were tested further through benchmarking, peer research, and ongoing rapid prototyping.

Perfecting Continuously

Lean does not assume that all problems can be solved at once. Rather, Lean asserts that making incremental changes can have a major cumulative impact. In addition to identifying and addressing which improvements need to be made immediately, Lean Design professionals should provide healthcare organizations with the capabilities to continuously perfect processes and address unforeseen challenges—long after a single building has been constructed or remodeled or a series of building projects completed.

When healthcare organizations use Lean and continuously perfect value streams, their buildings last longer. The building owners and managers are equipped with the strategies and tools they need in order to properly operate, maintain, and renovate or otherwise alter facilities over time. The facilities are designed to be durable, flexible, and adaptable so that they can better respond to constantly changing needs.[11]

Key Considerations

Design professionals take a number of key factors into consideration before recommending that the Lean Methodology be used to guide and inform the creative decision-making process. For example, if there is a lack of fit with the business model and culture of a clinic or if the potential for Lean principles to have a significant impact is very limited, the time and effort invested in Leaning work processes and the design of the built environment may not be justified.

Business Model and Culture

Lean Design cannot achieve its full impact without the support and leadership of key members of a healthcare organization's staff. Through their passion and commitment, these key leadership people ensure that the proper resources are in place at the correct time. Then they orchestrate the efforts of staff to implement improvements expeditiously. Thus, Lean Design professionals should consider a healthcare organization's business model and culture when they are assessing the extent to which they will be able to help catalyze and institute positive change.

Since Lean focuses on continually improving processes to advance toward an ideal state, it is a better fit for organizations that manage by process than it is for those that manage solely by objectives.

Management by Objectives

Management by Objectives (MBO) employs a top-down approach to decision making. Leaders of an organization set its objectives and define employee responsibilities for achieving these objectives. Hierarchies, roles, and expectations are well defined, but aspects of the MBO model make it difficult to achieve the flexibility and adaptability that healthcare organizations need.

In addition, the leaders' understanding of the culture of a particular healthcare facility, staff working conditions, and patient perceptions can be out of date if they do not have regular contact with caregivers and the patients they serve. There is often little incentive for employees at all levels to contribute creative ideas and make suggestions for improvements because they are compensated for doing exactly what is prescribed in order to achieve specific organizational goals.

Management by Process

Organizations that use the Management by Process (MBP) business model draw upon the knowledge, talents, and insights that staff at all levels can contribute to constantly improve the way they do business. They focus on the journey as well as on the destination.

Lean principles and practices are most effective for organizations that use a management by process model because Lean also focuses on the continuous improvement of an organization's processes and recognizes that the people who can best identify where processes are creating waste instead of adding value are the employees working on the front lines every day.

Lean views patients as the "primary customer" for healthcare organizations. Since care providers and other support staff provide healthcare services directly to patients, they have an immediate, firsthand understanding of what these customers need and expect. They also know which aspects of the built environment work well (and which do not), as well as what equipment, supplies, and other resources they need to provide the standard of healthcare services that their patients demand.

Lean also recognizes that care providers and staff members are motivated to improve the efficiency of their work environment because this can make their schedules more reasonable, eliminate fatigue and stress-related injuries and ailments, and provide them with the time and energy they need to work to the best of their abilities. Patients benefit by receiving better care, and healthcare organizations benefit from reduced costs and improved outcomes.

A key characteristic that distinguishes Lean from other management philosophies, such as Six Sigma, is that it relies as much on the knowledge, observations, and insights of care providers and support staff as it does on achieving "buy in" and advocacy from leaders at the top of a healthcare organization.

Lean experts recognize that other psychological factors can influence the results of their efforts, too. For example, clinicians and other staff asked to identify waste in existing processes may wonder: "What is in this for me? Is an industrial engineer doing this to me, or am I collaborating *with* Lean experts to improve processes and working conditions in ways that benefit me, as well as my employer?"

When staff members realize that they can play a role in improving their own working conditions and thus have more time to do the work they are passionate about, they are more likely to contribute to the Lean process and help enhance and sustain its success by continuing to identify opportunities for improvement.[12]

Potential for Impact

At a minimum, Lean Design professionals should be able to plant the seeds of change, and trust that when the resources needed to implement a plan or design become available, a healthcare organization will take the steps needed to advance toward its ideal future state.

For example, one leading Lean organization's goal is to reduce defects by 50 percent every year. Members of this organization's leadership know that the magnitude of improvement they can achieve will diminish as the total number of defects approaches zero, but they also know that the future state they have envisioned as part of the Lean process is an ideal.

Project Team Composition

In addition to building industry professionals, project teams that use Lean to improve the operations and design of healthcare facilities typically include:

- A representative from the healthcare organization's leadership team who will make sure that resources needed to implement improvements are in place at the proper time.

- A Lean facilitator, who plans and leads interactive sessions and orchestrates the efforts of all team members in order to make sure that research, planning, and implementation tasks proceed on schedule and are completed within the established budget.

- Care providers and other key staff who are knowledgeable about and have firsthand experience with processes that have been targeted for improvement. They should also be able to add value to these processes and be willing to implement Lean recommendations.

An implementation team of 7 to 12 people is usually formed by selecting key people from the larger project team who are directly involved with providing healthcare services and who can conduct rapid learning experiments to beta test ideas. This team then continues to measure, document, and report results once the final process changes and facility design (or remodeling) are implemented.

Credentials and Qualities

Lean Design professionals often have formal training and experience as industrial engineers, facilities managers, architects, and interiors designers. However, people with a variety of backgrounds can become Lean consultants or work as a member of a healthcare organization's in-house Lean team.

While there are a number of certification programs that provide a good introduction to the Lean philosophy and its tools, most Lean experts learn by doing. The ability to manage processes well and the commitment to continually improving these processes are key characteristics that individuals interested in applying Lean Methodology to the planning and design of healthcare facilities should possess.

Since the impact of Lean research and recommendations should extend well beyond the life of a single project or series of projects, Lean experts must be able to do more than deliver quality results in the short term. They should have the teaching and communications skills needed to equip care providers and other employees with the tools they need to continue eliminating waste and adding value to care delivery and operational processes.

External Consultants versus In-House Experts

A number of factors influence a healthcare organization's decision to establish a department dedicated to applying Lean Methodology, to hire Lean experts as consultants, or to use a combination of these approaches. What matters most is what works best for the culture of the organization.

Although occasionally a client may hire Lean Design consultants solely to improve the design or remodeling of a particular facility, this is not the ideal. The healthcare organizations that most benefit from Lean are those that invest in developing a strategic framework for continuous improvement and that implement the core strategies.

For example, two Midwest healthcare organizations located within five miles of each other embarked on distinctly different approaches to integrating Lean principles and values into every aspect of their operations. One hired a leading Lean consulting firm as its coach, and that partnership continues through today. The other built its Lean infrastructure from within. Both organizations are steadily achieving their Lean performance goals and thriving.

Technology

Technological innovations aimed at the efficient consolidation and accurate maintenance of medical records, as well as those improving the care delivery process and aiding "self-care," are profoundly affecting the design of clinics and other healthcare facilities. Lean Design professionals should consider how technology is being used (and can be used in the future) by a healthcare organization, and then factor this into the schemes they develop.

For example, some clinics have begun to use digital locator systems. Typically, these systems feature computer monitors at staff workstations that display a chart showing which exam rooms are occupied by whom. Computers in each exam room are connected to the centralized locator. When staff members complete part of a visit, they enter this information via the locator software program.

In addition to helping track progress of exams, digital locator systems can provide information about how long activities or procedures take. They can also streamline the care delivery process by helping various members of a patient's care team to arrive at the exam room prepared to carry out next steps. For example, a physician can use the locator to notify caregivers that a patient needs a shot or a blood sample so that a nurse can immediately prepare the syringe.

Summary

Today, clinics must be designed to accommodate and anticipate rapid changes in medical technology, procedures, and practices while addressing a major shift in the reimbursement model of the healthcare industry. Human and other resources—such as materials, equipment, and buildings and space—must be used to their top operational efficiency.

When Lean Design professionals are an integral part of the team for a remodeling or new construction project, they can make sure recommendations for streamlining operations are supported—and ideally enhanced—-by the physical qualities of the built environment.

Lean Design professionals are not expected to answer all of the questions that healthcare organizations have about how to improve efficiency and effectiveness. Rather, Lean Design professionals are master integrators who amalgamate information provided by care providers, patients, and others, and then use this as a basis for designing facilities that support Lean operations.

Lean Design professionals are most successful in the healthcare industry when they are aligned with a client's business model and expectations. This makes it more likely that the recommendations they develop will be implemented and that the healthcare organization will not only benefit from immediate changes but will also continue to use the philosophy, principles, and tools of the Lean Methodology to improve processes over the life of a facility.

Impact

The impact of implementing Lean recommendations can be measured and observed in a number of ways, including reduced costs, reduced errors, better infection control, better working conditions for care providers and other clinical staff, enhanced quality of care for patients, and the achievement of targeted health outcomes for the patient population a clinic serves.

The Life Beyond

Lean Design is best known for its goal of eliminating waste. This becomes more challenging and more valuable when a clinic's operational and healthcare delivery processes must remain flexible and adaptable to meet constantly shifting needs.

Thus, in addition to addressing immediate challenges, Lean Design professionals must also help healthcare organizations to build the capacity they need to continually reduce waste long after a single project or series of projects has been completed. Facilities last much longer than the people and processes that are performed inside of them. A building designed or modified using Lean principles has the potential to shape the culture of an organization well into the future.

BRENT PETERSON

Notes

1. NetMBA, "Frederick Taylor and Scientific Management," http://www.netmba.com/mgmt/scientific.

2. Jeffrey Liker, *The Toyota Way: 14 Management Principles from the World's Greatest Manufacturer* (New York: McGraw-Hill, 2004).

3. John Garven, "Administration Unveils New Rules for ACOs," http://benico.com/2011/04/administration-unveils-new-rules-for-acos.

4. Lean Enterprise Institute, https://www.lean.org.

5. Ibid.

6. Liker, 27–35.

7. Terra Vanzant-Stern, *Lean Six Sigma: International Standards and Global Guidelines* (Palo Alto, CA: Fultus, 2012).

8. Naida Grunden and Charles Hagood, *Lean-Led Hospital Design: Creating the Efficient Hospital of the Future* (Boca Raton, FL: CRC Press, 2012), 285.

9. Michael Kennedy, "Product Development for Lean Enterprises," *Oakland Press* (Oakland, CA), 2003.

10. Grunden and Hagood, 285.

11. Liker, 27–35.

12. Lean Enterprise Institute.

Select Bibliography

Liker, Jeffrey. *The Toyota Way: 14 Management Principles from the World's Greatest Manufacturer.* New York: McGraw Hill, 2004.

Worth, Judy. *Perfecting Patient Journeys.* Cambridge, MA: Lean Enterprise Institute, 2012.

Visualization Tools and Mock-ups

Overview

As design professionals conceptualize and develop a project, they rely on a number of tools to illustrate their intent and help clients visualize proposed spaces. These tools are essential for the design process because they help advance decisions and enable clients and designers to collaboratively shape a design.

Two-Dimensional Representations

Design professionals often use two-dimensional drawings, such as floor plans, elevations, and sections, to graphically present key aspects of a design, test functional relationships, and produce the building documentation needed for construction.

During the initial stages of a project, a conceptual "bubble diagram" may be used to represent the functional relationships between rooms, departments, or other project components. In these diagrams, the "bubble" size conveys the relative size of programmed spaces, and arrows or lines are used to indicate important relationships or processes (fig. 3-1).

An alternative to the typical bubble diagram is a magnetic board display that depicts rooms as boxes sized to represent their proportional

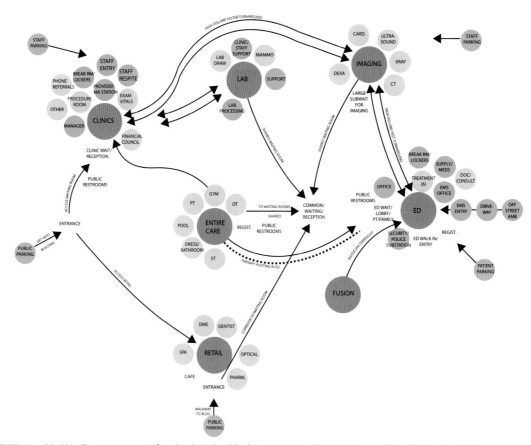

FIGURE 3-1: A bubble diagram represents functional relationships between rooms, departments, or other project components. Image courtesy of Hammel, Green and Abrahamson, Inc.

Previous page: Clinic design concept; Hammel, Green and Abrahamson, Inc.

relationships. This tool can be used interactively by client representatives and designers to quickly test a variety of space configurations. Bubble diagrams, lines or arrows may be used to designate key relationships (fig. 3-2).

Designers convert the information gathered from the initial diagramming process into a preliminary floor plan that shows rooms, departments, and circulation paths. As the design is further developed, additional project components, such as doors, structural elements, casework, and the like, are added to the plan (fig. 3-3).

Two-dimensional representations may be used to illustrate and document the entire project, including elevations for wall surfaces and reflected ceiling plans that show items overhead, such as lighting fixtures.

Three-Dimensional Representations

In addition to two-dimensional representations, designers frequently use three-dimensional (3-D) media to explore the relationships of room components and to realistically convey how a space "feels" as a result of the way forms, materials, and light are combined. Many designers also find that three-dimensional representations are better understood by clients than two-dimensional drawings and that using them can expedite the decision-making process.

Three-dimensional representations range from drawings and models to animations and full-scale mock-ups (fig. 3-4, 3-5).

One three-dimensional tool that is especially important for clinic design is an exam room model that includes easily moved representations of furnishings and equipment. This tool not only helps clients visualize the exam room and the relationships between room components but also offers the flexibility needed to quickly evaluate ideas. These models are often at a scale of one inch equals one foot, although other scales may be used (fig. 3-6).

Mock-ups

Mock-ups are models constructed to simulate real-life conditions in physical or digital form. Mock-ups are different from the three-dimensional tools described above because they are typically constructed at full scale to provide a realistic experience of a space or group of spaces.

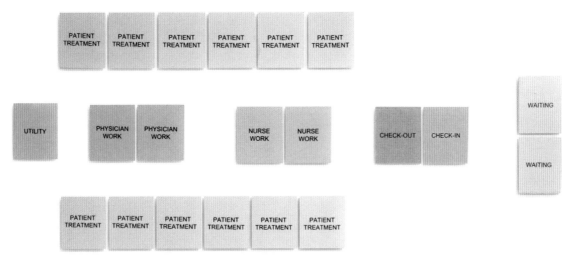

FIGURE 3-2: A magnetic board is an interactive way to represent key adjacencies and layout options. Image courtesy of Hammel, Green and Abrahamson, Inc.

FIGURE 3-3: Elements such as doors, columns, and casework are added to a plan once the design professional has established basic space relationships and required adjacencies.   Image courtesy of Hammel, Green and Abrahamson, Inc.

FIGURE 3-4: Three-dimensional renderings are useful to convey how a space will "feel" as a result of form, materials, and light.   Image courtesy of Hammel, Green and Abrahamson, Inc.

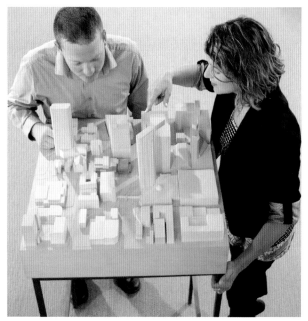

FIGURE 3-5: Models are easily understood by clients and encourage interaction.   Image courtesy of Hammel, Green and Abrahamson, Inc.

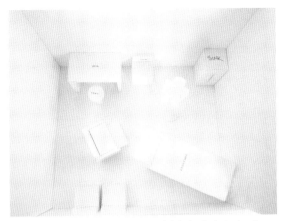

FIGURE 3-6: Interactive exam room models help clients to visualize relationships between room components and to quickly evaluate layout options. Image courtesy of Hammel, Green and Abrahamson, Inc.

Mock-ups enable clients and design professionals to test whether a room is adequately sized and properly configured, as well as whether or not equipment and supplies are within easy reach. Since mock-ups are full-scale, they typically involve one room (or a series of adjacent rooms), instead of an entire department (fig. 3-7).

Design professionals use mock-ups to test ideas and identify potential operational, work process, design, and implementation challenges before construction begins. Mock-ups can also be used to streamline and expedite the inception-revision cycle.[1]

Uses

From the rough mock-ups constructed of foam-core or cardboard to fully immersive and interactive virtual-reality experiences, physical and digital mock-ups can:

- Help design professionals anticipate the impact that their recommendations and decisions will have on a clinic's operations and care delivery processes.

- Enable healthcare organizations' leaders, staff, and donors to understand how a new or remodeled space will look and feel.

FIGURE 3-7: BIDMC Mock-up. Mock-ups enable clients and designers to test a room's size and configuration or specific room components at full scale. Image courtesy of Hammel, Green and Abrahamson, Inc.

- Make it possible for staff to rehearse scenarios that typically occur in a clinical practice before a facility is actually built or remodeled. Care providers can test various ways to accomplish tasks within a mocked-up space, interact with each other, move equipment, supplies, and furnishings around and thus, physically contribute their knowledge and experience to the development and refinement of a design.

- Remove healthcare and administrative staff from their everyday environment so that they can objectively evaluate aspects of their work routines and relate these to the built environment.

- Help to reduce the risk of adverse medical events occurring. In addition to these events being expensive in human and monetary terms, they can quickly cost a clinic its reputation. The number of adverse medical events that occur within a healthcare facility is tracked and reported on consumer information websites. Patient survey results are also routinely collected, synthesized, and incorporated into performance ratings and rankings that are shared online.

- Secure "buy-in" from a variety of stakeholders who cannot read architectural or engineering drawings as well as they can relate to seeing and, ideally, experiencing a physical or virtual representation of a space.

- Validate that a design will function as intended.

In addition to providing the opportunity to explore how spaces will work before a new clinic is fully designed and built, mock-ups can also be used to resolve problems with an existing space.

Considerations

Design professionals are responsible for presenting the costs and benefits of using mock-ups to their clients. Generally, the overarching goal of using mock-ups is to gather the information from hands-on interaction with a space as efficiently and cost-effectively as possible.

Depending on whom the client wants to engage during a particular phase of a healthcare construction project, design professionals can use a phased approach to developing mock-ups. Simple physical mock-ups are best for rapidly testing and revising early design decisions. Once the design has been finalized, a detailed or live mock-up can be used to build staff and community support.

Design professionals and their clients evaluate mocked-up spaces based on who will be occupying them at specific times or for defined durations. For example, questions design

professionals ask when reviewing an exam room concept could include:

- How is the patient zone affected when a care provider or family member enters the exam room?

- Does the exam table placement provide enough space for the care providers to work, and does it offer adequate privacy to the patient?

- How well does the space work when a physician and additional care providers are present? How many people can comfortably be in this room?

- Are there any obstacles in or conflicts between the zones (e.g., the care provider, patient, and partners-in-care zones)?

- What happens when various pieces of equipment or supplies are moved into or out of the exam room?

- Does working in the space call attention to any unforeseen safety concerns or reveal that awkward or overly strenuous movements will need to be made by staff to complete their routine tasks?

- How are supplies, equipment, and furnishings optimally positioned relative to the movement of people within and near the exam room?

- Are accessories such as sharps containers or gel dispensers and electrical outlets within easy reach?

Types

This chapter discusses the two primary types of mock-ups used by design professionals: physical and virtual.

Physical mock-ups are frequently constructed of foam-core, cardboard, or plywood. They provide stakeholders with the opportunity to interact with a design kinetically and by using all of their senses.

Virtual mock-ups, which can also be referred to as "virtual prototypes," are designed and constructed using computer equipment and software. They typically require little or no physical construction and can be created based on digital models that have already been developed using 3-D software.

Physical Mock-ups

Since physical mock-ups offer the chance for actual interaction with a design, they tend to elicit a high degree of engagement by research participants, who range from owners, care providers, administrative staff, patients, and other visitors to vendors and manufacturers.

Process

The process for creating physical mock-ups typically entails:

- Using the design concept(s) as a basis for constructing the mock-up.

- Defining what types of activities will be tested and evaluated within the mock-up.

- Determining the degree of detail and authenticity that need to be achieved based on the research goals, budget, schedule, type of spaces to be included in the clinic (are there, for example, a lot of repetitive spaces?) and major project goals.

- Verifying that the mock-up is accurately built and detailed to the level desired.

Categories

Physical mock-ups fall into three categories based on their level of sophistication: simple, detailed, or live. A life-size, physical mock-up is especially valuable for ensuring that rooms are the correct size.

- **Simple mock-ups** are typically life-size and made out of cardboard or rigid foam. They can contain simple props, and tape is often used on the floors and walls to designate the locations of furnishings, equipment, and supplies. Users can move props, which are often representations of furniture and equipment that have been constructed out of rigid foam or cardboard. Some mock-ups include the actual objects that will be used in the space (chairs, beds, or mobile medical equipment, for example). Design professionals sometimes use sticky notes or mount printed graphics to the wall of a mock-up to make it easy to experiment with the location of a light switch, sink, or other details by physically moving the pieces of paper that represent these objects. The major benefits of using simple physical mock-ups are that they are generally less expensive, easier, and faster to construct than detailed or live physical models. For these reasons, simple mock-ups are often used during the rapid prototyping phase of the Lean design process because they can quickly and rather inexpensively be modified to test new or revised design ideas in real time. Exploring options with simple mock-ups can help design professionals to prioritize where their remaining time and creative energy should be focused to efficiently advance a concept from design through construction documents (fig. 3-8).

- **Detailed mock-ups** more closely approximate how a space will actually appear and perform once it is constructed. They are usually made of fairly durable materials, such as plywood, and integrate furnishings and equipment that will be used in the completed facility. Healthcare organizations often invest in detailed physical mock-ups to make sure a space that is equipment-intensive, technologically advanced, or repeated multiple times within a module or facility functions well.[2] Physical mock-ups that have been refined to a high level of detail are sometimes used to train clinicians if the new layout or characteristics of the space vary significantly from the current environment in which they are accustomed to delivering care services.

- **Live mock-ups** are created when detailed physical mock-ups are "activated"—that is, are used as a fully functioning part of a clinic or other healthcare facility. Their plumbing, electricity, lighting, medical equipment, and any special systems are all operating so that staff can use them to treat patients. This type of mock-up works especially well for renovation and remodeling projects when the mock-up can replace a specific room and, thus, be integrated into the existing workflows to see if bottlenecks or other issues arise.

Integrating a live mock-up into an existing facility also allows design professionals and clinic staff to directly compare newly designed rooms to existing spaces. Design professionals define the metrics for these comparisons before the mock-ups go live and, thus, are able to evaluate a concept in

FIGURE 3-8: Simple mock-ups are useful for evaluating overall room size and configuration. Image courtesy of Hammel, Green and Abrahamson, Inc.

relation to the client's goals. Healthcare organizations can also use live mock-ups for staff education purposes.

To optimize the value of a live mock-up, it must be used long enough to gather statistically relevant data on events that rarely occur, such as adverse medical events. For this reason, some experts recommend having a live mock-up in use for a year or more so that research results can account for fluctuations in patient type and health status, as well as for seasonal variations in patient volume.[3] Portions of this time period can overlap with the design process because the initial use of live mock-ups is to test the efficacy of a design at the highest level of refinement before implementation.[4,5]

Advantages and Limitations

Some advantages that life-size physical models provide include:

- The ability to touch, see, navigate through, and generally interact with a tangible space.

- The opportunity for design professionals to adjust designs for practical reasons that may not have been addressed in a program document or during preliminary discussions with a client and various stakeholders.

- The chance to test concepts in actuality rather than hypothetically. For example, physical mock-ups enable design professionals to tap into the hands-on knowledge of staff and other research participants.

- The ability to test a space's design through complex simulations involving multiple participants. Clinical simulations may uncover issues undetected through general observation.

Limitations can include:

- Costs may be higher than those associated with generating 3-D digital models or creating virtual mock-ups.

- Physical mock-ups can take longer to build and, depending on their characteristics, may require approval by code officials.

- Physical mock-ups require physical space. They are frequently constructed in existing shell spaces, but clients with limited unused areas may need to rent space to accommodate construction of a mock-up. Depending on the length of time that the mock-ups need to remain in place, this can be inconvenient and costly.

- Not all spaces are feasible for mock-ups. For example, physical mock-ups of large spaces such as lobby areas are not feasible, and mocking up complex rooms such as operating suites can be very costly.

Virtual Mock-ups

The Merriam-Webster Dictionary defines virtual reality as "an artificial environment which is experienced through sensory stimuli… provided by a computer and in which one's actions partially determine what happens in the environment."

For decades, design professionals have explored ways to present the spatial attributes of a design digitally in order to take clients on a tour of a facility before it is constructed.

As the capabilities of virtual-reality technology continue to advance, design professionals are working on new ways for stakeholders to interact with and even alter a design in cyberspace. Although virtual mock-ups do not require costly construction, digital models that are complex and highly detailed can be time-consuming to design, build, and test.

Categories

There are two main types of virtual reality mock-up systems: desktop and immersive. Under the first, research participants sit or stand at a computer station and view the three-dimensional model on a screen.

In contrast, an immersive Virtual Reality (VR) system gives participants the sense that they are physically present in a virtual world. Some immersive VR mock-ups occur in CAVE (Cave-like Automatic Virtual Environment) systems, which are typically limited in scale and rely on screens to convey visual information. Recent improvements in technology, however, have led to larger-scale, fully immersive systems that permit users to navigate at will through virtual environments. Cameras are set up at different locations in an open room and send images to the stereoscopic goggles that participants wear to achieve the sense of movement in relation to the digitally created aspects of the mock-up. The Virtual Reality Design Lab at the University of Minnesota's College of Design is an example of this type of environment.

The level of interaction and immersion varies between the three major categories of virtual-reality experience, which are passive, exploratory, and interactive.

- **Passive (screen-based):** Users sit or stand in front of a monitor and watch scripted scenarios unfold on the screen. They select "play," watch the simulation, and—in the case of virtual mock-ups—provide feedback verbally or by way of a survey.

- **Exploratory:** Users navigate through a virtual environment, but they cannot physically interact with the model. They do, however, have the sense that they are physically moving around a space rather than passively watching what occurs within it, and they have some control over their direction of movement and experience.

- **Interactive:** Users can affect the virtual environment. For example, if they choose to pick up an object or push a button in the model, this action and its impact are recorded for analysis. Their movement in and interactions with the virtual mock-up are also reflected in what they are seeing and experiencing, so that any responses they have are authentic (figs. 3-9, 3-10).

FIGURE 3-9: A CAVE virtual-reality system (or Cave-like Automatic Virtual Environment) provides a realistic view of a proposed space using projected images. This image shows the CAVE system developed by Mortenson Construction. Image courtesy of Hammel, Green and Abrahamson, Inc.

FIGURE 3-10: The Virtual Reality Design Lab at the University of Minnesota's College of Design enables users to explore a large-scale virtual environment. Photography by Phil Rader

Advantages and Limitations

Some of the advantages of virtual mock-ups include that they:

- Offer a quicker, more cost-effective alternative than the design and construction of a physical mock-up, but with the same level of detail.

- Can be easy to manipulate and rapidly altered so that users can experiment with a variety of interior schemes that would take longer to test in a physical model.

- Make representation of colors and finishes less costly than in physical mock-ups, although the accuracy of color can vary greatly between computer displays, and the texture of a finish cannot be felt.

- Permit users to view a variety of options quickly.

- Are scalable and can be viewed from perspectives that are either too difficult or too costly to achieve with physical mock-ups.

- Make it feasible and affordable to explore spaces that would be too large to mock up physically, such as a main entry atrium. A virtual-reality mock-up of a department, floor, or entire building also makes sense in many instances because it would be too costly to build physically. In those cases, the effort spent on such a complex and large physical mock-up would be better spent on actual construction.

    Virtual mock-ups also present a number of unique challenges and have some limitations. For example, to obtain accurate, authentic responses from users, virtual mock-ups need to be as immersive and detailed as a physical mock-up.

Lessons Learned: Tips for Successful Mock-ups

Examples of key tasks that design professionals complete in order to create mock-ups that successfully achieve client goals include:

- Selecting which spaces are priorities for mock-ups.

- Setting goals and parameters for the assessment (for example, that no walls can be moved).

- Establishing the budget and schedule for creating and employing mock-ups.

- Planning scenarios to identify which equipment, furnishings, and staff need to be present. This sometimes includes buying or borrowing equipment and working in depth with the general contractor, equipment planners, vendors, and manufacturers to obtain specifications and photos.

- Determining which supplies are needed and purchasing them. Basic supplies typically include measuring tapes, sticky notes, blue tape, string, extension cords, markers, cameras, paper, comment forms, clipboards, and pens.

- Choosing which plans and elevations need to be available for reference, then printing and posting or displaying these.

- Identifying and assigning key roles. For example, team members are typically needed to take notes, record questions and suggestions, and photograph or videotape interactions within the mock-ups.

- Staging and running clinical simulations, giving tours, and holding discussions within the mock-ups. This typically includes kicking off the simulations with an orientation for staff that covers the design guidelines and explains what changes can or cannot be considered and made.

- Ensuring that all staff members who are needed are available and present for the simulations.
- Obtaining feedback from each and every participant.
- Making sure to achieve broad and consistent participation from a variety of people, such as:
  - Operations staff.
  - Front line staff and physicians (MDs, RNs, techs, RTs, PTs/OTs, and so forth).
  - Design team members (such as medical planners or architects).
  - Equipment planners.
  - Members of the construction team.
  - Selected manufacturers and vendors. Having equipment vendors present offers them the opportunity to provide direct feedback on what they can or cannot offer. It is important to clarify in advance, however, that vendors are there to observe and answer questions, not to pitch products.
- Establishing a process for reviewing and approving all comments and suggestions. Typically, clients make the final decisions about which changes they want to make based on the recommendations made by design professionals.
- Documenting whether ideas are accepted or declined.
- Communicating who is responsible for making any changes to the mock-ups/design and when the deadlines are for making these changes.

Value

In general, mock-ups are especially valuable for testing and exploring the design of:

- Unique spaces, such as a specialized procedure room that requires custom medical equipment, furniture, and/or technology.

- Spaces, such as universal exam rooms, that will be incorporated multiple times in a single clinic.
- Spaces that, when constructed as part of a new or remodeled facility, will have a major impact on the manner in which healthcare services are provided.

For example, design professionals use mock-ups to examine how a design relates to or affects:

- The flow of people, equipment, and supplies through a space.
- Staff interactions.
- Staff and patient interactions.
- The safety of patients, staff, and the public.
- Size and juxtaposition of spaces.
- Sightlines.
- Peak capacities.
- Cost reduction through improvement of the care delivery processes.
- Equipment placement, configuration, and clearances.
- The storage of supplies and equipment relative to where and when they are used.
- The integration of electronic health records and related digital tools, as well as other technological innovations, into the care delivery process.
- Color and finish preferences.
- The quality and level of illumination in a space.
- Acoustical and visual privacy.

Choosing the Best Option

Deciding when a physical or virtual mock-up is the most ideal to use for a particular project depends on the project's goals, budget, and schedule, as well as the availability of virtual-reality equipment and physical mock-up space.

Physical mock-ups are usually best for testing repetitive and team-based activities, infrequently occurring events (such as responses to emergencies), and the integration of complex technology into the care delivery process.

Improvements in virtual-reality technology have now made it possible for VR mock-ups to represent multiple people in a space, but the ability to interact with others and with room components is still not as realistic as it is with physical mock-ups.

Computer-Based Models and Simulations

The numeric data that design professionals input into a spreadsheet or other specialized software programs can be used as the foundation for creating computer-based models and simulations (CBS). These digital visualization tools help project teams and clients understand how an operational system works within a virtual environment.

For example, a design team and client representatives can use a computer-based simulation to envision how the care delivery process will occur in a specific clinic setting. This contrasts with virtual mock-ups, which provide each user with a personal experience of a space.

The two types of CBS that design professionals use to streamline and enhance the design and construction processes are static and dynamic, the latter of which is also known as "discrete event simulation models."

In general, CBS models take less time to create than physical mock-ups—although this depends on the amount of research and data input required to achieve a specific level of detail. As with all mock-ups and simulations, a CBS is only as useful as the information that design professionals incorporate into its

construction (for example, a CBS requires accurate assumptions related to patient volumes, staff schedules, and travel distances between points in a clinic).

In addition to helping design professionals and their clients predict and understand the impact that decisions about the built environment will have on the flow of people, supplies, and equipment through a clinic, a CBS can be used for forecasting future conditions (e.g., changes in the characteristics of the patient population) and for sequencing and synchronizing the details of construction so that this phase of a project advances smoothly and the design intent is accurately realized.

Static Simulation Models

Static simulation models present a system at a specific point in time. Thus, they do not typically account for the passage of time or for natural variations in actual operations. They generally take less time to create and use for analysis than dynamic simulation models.

Design professionals often use static simulation models to obtain a baseline forecast to determine if a dynamic simulation model should be created.

Discrete Event Simulation Models

Discrete event simulation (DES) models are dynamic. Since they show the progression of a process over time, they are typically animated. They are also "stochastic," meaning that they can have some degree of chance or variability built into them in order to mimic the randomness of real-world conditions.

DES models can be designed to study issues such as the efficiency of patient flow, wait times, and the introduction of new technology or equipment, as well as other issues of concern to clinic owners. Typically, the design professionals building the DES model, create a process flow chart, and then begin entering the specific data they need to run simulations.

An example of a DES program is MedModel, a simulation tool that design professionals use to visualize, analyze, and optimize hospital and clinic operational performance. Such programs enable designers and clients to quickly analyze operational processes under a variety of scenarios over various lengths of time, and thus identify any capacity issues or points of congestion (fig. 3-11).

Project Examples

The following project examples illustrate some of the ways design professionals and clients use mock-ups to evaluate and advance design decisions.

■ VERDE VALLEY MEDICAL CENTER (VVMC)
Sedona and Cottonwood, Arizona

VVMC serves Arizona's Verde Valley and surrounding communities through four campus locations: Cottonwood, Sedona, Camp Verde, and the Village of Oak Creek. The largest campus is located in Cottonwood and includes a 99-bed hospital, in addition to outpatient facilities. The other campuses primarily provide outpatient and emergency care services. The medical staff comprises nearly 100 physicians representing 25 medical specialties.

In 2013, VVMC decided to expand its outpatient services at the Camp Verde, Sedona, and Cottonwood campuses. Prior to commencing design, a rigorous Lean operational study was

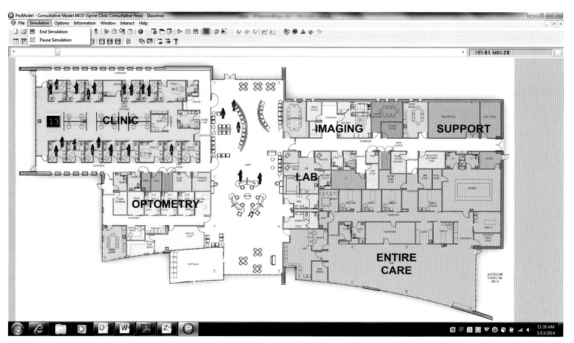

FIGURE 3-11: Computer programs such as MedModel help design professionals and clients visualize and optimize operational performance.   Image courtesy of Hammel, Green and Abrahamson, Inc.

completed with project stakeholders to identify ways for enhancing patient care and improving operational efficiency in the new facilities. As part of this study, the design professionals on the project team developed simple mock-ups to illustrate a variety of potential exam room layouts.

Mock-up Process and Results

Before constructing the mock-ups, the design professionals presented a range of exam room options to clinic staff, physicians, and administrators. Their presentation included identifying the pros and cons of each layout. VVMC representatives also outlined their requirements and preferences, which included:

- Physicians preferred to face patients directly during consultations.

- Physicians seated at the workstation needed the flexibility to consult with patients either sitting in chairs or on the exam table.

- Both physicians and patients needed to have clear views of the computer screen, regardless of whether the patient was sitting in a chair or on the exam table.

- The exam table needed to be positioned with the end away from the public corridor for privacy.

The design team and client also reviewed potential clinic modules at this time, as the configuration of exam rooms and overall clinic module are often related. For example, a single-door exam room requires that staff and patients share circulation, while a dual-door exam room permits the separation of public corridors from staff circulation and work spaces.

The client and design team identified three layouts that could meet VVMC's requirements and preferences. The following layouts were selected for mock-ups (fig. 3-12):

- Typical exam room with a single door

- Dual-door exam room

- Dual-door exam room with a separate consult space

To assess the layouts of the potential exam rooms, designers constructed simple mock-ups from rigid foam boards. The client provided actual equipment (such as exam tables) that helped to create an accurate representation of the proposed space.

The three exam rooms under consideration were constructed side-by-side, and detailed illustrations were provided for each mocked-up room. Clinic staff, physicians, and

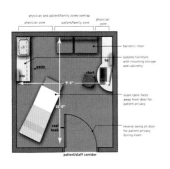 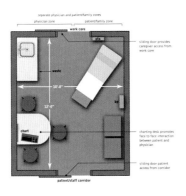 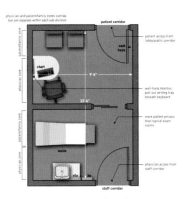

FIGURE 3-12: The design of VVMC's Camp Verde Clinic involved full-scale mock-ups. Design professionals and the client reviewed many potential exam room layouts, and three were selected for mock-ups. Image courtesy of Hammel, Green and Abrahamson, Inc.

administrators then evaluated each exam room layout against the criteria defined earlier in the process (fig. 3-13).

The client selected the dual-door exam room because it provided the preferred sightlines and privacy while enabling the separation of staff and patient circulation within the clinic module.

The option with the least favorable reviews was the dual exam room with the separate consult space. Despite being significantly larger than the other two options, the reviewers felt that the exam and consult areas both felt too tight.

This mock-up process helped VVMC quickly select an exam room layout and size early in the project. By the end of the Lean operational analysis, both the preferred clinic module and exam room had been selected, simplifying and accelerating the design process (fig. 3-14).

■ BETH ISRAEL DEACONESS MEDICAL CENTER (BIDMC)
Boston, Massachusetts

BIDMC is one of the nation's preeminent academic medical centers and a major teaching hospital of Harvard Medical School. In 2013, BIDMC began design of an integrated Breast Center to be located within an existing clinic building.

Mock-ups were used extensively during the predesign process to test exam room sizes and layouts, as well as provider workstation configurations.

Mock-up Process and Results

A key challenge during the predesign phase was to determine how to optimize the use of existing space. The client preferred exam rooms of 130 square feet, but the space available did not accommodate both the size and number of exam rooms desired. The design team used simple mock-ups to help the client quickly visualize

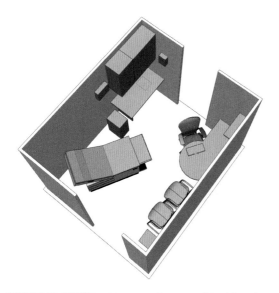

FIGURE 3-13: VVMC's exam room mock-ups were "simple" mockups constructed from foam with minimal detail. This 3-D diagram shows the elements that were constructed. Image courtesy of Hammel, Green and Abrahamson, Inc.

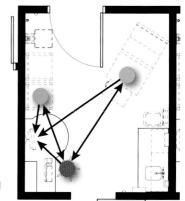

PATIENT

PHYSICIAN

FIGURE 3-14: The VVMC exam room design was modified during the mock-up process to meet the preferences of the clinic staff and the administration. The ability for the physician to communicate easily with the patient and the ability for both the physician and patient to see the computer monitor drove the layout. Image courtesy of Hammel, Green and Abrahamson, Inc.

various exam room dimensions and test their initial assumptions about the size of room needed.

The design professionals constructed these mock-ups from rigid foam boards to enable rapid reconfiguration while minimizing time and cost. Patients, physicians, and frontline clinical staff then reviewed the mock-ups to assess room size and configuration (figs. 3-15, 3-16).

As a result of the mock-up process, BIDMC determined that an exam room of 110 square feet functioned as well as larger exam rooms. As a result, the client was able to save space and money by avoiding overbuilding.

Summary

For many years, mock-ups and simulations have been used to test concepts in other fields, such as manufacturing, law, medicine, aviation, and the military. In the building industry, design professionals use these tools to streamline and enhance the creative decision-making process, as well as to develop and execute a detailed plan for construction or to envision how people, equipment, and supplies will flow through a building or space.

In effect, physical and virtual mock-ups allow design professionals to test-drive concepts and ideas, while the costs of exploration, discovery, and refinement are far lower than they would be if errors or inefficiencies are identified after construction has begun or a facility is occupied.

Mock-ups can have a substantial impact on the design of key rooms within a clinic (an exam room, for example) or a specific area (a clinic pod, for example) that will be repeated multiple times. Mock-ups can also prove to be valuable when design decisions have especially high financial or health consequences (such as for

FIGURE 3-15: BIDMC Mock-up. BIDMC used simple foam mock-ups to determine the best size for their exam rooms. Image courtesy of Hammel, Green and Abrahamson, Inc.

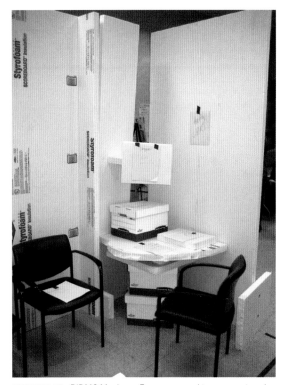

FIGURE 3-16: BIDMC Mock-up. Foam was used to represent equipment and work surfaces in the BIDMC mock-ups. Image courtesy of Hammel, Green and Abrahamson, Inc.

equipment-intensive spaces or when a clinic is being remodeled to improve safety).

Design professionals use mock-ups to foresee what the actual impact of a design will be on clinic operations. Mock-ups typically allow them to physically or virtually manipulate the designed environment and test possible changes before incorporating feedback, recommendations, and discoveries into a final design.

Healthcare organizations also use mock-ups and simulations for training staff, experimenting with new care delivery strategies, achieving stakeholder buy in, and raising funds.

Although the cost of creating and using mock-ups typically represents a small fraction of a project's total budget, it is important for design professionals to decide whether or not to use them as early in the planning process as possible so funds and time can be properly allocated to ensure their comfortable integration into the design process.

Well-planned and well-executed mock-ups can provide both immediate and lasting value for clients.

AMY DOUMA AND JENNIFER ROMER

Notes

1. Kathy L. Bell, "Mock-Ups: Giving Hospital Clients the Ultimate Reality Check," *Healthcare Design*, April 30, 2007.

2. Christine Guzzo Vickery, "Promoting Healthcare Innovation Through Facility Prototyping," *Healthcare Design*, November 21, 2012.

3. Erin K. Peavey, Jason Zoss, and Nicholas Watkins, "Simulation and Mock-Up Research Methods to Enhance Design Decision Making," *Health Environments Research & Design Journal* 5.3 (2012): 133–44.

4. Altug Kasali, Nancy J. Nersessian, and Craig M. Zimring, "Making Evidence Visible: Using Mock-ups in Healthcare Design," in proceedings of "The Visibility of Research," ARCC Architectural Research Conference, University of North Carolina at Charlotte, 2013, http://www.arcc-journal.org/index .php/repository/article/view/122.

5. Peavey, Zoss, and Watkins, 133–44.

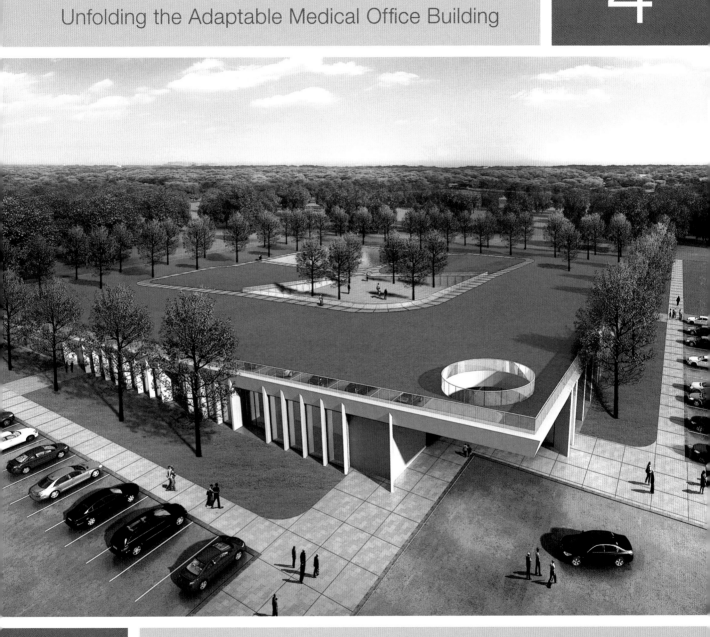

Overview

Buildings that are neither flexible nor adaptable can quickly become obsolete. This is especially true for healthcare facilities in the United States. Here, in addition to being subject to market factors, their effectiveness is currently being challenged by the transformation from how healthcare services are being delivered today to how they must be delivered in the future.

As the number of people with health insurance climbs and the provision of healthcare services continues to shift toward outpatient facilities, most clinics will need to serve more people for longer hours in a greater variety of ways than they have in the past. Since healthcare organizations are still developing and refining new care models to address these issues, clinic facilities must be able to respond to dynamically changing requirements and conditions.

Definition

In a conference presentation titled "What is the Meaning of Adaptability in the Building Industry?," researchers from the U.K.'s Loughborough University assert that "achieving adaptability... demands a shift away from [an] emphasis on form and function in response to immediate priorities, towards a context and time-based view of design."[1]

In other words, "adaptability" anticipates that buildings will need to change over time but recognizes that future needs and uses cannot be fully predicted. These are key characteristics of adaptability:

- **Scalability:** From the site selection and programming phases onward, design professionals consider how a clinic can be best expanded or remodeled.
- **Flexibility:** Spaces within a building are versatile (able to serve different functions with minimal or no change), convertible (able to be readily transformed to serve varying needs), and adjustable (have furnishings, equipment, and features that can be adapted to meet the unique needs of occupants).
- **Easily retrofitted:** It is easy to resize, reconfigure, or repair clinic spaces so that they can serve rapidly evolving work processes or be used for new purposes.
- **Movability:** Advances in modular design for healthcare facilities, as well as rapid innovation in medical and information technology, have expanded the range of building components and equipment that can be moved to include everything from high-tech diagnostic equipment to furnishings, casework, and walls to workstations and work zones.

Flexibility versus Adaptability

While the terms "adaptability" and "flexibility" are often used interchangeably, there is a slight but important distinction between them when they are applied to the design of buildings. An adaptable building is designed to accommodate *long-term* changes, such as conversion from a medical office building into an ambulatory facility or the addition of new, enclosed building spaces.

A building designed to be flexible can be changed in the *short-term* to easily meet immediate needs, such as transforming consultation rooms into a large group education space by moving demountable internal walls. Flexibility is usually a characteristic of an adaptable building.

Most clinic designs should be both flexible and adaptable so that they can meet immediate, rapidly evolving needs while also responding to longer-lasting changes in the delivery of healthcare services as these are sorted out and solidified over the next several years.

Goals

The overarching goal of designing for flexibility is to create clinics that can adapt over time to accommodate improved healthcare processes, achieve new efficiencies, integrate new technologies, and best serve a clinic's owner, staff, patients, and surrounding community. To accomplish this larger objective, design professionals consider the short-, mid-, and long-term goals of the healthcare organization that is constructing or altering a clinic facility:

- **Short term:** The maximum amount of flexibility requires that each room be designed, equipped, and staffed to serve any patient, in any room, at any time.

- **Midterm:** A clinic's groupings of treatment rooms and placement of core functions need to be designed to preserve flexibility and adaptability for one to five years after it has first been occupied.

- **Long term:** For a clinic to be adaptable in the long run (more than five years after it is first occupied), spaces within it should be able to be transformed for new purposes or expanded to serve a growing or otherwise changing patient population. The initial design should also facilitate alteration or expansion in the future.

Although some clinic spaces are more likely to change than others (waiting areas and medical records areas, for example), the degree to which flexibility and adaptability are needed will vary based on the patient-population characteristics, care philosophy and delivery process, business goals, and type of services offered by a clinic (figs. 4-1, 4-2).

Trends

Economic, legislative, demographic, and cultural factors, as well as advances in medical, information, and communications technology, are all contributing to an increased need for flexible, adaptable clinic facilities.

Economic

Macroeconomic factors, such as more limited access to investment funds during the Great Recession, as well as a significant jump in building costs arising from the increased

FIGURES 4-1, 4-2: Mayo Clinic Executive Health Program. This program offers individualized, coordinated, and time-effective evaluations catering to the unique needs of executives' busy schedules. Developed as a solution for business executives and corporations that recognize the importance of maintaining the health of their leaders, Mayo Clinic's Executive Health Program leverages Mayo Clinic's well-known diagnostic expertise with the latest in preventive medicine. Photography by Steve Henke global demand for construction materials, have prompted healthcare organizations and clinic owners to increase their scrutiny of capital budgets.

This means additional costs associated with investing in design features that make clinic buildings more flexible and adaptable must often be related to immediate returns on investment (e.g., measurable improvements in operational efficiency and productivity) or other pressing priorities (e.g., population-based health outcomes necessary to secure reimbursement).

Due to the magnitude of uncertainty in the healthcare industry, many design professionals are recommending that substantial investments in flexibility and adaptability only be made when a healthcare organization or owner knows that a clinic's design will need to be changed frequently, or within one to two years of the day it opens.

Legislative

Several aspects of the Patient Protection and Affordable Care Act (ACA) as well as other legislative requirements and federal incentives, such as those covered by the Americans with Disabilities Act (ADA) of 1990, the Health Insurance Portability and Accountability Act of 1996 (HIPAA), and the American Recovery and Reinvestment Act of 2009 (AARA), are driving the need for flexibility and adaptability in clinic design.

Healthcare Reform

As healthcare organizations test and refine new care models to comply with the requirements of the Affordable Care Act, clinic facilities must be able to adapt as the functions currently housed within them change, are transformed by technology, or are relocated.

Collaboration

In general, the Affordable Care Act focuses on making the delivery of healthcare services more collaborative and coordinated (versus siloed) and providing more emphasis on family-centered, multidisciplinary care and patient empowerment. The need for flexible work and exam spaces within a clinic is expected to continue as healthcare professionals work out the details of which disciplines and staff members will be working together in the same location.

Utilization

Since full implementation of the ACA is expected to result in 30 million more people having health insurance, most healthcare organizations are preparing for a major and sustained increase in patient volume. This and other factors have not only increased demand for outpatient facilities but also motivated clinic owners and design professionals to develop strategies for broadening and intensifying the utilization of all clinic spaces.

Single-use spaces are rapidly becoming luxuries of the past. For example, rooms that were once only used for waiting are being designed to serve as group education space after hours. One-stop and acuity-adaptable exam rooms are serving a wider variety of functions.

Reimbursement

In addition to the significant shift from healthcare providers being compensated on a fee-for-service to a patient-population/outcomes basis, the Centers for Medicare and Medicaid Services (CMS) began a three-year study in January 2013 to test a "bundled" approach to reimbursement. Referral requirements and which treatments, prescriptions, and procedures are reimbursed continue to change.

Bundling

Healthcare organizations that have agreed to participate in this bundling initiative will be compensated for full "episodes of care" that are based on national averages and reward the careful management of patient-population health outcomes across the spectrum of care. This includes all events leading up to and following care in hospitals, so services provided at clinics will be included, as appropriate. Experts expect bundled payments to lead to higher-quality, better-coordinated care at a lower cost. If this strategy is successful, private commercial insurers will likely follow suit.

Adverse Medical Events

Since 2008, Medicare has no longer reimbursed healthcare organizations for costs associated with a range of "adverse medical events" (or "reasonably preventable" secondary conditions).[3] As more healthcare services are provided in outpatient facilities (minor procedures, diagnostics, and lab tests, for example), clinic owners will increasingly focus on how their facilities, as well as care delivery processes, can be modified and improved to reduce or eliminate these medical errors.

Decentralized workstations, point-of-care testing and diagnostics, and standardization can all impact a clinic's bottom line by preventing or reducing the incidence of events for which payment can be withheld.

HIPAA and AARA

HIPAA requirements and incentives included in the American Recovery and Reinvestment Act of 2009 (AARA) are expediting the transition from paper to electronic medical records. As of 2015, care providers must demonstrate "meaningful use" of electronic medical record systems (EMRs) or pay steep penalties. Since the costs of investing in the hardware, software, and training needed to achieve these requirements can be high, the health-related portion of the AARA provides financial incentives to help make this transition affordable for Medicare- and Medicaid-participating providers.

While the conversion to EMRs is expected to reduce the space needed for the storage of printed medical information, it is increasing the need for spaces where computer servers can be securely and properly housed. The ventilation, cooling, and power requirements of server rooms are different than those historically used to store paper files. Clinic facilities must be able to respond to these changes as owners' strategies about how to best accomplish this conversion are finalized over time.

Demographic and Cultural

Patients who are better informed are also becoming more demanding. They expect the right care, at the right place, at the right time. Healthcare organizations and insurers are developing a range of strategies, such as adding health coaches to care teams and providing telemedicine options, to address these expectations. This makes plans to increase, automate, consolidate, and/or relocate the provision of these new services a critical factor to consider when assessing the level of flexibility and adaptability a clinic facility requires.

Staffing

Clinics are addressing which healthcare services are being provided by whom in a variety of ways. As the shortages of primary care physicians and nurses intensify, the roles of staff are morphing and traditional boundaries between caregivers are blurring. "Physician extenders," such as nurse practitioners and physician assistants, are taking on more tasks—especially in convenience care clinics. Flexibility in staffing requires flexibility in facilities—including shared offices and shared common and support areas between clinics.

New Generations of Staff

The expectations and priorities of healthcare professionals and other staff who work at clinics are changing as the general population in the United States ages. This means that a large number of healthcare workers are retiring at the same time that the demand for healthcare services is projected to increase. Occupations that require more education and lengthy training, such as physician and nurse, are at risk for being depleted more rapidly than openings can be filled.[4]

For example, physicians are among the oldest of the healthcare professionals, with 30 percent being 55 years of age or older (compared with only 14 percent of the general work force). Professional and technical positions that are relatively newer also tend to be filled by members of younger generations. Since many of the therapy professions did not exist 50 years ago, baby boomers were not even aware of these as career options.[5]

A major challenge design professionals face, then, is to design clinics that meet the demands of today's changing workforce while ensuring that these facilities can be easily and affordably modified to meet the workplace expectations of new generations of staff. Clinics that are flexible enough to accomplish these dual objectives will provide their owners with a competitive edge in recruiting and retaining top talent.

Gen Xers

Members of this demographic group were born between 1965 and 1980. They generally tend to work smarter than their predecessors because they are comfortable using technology to complete tasks better and more efficiently than in the past. They expect flexibility and adaptability in the workplace because they are used to being able to adjust their work environment to suit their individual needs and preferences.

Millennials

Born between 1981 and 1999, millennials are "digital natives." They grew up using computers and cell phones to communicate. They expect technology to become smaller, smarter, and more mobile and for technology to make their work easier and faster so that they can work reasonable hours. They are generally team-oriented and prefer collaborating with others, believing that "working together is far more effective than going it alone."[6]

To address these trends in workplace preferences and processes, design professionals identify where the most tasks are being (or will be) completed in a clinic, ask how and where these tasks will likely be carried out in the future, and design clinic buildings and interior spaces that can readily be altered to address anticipated changes.

For example, a clinic that needs a large, centralized nursing station based on current workflows may not need this in the future if its owners plan to invest in mobile digital technology to enable staff to communicate with each other from exam rooms and huddle spaces. In this instance, the central nursing station could be designed so that it can easily and affordably be transformed into a group exam room, conference room, telemedicine work areas, or space for other functions that will be in higher demand as the clinic's healthcare delivery process evolves.

Technological

Advances in medical technologies are radically changing how and where healthcare services can be provided. Thus, a key question design professionals ask during the preliminary phases of planning and design for a clinic facility is: "How can technology improve operational efficiency and the quality of care?"

Improvements in the design and capabilities of medical equipment as well as information and communications technology have generally made it easier and more affordable for clinics to automate routine tasks, eliminate redundancies, and bring care directly to patients. Since it is neither feasible nor prudent for a healthcare organization to retrofit a clinic each time it needs to adopt new technology, designers focus on how clinics can evolve so that new technologies can be either tested and phased in or fully integrated into the built environment. Planning ample space for information technology infrastructure is particularly important as more clinics convert from printed to electronic medical records.

Medical Equipment

Advances in the design of medical equipment are not only influencing how flexible and adaptable clinic facilities can be but have also had an impact on the characteristics of the spaces in which specific equipment is used.

Compact and Mobile

Medical equipment is increasingly being designed to be more compact and more mobile. Design professionals constantly evaluate how the size, configuration, and systems infrastructure of clinic spaces can best be designed to capitalize on these improvements. While manufacturers provide information about the space and systems requirements of specific products, it may make sense for designers to consult with a medical technology expert, depending on the complexity or novelty of the medical equipment a client plans to use in a clinic facility.

The amount of storage space required for mobile medical equipment and the ability to store it near where it will most frequently be used are critical factors for design professionals to keep in mind as they review information provided by manufacturers.

Self-Contained

Mobile medical equipment is also becoming more self-contained. This allows highly sophisticated technology to be brought to the patient and used in standardized exam rooms. For example, the walls of rooms with large-scale, fixed radiology equipment must be lined with lead and a separate viewing alcove/control room provided for clinic staff. The development of mobile C-Arms has now made it possible for x-ray technicians to simply cover areas of the patient that do not need to be exposed to radiation with a lead-lined apron or blanket. In the past, clinics needed a copper-lined room that had no fluorescent lights in it in order to use electrocardiogram equipment (EKG). Now, mobile EKG machines have shielding built into them.

Since the mix of fixed versus mobile medical equipment used by various clinics is likely to continue to change, design professionals are:

- Locating soft spaces near diagnostic departments and central labs when the client anticipates that the size of these will be reduced in the future.

- Avoiding designing the rooms where imaging technology is housed exclusively for one modality, although imaging rooms and departments are also often shared between clinics.

- Providing features such as technology docking stations that are adjacent to the imaging department. This consolidates systems-intensive infrastructure needs while enabling clinics to determine the right mix of fixed and mobile imaging technology at a particular point in time or to phase in new technology as finances allow.

Experience Levels and Preferences

Design professionals make sure to understand the experience levels as well as the personal preferences of the clinicians who will be using specific medical equipment. Generally, physicians prefer ceiling-mounted equipment if the mobile versions occupy too much floor space or otherwise inhibit the provision of care, can easily be damaged in transit, or require construction of specialized storage space.

Design professionals also assist owners with budgetary decisions. For example, designers typically ask questions, such as "How often will a mobile unit be used?" If the answer is "Not that often," then a mobile piece of equipment will be fine. If the piece of equipment will be used frequently, however, the cost of investing in an overhead model may be worth the expense.

Tracking Systems and Devices

A variety of devices and systems can now be used to track patients, staff, materials, and even specific tasks such as handwashing in a clinic, with the goal of optimizing work flows and eliminating wasted time, energy, and resources. These tracking systems collect information and relay it to workstations or other key locations where it can be viewed via a computer monitor. For example, tracking systems can help caregivers know when lab test and diagnostic results are ready, alert them to patient care needs, or help them locate another team member with whom they need to consult. This reduces the amount of time staff spends tracking down people and resources, expedites patient care, and, ideally, increases the amount of time caregivers can spend directly caring for and consulting with patients.

Bar Codes

Bar codes, which have long been used in commercial and corporate settings, are also being employed to track the flow of supplies, equipment, and people through clinics. Scanners or scanning software that can read bar codes are being incorporated into handheld digital devices and laptop computers.

Radio-Frequency Identification Devices (RFID)

The capabilities now exist for clinics to use real-time locations systems (RTLS) that employ radio-frequency identification devices (RFID) to track equipment, supplies, patients, and staff movements through a facility. This technology could aid just-in-time inventory strategies that reduce the need for in-clinic storage space. RFID systems use wireless technology to transmit information to computer monitors or handheld digital devices from tags or labels affixed to products and equipment or identification cards, badges, or wristbands. Scanners are located at key points throughout the clinic facility. A key advantage of RFID technology over bar codes is RFID's immediate and automatic data capture capabilities.

Digital Medicine

Technological advances in medical equipment are also making it possible for diagnostic imaging tasks and minor procedures to be completed by different staff using minimally or noninvasive techniques. For example, diagnostic computerized tomography scans of coronary arteries can be complete by radiologists in a less invasive manner than the angiography procedures performed by cardiologists.[7] Colonoscopies, which are now part of the routine preventative health regime for the growing portion of the U.S. patient population who are 50 years of age or older, can now use virtual technology that may eliminate the need for the invasive version of this procedure that is currently performed by gastroenterologists. Such advances are likely to accelerate the trend toward more care being provided in outpatient facilities.

As the amount of medical data available doubles every five years and medical decision making has become increasingly complex, efficient access to current information has become especially important for patients, care providers, healthcare organizations, and insurance companies. Thus, healthcare organizations and insurance companies are rapidly developing software applications, websites, and other methods for enabling patients to schedule appointments, preregister, communicate with caregivers, review and manage their health records, and purchase health products and services from remote locations, such as their home or office.

This means that as design professionals are developing and refining schemes for clinic buildings and spaces, they should also establish whether or not there will be a need for additional server rooms in the future. If so, they should make sure a clinic's design is flexible enough to meet this need by either planning to convert existing spaces that are likely to be used less over time or by building in extra capacity. Since nanotechnology continues to shrink the size of computers, other digital devices, and the dimensions of mobile medical equipment, some design professionals have addressed a projected demand for increased server space by adding storage rooms that can be transformed for this new purpose.

Data Access and Documentation

As computers have evolved from desktop to laptop to handheld, clinics have been able to move the collection and recording of patient data from check-in areas or centralized nurse stations to the point of care. Design professionals should still determine, however, if clinicians need some quiet, more private work areas with multiple electrical outlets where electronic equipment can be charged and mobile digital devices securely stored. Huddle spaces and work alcoves typically do not accommodate these special requirements.

The location, size, and other qualities of exam room documentation stations, workstations-on-wheels, or decentralized documentation alcoves must be carefully considered to make sure they in no way obstruct the flow of patients and staff through the care continuum. Other key design questions include:

- What preferences do patients and caregivers have for the orientation, sight lines, and ergonomics in regard to where and how data documentation tasks are completed within (or near) the exam room?
- How can the privacy of patient information be maintained while optimizing the flexibility of clinic space?
- Does it make sense to incorporate alcoves along the circulation paths that can serve as either team huddle space or data access and documentation work spaces?
- Where would workstations-on-wheels be stored when they are not in use?
- What impact would decentralization of data access and documentation have on the number of steps care providers and patients must take? How can these be minimized while still optimizing the flexibility and adaptability of the clinic facility?

Design Considerations

Factors designers consider when designing flexible, adaptable clinic buildings include: the type of services provided by and the care model of the healthcare organization that owns the facility, development costs, code and zoning requirements, and the project type (for example, new construction, adaptive reuse, or tenant fit-up).

Type of Services

Design professionals consider the type of services a clinic offers when determining how much flexibility and adaptability it will need. For example, experts anticipate a great deal of change will be occurring in primary care clinics that are being transformed into "medical homes" for their patients and bringing more disciplines under one roof.

Method of Care Delivery

The method of care delivery is a major factor influencing the extent to which a clinic is designed for flexibility and adaptability. For example, should all exam rooms be the same, or do they need to be sized, configured, and equipped differently to support the specific activities that occur within them?

Historically, both care models and the design of clinics have been physician-centric and thus designed around departments and specialized practices rather than in relation to patient needs (fig. 4-3). In recent years, however, there has been a clear shift toward designing "patient-centric" healthcare facilities (fig. 4-4).

Point of Care

Many of the technological advances mentioned earlier in this chapter are making it easier for medical equipment, supplies, and medical services to flow to where patients are receiving care so that they no longer have to move (or be transported) to different points along the care continuum within a clinic—or from clinic to clinic.

This can decrease the chance that ill or debilitated patients will fall or otherwise be injured in transit (adverse medical events), improve patient satisfaction,[8] and reduce staff fatigue because it typically takes less time and energy to transport equipment and supplies to the patient than to move the patient to a new location. The risk of medical errors can also be reduced because there are fewer "baton passes" between clinic staff.

Decentralization

Clinics choosing to bring more care to the patient are generally decentralizing workstations as well as equipment and supply storage rooms to keep these closer to patients. Thanks to the rapid advancement of wireless technology, care providers no longer have to be tethered to a central collaborative workstation by the need for a hardwired connection to a computer network. Rather, they can carry a tablet computer or other digital device with them to the point of care. A single handheld digital device can now replace multiple

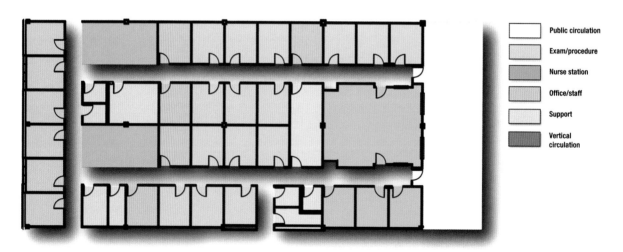

Public circulation

Exam/procedure

Nurse station

Office/staff

Support

Vertical circulation

FIGURE 4-3: Physician-centric floor plan. Physician offices are adjacent to their exam rooms. Offices are typically the same size as exam rooms, allowing for future flexibility. Image courtesy of Hammel, Green and Abrahamson, Inc.

pieces of equipment such as pagers, phones, and desktop computers.

Space Impact

While the use of mobile medical equipment and supply carts or cabinets increases flexibility, additional storage space may be needed to accommodate this strategy. Circulation paths must also be properly sized and configured to allow for the safe passage of patients, staff, and equipment. Some facilities provide hallways for physicians and other care providers that keep the flow of staff and equipment separate from the flow of patients. This helps keep patient areas quieter and allows clinicians to reach patients quickly. Each exam room has two doors: one that patients use to enter off the main hallway and one that staff members use to gain access from the private circulation corridors (fig. 4-5).

Development Costs

Development costs are influenced not only by site-specific conditions and market factors but also by the level of adaptability a clinic will need over time. Building areas with the shortest service life typically require more up-front

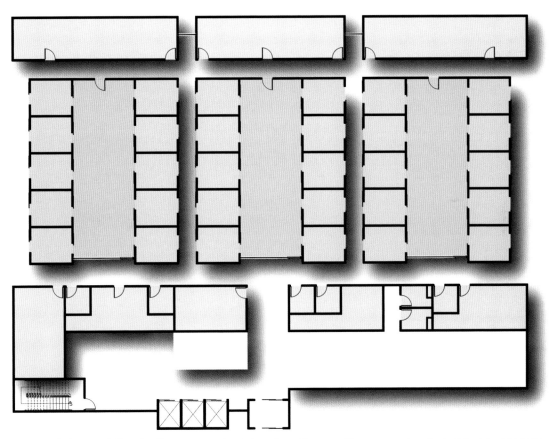

FIGURE 4-4: Patient-centric floor plan. Exam rooms are located near the waiting area with easy access for patients. Patients travel in their own corridors, reducing traffic and noise. Image courtesy of Hammel, Green and Abrahamson, Inc.

investment to reduce the costs of converting them for other functions in the future.

It can be especially challenging for design professionals to advocate for investing in flexibility and adaptability in the current economic climate when capital for investing in new construction is scarce. Also, when healthcare organizations keep their construction budgets separate from their facilities management and maintenance budgets, it is harder to justify higher investment in the short term when the majority of the cost savings will occur once the building is open and operating.

Materials and Resources

The development, construction, operations, and maintenance of buildings use an enormous amount of materials and resources. Design professionals not only assess the impact that materials can have on health outcomes in clinic facilities (avoidance of materials that off-gas or contain irritants, toxins, carcinogens, and the like) but also consider how to optimize the use of construction materials so that less money is spent of purchasing them and less waste is created from demolition and replacement activities over the course of the building's life. A clinic

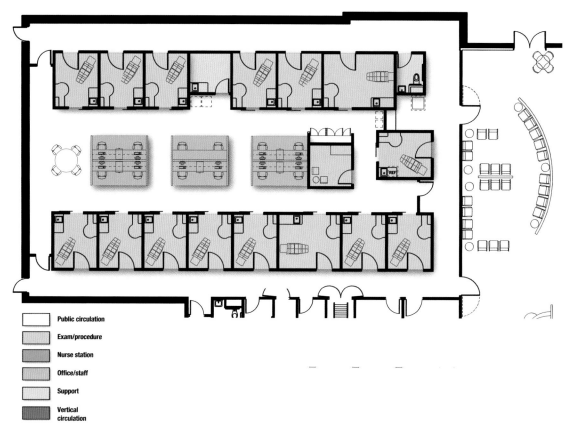

Public circulation
Exam/procedure
Nurse station
Office/staff
Support
Vertical circulation

FIGURE 4-5: Separation of patient flow from provider flow in this floor plan.   Image courtesy of Hammel, Green and Abrahamson, Inc.

designed to adapt to anticipated and unforeseen changes usually costs less to remodel, update, or otherwise alter.

Code and Zoning Requirements

Professionals designing adaptable clinic buildings begin by conducting a preliminary review of relevant building codes and zoning ordinances to establish what the height, massing, and buildable area limitations of different sites are, as well as to identify setbacks, easements, and other requirements for buildings that may need to be expanded or otherwise altered in the future.

Classification

It can be very expensive to upgrade a healthcare building's classification after it has been constructed and occupied. For example, it is easier to alter and expand a building to serve new healthcare functions if it is classified as an "ambulatory health" facility than if it is classified as a basic office structure. Fire protection, HVAC, and other code requirements are more stringent for healthcare facilities. Challenges related to building classification can extend beyond the bounds of the building, too. The number of parking spaces required for a medical office building is higher than the number needed for a basic office structure.

■ ESSENTIA HEALTH
Fargo, North Dakota

The 90,000-square-foot, full-service clinic building located on this medical campus is classified for ambulatory care while being designed for easy conversion to a basic office building if needs change. It was also designed to accommodate two additional floors of vertical expansion. The outpatient clinics were stacked to provide optimal horizontal adjacencies for providers, while

diagnostic and treatment spaces are centrally located (fig. 4-6).

Project Type

While greenfield clinic projects are still being planned and constructed, healthcare organizations in recent years have taken advantage of a downturn in the economy to open clinics in convenient locations by purchasing or leasing vacant properties.

Existing Buildings

A critical first step that enables healthcare organizations, designers, and real estate professionals to determine if an existing building and or tenant space can be adapted for use as a clinic is to complete a program document. This defines the type of services a clinic will offer, lists staffing, equipment, and resource requirements, provides hours of operation, and describes plans to include any specialized imaging, lab, treatment, or procedure areas.

Based on this document, owners and design professionals can then determine if the construction type of a building is suitable for

FIGURE 4-6: Essentia Health West, Fargo, North Dakota. Clinic building designed for flexibility by allowing for easy conversion to office space and structuring it for two additional floors.
Photography © by Don F. Wong

conversion into a clinic with the anticipated uses. They can also evaluate the value of a particular location in relation to any upgrade costs.

New Construction and Renovation

Regardless of whether a clinic project entails new construction or renovation, the shape, structure, and floor-to-floor height strongly influence its degree of adaptability.

Shape

Curvilinear or irregularly shaped buildings can be difficult to alter and/or expand in the future.[9,10]

Structure

The structural-bay size of an existing facility must be large enough to achieve the clinic's programmatic requirements. If it is too small or oddly shaped, this can lead to an inefficient use of space.

Floor-to-Floor Height

There must be enough above-ceiling space to route heating, ventilation, air conditioning, electric, voice/data, and lighting systems and accommodate materials used to reduce noise from mechanical systems or to achieve acoustical separation between spaces (fig. 4-7).

These issues are especially critical to address for clinics with labs, diagnostic equipment, or procedure rooms, as these have unique ventilation, cooling, and electrical system requirements. For that reason, design professionals often locate the most systems-intensive spaces on the first level of a structure, where ceilings are usually taller, in order to provide a sense of openness in entry areas.

Building Systems

Design professionals assess the condition and consider the costs of expanding, increasing the capacity of, and rerouting HVAC, electrical, and plumbing systems.

Tenant Spaces

While programmatic requirements and preferences vary greatly between clinics, some of the criteria design professionals commonly use to evaluate tenant spaces to assess if they can be adapted (or fit up) for use as a clinic include:

- Convenient access to and optimal visibility from elevators and stairs.
- The ability to have exterior signage displaying the clinic's name and/or logo.
- Proximity to parking areas or ramps.
- The existence of a separate elevator to serve back-of-house functions.
- The ability to provide bathrooms within the clinic's leased space rather than to share these with other tenants.

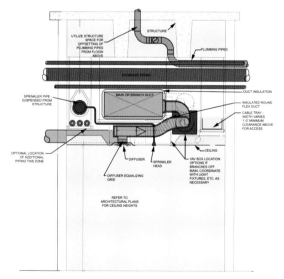

FIGURE 4-7: Typical building cross section showing the space needed above the ceiling for building and technical support. Image courtesy of Hammel, Green and Abrahamson, Inc.

- Flexible design standards for the main entry leading into the clinic and, ideally, a separate entry for staff.
- Opportunities for future expansion (swing space) or contraction.

Design Challenges and Strategies

One approach to designing a flexible, adaptable clinic is to imagine unfolding it to examine how each layer and piece should be designed. This builds upon architect Francis Duffy's concept of the "Six S's," which are: site, structure, skin, services, space plan, and "stuff." Duffy's basic belief was, "there isn't any such thing as a building. A building properly conceived is several layers of longevity of built components."[11]

Author Stewart Brand later reiterates this point in his book *How Buildings Learn,* writing: "The word 'building'...means both the action of the verb 'build' and [the noun] 'that which is built.'... Whereas architecture may strive to be permanent, a 'building' is always building and rebuilding. The idea is crystalline, the fact fluid."[12]

Since the magnitude and complexity of change in the healthcare industry are currently so high, many design professionals are recommending that decisions about the need for flexibility and adaptability be based on the changes clinic owners know will be required within the first one to two years after a building opens or tenant space is occupied.

■ WOMEN'S AND CHILDREN'S CENTER
Sacramento, California

The first building on this site was constructed over one half of a basement. The column grid as well as elevator and stairwell locations were built in the second half, which was otherwise left unfinished until funds could be secured to build a clinic structure above it.

Initially, this seemed like a sound strategy for roughing in the level of adaptability that would be needed to meet projected future needs. However, in the years that passed between when the first building was finished and when design development proceeded for the second building, the codes, funding sources, and space needs changed, making the built layout obsolete.

A major earthquake had occurred in the interim, and this prompted code officials to increase the lateral force distribution requirements for the columns. Changes in the leadership and the vision for this campus shifted, so program priorities were redefined. This, in turn, affected which organizations and individuals were willing to provide financial support. The original vision had called for the second building to be 8 stories, but actual needs led to the final building being 10 stories tall, with a heliport.

When the ways a clinic building will need to be altered and the timing of various changes is less precise, design professionals use broader strategies, such as increasing floor heights, using universal layouts, and/or maximizing the use of modular work space and furnishing systems to achieve the level of flexibility and adaptability a clinic owner desires while minimizing the risk of building in features that will not be needed in the future.[13]

Site

When purchasing land for a new clinic, it is good to plan for 50 to 100 years in the future while addressing the healthcare organization or clinic owner's goals and the immediate and the projected needs of the community.

Analysis

Design professionals can add lasting value to a project by identifying the advantages and limitations of various sites that are under consideration and defining the improvements required to make them suitable for construction of a clinic. The availability of utility connections and information about a site's topography, geology, hydrology, flora, fauna, climate, soil conditions, and other factors influence where a building should be placed and oriented so that anticipated alterations or expansions can be efficiently and affordably accomplished.

■ WHITTIER CLINIC
Minneapolis, Minnesota

The site analysis for Hennepin County Medical Center's (HCMC) Whittier Clinic entailed evaluating six sites based on the following criteria: service area for HCMC, amount of demolition required, amount of remediation required, height limits, and constraints for the building footprint.

Development was done in phases to allow the most pressing needs of the community to be addressed first. Phase I, which was constructed in 2010, includes a 60,000-square-foot medical clinic with 48 exam rooms, related support areas, and facilities for imaging, pharmacy, lab, and occupational and physical therapy (fig. 4-8).

Phase II will add approximately 8,700 square feet of street-level retail space, with 27,000 square feet of office space located above. A three-level parking garage is proposed for the southwest side of the site. One level will be underground and two above grade.

Planning

Once the purchase of a site is complete, design professionals and other members of the planning team consolidate their research findings and recommendations by developing a comprehensive

FIGURE 4-8: Whittier Clinic, Hennepin County Medical Center, Minneapolis, Minnesota. Prior to construction, this existing site was a brownfield industrial development that served as a meatpacking plant and trucking warehouse. Eventually it was abandoned. The community desired a facility that would reenergize an underdeveloped and gritty section of Nicollet Avenue, and hoped to build on the pedestrian-oriented character of the street's northern section. The result is a dynamic and colorful pedestrian-friendly design that encourages public interaction and celebrates the rich ethnic and cultural diversity of the neighborhood. Photography by Paul Crosby

plan for how the site can be developed over time. After identifying and envisioning scenarios for future alterations or expansions, the team members then collaboratively determine how these can be accomplished and include information about the phased implementation process on the site-planning documents.

The provision of adequate parking is often a key design challenge. For example, it may be necessary to purchase a larger property or adjacent land to allow for expansion of surface lots or the addition of parking garages needed to support expanded clinic buildings or medical complexes in the future.

■ OWATONNA HEALTHCARE CAMPUS
Owatonna, Minnesota

The two major facilities that merged into a single building on this campus are actually owned and operated separately: Owatonna Hospital is part of the Allina Health network; Owatonna Clinic is part of the Mayo Health System.

Allina and Mayo decided to colocate their facilities on this site when they both outgrew the properties they occupied in the town of Owatonna. The site's master plan included an integrated hospital and skilled nursing facility and accommodates future expansion of the clinic building. If expansion is not necessary in the future, peripheral portions of the site can be sold to developers for other purposes (figs. 4-9, 4-10).

Location Factors

Clinics should be located so that they are easily accessible and, ideally, so that staff, patients, and others have the flexibility to use different modes of transportation to reach them (using mass transit, driving a car, biking, or walking, for example).

FIGURE 4-9: Owatonna Healthcare Campus, Owatonna, Minnesota. The goal of this project was to address the need for an integrated healthcare campus that was more accessible to the region. Allina Health and Mayo Clinic Health System, Minnesota's two largest healthcare organizations, came together to develop a new healthcare campus. Photography by Steve Henke

FIGURE 4-10: Owatonna Healthcare Campus, Owatonna, Minnesota. One of the primary goals for the interior of the Owatonna healthcare campus was to create a community gathering place for health and wellness. On the north concourse, patients, family, and community members are encouraged to take advantage of such amenities as the cybercafé, family room, TV room, and the Pink Pantry. Multiple dining opportunities are placed along this corridor, including a chic indoor dining area and a sunroom. There is also an outdoor dining terrace. A reflection room and an indoor Wellness Walk overlook a spectacular view of the outdoor walking paths. Photography by Steve Henke

It is also essential to review current and projected demographic data, especially if there are major shifts predicted. Will the patient population served by this location be increasing, decreasing, or remaining approximately the same? Will its characteristics stay constant or be changing? How will age, ethnicity, economic status, and other factors affect the way that patients travel to the clinic and through its site? What is the payer mix? The answers to these questions all influence the current and future space needs and uses of a clinic facility.

Structure

In the United States, healthcare buildings are typically designed to last 50 or more years.[14] A key factor influencing the length of a clinic's useful life is the degree to which its structural system accommodates flexibility and adaptability.

Design professionals evaluate all structural system alternatives based on their initial costs, as well as on their safety, stability, and adaptability. Special code requirements, such as those governing the design and construction of buildings in regions where there are high seismic risks (California and Alaska, for example), must also be considered.

Clinic owners frequently want to avoid systems that use cross-bracing because the space underneath the cross cannot be used (or leased to others). The costs of building, heating, and cooling unusable space or of rental revenue forgone can add up to a point where it makes more sense to invest in a structural system with higher initial costs that maximizes the amount of usable (or leasable) space and provides greater flexibility and adaptability.

For example, design professionals and owners typically assume there is a cost premium associated with using a moment-frame versus a brace-frame structural system. Since moment-frame structures can have the open bays, they provide more flexibility for changing interior clinic spaces over time. While it is true that the labor costs and amount of steel required for a moment-frame system are higher, some of this can be offset by lower foundation costs.

Special Considerations

If a healthcare organization or clinic owner knows that a clinic will need to expand horizontally or vertically, the architects and structural engineers on the design team need to carefully coordinate the location of wind bracing during the planning phase because this key decision determines how adaptable the clinic building will be. The weight of mobile equipment and projected future occupancy levels must also be considered when calculating structural loads.

In zones where the risk of seismic events is high, architects and structural engineers must also factor the potential for building drifts into their recommendations. If a severe seismic event occurs, there could be more damage to the building's envelope, nonstructural elements, and contents if the structural system has been designed to maximize flexibility and adaptability. In these instances, it normally does not make economic

sense to increase the member sizes to improve the drift resistance of a moment-frame system to meet more stringent safety-code requirements.

■ OUTPATIENT SURGICAL CENTER
California

A Northern California healthcare organization purchased two existing office buildings across the street from one of its healthcare campuses with the goal of converting one into an outpatient surgical center with clinical spaces on the remaining floors and the other into an outpatient imaging center.

Unfortunately, extremely poor soil conditions had forced the original building to be constructed with an 18-inch-thick mat-slab foundation. A vacuum plumbing system had to be installed to minimize the need to penetrate the slab. The structural engineer determined how an opening could be saw-cut through the slab that was just large enough to provide sewer access for the new plumbing system, which had the additional capacity needed to serve day-surgery functions.

The location of the existing stairwell and use of wooden components in the building's original wall and floor assembly also presented challenges that added to the cost of retrofitting a basic office building to serve new medical functions.

The stairwell was located approximately 70 feet inside the edge of the floor plate, which meant that it became an obstacle for patients being moved from the operating rooms on one end of the outpatient surgical center to the recovery areas on the opposite end. Since, for infection control and other reasons, patients cannot be transported across nonmedical space, the interior stairwell had to be removed and an external, open stairway added to provide vertical circulation.

Although the skeletal structure of the building was constructed from steel, wood was used for the floor joists and decking. To achieve the two-hour fire rating required for the surgical center, three additional layers of drywall (with a ¾-inch gap between two of them) had to be added between the joists, and all building columns were coated with spray-on fireproofing.

It cost an unanticipated $1.2 million to complete the HVAC upgrades, stairwell relocation, and fireproofing needed just to prepare the building for remodeling.

Skin

Most building exteriors are designed to last at least 20 years. Fenestration, roofing, cladding, and other decisions about the design of a building's "skin" affect its ability to be altered or expanded over time. For example, using a unique material (such as titanium, for example) or a custom color can result in a need to purchase extra quantities up front so that patching related to future alterations and expansions can be seamlessly and affordably accomplished.[15]

In some instances, exterior wall panels can offer faster and more flexible installation options. Individual panels can also be temporarily removed and then put back into place when a large piece of medical equipment (an MRI machine, for example) needs to be moved in or out of a building. Storefront windows can also be strategically located for this purpose.

Design professionals consider how the size, location, and other characteristics of windows and doors relate to the standardized rooms used within the clinic module to maintain the flexibility to alter their uses in the future.

■ NEW CLINIC
Los Gatos, California

When development plans fell through for a prime site in the city of Los Gatos, a healthcare system based in Northern California purchased the property and worked with the site developer to adapt the current design of the building, which had already been approved by planning and zoning officials.

The irregular shape and fenestration of the building, however, presented major challenges for converting it into a clinic. The dimensions of the standard exam rooms and offices used by this health system did not relate to the placement of the exterior windows and the building's irregular shape. This would have created unused space. However challenging, the core and shell architects and the tenant improvement architects worked out a plan to use the space efficiently.

The floor-to-floor height of the first level had to be increased by a foot to accommodate the mechanical system–intensive medical functions. The elevator bank was originally positioned 10 to 12 feet back from the main entry doors, creating wasted space on all sides. By pushing the elevators closer to the back of this entry space, the designers were able to gain the usable space needed to create a main lobby.

Since clinic staff members prefer to be able to enter and exit the building without having to pass through the main lobby, the designers had to add an exit and connect it to a stairwell that leads directly into a parking garage that has been dug into the hill behind and under the building. (fig. 4-11).

Services

In the past, building systems were designed to last from 7 to 15 years before a major retrofit and upgrade were required. However, since the rate of technological innovation has been accelerating since the late 20th century, it is especially challenging for design professionals and owners to accurately predict the systems needs of clinics in the future. As Ray Kurzweil pointed out in a September 2001 article he wrote for *PC Magazine*: "When examining the impact of future technology, people often go through three stages: awe and wonderment at the potential; dread about the new set of grave dangers; and finally (hopefully), the realization that the only viable path is to set a careful, responsible course that realizes the promise while managing the peril."[16]

Design professionals employ a variety of strategies to address these uncertainties and make sure that the HVAC, plumbing, electrical, low-voltage electronics, and other systems serving a clinic are designed to achieve the desired levels of flexibility and adaptability established by the client, including:

- Designing the floor-to-floor height to allow enough above-ceiling space to reroute, expand, and reconfigure building systems as changing needs dictate. Space should also be provided to rough-in system components such as hollow conduit or electrical trays.

- Designing mechanical and electrical equipment rooms and shaft space to accommodate future expansion.

- Selecting modular workstation systems that are designed so electrical, lighting, and other systems can be easily routed through and to them.

- Routing plumbing and other systems through a fixed "spine" wall in combination with movable walls and casework that can easily be added, removed, or reconfigured to change how standardized rooms are used.

- Planning and designing for the appropriate amount of access to systems via ceilings, floors, and walls.

- Zoning building systems to allow for specific sections to be shut down for repair and to conserve energy when they are not in use.

- Providing additional fixtures so that equipment can be added without construction. Examples include additional electrical and communications outlets or roughed-in plumbing that allows an office to become an exam room.

- Identifying and planning for the full ranges of uses associated with specific rooms and spaces. For example, rooms that can be adapted and used for minor procedures may need to have exhaust fans installed.

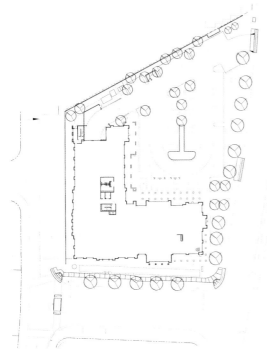

FIGURE 4-11: New Clinic, Los Gatos, California. An irregular building shape can be challenging for a medical clinic. A clinic's efficiency has a direct result on their bottom line. Therefore, the more irregular the building is, the more challenging the design will be. The designer's goal is to make the clinic the most efficient it can be for the physicians and medical staff. Image courtesy of Hammel, Green and Abrahamson, Inc.

■ MAYO MULTIDISCIPLINARY DESIGN CLINIC
Rochester, Minnesota

Mayo Clinic's Center for Innovation (CFI) includes the Design Research Lab, where design professionals and healthcare researchers rapidly develop and refine prototypes. Plumbing and electrical systems are routed through a spine wall that runs the length of the lab. Sinks are mounted to this wall. Researchers use a series of movable walls, a variety of fixtures, new technology, and signage to simulate different clinic settings and easily reconfigure the space to test new concepts.

While this facility was designed to maximize researchers' ability to reconfigure space, they have had to drill into the movable panels to mock up and equip clinic prototypes because the design of the modular system components had not fully anticipated these needs (figs. 4-12, 4-13).

Space Plan

One of the strategies design professionals use to maximize the flexibility and adaptability of a clinic is to standardize as many of its features as possible. This includes developing universal building layouts and standardized rooms so that spaces can easily be altered and adapted to address new and changing priorities.

Standard room dimensions and structural bay sizes make it easier to adapt clinic spaces because design professionals or facilities staff know what combination of standard-size rooms will fit within each bay. This makes relocation and reconfiguration of departments within a clinic or clinics within a module easier to achieve.

Standardization can help to systematize and streamline work processes by providing uniformly equipped and furnished designated spaces where tasks such as gathering data, taking vitals, examining patients, and adding information to medical records occur.

Universal Building Layouts

The first step design professionals take to develop a universal building layout is to develop a standard set of vertical and horizontal dimensions for the structural bays of a clinic building.

FIGURES 4-12, 4-13: Mayo multidisciplinary design clinic, Rochester, Minnesota. This area allows designers and healthcare researchers to rapid-prototype and test different clinic modules. A series of movable walls, furnishings, fixtures, technology, and signage simulate different clinic setups, from a three-part exam room to traditional exam rooms and group exam rooms. Physicians then meet with patients in prototype exam rooms while research teams follow up with a series of questions to evaluate design effectiveness. Photography by Steve Henke

These dimensions and other qualities of these bays should optimize the layout of standardized rooms and other spaces within a building's structural grid. Design professionals should be able to efficiently and effectively cluster exam rooms, staff workstations, and other support spaces into pods. Based on adjacency requirements, these pods can then be used to form clinic modules.

The development of universal building layouts also entails:

- Standardizing other qualities of a clinic's structural, circulation, mechanical, and electrical systems.
- Determining if the clinic owner prefers to provide access to windows by caregivers or patients.
- Planning for the use of "plug-and-play" medical equipment.
- Including open space plans that use movable partitions and modular workstations and furnishings to maximize flexibility.
- Juxtaposing "soft spaces" near the functions that are most likely to change over the life of the building.

Systems and Circulation

The layout of circulation systems and the placement of key elements such as entries, elevators, and stairwells should take into consideration a clinic's anticipated needs for reconfiguring, remodeling, or expanding spaces in the future. Elevators and stairwells as well as other fixed elements, such as mechanical and electrical chases or equipment rooms, should not encumber open space. Egress stairs and corridors must be designed to meet all codes and regulations associated with reasonably anticipated increases in occupancy loads or changes in the use of internal spaces.

Anticipating Future Needs

As healthcare organizations continue to experiment with ways to optimize the use of equipment- and staff-intensive space, design professionals should determine where services currently provided within a clinic building may be provided in the future.

For example, some clinics have begun to outsource scheduling and other telemedicine services, to consolidate their computer equipment in data centers, or to store supplies off-site in less expensive warehouse facilities. Some clinics have sublet vacated spaces to income-generating businesses, such as cafés and gift shops.

Since the aesthetic and HVAC requirements of retail or commercial tenants can be quite different than those of clinics, design professionals discuss potential future uses of spaces that will likely have the shortest clinical service lives with their clients and factor these into the layout and other characteristics of the building's design.

Standardized Exam Rooms

Designing exam rooms to be identical in their layout, equipment, furnishings, finishes, and other features not only makes it easier to reconfigure, relocate, or otherwise adapt them to serve changing needs but also helps to improve staff productivity because caregivers always know where the equipment and supplies they need are located (see chapter 6, "The Exam Room Today," for more detail on exam rooms).

The function of a standardized room can typically be changed by making a few adjustments and, as necessary, renaming it. For example, demountable walls used to separate two standardized exam rooms can be removed to create a conference room, or a group exam room could be subdivided to form four standard-size exam rooms.

Most clinics are including some larger standardized exam rooms in the layout of their modules in order to provide sufficient room for family members to remain with ill or injured patients. Caregivers who use specialized equipment often require larger exam rooms, too. However, there is still a need for specially designed and equipped rooms to serve disciplines such as otolaryngology.

Standardized exam rooms with fewer fixed elements can more easily accommodate the needs of specialists and mobile medical equipment. Care providers can enter any exam room knowing which basic components will be available, and then supplement these by wheeling in a cart with the instruments and supplies related to their particular practice.

Standardized rooms may or may not be designed to be "universal" or "acuity-adaptable."

Universal Exam Rooms

Instead of simply asking "How many physicians are there in a clinic and how many exam rooms do each of them need?" and then calculating total square footage requirements, design professionals planning universal exam rooms ask:

- What are the common tasks completed in all of this clinic's exam rooms?

- Who completes these tasks?

- How can a standardized exam room meet the most needs possible based on the services a clinic provides, its care philosophy, and the characteristics of its patient population?

- How can it be easily adapted to meet the unique needs of specialists who use it on a part-time basis or who join collaborative care teams as needed?

Once design professionals have identified which supplies, furnishings, and equipment are required by all caregivers who will be using a universal exam room, they can develop a standard design that has the same layout, dimensions, furnishings, and equipment. Specialized supplies or equipment can be brought to exam rooms as these are needed, and stored in mobile carts or in rooms that are less costly to fit out than exam space is.

The more versatile an exam room is, the greater the chance its utilization will be higher than if it had been designed to serve the needs of a single medical specialty.

Acuity-Adaptable Exam Rooms

Since "acute" and "acuity" are both used in the healthcare field, it is important to define these terms before relating them to the design of clinics. "Acute" is an adjective that means "very serious or severe," whereas "acuity" is a noun that signifies "a keenness of perception, sharpness, or the ability to hear, see, or understand something easily."

Acuity-adaptable exam rooms are designed so that they can be quickly adapted to treat patients who have illnesses and injuries resulting in varying levels of acuity. They are best suited for clinics where physicians and staff must quickly and accurately assess how serious a patient's condition is and prepare the exam room accordingly (urgent-care clinics, for example).

Key characteristics of acuity-adaptable exam rooms include:

- Their size, layout, and orientation are standardized. Acuity-adaptable rooms are typically laid out and configured to be uniform in relation to each other or to a group of rooms.

- They may be equipped with lifts to assist seriously injured or ill, disabled, or bariatric patients.

- Medical gases (e.g., oxygen canisters) can be routed to the rooms or brought in as needed.

- They need to be larger than the standard 100- or 110-square-foot exam rooms and have wider doors if mobile medical equipment will be used in them.

Work Zones

Design professionals can also address standardization at the zone level. For example, check-in or registration areas serving different departments within a clinic or different clinics within a building could all be the same size and use the same modular workstation components, finishes, and furnishings.

Zones within rooms can also be standardized. For example, the locations of the sink, storage units, desk or writing surface, and chair in the caregiver zone can be kept uniform, while the room dimensions and the equipment used in the patient zone could vary among different versions of a standardized exam room (fig. 4-14).

Pods

Pods serve as the main building blocks for clinic modules. Pods group together exam rooms and related functions, such as team workstations, conference rooms, physicians' offices, and other support areas.

■ WHITTIER CLINIC
Minneapolis, Minnesota

The clinic module for this healthcare facility clusters exam rooms around a central work area that is used by both nurses and physicians. This layout preserves clear sightlines between exam rooms and the central work area and improves staff coordination by facilitating communication among care providers.

Locating work areas within the exam pods frees the exterior wall from the procession of offices typically seen in clinic plans. Instead, the public views a busy staff corridor flanked with large-scale artwork, reinforcing a connection with street level activity (figs. 4-15, 4-16).

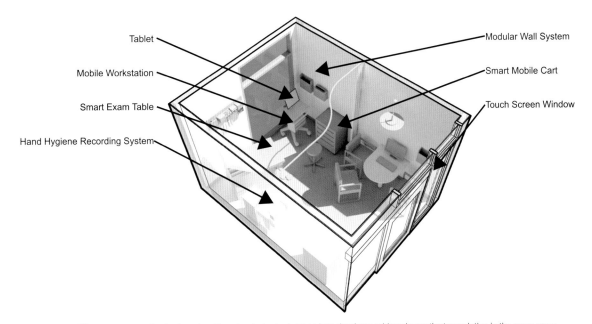

Tablet

Mobile Workstation

Smart Exam Table

Hand Hygiene Recording System

Modular Wall System

Smart Mobile Cart

Touch Screen Window

FIGURE 4-14: The exam room setup is changing. Here is a look at advances in technology, addressing patient population in the exam room, code requirements, and physician needs in the room. At the same time, patient satisfaction is the most important element in design and workflow.   Image courtesy of Hammel, Green and Abrahamson, Inc.

CLINIC MODULE

CLINIC MODULE

RESIDENCY WORK /
CLASSROOM /
INTERPRETERS

CLINIC
RESIDENCY
MODULE

LAB

DIABETES
EDUCATION

WAITING /
PUBLIC

OPEN TO
BELOW

ADMINISTRATION

FIGURE 4-15: Hennepin County Medical Center Whittier Clinic, Minneapolis, Minnesota. Floor plan. Image courtesy of Hammel, Green and Abrahamson, Inc.

Clinic Modules

The highest level of standardization occurs when spaces and rooms throughout a clinic are uniform according to their function—all exam rooms, workstations and zones, and support areas (see chapter 5, "Clinic Planning Concepts," for more detail on clinic modules).

Design professionals begin by identifying which rooms and spaces can be standardized and which cannot. They then group the standardized rooms together to form pods and arrange these pods within the clinic module to optimize the use of clinic space. The location of nonstandard rooms and spaces within pods and within or between clinic modules is determined by adjacency requirements. For example, an orthopedic

clinic is often located as close as possible to radiology and physical therapy spaces.

When calculating the total number of exam rooms needed, the goal should be to make sure that there are enough to serve all providers while optimizing the flow of patients through the clinic. Strategies for accomplishing this goal must be informed by the care philosophy and business model of a clinic as well as by other factors, including the characteristics of the clinic's patient population.

The characteristics of the clinic module influence options for expanding a building vertically or horizontally—and often dictate which of these two approaches should be planned for if a clinic owner anticipates a need for additional space in the future.

FIGURE 4-16: Whittier Clinic, Hennepin County Medical Center, Minneapolis, Minnesota. Central core work area with visibility of exam rooms. Photography by Steve Henke

Prototypical Layouts

Design professionals often show clients prototypical layouts to establish the level of flexibility and adaptability they want to achieve. Some examples of clinic module prototypes used for this purpose include the "on-stage/off-stage" layout and the "racetrack" layout.

Universal Layout #1 (On stage/off stage): The lobby and reception areas are at the front of the clinic, rows of exam rooms are in the center, and physician and other staff work areas are at the back and/or along the perimeter.

These zones are often separated by walls through which plumbing and other building systems are routed. This layout supports a linear approach to care and increases space needed for circulation by an average of 11 percent over clinics with similar functions and services (fig. 4-17).

Universal Layout #2 (Racetrack): This prototypical clinic module places exam rooms, consultation spaces, and physicians' offices around a central collaborative area. Using standardized exam rooms makes it easy to convert these into offices or combine them to create conference rooms or group meeting spaces (fig. 4-18).

Work Process

Standardizing the size, configuration, furnishings, and equipment of exam rooms can help streamline and improve operations. For example, staff will know exactly where supplies and equipment are kept and certain activities are expected to occur, so that less time is spent searching for items or locating members of a care team. Providing caregivers and other staff with the ability to adjust their work environment in ways that they feel enable them to do the best work possible generally improves their productivity.

■ BETH ISRAEL DEACONESS MEDICAL CENTER
Boston, Massachusetts

This owner initially wanted standard exam rooms throughout its facilities. Since it was not possible to design a universal prototype that could meet all of BIDMC's needs, the design team developed two universal exam rooms. By necessity, the clinic modules for Beth Israel also include specialized exam rooms.

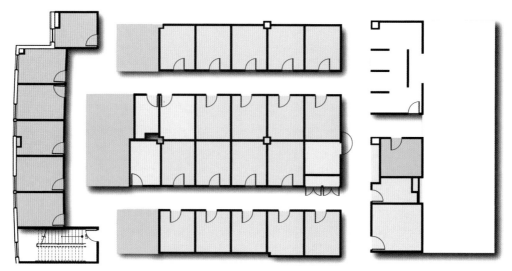

FIGURE 4-17: Universal layout #1.   Image courtesy of Hammel, Green and Abrahamson, Inc.

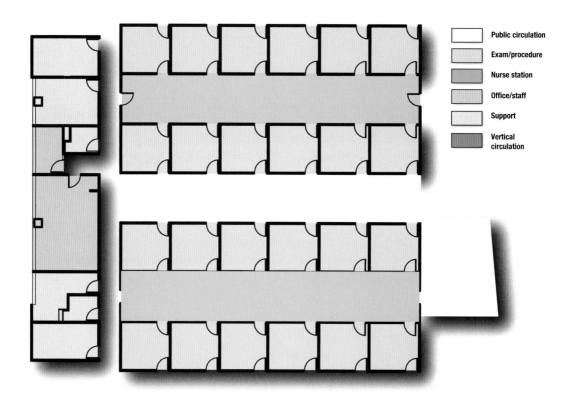

FIGURE 4-18: Universal layout #2.   Image courtesy of Hammel, Green and Abrahamson, Inc.

Thus, based on the research and recommendations of the design team, this healthcare organization's leaders chose the following standardized exam room layouts, which can be used in different combinations to suit the needs of each clinic:

- A 100-square-foot exam room.
- A 110-square-foot exam room.
- A 130-square-foot exam room, which can be converted into a procedure room according to the needs of the patient and the specialized expertise of the care provider.

Mobile carts are restocked each evening with the instruments, supplies, and other items needed by caregivers to treat patients who are scheduled to be seen in specific rooms the next day. This applies the just-in-time inventory strategy perfected by auto manufacturers to the design of clinics. It also helps to ensure that care is customized for each patient (figs. 4-19, 4-20).

FIGURES 4-19, 4-20: The user groups voted on the best room size for their department, and the final exam room design was selected. The team reached consensus on the universal option for the majority of clinics with a larger option for medical specialties. Addressing the needs of eight different user groups, this process resulted in only two different-sized exam rooms with an optional layout. Image courtesy of Hammel, Green and Abrahamson, Inc.

Stuff

While it used to take weeks or months to relocate, reconfigure, and otherwise alter the interior "stuff" found within clinics—such as partition walls and built-in casework or furnishings—advances in the design of modular systems have not only shortened the time needed to adapt interior spaces but have also expanded the palette of materials, forms, and finishes available.

It is worth considering the use of modular systems and furnishings when a clinic owner feels that there is a high likelihood that space needs will change; would like to be able to depreciate workstation components, furnishings, and equipment as part of a financial strategy; or is able to secure systems furnishings and components at a lower per-piece cost via a volume-buyer discount.

Modular Workstations

In addition to flexibility, some benefits of using modular workstation systems include:

- They can be disassembled, transported, and reassembled with minimal downtime. Minor remodels can be completed in a matter of days.

- Modular workstations can be assembled, mounted, and removed without significant patching and refinishing.

- The code review and approval process for remodeling and renovation projects is usually shorter than it is for projects requiring demolition and construction of fixed architectural elements and other built-ins.

- Using modular furniture systems can help to neatly organize and route electrical conduit, piping, wiring, and other building system components. Examples of this are the Herman Miller, Inc., "Canvas" workstation system (fig. 4-21).

Herman Miller Canvas Office Landscape Group-Based

FIGURE 4-21: Herman Miller Canvas Works. Herman Miller, Inc., modular "Canvas" furniture systems.   Image courtesy of Herman Miller

- Work-surface and other task lighting is (or can be) integrated into some modular workstation systems.

- Using prefabricated walls, power, networks, and millwork can offer substantial cost savings for clients, not to mention the ability to open clinics faster. For example, DIRTT can be cost-neutral, and in many cases, considerably less expensive when all factors are considered. It also provides very agile spaces that will handle future changes with ease. As an added benefit, DIRTT's revolutionary Ice Software is a planning tool used for real-time budgeting, live 3-D walk-throughs, and renderings (fig. 4-22).

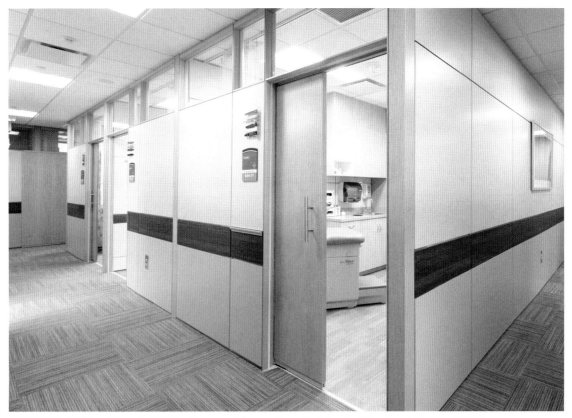

FIGURE 4-22: DIRTT modular walls. DIRTT walls can easily be reconfigured for future flexibility. Image courtesy of DIRTT

- It is easier to maintain the surfaces of drawers, cabinets, or other storage compartments that are part of modular systems than to dust healthcare equipment, instruments, and supplies that are stored in the open.

- Equipment mounting components are typically designed to be flexible so that users can adjust the height, orientation, and viewing angle of computer monitors—for example, to optimize ergonomics or to better engage patients during consultations.

- Components that have casters or glides make it easier to clean under and around them without damaging floor surfaces.

- Repairs can often be completed on-site.

There can also be some drawbacks or special challenges associated with using modular workstation systems, such as:

- The acoustical separation provided by movable walls and other modular system components varies. Not only can ambient noise levels become an issue, but preserving privacy is especially important for clinics, which must comply with HIPAA requirements.

- The visible impact of modular systems can detract from the overall sense of quality in a facility. These can look temporary or convey a lack of sturdiness and durability.

- The ability to hang light fixtures, storage units, shelving, art, computer monitors, and other items from modular wall panels varies greatly between systems.

The design of a replacement healthcare campus located in Santa Rosa, California, illustrates additional benefits that using modular systems can offer. In this instance, they are used throughout all facilities to maximize flexibility and adaptability.

■ SUTTER MEDICAL CENTER
Santa Rosa, California

After a thorough analysis of alternatives, the design team recommended Steelcase's Nurture workstation and furnishing systems for the facility for the following reasons:

- Steelcase's modular systems were the affordable and flexible option compared to the costs of labor, materials, and downtime associated with demolishing and constructing built-ins.

- In acute-care facilities in California, it can take six months or longer to obtain all the necessary approvals to replace a built-in nurse station. Modular systems simplify the construction approval process. It takes approximately a month to plan, design, and order the pieces needed to replace a nurse station using modular casework. (If system components are not in stock, it can take another four to six weeks for them to be produced and shipped to the site.) Installation typically takes less than a day; the code review is streamlined, as well, and usually requires very little lead time. Thus, using modular systems gives the client the ability to adapt spaces more quickly to changing needs.

- Since the modular units are floor-supported instead of wall-mounted, they are better suited for facilities in locations such as Santa Rosa, where there is a greater risk for a high-level seismic event.

Furnishings

Since clinic furnishings are subjected to a lot of wear and tear, designers are constantly researching how well they are constructed and whether or not their finishes and fabrics are resilient, easy to clean, and stain-resistant. The ideal is to select furniture that can be easily disassembled so that the legs, arms, seats, seatbacks, and cushions can be thoroughly cleaned, replaced, or refurbished individually. This enables clinics to avoid having to purchase an entire piece of furniture when one component is damaged or deteriorating faster than another. This saves money in the long run, while keeping clinic spaces attractive, up-to-date, and well maintained.

■ FAIRVIEW HEALTH SERVICES
Minneapolis, Minnesota

This healthcare system uses blends of built-ins and furniture systems to achieve a quality custom appearance while gaining the flexibility needed to quickly adapt spaces for changing functions and evolving processes. For example, the nurse stations located in Fairview Health Systems facilities often feature a custom-designed, built-in façade, with systems components behind. In some cases, the systems consist of work surfaces on standards. In other cases, the work surface is built in and combined with movable pedestals, keyboards, pencil drawers, or file cabinets.

Several of the benefits associated with selecting modular and/or mobile furnishings include:

- Staff and patients can easily create groupings for team huddles or for having family members and friends sit together.

- Seat heights, seatback angles, heights of work surfaces, and other aspects of modular furnishings can be adjusted to suit the demands of specific tasks and optimize ergonomics for users.

- They can be used for multiple functions. One example of this is the motorized IOA "Connect" patient chair, which can be easily converted from an upright or semi-reclining position to an exam table with a touch of a button (fig. 4-23).

- They can also help to organize the layout of the exam room and the supplies/equipment these activity-intensive spaces contain. This can help reduce negative distractions and ease the stress that patients typically feel when they are ill or injured and awaiting care.

Sensory Perception

Patients absorb a lot of information subconsciously as they progress along the care continuum in a clinic. The last thing they want to encounter is a cluttered exam room. The modular casework and furnishing systems that design professionals use to maximize flexibility in a clinic can also help to ease the tension created by the sight of medical instruments, equipment, and supplies (such as syringes, bandages, scopes, and scalpels) or by exposure to offensive smells or distracting noise.

Since modular workstations and furniture systems are designed so that items stored in them can be easily moved when a space is being reconfigured, doors, drawers, and specialized organizers provide specific places where exam room equipment and supplies are stored and thus hidden from view when they are not needed. This also keeps work surfaces clear of clutter, allowing caregivers to spread out printed materials during data gathering and consultation. A more organized exam room reduces the chance that important information and items being lost, as well.

■ THE MIND INSTITUTE
Sacramento, California

The MIND Institute, which is dedicated to the diagnosis and treatment of patients with autism spectrum and other neurological

FIGURE 4-23: The OA Connect patient chair can be easily converted from an exam table to an upright chair with the touch of a button. Image reproduced by permission of IOA.

disorders, effectively minimizes patient distractions. The sink is hidden behind cabinet doors because water is a distraction for many children with autism. The exam table is positioned along the wall and designed to be inconspicuous, since patients arriving at the Institute have often undergone a full battery of tests and assessments. If the exam table were the most prominent piece of furniture in the room, the sight of it could cause unnecessary stress. Warm wood finishes, soft lighting, subdued nonrepetitive patterns, and muted tones create a peaceful, familiar feeling that is calming for pediatric patients whose senses can easily be overstimulated. This design also demonstrates that aesthetics need not be compromised to achieve the flexibility and adaptability that modular furniture systems can provide (fig. 4-24).

Summary

One of the most daunting challenges that clinic designers currently face is helping their clients plan for a future that no one can fully predict. While it is clear that the increasing demand for clinics and the dynamic rate of change in the healthcare delivery process will continue for the next several years, no one knows how long it will take to complete the transformation that is currently underway, what all of the ramifications will be, and what the impact of these will be on design of the built environment.

A key strategy that many design professionals are using to ensure that clinics can continuously adapt to dynamically changing conditions and demands is to standardize as many aspects of a facility's design as possible. This helps to ensure that future alterations can be accomplished quickly and affordably, with minimal interruption.

DOUGLAS WHITEAKER

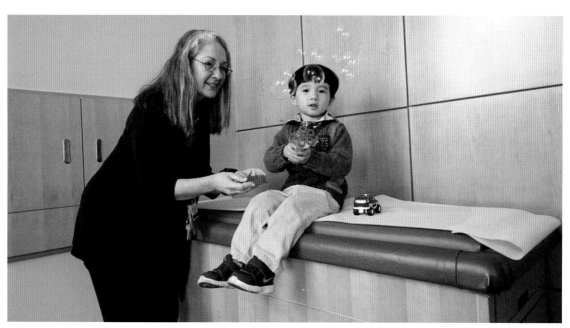

FIGURE 4-24: UC Davis MIND Institute. The exam table is positioned along the wall and designed to be inconspicuous. Typical exam room features are also designed to blend into the room aesthetics. This design also demonstrates that aesthetics need not be compromised to achieve the flexibility and adaptability that modular furniture systems can provide. Image courtesy of UC Davis MIND Institute

Notes

1. Robert Schmidt III, Toru Eguchi, Simon Austin, and Alistair Gibb, "What Is the Meaning of Adaptability in the Building Industry?" (paper presented at the CIB 16th International Conference, Bilbao, Spain, May 17–19, 2010).

2. "BPCI Initiative Episodes: Details on the Participating Health Care Facilities," Centers for Medicare and Medicaid Services, http://innovation.cms.gov/initiatives/Bundled-Payments/Participating-Health-Care-Facilities/index.html.

3. Jack Brown, Fred Doloresco III, and Joseph M. Mylotte, "Never Events: Not Every Hospital Acquired Infection is Preventable," *Clinical Infectious Diseases* 49 (2009): 743–46.

4. Center for Health Workforce Studies at the University Of Albany, School of Public Health, University at Albany, *The Impact of the Aging Population on the Health Workforce in the United States* (Rensselaer, NY: School of Public Health, University at Albany, 2006), http://www.albany.edu/news/pdf_files/impact_of_aging_full.pdf.

5. Ibid.

6. "Team Oriented," The Millennial Legacy, n.d., http://themilleniallegacy.com/?page_id=61.

7. Daniel Lee Kulick, "CT Coronary Angiogram?" MedicineNet, February 14, 2014.

8. HemoCue, "How Will You Benefit from Diagnostic Testing at the Point-of-Care?", http://www.hemocue.com/en/point-of-care-testing.

9. "Baylor Cancer Center," *Engineering News Record Texas & Louisiana*, June 1, 2010. http://texas.construction.com/texas_construction_projects/2010/0601_BaylorCancerCenter.asp.

10. Joseph Giovannini, "Lou Ruvo Center for Brain Health," *Architect*, April 7, 2011.

11. Wikipedia, "Shearing Layers," http://en.wikipedia.org/wiki/Shearing_layers.

12. Stewart Brand, *How Buildings Learn: What Happens to Buildings After They Are Built* (New York: Viking Press, 1994).

13. Christine Guzzo Vickery, "A New Look at Physicians' Workspaces," *Healthcare Design*, February 20, 2013. http://www.healthcaredesignmagazine.com/blogs/christine-guzzo-vickery/new-look-physicians-workspaces.

14. Robert F. Carr, "Health Care Facilities," *Whole Building Design Guide: National Institute of Building Sciences,* 2010, http://www.wbdg.org/design/health_care.php.

15. "Frank Gehry's Center for Brain Health: Ohio Photographer's Beautiful Shots of Masterpiece," *We Heart Magazine*, June 17, 2010.

16. Ray Kurzweil, "Accelerated Living," *PC Magazine,* September 4, 2001.

17. "Sutter Medical Center of Santa Rosa," *Steelcase Health* (blog), March 11, 2011), http://www.nurture.com/case-studies/sutter-medical-center-of-santa-rosa/.

Select Bibliography

Americans with Disabilities Act of 1990. P.L. 110-325. http://www.ada.gov/pubs/ada.htm.

Brown, Jack, Fred Doloresco III, and Joseph M. Mylotte. "Never Events: Not Every Hospital Acquired Infection is Preventable." *Clinical Infectious Diseases* 49 (2009): 743–46.

Keller, Amy, Anjali Joseph, Ellen Taylor, Xiaobo Quan, and Callie Unruh. *Promising Practices in Safety-Net Clinic Design: An Overview.* Oakland, CA: California HeathCare Foundation, 2011. http://www.chcf.org/~/media/MEDIA%20 LIBRARY%20Files/PDF/P/PDF%20 PromisingPracticesClinicDesignOverview.pdf

Schmidt III, Robert, Toru Eguchi, Simon Austin, and Alistair Gibb. "What Is the Meaning of Adaptability in the Building Industry?" Paper presented at the CIB 16th International Conference, Bilbao, Spain, May 17–19, 2010.

Overview

As the demand for clinic facilities has increased, healthcare organizations have realized that the physical qualities and features of this facility type must also evolve to address the ever-changing needs of a growing, more diverse, more informed, and aging patient population.

The increasing shift from a fee-for-service to a population-based compensation structure has further motivated healthcare organizations to make certain that every aspect of their business is working toward achieving optimal health outcomes. From this perspective, clinics can be designed as strategic assets that help make the provision of quality care affordable for patients, rewarding for care providers, and financially sustainable for healthcare organizations.

The overarching goal for design professionals as they develop clinic floor plans is to efficiently meet the programmatic needs of a clinical practice while maintaining (and ideally enhancing) the quality of the workplace for staff and the care provided for patients.

To this end, design professionals start by defining and refining a building program that addresses both standard and specialized functions of a particular medical practice. Activities that typically occur within clinics include check-in and registration, rooming the patients, the exam and consultation, and checkout or rescheduling.

Other factors determining the clinic floor plan are its business model and care philosophy, its location and the services it offers, the degree to which it uses new technologies, and how well these technologies are integrated into the care delivery process.

Since legislation and economic, demographic, and cultural trends influence clinic design generally, they must be considered at each step in the creative process—and especially during the space planning and schematic phases, when floor plans are developed.

The space allocation and layout of waiting rooms, offices, workstations, and exam rooms continue to evolve, while the location of where registration, rescheduling, and checkout tasks are completed has shifted.

Generally, there has been a trend toward reducing or eliminating the need for spaces dedicated entirely to waiting. Some clinics have reallocated space to provide a full range of activities in and around waiting rooms or lobbies. Others have implemented a self-rooming process or used technology to reduce or redirect waiting time. The success of these strategies depends on how well a clinic's operational processes and human resource policies support them.

For example, if self-rooming simply shifts the location of where waiting occurs to the exam room, this can be a less efficient use of space because exam rooms are designed and specially equipped for the purpose of conducting exams and facilitating consultations.

Increased collaboration between care providers and expansion of the core care team have affected the size and qualities of physicians' offices, influenced the grouping of disciplines within the clinic module, and generally created a need for more team-based work areas.

The shift toward providing patients with the information and tools they need to recover and maintain their health has altered the qualities of and expanded the need for consultation space. Clinics have also begun to include reference and resource centers—large meeting rooms where group visits, centering sessions, and/or health education and wellness programs can be held.

Trends

During this time of transformation, design professionals must identify and understand major trends that are having an impact on clinic

PREVIOUS PAGE: EAST TEXAS MEDICAL CENTER, PITTSBURG, TEXAS; HAMMEL, GREEN AND ABRAHAMSON, INC. PHOTOGRAPHY © BY GARY ZVONKOVIC.

design. Changes in the way healthcare services are being provided and by whom, as well as demographic and cultural factors, are clearly influencing the design of clinics today.

Staffing

New disciplines are being added to the core care team in clinics, and some existing roles are being expanded; consequently, healthcare professionals are focusing ever more specifically on the most skilled tasks sanctioned by their licenses (for example, physicians will not perform tasks that a physician's assistant, nurse practitioner, or RN can do, a physician's assistant will not perform tasks that a nurse practitioner can do, and so forth). At the same time, new staff positions are emerging to meet the dramatic growth in the patient population that is occurring just as a serious shortage of primary care providers has begun and is expected to intensify.

Primary Care Physicians

The shortage of primary care physicians that has existed in the United States for several years was worsening as of 2014. Nearly 20,000 more primary care physicians are already needed to meet existing demand. Professional organizations, such as the American Academy of Family Physicians and the Health Resources and Services Administration, predict that this shortage will grow to 45,000 by the year 2020 and reach 52,000 by 2025.

Nurses

Comparing changes in the nursing workforce to projected increases in the demand for healthcare services is more complicated. According to the AFL-CIO's Department for Professional Employees, nursing has been among the fastest-growing occupational fields in the United States since the 1990s. By 2011, the number of nurses employed across the nation had reached 2,724,570, which

represented an increase of more than 10 percent in less than a decade. The U.S. Department of Labor (DOL) expects this rate of change to more than double from 2010 to 2020, when employment of registered nurses will likely grow by 26 percent.[1]

Before the recession began in 2008, nurse shortages were common. However, the employment of RNs grew substantially during this economic downturn because some retired nurses and those who had left the workforce for other reasons returned to work to supplement their family income, the number of people who graduated from entry-level baccalaureate nursing programs more than doubled, and some nurses increased their working hours from part time to full time.[2]

Regardless of these increases in the total number of nurses providing care, experts are still projecting a shortage in some regions by 2020 because:

- The nursing population is aging. According to the American Nurses Association, approximately one-third of the RN workforce is between the ages of 50 and 64. Many of these RNs are expected to retire within the next five to ten years.[3]

- An economic recovery could prompt members of this mostly married, mostly female workforce to return to part-time work or quit.

- Implementation of the Patient Protection and Affordable Care Act (ACA) is expected to increase the number of U.S. residents who have health insurance by 30 million within the same time period.

Core Care Team

To address these shortages and the growing demand for healthcare services, clinics have begun to expand the core care team, which historically consisted of physicians and nurses, to include physician's assistants, medical assistants, certified nursing assistants, and health coaches. Organizations such as the Institute of Medicine of the National Academies are advocating that nurses be able to "practice to the full extent of their education and training."[4]

For example, since nurse practitioners have the professional education and skills needed to address most aspects of patient care, clinics are increasingly relying on them to provide diagnosis, treatment, and consultation services. Nurse practitioners can educate patients about preventative care and recommend treatments. In some instances, they can conduct physicals, order tests, prescribe medications, and serve as a patient's primary healthcare provider.

The role of registered nurses can extend beyond gathering and recording patients' medical information, taking their vital signs, and recording symptoms to include consulting with other members of the core care team to assess, formulate, and monitor the implementation of patient care plans. Registered nurses can also order, interpret, and evaluate diagnostic tests.

Healthcare specialists are being added to the core care team. These can include nutritionists, physical therapists, pharmacy technicians, chiropractors, and acupuncturists, as well as social workers, psychologists, and other behavioral health experts. Once sufficient research data are available to justify reimbursement from insurance companies, it is likely that other specialists, such as health educators, health education or patient care coordinators, and massage therapists, will be included on multidisciplinary care teams.

Demographic Factors

Life expectancy has steadily increased in the United States since the 1950s. Although the oldest members of the baby boom generation (1946–64), which represents 28 percent of the population, reached retirement age in 2011, most "zoomer boomers" want to remain active and continue feeling healthy.[5] Since improving health outcomes also requires patients to take charge of their own health and wellness, the trend toward clinics providing more education and wellness programs is likely to last for the foreseeable future.

The phased addition of about 30 million newly insured people to the total patient population in the United States is doing more than adding volume. According to a Price Waterhouse Coopers Health Research Institute report, the newly insured patients will be more likely to speak a language other than English and to be more ethnically diverse.[6]

Integration of Behavioral Health

A major shift in cultural norms and a better understanding of the mind-body connection prompted legislators to include mental health services in the "Essential Health Benefits" that the ACA requires insurers to offer by 2014. The broad impact that these factors are having on clinic design is evidenced by the use of the phrase "behavioral health" (instead of "mental health") and the fact that clinics treating patients of all ages are beginning to include healthcare professionals with this expertise on their core care teams.[7]

The stigma once associated with conditions such as attention-deficit disorder, depression, anxiety, physical and mental disabilities, addictions, and eating, personality, posttraumatic stress, and other disorders has begun to fade as researchers and healthcare professionals' knowledge about the relationship between mental health and physical health has increased.

At the same time, demand for behavioral health services has increased across the spectrum of care. For example, the July 2012 issue of the *Journal of American Medicine* (*JAMA*) published findings that behavioral health conditions have now displaced physical illnesses as the top five disabilities for children living in the United States.[8] Research has shown that approximately half of all lifetime cases of mental illness begin by age 14.[9]

Prevention and early treatment of pediatric behavioral health conditions in the clinic setting are expected to reduce both individual and public health costs. Currently, the majority of behavioral health patients are treated in emergency rooms, and many of those who fail to seek proper treatment or are unable to do so wind up being incarcerated.

Clinics are still determining how large a healthcare practice must be to support integration of behavioral health services. Characteristics of the patient population that a clinic serves also influence the timing and extent to which this integration will occur. It is clear, however, that spaces where behavioral health services are provided are generally designed to be calming and comfortable, with the clinic module including more group meeting rooms to serve patients with addictions and other disorders.

Technology

The rapid rate of technological innovation is not only improving the experience patients have while in the clinic and helping them to better monitor and maintain their personal health. It is also having a significant impact on space allocation and layout within the clinic module.

Electronic Medical Records

A number of factors have converged to shrink the amount of space clinics need to store paper medical records on-site. Some clinics are outsourcing file transcription and telephone scheduling. The transition from printed to electronic medical records (EMRs) is well underway, and advances in nanotechnology are shrinking the size of computers and peripheral equipment needed to update and maintain EMRs. Generally, archival information is being scanned and stored electronically, while the paper copies are destroyed.

As a result, file and computer server rooms at clinics can be smaller, and the extra square footage can be eliminated from space programs for new clinics or retrofitted to meet changing needs within existing clinics. Although instituting an EMR system requires substantial investment in computer hardware and software, the labor cost savings and reduced space needs can balance this over the long term.

Electronic Triage and Consultations

While patients have been able to consult with a nurse or physician via phone for many years, until recently healthcare professionals have only been paid for treating patients in the clinic. Now that using telephones and interactive video to provide healthcare services from remote locations can be reimbursed, some clinics are integrating these strategies into their care delivery process. Used properly, they can provide patients with convenient access to basic healthcare services while eliminating travel time and expense.

The steady growth in electronic triage and assessment services has already led to the creation of spaces that facilitate the work of telephone triage nurses who answer health-related questions over the phone, assess the level and urgency of treatment a patient requires, and recommend where and when a patient should seek care.

A video consultation provides valuable visual information that care providers can use to determine whether or not a patient should be seen in person. Patients can provide information about their vital statistics from remote locations, such as wellness rooms in workplaces that are equipped with an automatic blood-pressure cuff, thermometer, and video equipment.

Video technology is also making it possible for healthcare professionals with highly specialized expertise to consult remotely with patients and other care providers who are located great distances from where the specialists are based.

As clinics shift toward completing basic assessment, diagnostic, and triage tasks via the telephone and the Internet, design professionals are integrating spaces for new staff positions such as health educators, health education or patient care coordinators, telephone triage nurses, and healthcare information management professionals in the clinic floor plan.

For example, a primary care clinic located near Sacramento, California, includes five work-stations for "educational consultants," who are qualified to ask patients the basic questions needed to make triage decisions.

Specialized Websites and Software Applications

Healthcare organizations, insurers, public agencies, and private businesses have developed websites, web portals, and software applications that help patients assess the urgency and severity of their symptoms and obtain self-care information or, if they need to see a healthcare professional, determine where the kind of treatment they require is available and when. Depending on the website or software application, patients can also obtain information about a full range of illnesses, injuries, and chronic conditions.

For example, the goal of the i-Triage website (itriage.com) is to provide "care on demand" and shorten the patient-to-provider pathway. Patients begin by entering information about their symptoms. They then receive basic diagnostic information (e.g., fracture or muscle sprain or similar) and a general recommendation about the type of facility where they should seek care (urgent-care clinic, retail clinic, and so forth). Once patients have selected the

recommendation they prefer, they type in their zip code and are presented with a list of clinics and other healthcare facilities, with associated distances and a link to additional information.

MyChart and related software applications enable patients to review information from their healthcare provider. They are able to view their electronic medical records using a computer or digital mobile device. MyChart helps patients connect through the Internet with their doctors to view appointments and see their health history or get test results and renew prescriptions online any time. By providing self-service convenience for patients, this technology can reduce the amount of time clinic staff spends answering patients' questions by phone, by email, or in person. This can have an impact on the check-in, rescheduling, and checkout functions (and their related spatial needs and features) in clinics.

Although the i-Triage and MyChart examples illustrate *some of* the capabilities of Web-based healthcare services and software applications, new options are being developed so rapidly that design professionals must constantly assess how current and future technologies can influence clinic design.

Kiosks

In addition to providing clinic visitors with way-finding information, kiosks can also be designed and programmed to enable patients to complete basic registration, check-in, rescheduling, and checkout processes on their own. The kiosks of the future will likely be even more "multimodal" than they are today. In addition to providing keyboards for entering information directly into electronic forms, they will be equipped with scanners that can read bar or QR codes and software applications that will allow the kiosks to synch directly with "smart" mobile devices.

Healthcare and design professionals have given mixed reviews of how useful kiosks are. Most experts have observed that kiosks cannot completely eliminate the need for a staff person. There are exceptions: Vanderbilt Medical Group and Clinic, located in Nashville, Tennessee, has been successful using only kiosks.

Attitudes are continuing to evolve as more people become familiar with using kiosks in a variety of other settings, such as airports, and as the percentage of patients accustomed to using technology in all aspects of their lives increases.

Once a clinic decides to install kiosks, design professionals focus on determining the optimal placement of these electronic information hubs and planning space in ways that optimize the current and future ratio of staffing to kiosks.

Notebook and Tablet Computers

The use of notebook and desktop computers in clinics ranges from serving as a registration and wayfinding device to being used as an education tool in the exam room. Patients can use these electronic devices to obtain answers to health questions as well as to locate and review graphics that explain illnesses and injuries.

The touch-screen feature of tablet computers makes them easier to use by some patients with disabilities because fine motor skills are less important than they are for entering information via a keyboard.

Since information entered by the patient into electronic forms can be added to electronic medical records directly, there is less of a chance for errors to arise than when answers are entered by clinic personnel who are typing information from printed forms that have been completed by hand. The cost of purchasing tablet computers may be offset in part by the reduced administrative labor and printing costs as well as by a decrease in the amount of space needed to store hard-copy medical forms in files.

A February 2012 report by BizTechReport, an independent research agency, indicated that while physicians and care providers found the flexibility and user-friendly interface of commercial notebook computers beneficial, healthcare information technology (HIT) leaders were hesitant to recommend using these in clinical settings because of concerns about governance, security risks, and durability.[10]

Governance is the collection of rules that dictate what clinic staff at all levels can and cannot do. As discussed earlier in this chapter, the Health Insurance Portability and Accountability Act of 1996 (HIPAA) has had a major impact on the governance of healthcare organizations by requiring them to share data while ensuring its security and privacy.

HIT personnel interviewed for the BizTechReport study questioned whether commercial notebook computers had been properly designed and programmed to address the risks of patient data being leaked, overseen by others, or shared beyond established boundaries. Other issues range from durability to ease of cleaning needed to mitigate disease-transmission risks.

Design Considerations, Challenges, and Strategies

Safety, privacy, acoustics, universal accessibility, and wayfinding are key design considerations for all clinic types, with the emphasis given to each of these issues varying by a clinic's staffing model and the type of services it provides, the clinic's location, and the characteristics of the patient population that it serves.

Safety

Concerns about safety in clinics that have arisen in recent years are now routinely addressed from the programming and space planning phases of the design process onward. For example, a greater awareness of and knowledge about how diseases spread has led to the separation of patients with infectious diseases from others who have noncontagious conditions. Strategies that some clinics have used to accomplish this range from having triage staff members evaluate patients' symptoms by telephone or in person, to providing "sick" and "well" waiting rooms.

As more healthcare services are provided in clinics, the attention paid to ensuring the safety of patients who have been weakened by illness or injury and protecting other visitors, staff, and clinic assets will continue to increase.

Hand Hygiene

Ensuring that all visitors and staff have easy access to hand hygiene equipment and supplies throughout the clinic module has become a top design consideration. The investment in additional sinks and sanitizing solution dispensers can be minimal, yet these interventions have been shown to greatly reduce healthcare-associated infections.[11]

There are a number of design features that can help promote good hand hygiene. Sinks and hand-sanitizing stations should be visually obvious, in a clear line of sight for visitors and clinic staff. Consistently placing hand-sanitizer dispensers along corridors and at team workstations can help care providers to more easily integrate hand sanitizing into their regular routine.

Sinks and hand-sanitizer dispensers should be in the same location in every exam room, with sinks positioned and oriented so that care providers can maintain eye contact with their patients. Patients should be able to observe care providers washing their hands. Signs encouraging all visitors and staff to use hand sanitizers and signs that describe the hand hygiene practices of a particular clinic should be posted as needed.

Other Safety Features

It is also important to provide clinic staff with clear, unobstructed views of people who are entering and exiting the building as well as of the paths of patients and other visitors as they move between interior spaces.

Design professionals should consider how people arrive at and depart from a clinic. The surfaces of pedestrian and vehicular pathways should be designed to provide good traction at all times, with attention given to the climatic challenges of a particular clinic's location, such as ease of snow removal. Parking areas, ramps, and pathways should be well lit, yet the lighting should not create so much contrast that people cannot distinguish forms or movement in surrounding and adjacent spaces.

While providing a lot of glass in entry and lobby areas can make it easier to monitor activities occurring outside of a building, design professionals should consider the likelihood that patients who have driven themselves to a clinic in a weakened state could pass out or lose control of a vehicle and accidently drive it into a building. In some instances installing bollards or other landscaping and site features can prevent this from happening (fig. 5-1).

It makes sense to provide handrails near seating areas and at major transition points throughout the clinic module, especially when a clinic primarily serves elderly or chronically ill patients or people with disabilities. The aging population and other factors, such as the percentage of people living in the United States who are obese, are making handrails a more standard feature for all clinics.

Privacy

The HIPAA has heightened care providers' awareness of privacy issues and prompted design professionals to pay particularly close attention to spaces where confidential patient information is exchanged or recorded. By combining space layout decisions with architectural and interior design features and thoughtfully specifying equipment and materials, design professionals can achieve the level of acoustical and visual privacy that their clients require.

Patient Interaction Areas

The spaces where clinic staff interact with patients should be designed to facilitate the private exchange of personal information, such as the patient's identification and insurance data, a description of symptoms, existing medical conditions, and lab or diagnostic results.

Work Areas

The focus on privacy extends into work areas where staff members complete tasks that do not involve face-to-face interaction with patients. Patients should not be exposed to other details of

a clinic's practice beyond those that affect them personally (figs. 5-2, 5-3).

For example, a clinic located in North Dakota removed all of the nurse pass-throughs that were installed when the building was first constructed after staff members realized that noise and nearby conversations "passed through" these openings, too. While pass-throughs make sense in many hospital settings, supplies can be restocked at night during the hours this clinic is closed.

Other Privacy Features

The highest degree of visual and acoustical privacy can be achieved by providing a fully enclosed room with a door. Walls should reach to the deck or have acoustical ceiling tile with

FIGURE 5-1: Allina Health's Owatonna Healthcare Campus, Owatonna, Minnesota. Landscape walls, entry canopy, and bollards help to define the entry to this facility. Photography by Steve Henke

a bulkhead dropped in the plenum space to be flush with the top of each wall. The bottoms of walls should be sound-sealed prior to installation of the base. All openings—doors, windows, electrical outlets, recessed lights, and so forth—should be sealed to reduce the degree of sound leakage. For example, 10 decibels (dB) of sound can leak through a ½″ gap under a door and into adjoining spaces or corridors.

When possible, heating, ventilation, and air conditioning (HVAC) systems should use boots, baffles, and fully ducted returns.

The sound absorption average (SAA) is a single-number rating that designates the level of sound absorption a particular product provides. Products with high SAA ratings should be specified to reduce the amount of sound traveling between clinic spaces. However, if all materials in an open area are absorptive, the base level of sound can become so quiet that even conversations in lowered voices can be overheard.

The acoustical privacy levels of clinic spaces can be tested after they are constructed by taking an ambient decibel (dBA) reading and then a noise isolation class (NIC) reading to calculate a speech privacy reading. Speech privacy is achieved with a privacy index rating of 80 and above, with confidentiality attained at 95 or greater.

FIGURE 5-2: Mayo Clinic Health System, Albert Lea, Minnesota. At this facility nurse work areas are located across from physician offices and away from patient care areas to enhance privacy. Photography © by Dana Wheelock

Best-practice standards for design focus on ensuring that staff members obtaining private information can be standing or seated close enough to patients to interact comfortably while maintaining acoustical privacy. Adjacent seating should face away from these patient interaction areas. Registration, rescheduling, and checkout functions should be physically separated from lobbies and other high traffic areas.

There should be a minimum of 8′ between registration/checkout desks and the closest waiting room chair or person standing at the front of a queue. A minimum width of 5′ should be provided between privacy panels for seated check-in areas, with 42″ widths being common for stand-up check-in areas. Procedure rooms should not share walls with waiting rooms or other spaces where patients linger for activities such as check-in and checkout.

The height of the acoustical portion of privacy panels should be 42″, with solid materials extending past this to a minimum total height of 5′-6″. Combining the use of fabric-wrapped, high sound-absorbing panels with the installation of high noise-reduction coefficient (NRC) ceiling tiles contributes to achieving acoustical privacy

FIGURE 5-3: Altru Health System, Devils Lake, North Dakota. HGA led the physician group through a process that focused on creating patient-centric clinical models. Private offices were eliminated in favor of multi-teaming areas to encourage collaboration and knowledge sharing. Exam rooms now reflect current practice requirements and are standardized to encourage multiple physicians to use the same space. Clear circulation routes provide for a separation of staff and public areas, while natural light floods both the waiting areas and the caregivers zone. Photography by Paul Crosby

objectives and also dampens harsh or annoying sounds.

Design strategies that help preserve privacy of staff work areas include locating telephones used for triage, health coaching, or other discussions related to patient's medical information away from the patient interaction areas (ideally in a soundproof office); providing a space where documents with protected health information can be properly shredded; and making sure that medical records can be securely stored in locked file drawers or in a pass-card-protected room. Huddle spaces should be located away from the main traffic flows and exam room entries so that discussions occurring within them are not overheard by patients and other visitors.

Electronic Transactions

The trend toward conversion to electronic medical record systems at clinics has raised additional concerns about patient privacy. HIPAA's privacy rule mandates that healthcare organizations conducting certain financial and administrative transactions electronically provide safeguards to prevent intentional or unintentional disclosure of protected health information.

Design professionals must pay close attention to the placement of electronic equipment in patient interaction areas, making sure that computer monitors used by staff face away from the queuing and waiting areas. Selecting monitors that can be easily rotated makes it easier for staff to have patients review updated or new information. Shared printers, scanners, and fax machines should be located in places that are physically and visually separated from public areas. with access restricted to the clinic's staff.

Acoustics

Since noise can cause anxiety and distract patients and clinic staff, design professionals employ a combination of space-planning,
architecture, and interior design strategies to mitigate any negative effects of unwanted sound. Architects and interior designers often collaborate with acousticians on the design of clinic spaces where sound attenuation is especially critical.

Floor and Wall Finishes

Some strategies for controlling and reducing noise throughout the clinic module include selecting floor and wall surfaces that help to dampen sound and installing sound-masking systems to serve patient interaction areas, team workstations, and high-traffic public spaces. While carpet absorbs noise better than tile and sheet vinyl, it should not be relied on for sound control. Noise reduction coefficient (NRC) ratings of 0.80 and better are considered "good" sound absorption. Since carpet typically has an NRC rating of 0.20 to 0.30, it is only part of an acoustical design solution. Acoustic wall panels can reduce the amount of reverberation in a space.

Building Systems

When developing the clinic layout, architects and interior designers should confer with mechanical engineers, lighting designers, low-voltage electronic experts, and other specialists to make certain that building systems do not create noise.

Locating mechanical rooms and major noise-producing system components away from occupied spaces, making sure that machine and call-system alarms use light rather than sound signals, specifying a maximum noise level for safety alarms, and using baffled fluorescent fixtures or fixtures with grated light diffusers are all examples of strategies that multidisciplinary design teams can use to create an acoustically optimal clinic environment.

Sound Masking

Sound masking integrates ambient background noise into a space to make speech unintelligible after a specified distance. Sound masking systems, which are often installed in ceilings, can produce white or pink noise. White noise is perceived as a constant background buzz that is used to make unwanted sounds less audible, whereas pink noise is a frequency-specific sound that is used to cancel out sound. One downside of using pink noise in a clinic setting is that it can make sounds that staff and patients need to hear, such as alarms, either difficult to hear or nondirectional.[12]

Sound masking systems can be especially helpful for making voices and distracting noises less audible in clinic spaces that require a high degree of acoustical privacy but are not fully enclosed—reception, check-in, and checkout areas, for example. HVAC systems can also provide sound masking by providing ambient background noise.

Universal Accessibility

The Americans with Disabilities Act (ADA) of 1990 defines a person with a disability as someone who has a physical or mental impairment that substantially limits one or more major life activities. The ADA greatly affects the design, construction, and operation of clinics because it mandates that certain requirements be met to ensure that people with disabilities can gain access to buildings and interior areas. For example, the ADA requires that all clinic exam rooms must be universally accessible, in contrast to hospitals, which have designated ADA-compliant patient rooms.[13]

Often design decisions that comply with the ADA make a clinic safer and more welcoming for all patients. For example, entry-door thresholds designed to make it possible for a wheelchair or scooter to traverse them safely and easily also facilitate passage of baby strollers and reduce the risk of falling for patients who are infirm or elderly. For legal and practical reasons, then, all clinics are designed to be universally accessible.

Design professionals begin by identifying and analyzing any existing or potential barriers to access at all points along paths to, through, and away from a clinic. Based on the results of their analysis, members of the design team then develop an implementation plan that describes and illustrates what features and equipment must be provided or which alterations must be completed.

There are times when the experiences design professionals encounter while applying ADA (or other code) guidelines motivate them to develop "best-practice" standards that exceed what is required.

For example, a major Midwestern architectural firm had to keep correcting work during construction even though the plans it prepared met the ADA's 5′ turning-circle requirement for toilet rooms. This firm now recommends increasing this dimension to 5′-1″. This takes construction tolerances into account and allows enough space for finishes, such as tile on the walls, while achieving the full 5′ of clear space needed for people in wheelchairs to comfortably enter, move around in, and exit toilet rooms.

In addition to addressing architectural and interior design decisions for the clinic module as a whole, universal access plans should focus on areas and features where complying with ADA and building code requirements is especially critical, such as entries, transitions, and registration and checkout areas.

A number of architecture and interior design strategies can be used and combined to help ensure that clinics are universally accessible and welcoming for all visitors and staff. For example, space should be allotted for wheelchairs at arrival and departure points as well as in lobbies and other waiting areas.

The fact that approximately 26 percent of the U.S. population is obese and another 36 percent is classified as overweight continues to have a significant impact on the design of clinics.[14] Bariatric seating should be provided where patients and other visitors tend to linger in the clinic module.

The amount of space provided to meet these specialized seating requirements will vary according to the characteristics of the patient population a clinic serves, with more space generally made available in bariatric, geriatric, and orthopedic clinics. As the medical home care model becomes more common, design professionals developing plans for primary and multidisciplinary clinics will need to address this design consideration in greater detail.

Entries, Transition Points, and Core Amenities

Ramps, entry doors, flooring, and other design features should work together to ensure that building entries, transition points, and basic amenities are universally accessible for all visitors and staff members.

Ramps designed to provide wheelchair and wheeled-equipment access to main entries should have a maximum grade-level-change ratio of 1:20, with the ratio for shorter ramps used to travel between buildings and interior spaces not exceeding 1:12.

Building entries should have automatic hinged or sliding doors that close in no less than three seconds or wide revolving doors that are designed to easily allow the passage of wheelchairs. Exterior doors should have at least a 32″ clear width measured from the surface of the door to the surface of the stop when the door is opened to 90 degrees, with doorways deeper than 24″ having at least a 36″ clear width. Hardware should not require tight gripping or twisting for people to be able to open a door. Walls, door jambs, doors, and baseboards should be distinctly different colors or textures to facilitate visual orientation and balance.

The qualities of flooring materials should not obstruct or impede the movement of people with disabilities throughout a clinic. In general, transitions between changes in floor surfaces should be smooth and gradual. Changes in floor surface levels between ¼″ and ½″ need to be beveled with a slope no greater than 1:2, and changes in floor surface levels that are greater than ½″ must be accomplished with a ramp.

When there is a carpet-to-solid-surface floor connection, it should be feathered or a threshold or trim should be used. Carpet with a pile up to a height of ½″ is allowed. Carpet and carpet tiles need to be securely attached and have a firm backing. They should also have a level loop, textured loop, level cut pile, or level cut/uncut pile no greater than ½″ in height.

In addition to meeting basic federal and local requirements, professional designers should consider the type of care being provided in a specific clinic to make sure that these guidelines accomplish the level of accessibility appropriate for the patient population being served.

There are times when it makes sense to go beyond meeting basic ADA requirements in order to meet the unique needs of the patient population served by a particular clinic. For example, for clinics that provide radiation and other therapies that can lead to patients feeling weak when they leave, design professionals should consider trying to further reduce the risk of patients tripping and injuring themselves by specifying flush thresholds.

Drinking fountains must be installed at two heights, with the lower drinking fountain accommodating patients using wheelchairs or scooters.[15]

Registration and Checkout Areas

At least one area of a registration or checkout station should have a lower counter with a minimum knee clearance of 27″ and with the top-of-counter or desk height between 29″ and 30″ to accommodate patients using wheelchairs or whose health condition requires them to remain seated. There should be a visual as well as an audible method for calling patients.

Sufficient space should be provided so that patients in wheelchairs can turn as necessary to enter and exit the reception and check-in areas. The turning space should be a minimum of 5′ in diameter. T-shaped turning spaces must be at least 5 square feet in size. Each arm of the "T" should be clear of obstructions for a minimum of 12″ in each direction, and the base should be clear of obstructions for a minimum of 24″.

The minimum width for alcoves is 36″ where the depth exceeds 24″. Alcoves should be a minimum of 60″ wide where the depth exceeds 15″.

Signage

The ADA includes specific requirements for signage. Characters and symbols used on signs should present a high contrast to the background. The field onto which a symbol is placed should be a minimum of 6″ high so that raised text or Braille descriptors of the symbol can be placed below the symbol. Braille dots should be positioned below the tactile characters, with a ⅜″ space around all fours side of a dot cluster.

Standard 7 of the National Standards for Culturally and Linguistically Appropriate Services (CLA) in Healthcare recommends using Grade 2 Braille (American Edition). Raised characters and symbols should be a minimum of ¹⁄₃₂″ above a sign's surface.

The level of the finished floor surface and the viewing distance affect the design of signs in several ways. Signs should be placed 48″ to 60″ above the finished floor surface (AFF) measured from the bottom of the lowest tactile characters on the sign. Signs providing information about entering, exiting, and moving through the clinic should be placed low enough on walls to enable people in wheelchairs to reach them. A tactile sign should be located on the latch side of a door and should have an 18″ by 18″ square of clear floor space, on center, in front of it.[16]

Wayfinding

Wayfinding is the process by which people find their way to and through a building. Transitioning occurs when people move from one point to the next, such as from the front entry to the check-in area. People visiting clinics can become stressed or feel uncomfortable when they must struggle to find their way. This usually happens when wayfinding cues are absent, confusing, or difficult to understand. Well-designed wayfinding helps to alleviate this discomfort by making visitors feel welcome and confident that they can efficiently reach their desired destinations.

People obtain information about how to enter and chart a path through a clinic in a variety of ways. For example, some people rely on spatial layout and organization to find their way, while others depend on signage or memorable visual cues such as art. In general, design professionals should provide wayfinding information via media that serve a wide range of ages and abilities (figs. 5-4, 5-5).

Demographics

Design professionals should consider the demographic characteristics of a clinic's patient population and surrounding community when developing wayfinding systems. For example, if the patients for a particular clinic have a limited ability to read English, pictograms may be more effective than text for signage.

Standard 7 of the National Standards for Culturally and Linguistically Appropriate Services (CLA) in Healthcare recommends posting signage that provides directions to specific clinic areas and instructions for registering and receiving service in the languages of the three to five most populous groups in the clinic's service areas. Signs with this information should be located near all major entry points.

Design professionals may consider installing informational telephones that can provide auditory directions for visitors. People with limited English-speaking abilities can pick up a telephone, press the appropriate button, and obtain directions in a language they fully understand. Auditory directions are also helpful for people who are visually impaired or disabled.

Generational differences influence how patients and visitors seek and prefer to obtain wayfinding information. For example, research has shown that elderly people (born before 1946) prefer well-marked signage or like to be assisted by a staff member when they are trying to find their way. Baby boomers (born 1946 to 1964) also prefer personal interaction, but will use technology as necessary. Members of Generation X (born 1965 to 1979), Generation Y/millennials (born 1980 to 2000), and Generation Z/boomlets (born after 2000) are tech-savvy and often prefer to obtain information by using technology rather than face-to-face.

Technology

Most of the innovation occurring in wayfinding design is being driven by technological advances. In addition to posting wayfinding information on websites and sending directions to patients via e-mail or text messages, clinics are installing

FIGURE 5-4: Hennepin County Medical Center Whittier Clinic, Minneapolis, Minnesota. An example of a nature-themed wayfinding system using color and images of nature to guide patients to their destination.   Photography by Steve Henke

kiosks, providing interactive digital maps, and exploring ways to integrate mobile digital devices into wayfinding systems.

The self-help touch-screen kiosks and wall-mounted interactive digital screens now found in main entry areas are becoming more advanced, providing basic information about services, procedures, and events, as well as about the locations of departments, bathrooms, and amenities.

Kiosks and screens should be easy to find, easy to use, and flexible in function. They should be located so that visitors see them immediately upon entering a clinic. In addition to providing wayfinding information, they can welcome guests, recognize donors, announce events, and provide educational information about the clinic, its staff, and the services it offers.

Some drawbacks associated with the use of kiosks and wall-mounted interactive screens include limitations on the quality and complexity of directions they can provide, the costs of purchasing the digital equipment and installing the low-voltage electronic systems to support it, the ongoing costs of operations and maintenance (e.g., keeping information current and resolving malfunctions), and infection control concerns.

Design professionals have also been collaborating with clinic owners and staff to find ways to integrate smartphones and other mobile digital devices into wayfinding systems. Quick

FIGURE 5-5: Hennepin County Medical Center Whittier Clinic, Minneapolis, Minnesota. Each clinic entry is assigned a vibrant color, reinforced by an overscaled graphic image to aid in wayfinding—especially important given the number of languages spoken by patients in this community. Within each clinic module, exam rooms cluster around a central work area to facilitate visibility and team communication. Photography by Steve Henke

Response (QR) codes are being included in print advertisements and at main entries for clinics. People who own smartphones and other mobile digital devices can simply take a photo of the QR code to gain access to and instantly upload wayfinding information, such as directions to a clinic or, in the near future, interactive digital floor plans.

Some clinics have considered giving patients a preprogrammed tablet computer when they enter a clinic facility. The tablets could direct people to their destination via voice and visual commands. The application used on this tablet could be made available to patients who prefer to use their own smartphone or tablet computer.

Environmental Graphics

A well-designed signing and environmental graphics system addresses legibility, visibility, clarity, consistency, quantity, frequency, spacing, and flexibility.

No more than two different fonts should be used. Sans serif fonts, such as Helvetica and Arial, help optimize legibility. Characters can be uppercase or lowercase, but should not be italics, or decorative or distorted in form. Unique visual and verbal cues, such as the clinic's name and logo, as well as typography and terminology, should be used consistently across all aspects of a clinic's wayfinding system. Achieving consensus on terms and phrases used to provide directions and name areas is especially important. For example, a clinic may decide to use the phrase "Ear, Nose, and Throat Care" rather and "Otolaryngology."

A picture is definitely worth a thousand words when visitors to a clinic range in age, ability, and language skills. People can find their way more quickly when symbols are included on signage. Symbols fall into two categories: image-related/concrete, in which a picture clearly resembling the subject represented is used, and concept-related/

abstract, in which an abstract relationship between the symbol and the subject is represented, but the symbol's meaning can be taught and recalled (the biohazard symbol, for instance). Both categories are acceptable and are commonly used in signing and environmental graphics systems.

Since different cultures associate varying meanings with images and symbols, design professionals must be cognizant of cultural taboos. At a minimum, symbols should be understood by cultures represented in the patient population of a clinic. The educational level of the viewer should not be an important factor in understanding a symbol; rather it should be easily read and understood.

Signage should be placed at key decision-making points and posted or hung perpendicular to the path of travel, above eye level. Overhead signs tend to be more effective than wall-mounted signs. Elevator directories are often ignored or unseen unless the type size is very large, additional design elements are added, or the directory is coordinated with symbols found on maps and signage. In a multistory clinic, a directory pertaining to each floor should be placed just outside the elevator to assist visitors.

Stationary maps located at key decision-making points should include the name of the facility, along with the logo or other branding graphics. An arrow indicating which direction is north, a "You are here" marking, and major anchor points (for example, landmarks and destination zones) should also be included on the map. Information should be keyed to directories and should highlight the location of help desks and kiosks, restrooms, key amenities, and emergency shelters.

Determining the ideal number of wayfinding strategies and cues presents a major design challenge: too many can be overwhelming and too few can leave visitors stranded. Generally, the number of signs used should be limited to essential markers. Information included in directories should be clustered in groupings of five items or less. Larger clinics may consider including the distance to the specified destination on signage (for example, Ear, Nose, and Throat Care, 100 Feet).

Just as a two-dimensional graphic must include white space to balance the composition, there must be calming space between signs and directional cues. Design professionals often use "progressive disclosure," a design strategy that gives people just enough information to transition to the next decision-making point.

Signage systems with removable faceplates enable clinics to quickly and easily make color changes, indicate when departments or staff have been relocated, and identify room types.

Architecture, Lighting, and Landscaping

Wayfinding design for clinics encompasses more than graphic artistry and the strategic placement of site and building signage. Architecture, lighting, and landscaping can be designed and orchestrated to make wayfinding feel more intuitive for visitors and staff.

When developing the spatial layout for a clinic, design professionals should identify ways to minimize travel distance, turns, and intersections. This goal can be achieved by organizing areas according to the order and path visitors will travel and by placing windows in corridors to provide exterior views that help visitors to further orient themselves. Plantings and landmarks, such as water elements or art, should be distinct in color, size, and shape so that they are memorable.

Symmetry, regularity, continuity, and simplicity in spatial layout can make it easier for visitors to find their desired destination. However, while symmetry makes a building's layout easier for people to understand, it can also create a monotonous environment if too many repetitive elements are used. Asymmetry, if not overly complex, can hold visitors' attention and facilitate wayfinding.

Building entries should be highly visible and should clearly communicate where patients, staff, and other visitors should enter. The main entry is typically designed to be the most prominent one so that it will draw patients and other visitors to the "front door" of a clinic, whether it is a stand-alone structure or part of a larger healthcare complex.

For example, at the Albert Lea Medical Center in Albert Lea, Minnesota, a dramatic stone-and-glass entry rotunda conveys that this renovated facility is a major regional hub for healthcare services (fig. 5-6).

FIGURE 5-6: Mayo Clinic Health System, Albert Lea, Minnesota. The building entry is clearly defined for this healthcare facility. Photography © by Dana Wheelock

A hierarchy of architectural forms at the East Texas Medical Center in Pittsburg, Texas, combines with site features and lighting to punctuate the main entry while clearly indicating where staff and patients with life-threatening injuries or conditions should enter.

Three porte cocheres with columns and oversized roofs, a grand circular entry drive with flagpoles and a fountain, and warm-hued uplighting accentuate these three heavily used entries. The scale of the largest porte cochere and its central position highlight the location of the main public entry. The emergency entry is clearly marked with a glowing red Emergency sign. The staff entry is the least conspicuous of the three and is located immediately adjacent to the separate staff parking area (fig. 5-7).

A slight curve in the wall, an arched pathway, or varied ceiling heights can help wayfinding feel more intuitive. A design trend for new healthcare campuses is to connect buildings with corridors that provide exterior views and introduce natural light. In addition to making movement through the site and multiple structures more relaxing and pleasant, this design strategy makes wayfinding more intuitive. Exterior and interior details can both serve as mental markers. People naturally associate wider corridors that have exterior views with a high level of importance in a circulation hierarchy.

Changes in wall and flooring colors or materials can convey directionality. For example, a different color or pattern could be designated for each department in a clinic. A change in

FIGURE 5-7: East Texas Medical Center, Pittsburg, Texas. The hierarchy of entries helps to define the main entry.   Photography © by Gary Zvonkovic

flooring material can distinguish the circulation path from adjacent open spaces, such as waiting rooms or reception areas. An inlaid floor pattern can function as a memorable landmark.

Color selection should use a limited palette that enables signage to be integral to the architecture and interior design scheme. The colors used in directories and maps should be coordinated with those used in the finishes and furnishings of corresponding clinic spaces. Some healthcare organizations have preset colors (and typography and symbols) that are part of the brand standards they use for all communicating purposes, including signage. A color contrast of

75 percent between the background and foreground should be achieved. Color should always be used in combination with other wayfinding components and strategies so that people who have color vision deficiencies do not become confused. Color vision deficiencies affect at least 8 percent of males and 2 percent of females.[17]

Lighting plays a key role in making sure that clinic interiors and wayfinding systems reinforce each other. It can be used to accentuate circulation paths and exiting areas, landmark signage, or other wayfinding components. Various combinations of lighting and materials can create undesirable effects, such as shadows, surface

FIGURE 5-8: Mayo Clinic Health System, Owatonna, Minnesota. Retail components for dermatology and optical services are easily visible and accessible from the public areas.   Photography by Philip Prowse Photography

glare, and low contrast values. Sign surfaces should be evenly illuminated in the range of 100 to 300 lux (10 to 30 foot-candles). Illumination levels of at least 500 lux of ambient light and 2,000 lux in activity/task areas ensure that people can safely move from one space to the next.[18]

Three clinics designed by HGA provide examples of how spatial layout and interior features can work in concert with other components of a clinic's wayfinding system.

At the Owatonna Clinic in Owatonna, Minnesota, visitors are given several visual cues that direct them to specific check-in and waiting areas. Retail displays with products related to a specialization—such as dermatology or ophthalmology—line the main concourse. Reception desks located behind the retail displays have signage describing the type of healthcare services being provided in a particular zone. A small waiting area is located near each reception desk (fig. 5-8).

Fairview Medical Center in Maple Grove, Minnesota, is also zoned by area of specialization, such as cardiology, endocrinology, medical oncology, urology, and primary care. Clear sightlines from the main concourse make it easy for patients to locate the check-in and related waiting areas for each specialty (fig. 5-9).

A curved ceiling soffit and double glass door entry accentuate the location of the Children's

FIGURE 5-9: Fairview Maple Grove Medical Center, Maple Grove, Minnesota. Main concourse provides visual connection to clinics on the second level. Photography © by Dana Wheelock

Specialty Clinic within this medical center. The floor tile pattern beneath the soffit creates the appearance of a pond with fish and other creatures (fig. 5-10).

Spatial layout, color, and branding combine to clarify wayfinding at Hennepin County Medical Center's Whittier Clinic (HCMC) in Minneapolis, Minnesota. The colors in the logo that HCMC uses on signs and ambulances—blue, orange, green, and purple—appear in separate waiting area zones, each of which serves a set of medical specialties. Since this clinic is located in a culturally diverse urban neighborhood where many of the patients speak little or no English, HCMC staff can hand patients who speak little or no

English a colored, laminated card that they can use to find the same-colored check-in and waiting areas (figs. 5-11, 5-12).

Connecting to Other Structures

The Warren Medical Office Campus in Tulsa, Oklahoma, illustrates how important it is for designers, when developing wayfinding systems, to consider the entry sequence that connects parking ramps or other buildings to clinics.

The existing campus had three medical office towers that were built in the 1960s and 1970s. The revitalization plan for the campus included relocating surface parking, constructing a new medical office building with an attached parking

FIGURE 5-10: Fairview Maple Grove Medical Center, Maple Grove, Minnesota. Playful graphics identify this area as a children's clinic.   Photography © by Dana Wheelock

garage and four skywalks, and creating a park like setting to provide attractive views for people who are approaching, departing, or remaining within the buildings.

The new parking garage is easy to reach from the main boulevard. It provides covered access directly into the medical office building. Parking levels are organized to correspond with treatment levels.

When patients visit this medical office building for the first time, they typically park on the first floor and enter via a corridor that has overhead signage and a rhythmic floor pattern that visually communicate that patients should keep walking toward the building's interior.

At the end of the corridor, a receptionist stationed at a desk provides directions and tells patients which level of the parking garage will bring them closest to their destination in the future (fig. 5-13).

Clinic Module Prototypes

The following clinic modules amalgamate attributes and efficiencies gleaned from extensive project experience, original research, and observations. Lean design principles aimed at

eliminating waste, overburdening, and unevenness in the use of human and other resources also guided the development of these prototypes. The floor plans provide a visual reference for exploring the impact of current and future healthcare trends in the design of clinic modules.

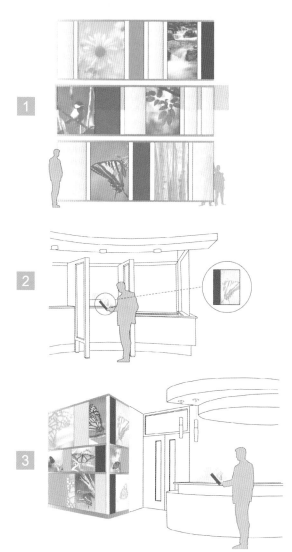

FIGURE 5-11: Hennepin County Medical Center Whittier Clinic, Minneapolis, Minnesota. Color, lighting, and images of nature provide visual cues to guide patients to their destinations.   Photography by Steve Henke

FIGURE 5-12: Hennepin County Medical Center Whittier Clinic, Minneapolis, Minnesota. Wayfinding system starts at check-in and registration.   Photography by Steve Henke

Academic Clinic Modules

A key question that design professionals ask when they are developing clinic modules for academic clinics is: Should all academic offices be clustered together, or should they be interspersed with other clinic spaces? Answers to this question often vary by discipline.

FIGURE 5-13: Natalie Office Building, Warren Medical Office Campus, Tulsa, Oklahoma. The design of the 178,880-square-foot building integrates the existing hospital and medical offices with the new medical office and parking garage through an elevated skywalk. The campus was converted from a sea of parking lots into a park-like environment with a major lake and a grove of trees to enhance the patient experience, allowing all medical offices direct views and access to the park and lake. The garage allows for clear and direct access onto the campus from the main boulevard and provides covered access directly into the medical offices. A major four-story atrium becomes the focal point for the campus, relating to the main entry, the new medical office, to retail space, to the lake, and to the park. As a symbol for the renewal of life, the atrium provides spaces for reflection and interaction. Siting, building orientation, landscaping, building systems, daylighting, energy use, material selection, and indoor air quality were all carefully considered during the design phase. Photography by © Gary Zvonkovic

Surgeons and doctors in "disease-oriented groups" (DOGs) generally like to have their offices near each other in a more private area of the clinic module. Specialists (such as pharmacists and dieticians) who are called into collaborative consults tend to have their offices interspersed with exam rooms.

Academic—Module A

The benefit of this model is threefold. It places all support spaces at the back, in order to have exam rooms closer to the waiting area. Exam rooms are visible from a central shared work area. And flexible space is provided for patient or resident education sessions.

The exam rooms are standardized to improve acoustical separation. Windows that line the staff corridor provide all employees with access to daylight and exterior views. Centering one of these windows at the end of the two major exam room corridors enables these to serve as way-finding references.

There are 12 exam rooms to serve four collaborative care teams. Each team can visually monitor the three exam rooms assigned to it (fig. 5-14).

Academic—Module B

This model features a large, centrally located teaching zone that could also be used for group educational sessions, depending on the care delivery processes of a particular clinic. While it is easy for patients and staff to find this area, acoustically isolating it and securing it for evening group sessions would be difficult.

Nurses' stations have clear sightlines to exam rooms and immediate access to alcoves located along two of the corridors where care providers can take patients' vitals.

The faculty zone is physically separated from the exam and teaching areas. It features a mix of private offices and open office areas (fig. 5-15).

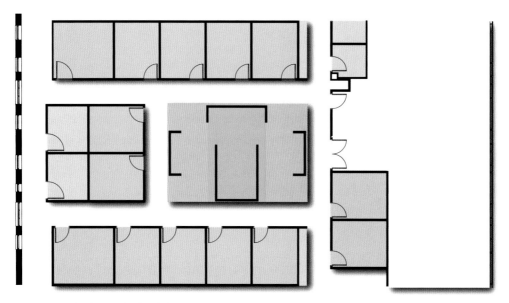

FIGURE 5-14: Academic—Module A. Central work core provides excellent direct visual observation of all exam rooms.
Image courtesy of Hammel, Green and Abrahamson, Inc.

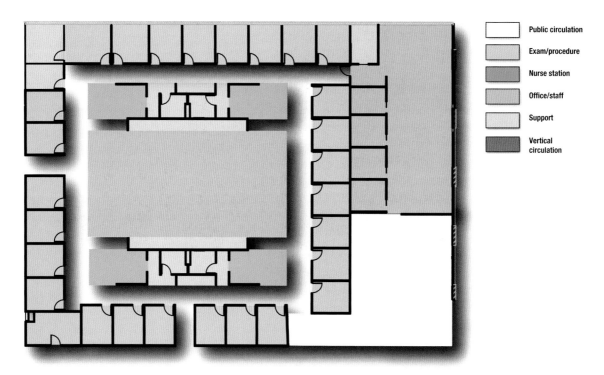

	Public circulation
	Exam/procedure
	Nurse station
	Office/staff
	Support
	Vertical circulation

FIGURE 5-15: Academic—Module B. Centrally located teaching zone can be used for group educational sessions prior to an exam room visit. Image courtesy of Hammel, Green and Abrahamson, Inc.

Patient Self-Rooming Clinic Modules

Clinics using the self-rooming process give patients instructions when they check in so that they can locate and travel to the specific room where they will be examined. The receptionist electronically notifies nursing staff which patient is being sent to a designated exam room.

Self-rooming works best for routine visits. It is not as likely to work well for urgent-care clinics where patients do not want to lose sight of clinic staff in case their condition worsens suddenly and unexpectedly.

Patient Self-Rooming—Module C

Key attributes of this clinic module are that it minimizes space used for waiting, locates all staff support areas at the back, provides direct access to exam rooms from shared provider work areas, and separates patient and staff traffic flows.

All work areas are open, making it easy to locate clinic staff visually. Acoustical separation is more difficult and expensive to achieve, however, because there are two doors serving each exam room.

An exterior window at the end of each exam room corridor aids orientation. Staff support areas are located close to the entries for each shared workstation. Patients travel the greatest distance.

A variation of this clinic module is referred to as the on-stage/off-stage clinic module. It organizes spaces from the most public to the most private so patients do not see all the behind-the-scenes activities carried out by clinic staff. It also provides separate access to each exam room for patients and staff. However, exam rooms are arranged in a doughnut shape around a central work core. A public corridor runs along the outside rim of the exam rooms. Patients enter exam

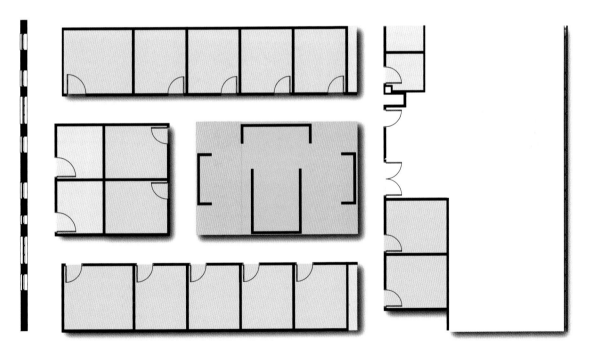

FIGURE 5-16: Patient Self-Rooming—Module C. Separation of patient flow from provider flow. Image courtesy of Hammel, Green and Abrahamson, Inc.

rooms from this corridor, which gives them access to daylight and exterior views.

While the on-stage/off-stage clinic module reduces travel time for physicians and other caregivers, the public corridor increases the total circulation space by an average of 5 percent over clinics with similar functions and services (fig. 5-16).

Patient Self-Rooming—Module D

This model locates staff workstations and waiting areas next to each other and near exam room entries, which presents major acoustical and visual challenges. Staff and patient conversations are more likely to be overheard. A shared office area for physicians is located close to amenities and support areas (such as locker and conference rooms) at the back of the module. A private space is provided for electronic or telephone consultations (fig. 5-17).

Physician-centric Clinic Modules

The physician-centric module has been used for many years. It reduces the travel for physicians by creating an efficient work triangle. Travel distances for patients are longer. Collaboration is more difficult.

Physician-centric—Module E

The decentralized nurse stations in this module are close to the offices of physicians with whom they need to consult about various patients'

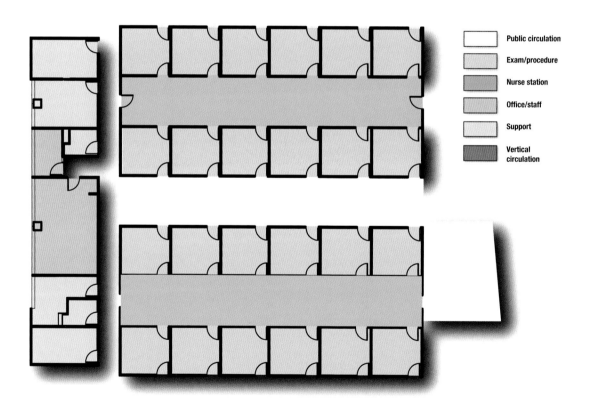

Public circulation

Exam/procedure

Nurse station

Office/staff

Support

Vertical circulation

FIGURE 5-17: Patient Self-Rooming—Module D. Patient waiting occurs in expanded patient corridor.   Image courtesy of Hammel, Green and Abrahamson, Inc.

conditions, near supplies, and within varying travel distances to exam rooms.

Registration is centralized. Patients must pass by rescheduling/checkout alcoves as they enter and exit the exam room area.

Physicians' offices are private and dispersed throughout the module so that they are next to the three exam rooms assigned to them. Four out of the five physicians' offices are located near the nurse stations. Travel distances for patients vary greatly (fig. 5-18).

Physician and Staff Collaborative— Module F

As the collaborative care model is becoming more prevalent, designers have been creating modules that locate nurse stations and physicians' offices close to each other or that eliminate private offices for physicians and provide a shared work area instead. In this example, Physicians' offices are private, yet located near each other and the nurse stations to encourage collaboration. All fixed elements in the nurse stations are on one wall to keep these spaces as flexible as possible.

Registration and rescheduling occur in the same area to use staff and space efficiently. Although there are no dedicated teaming areas, care providers partner with other staff throughout the day. The physician is brought into exams and consultations for complicated cases (fig. 5-19).

Physician and Staff Collaborative— Module G

The central work zone for this module includes space for physicians, nurses, and other care providers to collaborate. Physician work areas are also provided in the staff work zone at the back of the module. Specimen collection toilet rooms are located next to the centralized work zone.

While most of the exam rooms are standardized, four serve special functions. One can serve as a procedure or team-consult room. There are rooms for exams where multiple family members are present or for specialists, such as pharmacists or dieticians.

The larger exam rooms and the conference room could provide core space for clinics using

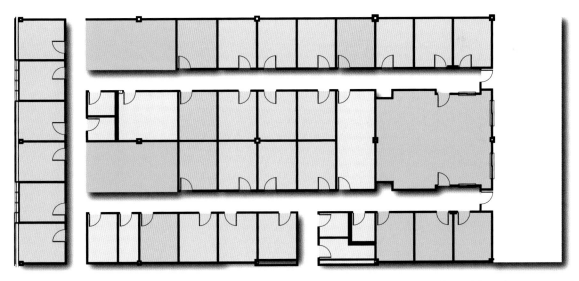

FIGURE 5-18: Physician*centric—Module E. Exam rooms are located near physician offices to reduce travel for physicians. Image courtesy of Hammel, Green and Abrahamson, Inc.

the medical home model. A dietitian, primary care physician, and other members of a collaborative care team could meet with patients and their family members in these rooms (fig. 5-20).

The Neighborhood Clinic

There has also been a shift towards healthcare services being provided in community-based, neighborhood clinics. These are generally family

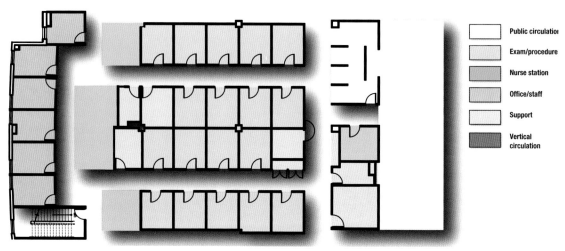

Public circulation

Exam/procedure

Nurse station

Office/staff

Support

Vertical circulation

FIGURE 5-19: Physician and Staff Collaborative—Module F. Physician offices are located at the back, adjacent to the nurse station, to promote collaboration. Image courtesy of Hammel, Green and Abrahamson, Inc.

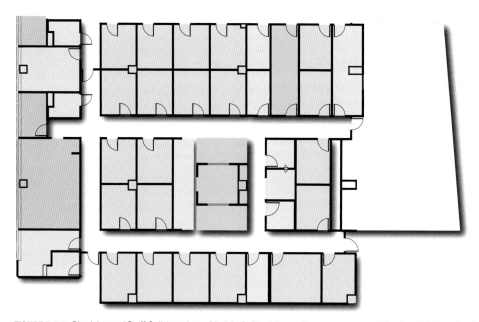

FIGURE 5-20: Physician and Staff Collaborative—Module G. Physician work area and nurse station located at center of module for easy access to exam rooms. Image courtesy of Hammel, Green and Abrahamson, Inc.

practice, pediatric, internal medicine, or women's health clinics that have a lobby/reception area, exam rooms, physicians' offices, bathroom, and supply storage area.

Neighborhood Clinic—Module H

Registration, check-out, rescheduling, and other administrative tasks are usually completed at the same workstation. Privacy is assured by strategic location and orientation of this multipurpose administrative work station relative to high-traffic corridors and by providing sufficient separation from queuing and lobby seating areas.

Some neighborhood clinics include an x-ray room or small lab so that basic diagnostic and testing activities can be completed on site. There has also been a trend toward having a mobile C-arm available to move in and out of exam rooms as needed. These technologies can improve the quality of care by making results available to physicians and nurses during the assessment and consultation portions of an exam (fig. 5-21).

FIGURE 5-21: HealthEast Grand Avenue, St. Paul, Minnesota. The Neighborhood Clinic—Module H. Privacy is assured by strategic location and orientation of this multipurpose administrative workstation relative to high-traffic corridors and by providing sufficient separation from queuing and lobby seating areas.

Physician's Practice in a Medical Office Building

This module includes the same basic spaces as the neighborhood clinic, such as exam rooms, physicians' offices, and supply storage areas.

Physician's Practice—Module I

Visitors typically enter from a shared corridor directly into a combined reception, check-in, waiting, and rescheduling/ checkout area.

However, this module shares some amenities, such as public bathrooms, with other building tenants. Diagnostic imaging and lab tests can be provided by small rooms dedicated to these purposes within the clinic module or by other building tenants who specialize in the provision of these services (fig. 5-22).

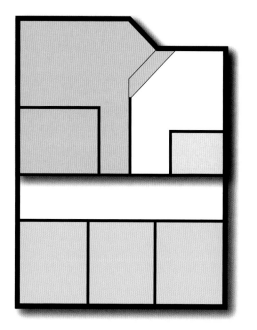

FIGURE 5-22: Physician's Practice in a Medical Office Building— Module I. This module contains basic spaces needed for a single physician.   Image courtesy of Hammel, Green and Abrahamson, Inc.

Emerging Clinic Modules

New models of care are being explored within the framework of the clinic module. As more primary care clinics evolve toward the medical home model (see chapter 6, "The Exam Room Today"), healthcare organizations and private practitioners are developing new strategies for combining primary, specialized, and complementary care services.

Design professionals must keep pace with the unique requirements of clinics that are rapidly creating new care models in order to develop the efficient, innovative space plans needed to support them.

Group Exam Space—Module J

Some clinics have begun to host group exams. These typically begin with or are preceded by individual assessments. Then a certified healthcare professional presents an educational program and facilitates a group question and answer period that is followed by time for informal discussion.

Patients who benefit the most from group visits are those who can learn by sharing information and experiences with other individuals who have similar medical conditions or chronic diseases. This approach can also be used to provide care that is culturally appropriate for language-specific groups.

Flexibility can be achieved for clinics experimenting with this care delivery strategy by designing group exam rooms that are multiples of the standard exam room dimensions. If necessary, the group exam rooms can be converted into individual exam rooms in the future.

Group exam rooms are typically located close to the main waiting room and shared amenities, such as public bathrooms, for convenience and optimal traffic flow (fig. 5-23).

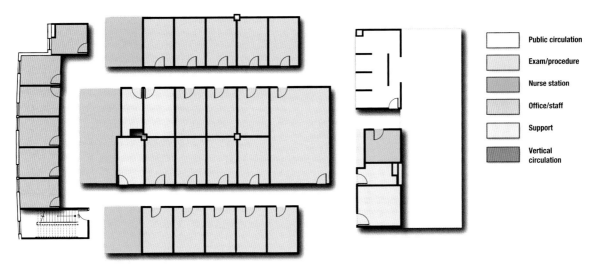

	Public circulation
	Exam/procedure
	Nurse station
	Office/staff
	Support
	Vertical circulation

FIGURE 5-23: Group Exam Space—Module J. Group exam space located near entry for easy access. The space is designed to be easily converted to typical exam rooms.   Image courtesy of Hammel, Green and Abrahamson, Inc.

Multiple Specialists, Single Discipline— Module K

Healthcare professionals specializing in an area such as cardiology are beginning to pool resources and purchase sections of medical office buildings (or excess space that is available in some hospitals) as a commercial condominium that each specialist can use a couple of days per week to "see patients in clinic."

The exam rooms are designed to meet unique needs of the specialists and their patients. Core amenities such as lobby and reception space, nurse stations, bathrooms, diagnostic imaging rooms, and small-scale labs are shared (fig. 5-24).

Multiple Specialists, Multiple Disciplines— Module L

Depending on their areas of expertise, healthcare professionals from different disciplines can also use the condominium/rotating schedule approach to create a specialized care clinic. This

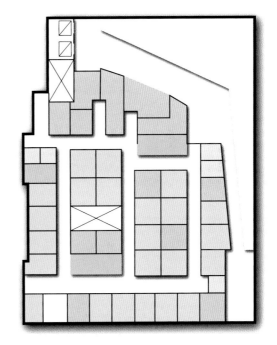

FIGURE 5-24: Multiple Specialists, Single Discipline—Module K. This clinic is designed to allow multiple physicians to practice in the same space on different days or in half-day shifts.   Image courtesy of Hammel, Green and Abrahamson, Inc.

can be accomplished through the use of mobile furnishings and equipment that are wheeled in and out of exam rooms, according to the needs of a particular specialist on a given day.

Sharing point-of-care lab and imaging rooms, administrative and team work space, and core amenities could make this model worthwhile, although space for storage of mobile furnishings and equipment would need to be provided.

This strategy is least likely to work well for specialized healthcare services that require highly customized furnishings and equipment (Ear, Nose, and Throat, for example) (fig. 5-25).

Dental Clinics

Dental care is gradually being colocated with other medical specialists in clinics because of an increased focus on the relationship between dental health and overall wellness. Dental health problems can cause chronic pain and lead to problems with eating, speaking, thinking, and learning. For example, studies have shown a link between periodontal diseases and diabetes, heart and lung diseases, strokes, and other health issues.[19]

Public and nonprofit healthcare organizations as well as private dental practices, are all

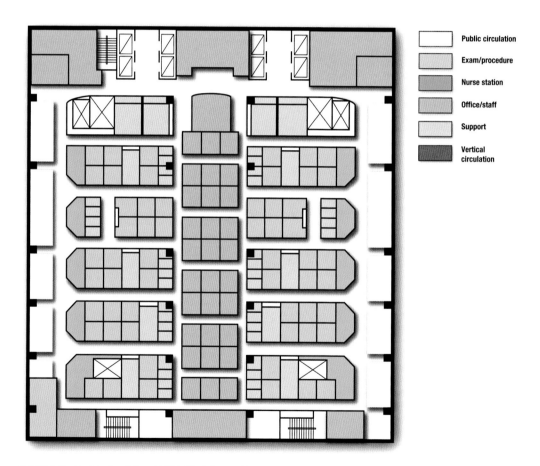

FIGURE 5-25: Multiple Specialists, Multiple Disciplines —Module L. Physicians share point-of-care lab and imaging rooms. Image courtesy of Hammel, Green and Abrahamson, Inc.

developing new models of care to meet the needs of specific patient populations and respond to new market demands.

Dental care services are also now being included in safety-net clinics and in-school clinics to address the epidemic levels of dental diseases among children, adolescents, and low-income people.

Primary Care Clinic with Dental Services

Many adult and pediatric primary care clinics provide additional specialty care. These services could include dental, psychiatric, and social work services, prenatal and postnatal care, family planning and birth control counseling, and group education and recovery programs for substance abuse and smoking cessation, nutritional education, and chronic diseases, such as diabetes.

Dental Clinic with Multiple Specialists

Some nonprofit dental practices provide care in a multispecialty format designed to provide affordable services to patients who typically do not have access to dental care, such as the elderly, the poor, and the homeless.

In addition to basic preventative, maintenance, and sedation dentistry, these clinics also provide denture fitting, relines, and repairs. Digital imaging services are performed within the clinic to inform care decisions and better integrate the services provided.

Summary

This chapter has addressed how legislative, economic, demographic, and cultural factors are broadly affecting clinic design across the United States.

The phased implementation of the Patient Protection and Affordable Care Act (ACA) and the escalating costs of healthcare have increased the demand for clinics by motivating healthcare organizations to shift care away from inpatient facilities that are more expensive to operate and maintain.

The major shift from fee-for-service to value-based compensation structures associated with the ACA has prompted care providers to better coordinate care and to use a team-based approach to optimize health outcomes for their patients.

A shortage of primary care physicians has expanded the responsibilities of care providers such as nurse practitioners and registered nurses and has led to the creation of new staff positions that enable clinics to best utilize the time of highly trained professional staff and keep labor costs in check.

These changes in the delivery of healthcare services and the size and composition of core care teams, combined with technological advances, have generally eliminated or decreased the size of private physicians' offices, reduced or eliminated the amount of space dedicated entirely to waiting, increased the amount of space needed for teamwork and consultations, and led to the evolution of new spaces, such as those that serve telephone triage nurses and health education consultants. Since advances in technology have made point-of-care testing more feasible and affordable, small labs and diagnostic imaging rooms are increasingly being included.

Safety, privacy, acoustics, universal accessibility, efficiency, and wayfinding remain top design considerations for clinics. The emphasis given to each of these factors varies according to the care philosophy and healthcare delivery process of a specific clinic, the type of services it provides, its location, and the characteristics of its patient population (table 5-1).

Legislation such as the Health Insurance Portability and Accountability Act of 1996 (HIPAA) and the Americans with Disabilities Act of 1990 (ADA) guide the majority of design decisions related to protecting the privacy of patient information and ensuring that clinics are universally accessible to all visitors and staff.

GARY NYBERG

TABLE 5-1: CLINIC MODULES COMPARISON

Clinic Module	Traffic Patterns (Staff / Patient)	Visibility From Team Work Area	Patient Wayfinding	Staff Collab. Space	Group Exam Space	Acoustical Privacy	Flexibility Use By Mult. Phys.
A	Shared	Corridor / All Exam Rooms	Complex	Central		Full Privacy	High
B	Shared	Corridor / All Exam Rooms	Complex	Central	Buried in Dept.	Full Privacy	High
C	Separate	Exam Rooms	Complex	Central		Two-Door Exam Rooms Limit Privacy	High
D	Separate	Exam Rooms	Simple	Central		Two-Door Exam Rooms Limit Privacy	High
E	Shared	Corridor / Some Exam Rooms	Simple	Back		Mirrored Corridor Doors Limit Privacy	Limited by Office Location
F	Shared	None	Simple	Back		Mirrored Corridor Doors Limit Privacy	High
G	Shared	Corridor / Some Exam Rooms	Simple	Central		Full Privacy	High
H	Shared	Limited	Complex			Full Privacy	High
I	Shared	None	Simple			Full Privacy	None
J	Shared	None	Simple	Back	Front of Module	Full Privacy	High
K	Shared	Limited	Complex			Unknown Door Location	Limited by Office Location
L	Shared	Limited	Simple			Unknown Door Location	High

Courtesy of Hammel, Green and Abrahamson, Inc.

Notes

1. AFL-CIO Department for Professional Employees, "Nursing: A Profile of the Profession" (Fact sheet, 2012), http://dpeaflcio.org/wp-content/uploads/Nursing-A-Profile-of-the-Profession-2012.pdf.

2. Nicole Ostrow, "Nursing Shortage Is over in U.S. until Retirement Glut Hits," *Bloomberg News,* March 21, 2012, http://www.bloomberg.com/news/2012-03-21/nursing-shortage-in-u-s-is-over-temporarily-researchers-find.html.

3. Ibid.

4. Institute of Medicine, *The Future of Nursing: Leading Change, Advancing Health,* (Washington, DC: The National Academies Press, 2010), http://www.iom.edu/Reports/2010/The-Future-of-Nursing-Leading-Change-Advancing-Health.aspx.

5. Babyboomer Magazine.com, "The Influence of the Baby Boomer Generation." April 14, 2013, http://www.babyboomer-magazine.com/news/165/ARTICLE/1207/2013-04-14.html.

6. Health Research Institute, PricewaterhouseCoopers, "Health Insurance Exchanges: Long on Options, Short on Time" (working paper, October 2012), http://www.pwc.com/us/en/health-industries/health-insurance-exchanges/assets/pwc-health-insurance-exchanges-impact-and-options.pdf.

7. Stacey Bumpus, "Mental Health Care Now Covered Under Affordable Care Act's Essential Health Benefits Package," *Go Insurance Rates* (February 22, 2013), https://www.goinsurancerates.com/health-insurance/mental-health-care-coverage-affordable-care-act/.

8. Anita Slomski, "Chronic Mental Health Issues in Children Now Loom Larger than Physical Problems," *Journal of the American Medical Association* 308 (2012): 223–25.

9. R. C. Kessler, W. T. Chiu, O. Demler, K. R. Merikangas, E. E. Walters, "Prevalence, Severity and Comorbidity of 12-month DSM-IV Disorders in the National Comorbidity Survey," *Archives of General Psychiatry* 62 (2005): 617–27.

10. Gabriel Pema, "Compliance, Durability Concerns Holding Back the iPad in Healthcare," *Healthcare Informatics* (February 14, 2012),. http://www.healthcare-informatics.com/article/compliance-durability-concerns-holding-back-ipad-other-tablets-healthcare.

11. Centre for Healthcare Related Infection Surveillance and Prevention, "The Effect of Hand Hygiene on Healthcare Associated Infection (HAI)" (September 2013), http://www.health.qld.au/chrisp/hand_hygiene/HH_HAI_fsheet.pdf.

12. Susan E. Mazer, "What Is at Stake in the Sound Environment?" *Healthcare Design*, November 1, 2001.

13. Americans with Disabilities Act of 1990, P.L. 110-325, http://www.ada.gov/pubs/ada.htm.

14. Alyssa Brown, "In U.S., Obesity Rate Stable in 2012: Nearly 4% of All Americans Are Morbidly Obese," *Gallup* (January 23, 2013), http://www.gallup.com/poll/160061/obesity-rate-stable-2012.aspx.

15. Adaptive Environments Center Inc., "Checklist for Existing Facilities," National Institute on Disability and Rehabilitation Research (August 1995), http://www.ada.gov/racheck.pdf.

16. Ibid.

17. Patricia Salmi, "Wayfinding Design: Hidden Bariers to Universal Access," *Informed Design* 5, no. 8 (2005).

18. Gary A. Nyberg and Christine Guzzo Vickery, "Clinic Design: Enhancing the Patient Experience Through Informed Design" (working paper, Hammel, Green and Abrahamson, Inc., Minneapolis, MN, 2011), 276.

19. Edwin Jones, "How Not Brushing Your Teeth Could Cause a Heart Attack and Other Diseases" (April 21, 2010), http://ezinearticles .com/?How-Not-Brushing-Your-Teeth-Could-Cause-a-Heart-Attack-and-Other-Diseases&id=4144395.

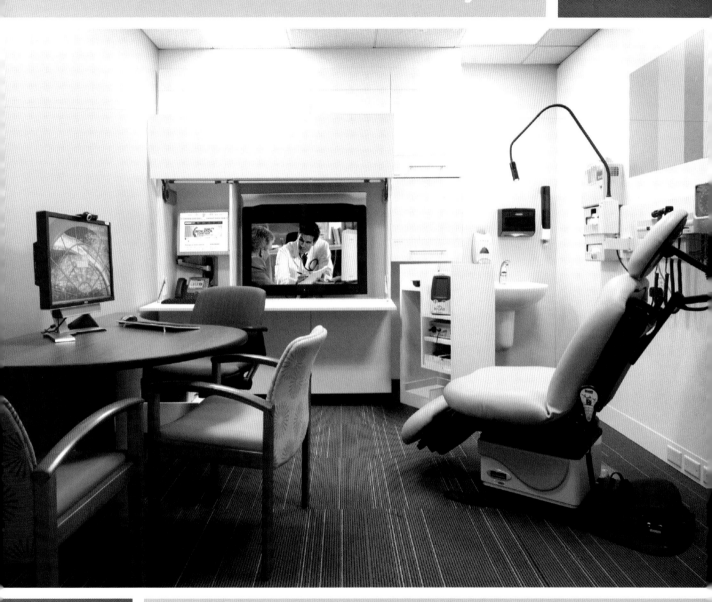

Overview

While the basic components of exam rooms remain familiar in appearance, their size, layout, and other design features are evolving rapidly to address the significant changes in the activities occurring within them.

The features of the exam room can dictate the size and layout of a clinic facility. To set priorities for these features, design professionals must first understand the end users' needs—the patient's as well as those of clinic staff—and evaluate these within the context of the care philosophy and business goals of the healthcare organization or medical group that owns a specific facility. For example, physicians may each want exam rooms of different sizes or with different features, but a health system may override these requests to provide standard rooms that its leaders believe will better support the overall operations of a clinic. Recognizing when these differing perspectives exist and understanding the rationales behind each of them sets the stage for the remaining phases of the design process.

There are some commonalities across all exam rooms, however. For example, there are activities that occur in most exam rooms and these require, at a minimum, an exam table or chair, a work surface and seat for the care provider, and a sink or hand-sanitizing station.

Although the length of time allotted to the following exam room tasks and the staff person who completes them varies among clinics, a standard turnover cycle of 40 to 50 minutes typically includes:

- 5 minutes for self-rooming or being escorted to the exam room.
- 5 minutes for a medical assistant or nurse to obtain key assessment information and take vitals.
- 5 minutes for the patient to disrobe and store personal items, if needed.
- 10 to 15 minutes for exam, treatment, and consultation with physician.
- 5 minutes for patient to get dressed and collect personal items.
- 5 to 10 minutes for instructions and other follow-up tasks by the medical assistant or nurse.
- 5 minutes to clean and prepare the room for the next patient.

Exam rooms also typically have three main zones: the patient zone, the care provider zone, and the partners-in-care zone. The patient zone is also the "point of care." This is where the highest value time is spent during the patient visit. The partners-in-care zone is the area where family (or other guests who accompany patients) can sit. The care provider zone is where the physician consults with the patient and family and completes any paperwork that they need to take with them when they leave the clinic. The larger the exam room is, the more these spaces will be separate. The smaller the exam room is, the more they will overlap.

In the past, most of the other tasks completed along the care continuum took place at different locations in a clinic. Patients would check in at a reception desk, complete forms to make sure the medical information in a printed file was updated, and then wait in a lobby until a nurse called their name.

After reviewing information added to the medical file by the nurse, the physician would complete a physical exam, provide any immediate care that was required, and discuss the need for medications, follow-up activities, or referrals to specialists. The physician would either complete the prescription slips and other forms on the spot or leave these at the checkout desk for the patient to collect on the way out of the clinic.

This flow of activities from point-to-point within a facility still occurs at many clinics.

However, the "who does what, when, and where" is changing. As more health services flow toward the point-of-care, the exam room is becoming the place where most of the work is accomplished.

Trends

On average, design professionals are addressing the following trends by designing larger, more flexible clinic exam rooms so that a greater number and greater variety of tasks can be completed within them.

Technology

The size, layout, and adjacencies of exam rooms have been affected by steady improvements in medical, health information, and communication technologies—not all of which have to be highly sophisticated to be effective. In fact, some low-tech modes of communication, such as whiteboards, can be more engaging for patients.

What matters most from the standpoint of design is how physicians and other care providers choose to use the tools available to them in the exam room as well as the overall degree to which a clinic plans to automate its medical record and care delivery processes.

For example, a clinic may choose to use digital locators to facilitate an "open rooming" strategy, with the goal of improving exam room utilization. Open rooming allows care providers to use any exam room that is available. This strategy works best with universally designed exam rooms that have standardized layouts, equipment, and furnishings. A digital locator system is then used to monitor and optimize the flow of people, equipment, and supplies into and out of these exam rooms. Computer monitors located in staff workstations display a chart that lists all exam rooms and indicates which patients and staff members are in them.

When staff members complete part of a clinic visit, they enter this information into a computer in the exam room so that the progress of exams can be tracked and requests for additional care or supplies communicated electronically. For example, a physician can use the locator to indicate that a patient needs a shot or a blood sample. A nurse then knows to prepare a syringe.

By helping to track the progress of exams, digital locator systems can help clinics to streamline the care delivery process by letting various members of a patient's care team know when to arrive at the exam room and providing them with the information needed to most efficiently complete the next steps in the care delivery process.

Legislation

Two major pieces of federal legislation that have affected exam room design in the United States are the Health Insurance Portability and Accountability Act of 1996 (HIPAA) and the Patient Protection and Affordable Care Act, which was signed into law in 2010.

HIPAA's privacy rule mandates that healthcare organizations take steps to protect the confidentiality and security of patients' health information in spaces where it is exchanged or discussed—including exam rooms and adjacent areas. This has made achievement of acoustical and visual privacy a top design criterion for exam rooms and adjacent areas, such as shared work areas where care team members may need to discuss patients' conditions and health histories.

The Affordable Care Act has generally led to more time in the exam room being spent on consultation and education tasks. This has increased the size of the care provider work zone so that patients and their guests or multiple members of an integrated care team can participate in consults. At a minimum, the care provider zone now needs to be large enough and provide sufficient seating for the doctor (or nurse practitioner) to sit next to the patient and maintain eye contact while reviewing health information on a computer monitor.

The fact that healthcare reform has also eliminated reimbursement for adverse medical events (errors and injuries, for example) has helped drive the trend toward bringing more care to patients in exam rooms. This, in turn, has led to an increase in the average size of exam rooms as the range of tasks completed within them has expanded. The Affordable Care Act's emphasis on collaborative care has also led to a need for more space and additional seating to be provided in the exam room to accommodate multiple members of integrated care teams. The need for group exam rooms is also growing as clinics search for ways to optimize the health outcomes that are now used as a basis for reimbursement.

Demographics

Changes in the characteristics of the patient population served by clinics are having an effect on the design of exam rooms. High obesity rates, for example, have led to a need for bariatric-ready exam rooms that come equipped with patient lifts, power exam tables, wider doors, and benches without arms or other specialized seating. Acoustical design is becoming more challenging in clinics that treat elderly patients because the hearing loss associated with an aging population requires care providers to speak louder to be understood, while at the same time confidential conversations about a patient's health should not be overheard by people in adjacent clinic spaces. The increasing diversity of the patient population in the United States has also led to a need to provide space in the exam room for an interpreter to accompany patients for whom English is a second language.

Culture

The increased awareness and recognition of the positive role partners-in-care (PICs) can play in supporting patients and helping them to recover and manage their health is having an impact the design of exam rooms, which now often include sufficient space to allow PICs to remain in the exam room throughout a clinic visit. This means that design professionals address how to maintain visual privacy so that the patient can disrobe, be examined, and get dressed while family members or other guests are present.

Care Delivery Process

The shift toward more team-based care has created a need for consult rooms that can also be adapted for other uses, such as e-visits or phone triage, when they are not being used for consultations. New prototypes are also being developed that meet the specific needs of convenience, boutique, and executive care models.

One example of an innovative care delivery process that is being used today is the patient self-rooming model. A staff member at a reception/check-in desk simply provides patients with instructions so they can locate and travel to the specific room where they can wait privately to be examined. The receptionist electronically notifies nursing staff which patient is being sent to a designated exam room. A clinic could also use a radio-frequency identification device (RFID) or other method of tracking the patients' locations to make sure that they are given prompt and proper care.

Self-rooming works best for routine visits or at convenience care clinics. However, it is not as likely to work well for urgent-care clinics where patients do not want to lose sight of clinic staff in case their condition worsens suddenly and unexpectedly.

Staffing

The roles of clinicians such as nurse practitioners, physician's assistants, and other "physician extenders" continue to evolve to help clinics address the shortage of doctors, the shift in the provision of healthcare services from inpatient to outpatient facilities, and the growing demand for these services as the patient population in the United States ages and increases. For example, the emerging role of "personal medical assistants" affects the design and technological needs of exam rooms in clinics that combine this staff function with the one-stop delivery model.

Personal Medical Assistants

This model combines single-stop convenience with changes in clinic staffing and procedures. A medical assistant meets the patient at the door, takes him or her to an exam room, reviews health history information, obtains the patient's vital stats, and enters these into an electronic medical record.

The medical assistant remains in the exam room to take notes during the exam and consultation, obtains signed prescriptions from the doctor, prints any additional information needed, schedules return visits, and escorts the patient to the pharmacy and then to the exit. Exam rooms for clinics that employ personal medical assistants in this manner would require seating and space for the medical assistant and the digital equipment that makes it possible for this staff member to obtain and enter patient information electronically.

The advantages of this care model include reducing or eliminating the need for a receptionist, a medical records person, and a waiting room.

Standardization

Standardizing the size, configuration, furnishings, and equipment of exam rooms helps to streamline operations by making it easier for staff to locate supplies and equipment regardless of which room they are using. It can also increase exam room utilization, simplify purchasing procedures, and reduce costs by allowing clinics to order quantities that are large enough to warrant a volume discount. As new team-based models of care, such as the medical home, are being tested, more clinics are experimenting with the development and use of standardized, universally designed exam rooms because these can be used by a broad range of clinicians and support staff.

Design Considerations

Exam room functions vary greatly between clinics depending on their care delivery processes and the types of services provided. In addition to considering these factors, key questions design professionals ask to determine how exam room design can aid and enhance clinic operations include the following:

- How can interior details establish comfort and help to alleviate "white coat anxiety"?
- How can the layout of exam rooms contribute to the overall efficiency of clinic workflows?
- How can privacy, safety, and universal accessibility be achieved so patients feel comfortable and welcome?
- How can new technologies be seamlessly integrated to improve the quality of care?

Care Model

The activities completed in exam rooms and the degree of flexibility and adaptability these require vary according to a clinic's care model.

For example, exam rooms in convenience care clinics are typically smaller, with just enough space for essential technology, equipment, supplies, and furnishings, because the services provided within them are limited to preventative care, as well as diagnosis and treatment of common ailments, such as colds, sore throats, ear infections, and the flu (see table 6-1).

Comfort

One of the ways design professionals can improve the patient experience is create exam rooms that increase comfort and counteract the "white coat effect." This syndrome occurs when patients' anxiety related to an upcoming exam or procedure causes blood pressure levels taken in clinic exam rooms to be higher than those taken outside of a medical setting. This effect is more prevalent in women than men, in older than younger patients, and in patients with hypertension.

Although research indicates that the white coat effect is associated with the act of a care provider, measuring the patient's blood pressure, the physical environment of an exam room may also trigger a conditioned response that causes or exacerbates anxiety. Thus, design professionals use a range of strategies for helping to establish a comfortable exam room environment. These include:

- Providing positive distractions or familiar details, from fabrics and finishes to wall art.
- Neatly displaying educational information and materials that may be of interest to patients.
- Ensuring that the exam room is properly heated, cooled, and ventilated.
- Mitigating or eliminating negative distractions, such as ambient noise.
- Providing comfortable furnishings.

Safety

The design and adjacencies of clinic exam rooms should help to prevent medical errors and injuries, as well as keep patients safe and their possessions secure. Design professionals address safety in and around exam rooms by:

- Providing clear sightlines between staff work areas and exam rooms that allow clinicians to be certain that patients are being treated promptly and that care delivery processes are being executed properly.
- Specifying the use of locks for drawers or cabinets where supplies or equipment that could be dangerous are stored. The design of exam rooms for behavioral health clinics often takes the extra step of sectioning patients off from equipment and medical supplies by way of a door that can be pulled down from the ceiling.
- Selecting furnishings with radial corners and providing one guest chair with arms and one without arms to accommodate individuals with a variety of physical conditions.
- Using same-handed exam rooms in clinics where patients with high or greatly varying levels of acuity are treated. Since these exam rooms are uniformly configured, furnished, and equipped, care providers can quickly locate the proper medical instruments and supplies they need to treat patients.
- Providing a minimum seat height of 18 inches for a typical exam room. However, in specialty facilities such as orthopedic clinics, a seat height of 20 to 21 inches has been found to be more comfortable for patients.

Infection Control

Intensified utilization and the presence of more people in a confined, enclosed space have increased the risks for spreading infections in exam rooms. Design professionals can address this issue by:

- Selecting exam room furnishings made with materials designed to inhibit the spread of bacteria. Experts recommend the use of a moisture barrier for seats of chairs and fabric with an easily cleanable surface for the backs of chairs. Seating with an opening between the back and seat should be used to prevent the build-up of dust and crumbs, etc.

- Strategically placing sinks or sanitizing stations in exam rooms to promote proper hand hygiene practices. Sinks or hand sanitizer dispensers should be located in the care provider zone of an exam room so that physicians can scrub their hands prior to performing the physical exam. Locating the sink near an entry door encourages care providers to wash their hands when they enter and exit an exam room. Placing sinks near the back of an exam room can impede (or de-emphasize) compliance with hand hygiene policies by requiring care providers to cross through the patient zone to wash their hands before conducting the physical exam.

- Separating sinks from the care provider's work surface. When these are integrated or located closely together, liquid splashed from the sink can contaminate work surfaces.

Some clinics have opted to place hand sanitizer dispensers throughout exam rooms by mounting them near entries, exam tables, and/or care provider work surfaces.

Privacy

HIPAA's privacy rule states that healthcare organizations completing financial and administrative transactions electronically must provide safeguards to prevent intentional or unintentional disclosure of protected health information. Since the exam room is becoming the place where the majority of confidential patient information is gathered, input, retrieved, and reviewed, design professionals who once focused primarily on achieving physical privacy for patients now simultaneously consider how to protect their health information. The types of activities that occur within an exam room, the extent to which a patient will need to disrobe, and the functions of adjacent spaces influence design professionals' decisions about how to achieve a clinic's desired level of visual and auditory privacy within exam rooms.

Acoustical Privacy

Patients and other people visiting a clinic should not be able to distinguish words from conversations occurring in and around exam rooms. Acoustical separation of exam rooms has become more challenging to achieve as the range of activities that occur within these spaces has expanded and more clinics have shifted to a team-based care model that relies on frequent verbal communication between care providers.

Design professionals use a range of strategies in varying combinations to provide acoustical privacy for patient–care provider conversations that occur within exam rooms. These include:

- Carefully configuring exam rooms to balance the goal of preventing confidential discussions about a patient's health from being overheard with patients' desire to have direct visual access to the corridor.

- Using a solid-core, hinged door that has sound-sealing gaskets at door jambs and automatic-drop door bottoms to provide additional acoustical privacy. New sliding doors with sound-sealing gasket features can also mitigate the transfer of noise from adjacent spaces.

- Making sure that the wall studs and gypsum board extend all the way to the underside of the deck.

- Using high-mass drywall and dense, acoustic-quality insulation between the studs.

- Minimizing the need to punch through, and then seal around punctures in vertical surfaces such as walls or doors.

- Selecting and specifying the use of proper sound sealants when vertical surfaces must be punctured by pipes, ductwork, electrical conduit, and doors, for example.

- Installing sound-masking systems that serve exam rooms or dampen sound in adjacent spaces.

- Providing extra ceiling space for sound attenuators.

- Providing sound boots and baffles at openings in plenum wall/return air registers.

- Installing ceiling tile with a good ceiling attenuation class (CAC) rating, which measures the sound traveling to adjacent rooms or to the room above a space. A CAC rating of 25 or less is considered to be "low performance," while a CAC of 35 is considered to be "high performance."[2]

- Considering the use of carpet in lieu of hard-surface flooring.

- No back-to-back outlets.

Acoustical privacy is better in universal exam rooms that are also laid out in a "same-handed" configuration within a clinic module—especially when design professionals also stagger the door openings of these exam rooms. Since the care provider work areas are at least 10 feet from each other in same-handed, universal exam rooms, private conversations between physicians and patients are less likely to be overheard than those occurring in exam rooms configured as mirror images to each other.

Sound Transference

In addition to creating a negative distraction and adding to the anxiety patients often experience in exam rooms, high levels of ambient noise potentially can make it difficult or impossible for building occupants to hear alarms or calls for assistance.

Since auditory levels in a clinic depend on both the strength of the signal and the level of ambient noise, noise reduction is best accomplished with a combination of operational policy measures and strategic design decisions that address issues such as the need to provide a clear auditory pathway between the exam table and the corridor to ensure patient safety while also maintaining the privacy of confidential conversations occurring in the exam room.

■ SUTTER MEDICAL CAMPUS
Novato, California (Acoustical Study)

Key goals of this study were to define the acceptable levels of sound transference between exam rooms and adjacent spaces in order to determine an appropriate design that would ensure patient privacy and confidentiality.

The owner and design team members assumed that sound was traveling through glass doors and walls. The design team's research on the proper materials and STC ratings for this type of installation made it clear that there were other factors at play. The contractor initially recommended:

- Removing laminated glass walls in exam rooms. These had been installed in response to an orthopedic physician's request for a larger marker board surface in exam rooms.

- Removing all glass in exam rooms and office doors.

- Increasing the amount of gypsum board used for replacement walls.

Since these actions would diminish the design quality of the exam rooms, increase construction costs and time, and further delay clinic operations, the designers and owner decided to try an evidence-based design approach (EBD) to determine exactly where the sound was leaking. They hypothesized that the sound was traveling through the ceiling tiles and the plenum more than through the glass in the doors and the glass wall within each exam room. They conducted a field study to determine if these components were holding an appropriate STC rating and discovered that:

- The doors were a main source of sound leakage, specifically, the gap under the door. In this case, the doors were undercut too much, which often goes unnoticed.
- Laminated glass that was ¼" thick maintained a sufficient STC rating.
- There were several holes in the walls. A hole as small as ½" proved as adverse as a 24" hole, as sound travels like water through cracks and openings.
- The larger the gauge of steel used for wall studs, the more sound would travel through it.

The acoustician on the project team recommended:

- Providing boots and baffles at all HVAC open-plenum locations.
- Making sure a minimum of three walls met the underside of the deck.
- Providing a sound-masking system.
- Adding door-bottom gaskets and door seals to all exam rooms, offices, and restrooms.

These recommended measures were in addition to the standard steps already undertaken to reduce ambient noise and preserve acoustical privacy, such as using sound sealant on the top and bottoms of walls and installing acoustical ceiling tiles with a good STC rating. However, given that implementing the additional recommendations would still be cost-prohibitive, the team examined sound transference in multiple suites and determined that:

- All doors and walls required mitigation measures. For example, holes in the walls were filled with acoustical sealant.
- The glass in the doors and exam room walls was not an issue.

The final recommendations by the team were to install bottom gaskets on selected exam room and office doors throughout the clinic, provide seals for these specific doors, seal all penetrations in full-height walls, and provide rubber transition strips for all doors and door-bottom gaskets.

A follow-up sound study verified that speech privacy requirements were met, proving that the effectiveness of the door seals related to how true a door was installed in relation to the wall surrounding it. A simple alteration of the installation design for the gaskets was needed to achieve a proper seal. Using this EBD approach resulted in a 25 percent cost savings for the completion of remedial work. These savings were closer to 75 percent, however, when compared with the cost of fully remodeling the walls and doors.

Visual Privacy

Design professionals use the strategic placement of the entry door, the direction of its swing, and the location and orientation of the exam table to achieve proper visual privacy in exam rooms. As needed, they also recommend the use of privacy curtains or other room dividers.

Entry Doors

An exam room door can be hinged to swing into the room in one of two ways: against the wall opposite the exam table, or toward the exam table to block a direct view of it from adjacent areas. Most clinics find doors up to 42 inches wide manageable. Reverse-swings toward the exam table work only with doors that are 36 to 42 inches wide, and the standard swing is best for a 42-inch-wide door.

A clinic's culture influences design decisions about the direction in which exam room doors should swing. For example, when interviewed in conjunction with the development of a five-year strategic facilities plan, Mayo Clinic physicians in Rochester, Minnesota said they did not need the reverse door swing because people knock before entering exam rooms.

Sliding doors save space because the clearance area needed to accommodate a door swing is eliminated. Clinics that use an on-stage/off-stage layout often use sliding doors for clinician entries from private work corridors. However, these types of doors are rarely used for the patient entry into an exam room due to noise transmission from public areas. Sliding doors generally require more maintenance and repairs (see fig. 6-11).

Exam Table Layouts

The placement and orientation of the exam table affect the level of visual privacy afforded patients. These decisions are influenced by factors such as the type of services a clinic provides and the characteristics of its patient population. For example:

- OB/GYN physicians and patients prefer to have the foot of the exam table face the wall opposite the entry door.

- Exam tables in primary care rooms are usually set at an angle to the adjacent walls to provide physicians with easy access to both sides of the patient.

- Pediatricians have the exam table placed against the wall to prevent patient falls.

- Otolaryngology (ear, nose, and throat) exam rooms provide healthcare staff with 360-degree access to the exam chair.

- Exam rooms in orthopedic clinics provide access for the care providers to work from all sides of the exam table—top, bottom, left, and right—so that they have easy access to the precise location of a fracture and can also test a patient's range of motion.

Positioning the exam table near the back of the room de-emphasizes the physical exam portion of clinic visits (Mayo Clinic 2006), which can help to alleviate stress.[3] It also positions the physician zone toward the front of the exam room near the patient entry and thus allows care providers to avoid the need to cross past the patient and partners-in-care upon entering the exam room. However, this design strategy compromises patient privacy if the patient entry door is opened during the physical examination.

Cost, cultural norms, care delivery processes, type of services provided, and patient population characteristics also influence decisions about which exam tables should be used and how they should be positioned in a clinic's exam rooms.

Curtains and Room Dividers

Approaches to providing a private place for patients to change clothing include installing privacy curtains or using movable partitions.

Privacy curtains can be installed so that they surround the entry arc created by the door swing or to completely section off the patient zone of the exam room from the entry area. While curtains are often used to provide an extra degree of privacy, some clinics are wary of using them because they add another exam room component that must be cleaned and maintained. Design professionals considering this option should thoroughly research the materials used to fabricate various curtains, analyze the qualities of the track or rod system used to hang them to avoid creating potential breeding grounds for bacteria, and make sure that final choices are made in relation to the clinic's ability to adhere to a regular cleaning schedule.

Some clinics create an efficient dressing area by hanging a curtain in a corner of the exam room that is remote from the entry door and providing a locker or hooks for storing personal items. This design helps to minimize or eliminate the need for patients to move from a dressing room elsewhere in the clinic to the exam room.

Depending on the relative locations of the care provider and patient zones, using a curtain to divide the interior space can allow physicians to remain in the room and to complete charting or other tasks while a patient is undressing or getting dressed. This can reduce wait time and increase throughput (fig. 6-1).

Windows

The use and placement of exterior windows in exam rooms should relate to the location of the

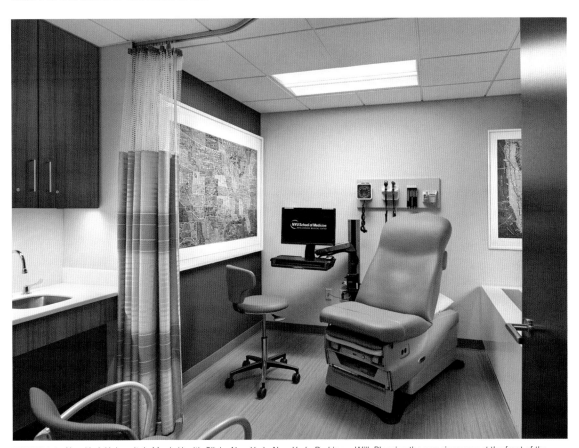

FIGURE 6-1: New York University's Men's Health Clinic, New York, New York; Perkins + Will. Planning the caregiver zone at the front of the exam space allows for easy access to the handwashing station. The privacy curtain location allows for patient privacy while accommodating family or a translator. Products such as this exam table that easily converts from chair to a fully reclining table provide flexibility for patient needs and add to patient comfort. Photography © by Halkin Mason Photography

exam table and dressing areas—especially when a clinic's exam rooms are on grade.

Lighting

Lighting should be evenly diffused and provide the proper color rendition, which for the typical exam room requires achieving a color rendering index score (CRI) of 80 or greater. The CRI score conveys the ability of a light source to render an object in true colors when compared to incandescent light, with higher scores on the scale of 0–100 indicating more accurate color rendition.[4]

Since the moderately higher cost of using indirect lighting can often be justified by improved patient satisfaction, design professionals have introduced more lighting with features that shield the light source to prevent patients from having to look directly into an uncovered lamp when they are lying on an exam table.

Specifying ambient light sources that are warmer in color temperature and that avoid creating a high contrast has a softening effect in exam rooms. Recessing lights and keeping angles at a high level to bounce light off of walls minimizes shadows while evenly dispersing light over interior surfaces.

Exam room lighting decisions need to be carefully coordinated to avoid creating glare, which can cause eyestrain, fatigue, and headaches. For example, design professionals pay special attention to wall-mounted lighting because in addition to generating glare, light fixtures in various parts of the exam room can project hot spots onto monitors, whiteboards, and other exam room features and, thus, create a negative distraction. The optimal illumination level is 75 foot-candles at three feet above the ground. This is easiest to accomplish when the (shielded) light source is positioned directly above the exam table.

Task lighting over work surfaces should provide high enough illumination levels and contrast to facilitate reading printed materials. These objectives can be accomplished while achieving an even dispersion of light by locating task lighting on the bottom of a wall-mounted cabinet or integrating it into workstation millwork.

Decisions about how to illuminate the tasks that occur in the exam room vary significantly in relation to the type of practice a clinic serves. For example, ophthalmologists prefer to have dimmable can lighting that they can adjust as needed to decrease or increase illumination levels depending on the condition of the patient. Dermatologists prefer to work in spaces illuminated with natural light or artificial light with a CRI of 90 or greater.[5]

The energy efficiency of fixtures, lighting system components, and sources should be considered throughout each phase of the planning and design process. This analysis can include consideration of lighting control systems, although most clinics prefer to use these in public areas, which are subject to greater variations in occupancy levels throughout the day.

Daylight is generally introduced into the public and staff areas of clinics rather than exam rooms to preserve patient privacy. Natural light can be borrowed from these spaces, however, via a transom, skylight, or clerestory windows. When natural light is introduced into exam rooms, the design of artificial lighting systems must take this into account to avoid creating glare while ensuring an even distribution of ambient light as the amount of daylight available varies. Blackout or room-darkening window treatments that allow no more than 0 to 1 percent of natural light to enter the room are recommended (figs. 6-2, 6-3).

The ease of finding replacement lamps and components is a key consideration when making lighting selections.

Universal Accessibility

Clinic exam rooms must be universally accessible so that patients receive the same quality of care at any time regardless of their physical and mental capabilities. The basic design guidelines for achieving this goal and complying with ADA requirements for exam rooms include:

- Providing a five-foot-diameter turning circle or five-square-foot T-shaped turning area to accommodate patients in wheelchairs or those who use scooters. Door swings are allowed to overlap the turning area.

- Equipping at least one exam room with a motorized exam table for patients who have limited strength and mobility as well as to accommodate bariatric patients.

- Providing at least a 30″ by 48″ area of clear floor space alongside the exam table.

FIGURE 6-2: UMP Mill City Clinic, Minneapolis, Minnesota; Perkins + Will. Comfortable seating and varied natural and artificial lighting create a warm ambience. Lowered ceiling planes and varied light sources differentiate public from clinic zones. Clerestory windows allow for natural daylight to be shared between public and private spaces without compromising patient privacy. Photography © by Christopher Barrett

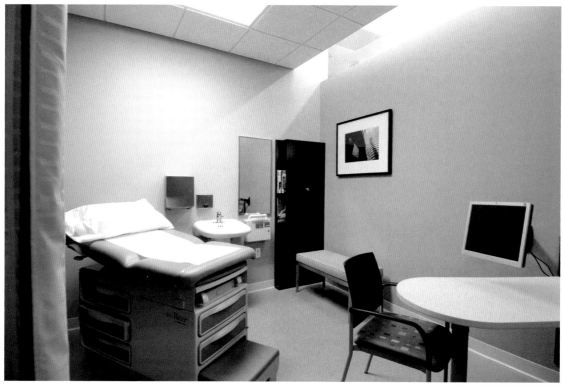

FIGURE 6-3: UMP Mill City Clinic, Minneapolis, Minnesota; Perkins + Will. Exam rooms feature consultation space for patient, family, and care-giver. Clerestory windows allow for natural daylight while maintaining patient privacy.　Photography © by Christopher Barrett

- Equipping at least one exam room with a power lift. These can be ceiling-mounted or portable. Ceiling-mounted lifts do not require additional floor clear space; but they are typically more expensive than portable lifts, which can be used in more than one room. However, portable lifts require storage space and occupy floor space when not in use.

- Installing medical equipment so that it will not obstruct patients' access or the doctor's ability to conduct examinations.

- Designing door openings to achieve (or exceed) the ADA minimum requirement of a 32-inch width. Using a 42-inch width as a standard better accommodates wheelchairs, mobile supply carts, and mobile medical equipment. It also makes it easier for bariatric patients to enter and exit an exam room.[6]

- Placing a handrail on the wall above or next to the exam table to provide assistance for patients who need to change position, transfer to a wheelchair, or steady themselves before using crutches, a walker, or other piece of mobility-related equipment.

- Providing a minimum clearance of 29 inches below care provider work surfaces (desktops, for example).

Impact of Technology

Seamlessly integrating basic building systems as well as medical, health information, and communications technology into the design of exam rooms requires close collaboration between design professionals with a variety of backgrounds—from architects and interior designers to mechanical and electrical engineers, technology consultants, and lighting designers. These experts collaboratively address issues such as:

- Providing sufficient floor-to-ceiling height so that electrical and heating, ventilation, and air conditioning (HVAC) systems can be properly routed and sized to achieve desired temperature and lighting levels, as well as proper air quality for exam room occupants.

- Determining how electrical conduit, outlets, switches, and other related details are best coordinated with equipment locations, furnishings, and furniture systems.

- Relating lighting design to the use of technology in the exam room to provide appropriate illumination and avoid creating glare.

Use of Computers

Openness and an interactive exchange of information are essential for building long-term, trusting relationships among patients, physicians, and other healthcare professionals. This has made design decisions about how to best integrate computers into the care provider zone of exam rooms as important as those made about the features and location of the exam table. Clinicians now need access to a computer for everything from real-time charting to the review of patient health history data, lab and diagnostic test results, and educational information.

Today, many patients complete research online in advance of a clinic visit in order to be able to ask informed questions. This can enrich consultations and build comfort between the care provider and patient as they jointly review information that supplements the preexam research and discuss the patient's condition and care plan.

While patients' attitudes toward exam room computers are generally positive, their perceptions are strongly influenced by the design of the exam room area where a computer is located (as well as the digital skills of the care provider). Generally, design professionals have found that:

- The computer should never become a barrier between the care provider and patient.

- Care providers should not need to turn their backs on patients to work on the computer. A partial turn of 90 degrees is acceptable during the time the care provider is working online. But during the consultation, everyone in the room should be able to make eye contact and view information on a computer screen.

- Wall-mounted monitors are ideal for providing clear sightlines for multiple people. Using a swivel-arm wall mounting also makes it easy for the physician or nurse practitioner to switch between screens privately and then move the monitor into a position that makes shared viewing possible during the collaborative portion of the consultation.

- When the patient and physician can be seated next to each other with the computer monitor viewable by both, there is more eye contact between them and the physician can more easily shift attention back and forth between the patient and the computer.

- Locating the patient seating area next to the physician zone where the computer is located places care providers in front of the computer while allowing them to glance over to the patient seating area.

- Docking stations could be integrated into the design of the work/consult table for clinics making the transition to using tablets or laptop computers. This would make it possible for mobile digital devices to be recharged during the physical exam and to connect these to a keyboard, mouse, or large-screen monitor.

Since the care provider's ability to use technology influences patients' perceptions of the quality of care they receive, it is important to review strategies for integrating technology into an exam room's design with clinicians in order to make sure that these support the way the physician intends to use computers and other equipment.[7]

Design Challenges and Strategies

For many years, the design of exam rooms for clinics was quite straightforward. The total quantity of exam rooms was based on how many each physician needed since most of the time patients spent in exam rooms was dedicated to the assessment, physical exam, treatment, and consultation activities completed by doctors.

Now the utilization of exam rooms varies greatly based on a clinic's provider mix, care model, range of services, and the characteristics of its patient population. The wide range of ways clinics use exam rooms affects every detail of their design, from the ratios established to calculate the total number of exam rooms needed to their size, shape, layout, configuration, and furnishings.

Utilization

In the past, exam room utilization was based on the stated needs of doctors. If a medical practice had four physicians and each one required 3 exam rooms, then design professionals would focus on how to most efficiently include 12 exam rooms in a clinic facility's design.

This model can still work well if all of the physicians are scheduled to see patients throughout all clinic hours, every day of the week. However, if one or more of the physicians only sees patients on certain days or for specific hours of the day, this leads to underutilization of exam rooms, which are typically the most expensive spaces to equip and fit out in a clinic.

To rectify this situation and optimize utilization, design professionals thoroughly research the provider mix, healthcare delivery processes, services provided, and patient population characteristics associated with a specific clinic to design exam rooms that meet its unique needs. For example, the fact that nurse practitioners and other clinicians can also use exam rooms to provide care has an impact on exam room ratios (see the cycle time chart, in fig. 2-2).

Ratios

A number of studies have been completed in an attempt to determine how exam room ratios are influenced by factors beyond the number of physicians a medical practice has. For example, in 2012, the Oakland University School of Business used a simulated computer model to identify ways to streamline and improve the performance of different healthcare system scenarios. The number of exam rooms per provider was examined in combination with the following factors to determine their effect on wait time:

- Number of support staff.
- Location where vital signs are taken.
- Duration of exam.
- Scheduling method.

The computer model explored three different scenarios where these variables were all similar (i.e., two exam rooms per provider, 13-minute exam periods, 6-minute duration for vital signs) *except* that the number of support staff was increased from two to three to four between scenarios.

The initial time patients spent in the waiting room and provider wait time in the exam room were greatest when there were only two support staff per physician. For this scenario, as the number of patient visits per day increased, the wait time also increased significantly. On the other hand, there was noticeably less time spent waiting when three or four support staff were assigned per physician.[8]

Size

The first critical step for establishing the proper size of exam rooms is to identify the specific activities that will occur within them. For example, convenience care clinics usually provide a limited range of care services and, thus, feature compact exam rooms that have just enough space for an exam table, basic seating, and a small work surface for the care provider. On average, however, exam rooms are increasing in size, for the following reasons:

- Healthcare experts and care providers recognize the positive role that family members, friends, and other partners-in-care can play in providing support as part of a patient's treatment and recovery plan. This has prompted clinics to expand the seating and consultation areas of exam rooms so that more people can be present during the physical exam and ensuing consultation period.

- The general trend towards more collaborative care has led to a need for sufficient space in the exam room to accommodate multiple members of a patient's care team.

- More tasks are being completed in exam rooms—from checking patients in and obtaining lab specimens to conducting exams and consultations, providing educational materials and prescriptions, and scheduling follow-up tests, procedures, or appointments.

- More space is being dedicated to consultation and education areas in exam rooms as reimbursement structures shift from rewarding

care providers for the number of clinic visits they complete within a specified time period to the quality of their patients' health outcomes.

The average exam room now ranges from 100 to 120 square feet in size. The size of exam rooms can be larger than the top end of this range when they serve medical homes, multispecialty practices (such as pelvic floor clinics and spine clinics), and clinics that complete lab tests, imaging, and noninvasive or minimally invasive procedures in exam rooms.

Storage Requirements

In certain types of exam rooms, providing a private space for disrobing, dressing, and storing clothing and personal items sends a message to patients that a clinic cares about their comfort and privacy. Efficient, appropriate, and secure storage areas or containers should:

- Provide the volume of storage space needed to accommodate the personal items of an average patient and family members.

- Help keep exam rooms free from clutter.

- When possible, optimize the use of available space by using overhead areas as well as those beneath work surfaces. Exam tables with storage drawers, for example, can improve the efficiency of an exam room's design.

- Avoid creating any circulation conflicts that could hamper patient care.

Design professionals devising exam room layouts should factor these specialized needs into their space calculations for clinics that serve a high number of patients who must temporarily store special equipment, such as strollers, baby carriers, wheelchairs, and walkers.

Medical Equipment

The characteristics of medical equipment used in exam rooms have an impact on the size, configuration, and furnishing of exam rooms. Sufficient clearance, for example, must be provided for the movement of mobile medical equipment, and design professionals must also determine if it is best stored in an exam room or elsewhere. The location of power receptacles, as well as the routing of mechanical, electrical, and other systems, also influences the exam room configuration and furnishing choices.

To ensure that medical equipment enhances rather than becomes an obstruction to the smooth flow of exam room activities, design professionals consider:

* The dimensions of "plug-and-play" requirements, and storage requirements for mobile medical equipment. These factors influence design decisions about systems capabilities and routing as well as the placement, orientation, and characteristics of exam tables, the sizing and configuration of exam room space, and the width of entry doors and direction of the door swing.

* The range and type of services provided in the exam room. Care providers must have direct and easy access to the patient at all times and, thus, must be able to easily move medical equipment—fixed or mobile—out of the way.

* The ergonomic issues related to the use of ceiling- or wall-mounted medical equipment. For example, to reduce the risk of staff injuries, such as strained backs, ceiling-mounted lifts are recommended for bariatric-ready, universally accessible exam rooms.

Shape

Unique activities that occur within exam rooms serving specialized medical practices can influence the shape (or relative dimensions) of these spaces. For example, if exam rooms in an ophthalmology clinic include eye charts, these typically have to be mounted a distance of 20 feet from where the patient will be using them.

Layout

The pressure that healthcare organizations and care providers are experiencing to "do better with less" has encouraged more clinics to "lean" the layout of exam rooms to optimize the efficiency of tasks completed within them. Some strategies for achieving this objective include:

* Locating the sink or sanitizing module as close to the entry door as possible so that clinicians can disinfect their hands en route to examining the patient. This reduces the total number of steps care providers make.

* Using a universal (same-handed) layout where everything in the room is identical makes it easier for care providers to quickly and easily find standard instruments and supplies that are stored in a clinic's exam rooms.

* Using mobile supply carts that are stocked only with the items needed to address the needs of the patients who will be seen in specific exam rooms the next day.

A well-designed exam room should have functional patient and care provider zones with unobstructed access between these realms.

Patient/Partners-in-Care Zone

While guests accompanying patients to clinics most commonly are family members or friends, the phrase "partners-in-care" (PICs) encompasses a wide range of people, such as translators, social workers, or others who play an important role in helping patients to manage their health and wellness. Design professionals address this by providing sufficient space and seating to accommodate these guests in the exam room. The partners-in-care zone is typically located near the exam table, with a curtain or other room divider used to provide privacy for patients when they are disrobing, being examined or treated, or getting dressed (see fig. 6-15).

Care Provider Zone

As more clinics use a team-based approach to providing healthcare services the care provider zone has grown from a simple physician's workstation with desk and chair to a collaborative work area where members of an integrated care team (or family members) can join the physician and patient during a consultation. The degree to which a clinic uses electronic health records and includes health education as part of consults also influences how the care provider zone of an exam room is furnished and equipped.

When determining how to size, configure, furnish, and equip care provider zones in exam rooms, design professionals:

- Often must include sufficient space and seating to accommodate multiple members of a care team or partners-in-care.

- Provide adequate space and choose furnishings and equipment that allow the patient to sit next to the care provider during a consult.

- Avoid creating any unnecessary obstructions inside or immediately outside of the caregiver zone. For example, the placement of the sink or supply storage should allow enough room for additional clinicians to participate in a collaborative consult. Depending upon the size and configuration of the exam room, furniture that is located next to the care provider zone can create a barrier and reduce the efficient flow of exam room activities.

The size of desktop computers has been reduced to the point that they no longer need to occupy a major portion of a work surface in the care provider zone of an exam room. Since there is now sufficient area for patients to have a clear, flat surface for taking notes, many clinics have begun using work surfaces instead of desks in the care provider zone because these can often double as consultation tables.

Half-round or peninsula-style tables are frequently used in exam rooms where multiple people are likely to participate in a consult because these shapes make it easy for two to three people to view information on a computer monitor. In orthopedic exam rooms the desk or consultation work surface can double as a place to assess hand and arm issues.

Seating

Today, manufacturers specializing in the design of healthcare furnishings offer a broad range of products that are comfortable, attractive, durable, and adaptable. For example, some companies now produce upholstered chairs that recline to a variety of angles, including a fully horizontal position so they can be transformed into an exam table. Others produce chairs that can be converted to wheelchairs or gurneys for transporting patients from the exam room to outpatient procedure and recovery areas of the clinic.

A clinic's care model and characteristics of the patient population influence the type of seating design professionals specify for an exam room. Seating should be provided to accommodate various types of patients and guests. For example, with more than one-third of the U.S. adult population over the age of 20 being overweight or obese, designers are now recommending that clinics provide either bench seating with a high weight capacity or a combination of one bariatric chair without arms and one standard chair with armrests for patient/guest seating in the typical exam room. Seats that are wider and deeper with strengthened support best accommodate bariatric patients.

Seats with arms are important for elderly patients (or those who are in a weakened condition) to assist them in getting out of the chair.

Benches also allow family members and friends who have accompanied a patient into the exam room to comfort them, if necessary (see fig. 6-17). Fold-up seating can be used in compact exam rooms, such as those used by convenience care clinics. When fold-up seats are not in use, the floor space can be used to temporarily store equipment such as walking canes, strollers and baby carriers, or wheelchairs.

Types of Exam Rooms

Design of the following types of exam rooms has evolved over the past several years to address the wide range of ways that clinics use these spaces.

Universal Exam Room

The design of these exam rooms is standardized and flexible in order to maximize the number of clinicians who can use them and the range of patients who can be treated within them. Clinic owners and care providers decide which equipment, supplies, and design features should be standard in the exam rooms based on the type of services that a clinic offers, its staffing strategies, and the characteristics of its patient population.

One-Stop Exam Rooms

One-stop exam rooms are designed to maximize the range of clinic tasks that can be performed within them. Depending on the specific needs of a clinic, registration, tests and diagnostics, minor procedures, checkout, and other activities that used to occur elsewhere in a clinic can now be completed in one-stop exam rooms.

Once a nurse or other staff member has taken the patient's vital signs and updated health history information, the physician enters and completes the exam, treatment, and consultation. Specialists can also enter the exam rooms to obtain lab samples, to use mobile imaging

equipment to take x-rays, to complete a minor procedure, or to discuss dietary, pharmaceutical, behavioral health, or other issues related to an illness or injury.

Design professionals focus on comfort as well as flexibility when designing one-stop exam rooms because their increased range of uses typically leads to patients spending more time in these clinic spaces than they had in the past.

The benefits of one-stop exam rooms are that they provide patients with a private place to wait and to discuss personal information. They may also help to reduce medical errors and injuries because the patient is not handed off between departments.

However, the additional costs associated with one-stop exam rooms can be high. For example, since research has shown that patients dislike being weighed in public hallways, some clinics equip each of their one-stop exam rooms with a scale. Other clinics include printers in one-stop exam room so that prescriptions, educational materials, and information about follow-up appointments can be printed and signed on the spot by physicians or nurse practitioners.

The investment in additional equipment, maintenance, supplies, and energy costs associated with providing printers in all exam rooms may be justified by a reduction in labor costs if staff members no longer have to spend extra time walking to and from a shared printer or if printing costs decline because brochures, FAQ sheets, and other medical materials are now only produced "on demand." The risk of confidential patient information inadvertently winding up in the wrong hands is also reduced through use of a printer in the private consult area of a one-stop exam room rather than in a shared work area.

Consult Rooms

Care providers use consult rooms to discuss diagnoses and care plans with patients and their families.[9] Due to an increased focus on the importance of health education and home care, the design of consult rooms is evolving as quickly as the design of exam rooms. Consult rooms are usually the same size as exam rooms (for future versatility), but have softer lighting and more comfortable furniture. They may not need to have a sink, but they should at least be equipped with a hand sanitizer dispenser.

Research conducted by the Mayo Clinic Center for Innovation indicated that patients' responses to rooms that were specifically designed for consultation activities are overwhelmingly positive. Researchers recommended the following:

- Making consult rooms smaller than exam rooms in order to provide the intimacy appropriate for face-to-face conversations. However, this strategy is not likely to work well for clinics that use a team-based approach to care or that serve patient populations that require or expect translators, social workers, family members, or other partners-in-care to be present during consults.

- Designing exam rooms to deemphasize the exam table (and thus the physical part of the exam).

- Integrating mobile tools into the care process to minimize the patient's need to move.[10]

By simply separating patients from the area in which they have been examined or a minor procedure has been completed, consult rooms (or areas) help to reduce stress.

Telehealth Rooms

As provisions in the Affordable Care Act have made it possible for care providers to be compensated for providing e-consults, the demand for telehealth rooms in clinics is likely to increase. In anticipation of this, some clinics are testing models for providing exams or consultations from a remote location by using videoconferencing equipment or web-based communication options, such as Skype. In some instances, these telehealth rooms are used to complement the activities that occur in adjacent areas of a clinic (at the South Central Foundation Primary Care Center in Anchorage, Alaska, for example).

■ MAYO CLINIC INNOVATION CENTER E
Rochester, Minnesota (Consult Room)

This is one example of a telehealth room and illustrates how technology can be hidden during in-person consults and revealed when needed to conduct remote consultations or e-visits. The videoconferencing equipment is stored in a wall cabinet that conceals the equipment when not in use. A cart that stores vital equipment is integrated into the bottom right-hand corner of the casework. It can be pulled out and moved into close proximity to the exam room table. The video monitor has a camera attached to the top of the screen. There is also a computer monitor, a dialer, and a switching device in the middle portion of the casework, with the computer tower and codec machine concealed in the lower portion.

An exam chair is included in the room and has task lighting provided by a wall-mounted exam light nearby. Dimmable 2′-by-2′ LED light fixtures provide ambient illumination that can be adjusted as needed.

Care Suites

Some clinics have elected to combine consult and exam rooms into care suites. This configuration typically works better for specialized practices than it does for primary care clinics, which tend to have a higher percentage of patients requiring physical exams than consultations.

Furnishings in the consult room of a care suite are arranged so that the physician and patient sit side by side and discuss test or exam results over a shared work surface or a coffee table. Finishes and furniture are similar to what is typically found in a waiting room or office. Patients have the chance to view educational videos while they wait in the consult room. Specialists can enter the exam room as necessary to complete tasks such as blood draws or to participate in multidisciplinary consultations.

The consult and exam rooms in care suites are typically positioned back-to-back. To gain access to the exam room, patients must go through the consult room. However, this model is evolving from a one-to-one to a two-to-one ratio of consult to exam rooms for practices that conduct a higher number of consultations than physical exams. A prime example of this is a three-part exam room prototype pioneered by Mayo Clinic.

The Three-Part Exam Room

Two consult rooms are located on each side of an exam room to form this care suite. A curtain separating the entry area of the exam space from the exam table allows partners-in-care to be present during the exam without compromising patient privacy.

The consult rooms feature peninsula-shaped tables that facilitate interaction between patient and physician, a whiteboard, corkboard, and wall-mounted computer monitor. Since the consult rooms do not require a sink or exam table, this prototype reduces plumbing and equipment costs for practices that provide a high percentage of consultative care.

The comfortable, less institutional design of the consult areas encourages patients to be more engaged than they might be in exam rooms where exam tables (or chairs) and medical instruments, equipment, and supplies are more conspicuous and, thus, more inhibiting. The time that patients spend in the exam room section of the care suite is limited to when they are being physically examined or treated by a clinician.

On days when a high number of predictable clinic visits are expected to occur, all three spaces can be scheduled to serve the varying needs of patients. The doors connecting the exam room to the consult rooms on either side can be locked, and patients and care providers can enter each room directly from the main corridor. Small group staff meetings or group consultations can also be held in the consult rooms.

Being able to close off the three parts also makes cleaning and preparing the room for the next patient easy and efficient (fig. 6-4).

Early feedback from users who have tested this prototype indicates that it has improved efficiency for internal medicine physicians. It does not, however, suit the needs of family practice physicians as well because it generates too much movement and information to track. The room sizes are also too small for population groups who expect family members to accompany patients.

Group Exam Rooms

As healthcare experts have observed how group interactions can help patients stay healthy and manage illness, some clinics have begun offering group visits for patients with similar conditions (pregnancy, for example), chronic illnesses (such as diabetes) or behavioral health issues (such as drug or alcohol rehabilitation).

Health experts lead group sessions during which patients learn about preventative care options and health maintenance measures. If private exams or consults are needed, these are provided in an adjoining room that is separated from the group meeting area by a wall with a curtain or door. Formal health education sessions are typically followed by a period where patients can share information informally and learn from each other's experiences.

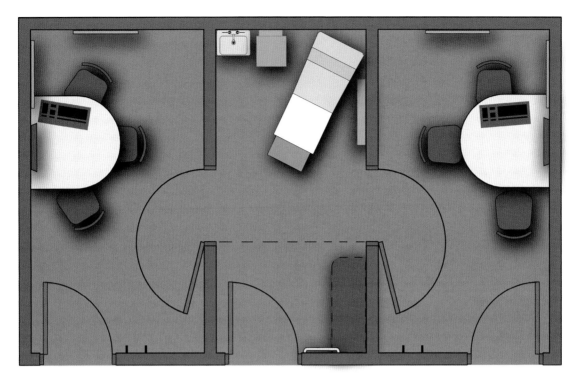

FIGURE 6-4: Three-Part Exam Room N. Two consult rooms are on either side of an exam room. This configuration works well for specialties that have a longer consultative appointment. Image courtesy of Hammel, Green and Abrahamson, Inc.

Group visits are most often used by specialized clinics that have a high volume of patients who have similar ailments or are treated by consultative medicine. Group exam rooms are typically planned as a module of two or four standard exam rooms, allowing them to be converted back to serve as individual exam rooms if needed (fig. 6-5).

An individual exam space with a sink is located at one end of this large room to allow physical assessments to occur at the same time that a discussion is taking place in the group meeting space. A combination of a partial wall and a curtain provides visual privacy while still allowing a patient who is being examined to hear the conversation or presentation in the neighboring space.

Seating is provided for one or two care providers and a group of patients. A screen or large wall-hung monitor, computer, whiteboards, and other presentation aids, as well as educational materials, are often included in these exam rooms.

The staff entry leads directly into the individual exam area. Patients and partners-in-care enter the large group area through a door connected to a public corridor that leads to the lobby. A second sink and countertop serve the large group meeting area (fig. 6-6).

This layout allows the charting desk and sink to be shared by the exam room and group space when the curtain is open. Seating for 12 patients is provided in a classroom-style arrangement. There are also three seats provided for healthcare professionals near a rectangular presentation table. A computer on top of this table is connected to a presentation monitor.

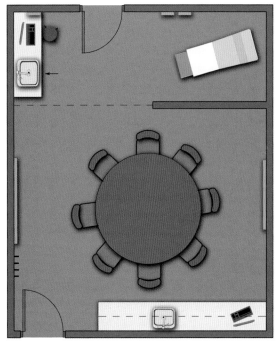

FIGURE 6-5: Group Exam Room Q. This exam room configuration is appropriate for group consulting activities such as smoking cessation. Image courtesy of Hammel, Green and Abrahamson, Inc.

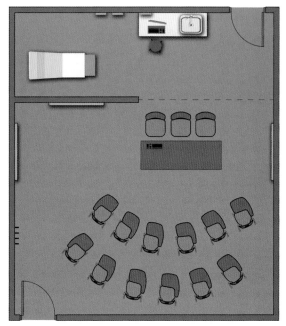

FIGURE 6-6: Group Exam Room R. This exam room configuration is appropriate for educational sessions, such as diabetes education. Image courtesy of Hammel, Green and Abrahamson, Inc.

This group exam room was created by removing a wall between two standard exam rooms so that the owner can convert it back into individual exam rooms if that is necessary in the future. (fig. 6-7).

Exam+ Rooms

This prototype is typically 20 to 30 square feet larger than the average exam room because it includes sufficient space to accommodate multiple care providers (or partners-in-care) in the consultation area and provides a full-height, insulated wall with a sliding door to separate the exam and consultation zones. Partners-in-care can wait in the consultation area while the patient is examined in private. By adding a second door that allows care providers to enter the examination section of this room from the staff

corridor or work core, this prototype can be integrated into an on-stage/off-stage clinic module (fig. 6-8).

The physician and family zones overlap, but are separate within each subdivision. One of the two entry doors connects the consult section of the room to the patient corridor; the second provides physician access from the staff corridor to the exam area. The care provider zone in the consult area features a peninsula-shaped work surface and chairs to accommodate a care provider, the patient, and a partner-in-care or other medical specialist. The sink, waste receptacle, and equipment for taking patient vital signs are located in the exam area of this prototype, adjacent to the patient and near the care provider's entry. Clothing hooks are provided on the wall and on the back of the patient's entry door. This prototype provides more privacy than typical exam rooms because the exam and consult areas are separated by a wall and a sliding door.

Procedure Rooms

With proper equipment, one-stop exam rooms that range from 120 to 130 square feet in size and are bariatric-ready and ADA compliant can be used for noninvasive and minimally invasive procedures. Procedure rooms have power tables, patient lifts, wider doors, and enough floor area to accommodate the movement and temporary storage of wheelchairs, other access devices, and mobile medical equipment.

Bariatric-Ready/Universally Accessible Exam Room

In addition to the need to accommodate patients who have physical disabilities, these specialized exam rooms have evolved to address major demographic shifts in the United States, including the increased rate of obesity for patients of all ages as well as the needs of elderly patients and wounded veterans. Bariatric-ready/universally accessible exam rooms feature power exam tables and lifts. Their doors are wider than those of standard exam rooms. Since the storage space that is typically integrated into the design of standard exam tables cannot be included in power tables, design professionals must determine how to provide this elsewhere in the exam room (fig. 6-9).

The door swing for this prototype does not provide privacy. The casework is built-in. This prototype features a power exam table with an integral scale that not only can be adjusted to different heights but also can be reclined to achieve elevated seated, low seated, supine, and

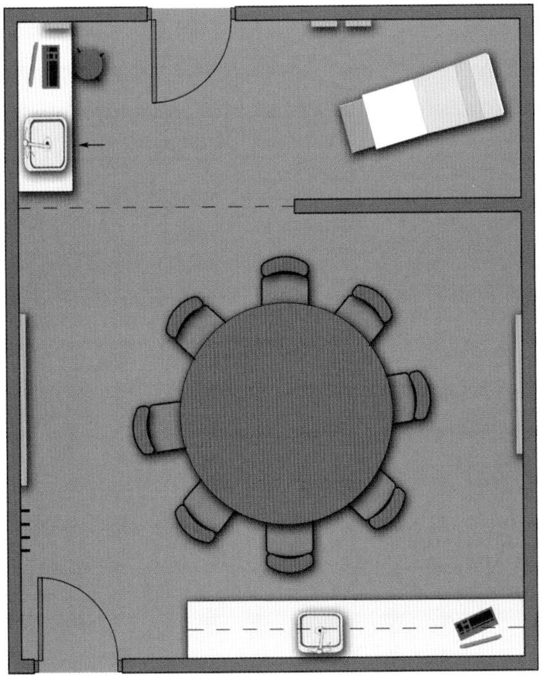

FIGURE 6-7: Group Exam Room S. This exam room configuration is for smaller groups and takes up the space of two exam rooms. Image courtesy of Hammel, Green and Abrahamson, Inc.

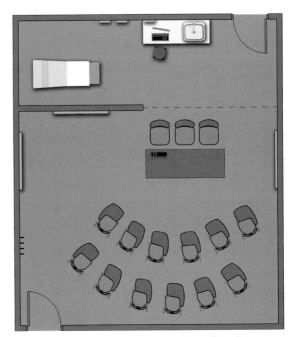

FIGURE 6-8: Split Exam Room M. This room is configured to provide a separation of the exam and consult functions to address the "white coat effect." This room requires significantly more space for appropriate clearances around the exam table and the consult desk. Image courtesy of Hammel, Green and Abrahamson, Inc.

lithotomy positions. Vitals can be taken in the exam room to streamline clinic visits.

This exam room is approximately 33 percent larger than a typical exam room and thus provides a 30" by 40" clear floor space for patient transfer that also makes it easier for patients in wheelchairs or who use scooters to maneuver once they have entered. The door width shown is 48" to better accommodate access devices as well as mobile medical equipment or supply carts (fig. 6-10).

Exam Rooms for Specialty Clinics

The design of exam rooms for specialized care continues to evolve in ways that better align features and equipment with the unique needs of the patient population being served.

Women's Clinics

Clinics focused on addressing the specialized health needs of women have been reviewing the possibility of having two exam rooms flank a common dressing room that can also serve as a consult space. This would eliminate subwaiting rooms and their adjoining locker areas, making it possible to reallocate this space so that it can be more fully utilized.

Behavioral Health Clinics

Designing a behavioral health clinic is different than other clinics. The patients all have varying degrees of mental health issues. Some will wander the halls, pick at laminates, open and shut doors, and pull items such as soap dispensers off walls. These rooms must be designed with this type of patient in mind. Safety, durability, and suicide prevention are all factors to be considered. Antiligature fixtures must be specified

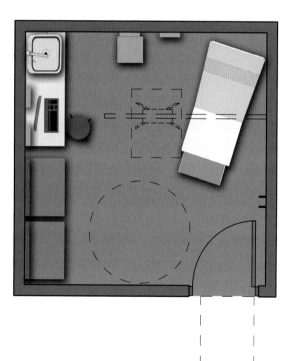

FIGURE 6-9: Bariatric Exam Room O. The doors are 42" wide on this exam room and there is an overhead lift to assist with patient transfer. Image courtesy of Hammel, Green and Abrahamson, Inc.

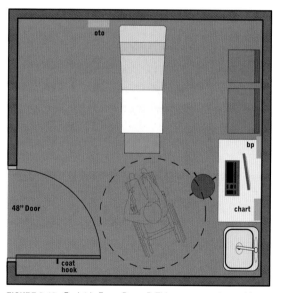

FIGURE 6-10: Bariatric Exam Room P. This exam room is roughly 33 percent larger than a typical exam room in order to accommodate various assist devices. Image courtesy of Hammel, Green and Abrahamson, Inc.

so that no cords or strings are used, there is no risk of loose parts, and no gaps are created that could be used by patients to wrap or hang items in order to harm themselves.[11]

It is good to limit the use of patterns that can be overstimulating, to use radial or beveled edges in millwork to eliminate sharp, potentially dangerous corners, and to use soft lighting in quiet rooms, muted colors, and warm wood finishes that have a calming effect in exam rooms serving behavioral health patients. Supplies are kept out of sight and in locked drawers or cabinets in case a patient is left alone or has an outburst. There are no glass mirrors, and if there are windows in the room, they should be inoperable with integrated blinds (eliminating cords or pieces that could be used as weapons) and made of a shatterproof, transparent material. Ceilings are made of gypsum board, and wall protection is provided with acoustical panels used to help absorb sound. An integral base is important here for safety reasons, as it prevents the risk of a standard base being pried loose.

Pediatric Exam Rooms

The exam table is typically pushed up against the wall in pediatric exam rooms to help prevent patient falls. Some clinics choose specially designed exam tables with flip-down stools that enable kids to climb onto them with little to no assistance. A bench or small sofa is a nice solution for the partners-in-care zone so that a parent can sit next to and comfort a child before and after the physical exam. Exam rooms serving teens and adolescents in pediatric clinics usually feature a curtain or other room divider to provide privacy during the physical exam and while patients are disrobing and getting dressed.

The Retrofitted Office/Exam Room

Some existing clinics are addressing the need for more consultation space within a limited building area by subdividing physicians' offices and using one side for exams and the other side for combined office and consultation functions. This strategy is facilitated by the use of electronic health records, which reduces the amount of space needed for file cabinets and frees up space for additional seating and replacement of a desk with a consultation table.

Drawbacks to this strategy include the fact that even when a wall or other room divider separates the exam and consultation areas, patients can feel awkward disrobing in a space that still partially functions as a private office. During the consultation, the doctor's personal items, such as photos, are often in sight. Since not every consultation requires an exam, designating a space for this distinct function means there will be periods when it is expensively equipped but not used. There are also periods when doctors need to work in a private space, so neither consultations nor exams could occur during these times.

Exam Room for the Near Future

The exam room of the near future will be more technically advanced and technology-integrated. It will be designed for complete flexibility, with no fixed equipment or furnishings except the sink. It will have distinct zones, and supplies will be provided on a just-in-time basis.

This prototype will provide an egalitarian setting for consultations and emphasize the sharing of information via all available media—from magazines, FAQ sheets, and brochures that are displayed on wall-mounted racks to a smart mobile cart that can be moved near the patient to stream vitals directly into an electronic health record system. A computer and monitor are also integrated into the consult area.

Modular wall systems will provide the flexibility to easily combine or subdivide exam room areas of the clinic module. They will afford acoustical privacy, but be thinner than fixed walls and thus allow for more space within the exam room. Proper hand hygiene practices will be recorded by a smart sink that also has a motion sensor for hands-free operation and water conservation (fig. 6-11).

Exam Room Prototypes

During the preliminary programming and conceptual design phase of a clinic project, design professionals often review a series of exam room prototypes with clinic clients in order to set priorities for the space allocation and layout, furnishings, equipment, and other key features.[12]

Separate Care Provider and Patient Zones

The following prototypes all separate the physician zone from the patient/partners-in-care zone to some extent. They vary in size, flexibility, and degree of visual privacy provided.

Exam Room H

A reverse-swing door provides visual privacy when a patient is on the exam table, which is oriented to face away from the door. The caregiver can enter the room and directly access the workstation without crossing in front of the patient. However, the provider must pass by the patient and family members to reach the sink. This exam room is at the lower end of the average size range, providing just less than 100 square feet of space within its walls (fig. 6-12).

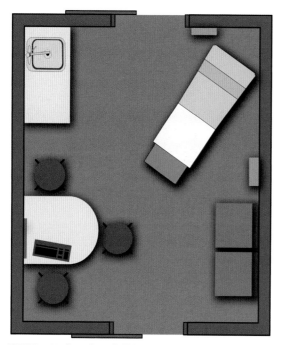

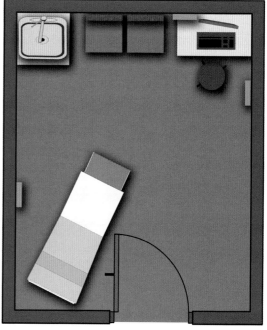

FIGURE 6-11: Exam Room L. This exam room has begun to be implemented at a number of healthcare locations. It is well suited for the on-stage/off-stage planning concept. Some locations have allowed two sliding doors. However, many code officials will require one swinging door on the patient-access side. Image courtesy of Hammel, Green and Abrahamson, Inc.

FIGURE 6-12: Exam Room H. This is a variation of the most common exam room design that exists. The variation switches the location of the caregiver workstation and the patient seating area for more efficient access by the provider. Image courtesy of Hammel, Green and Abrahamson, Inc.

Exam Room B

Floor space is allocated for a mobile supply cart that can be custom-stocked according to the needs of the care provider using this room on a specific day. A privacy curtain blocks a direct view of the exam table from the entry door and also allows partners-in-care to remain present during the dressing periods or physical examination without compromising patient privacy. To maximize flexibility, the sink is the only fixed element in the exam room (fig. 6-13).

Exam Room C

The physician can walk directly to the care provider's work zone at the back of this exam room without having to cross between the patient and partners-in-care zone. The sink and desk are the only fixed elements in the room. The door swing compromises visual privacy (fig. 6-14).

Exam Room D

A curtain allows for privacy from the entry door and from partners-in-care seating area during clothes changing and the physical exam. The physician must cross in front of the patient and family members to reach the workstation and sink (fig. 6-15).

Exam Room E

A bench provides seating for more than one person or a patient who needs more space. The physician's workstation is close to the entry door for

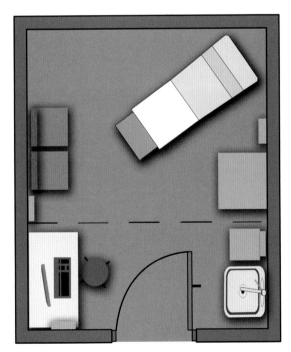

FIGURE 6-13: Exam Room B. This exam room design locates the provider work surface closest to the door. The provider uses a hand sanitizer station right inside the door upon entering. The sink would only be used when the door is closed.   Image courtesy of Hammel, Green and Abrahamson, Inc.

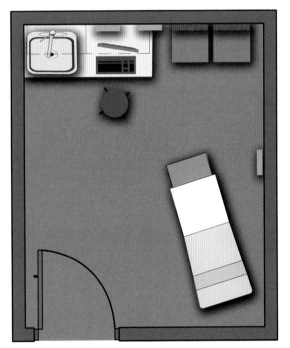

FIGURE 6-14: Exam Room C. This exam room design provides for direct access to the sink for the provider when entering the room. The door swing is standard, which improves the flexibility of room usage.   Image courtesy of Hammel, Green and Abrahamson, Inc.

easy access. The sink is the only fixed element in the exam room to maximize flexibility for future changes. Supplies are stored in an overhead cabinet (fig. 6-16).

Exam Room F

By moving the bench closer to the desk in the care provider's work area, sufficient space can be made for mobile medical equipment or for temporary storage of assisted devices. The patient zone is easily accessed upon entry into the exam room. The sink is still rather close to the entry door (fig. 6-17).

Overlapping Care Provider and Patient/Family Zones

The care provider, patient, and partners-in-care zones overlap in the following prototypes, but their configurations, size and design features vary.

Exam Room G

The physician can pass directly to the workstation at the back of this exam room without having to cross through the patient zone. Care providers must, however, walk past the partners-in-care seating area and through the patient zone to reach the sink and waste receptacle. The sink is the only fixed element in the room. The combination of a reverse-swing door and the orientation of the exam table provide visual privacy during the exam (fig. 6-18).

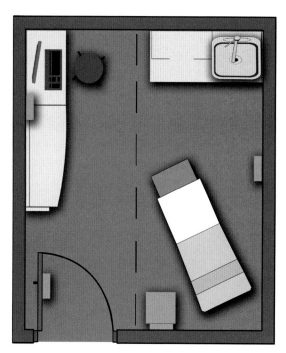

FIGURE 6-15: Exam Room D. The table is oriented for privacy, which is enhanced by the cubicle curtain. A fixed bench is designed for patients, with storage of gowns and supplies below.   Image courtesy of Hammel, Green and Abrahamson, Inc.

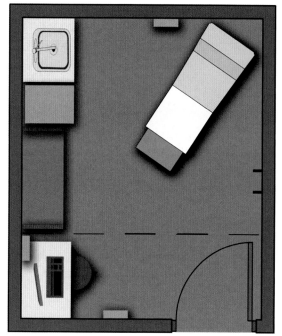

FIGURE 6-16: Exam Room E. The provider workstation is located immediately inside the door. A privacy curtain provides an area for a family member or interpreter during an exam. The sink is located to support the provider during the exam portion of the patient visit.   Image courtesy of Hammel, Green and Abrahamson, Inc.

Exam Room I

The physician must cross in front of the patient and family to gain access to the workstation and charting area. There is less privacy for the patient when the entry door is open. The sink and waste receptacle are near the door to facilitate proper hand hygiene practices (fig. 6-19).

Exam Room J

A combination of a reverse door-swing and the orientation of the exam table provides visual privacy for the patient. The sink is located close to the door for convenient access when entering the room and from the exam table. The patient zone is at the furthest corner, which provides extra storage space for strollers or assist devices (fig. 6-20).

Exam Room K

The provider work area is closest to the door in this example. The sink is also adjacent to the entry door for good hand hygiene practices. The exam table is visible upon entering the room. The patient area is private and at the back of the room. The provider workstation is arranged to permit more conversation with the patient, and the computer monitor is mounted on the wall for visibility to both the patient and provider (fig. 6-21).

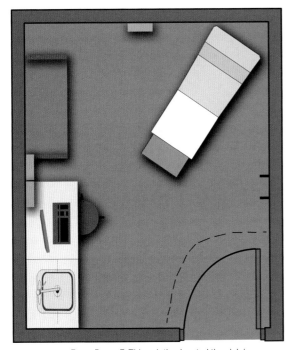

FIGURE 6-17: Exam Room F. This solution located the sink immediately inside the door for providers to wash their hands. The workstation is adjacent to the sink and the patient seating area. There is more patient space in the back of the room to accommodate strollers, assist devices, and the like. Image courtesy of Hammel, Green and Abrahamson, Inc.

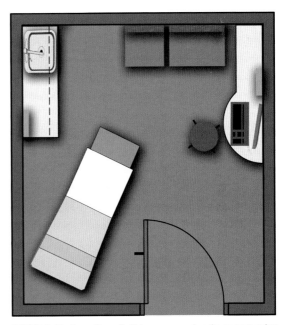

FIGURE 6-18: Exam Room G. This exam room has the reverse swing for privacy, but also provides easy access for providers. The desk has a curved shape so that the provider can sit face-to-face with the patient. Image courtesy of Hammel, Green and Abrahamson, Inc.

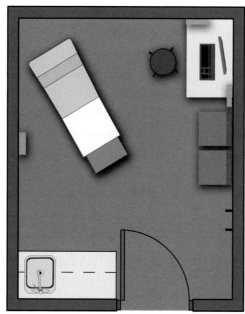

FIGURE 6-19: Exam Room I. This design includes the reverse swing door, which provides some privacy; however, the sink is behind the door. The provider can move easily from the workstation to the exam table. Image courtesy of Hammel, Green and Abrahamson, Inc.

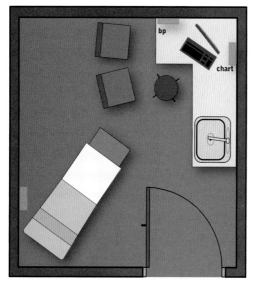

FIGURE 6-20: Exam Room J. This design provides a comfortable consulting environment where both the provider and patient can view the monitor together. Image courtesy of Hammel, Green and Abrahamson, Inc.

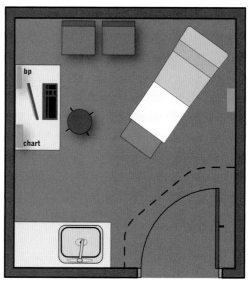

FIGURE 6-21: Exam Room K. The patient zone is more private in this example. The provider can speak face to face with the patient and partners-in-care whether they are on the exam table or in the chairs. Image courtesy of Hammel, Green and Abrahamson, Inc.

Project Examples

The following projects illustrate how design professionals have used prototypes as a reference for developing exam room designs customized to meet the specific needs of clinic clients.

■ BETH ISRAEL DEACONESS MEDICAL CENTER (BIDMC)
Boston, Massachusetts

BIDMC designed a 30,000-square-foot facility in approximately one month. The approach was to facilitate a Lean Process Improvement (see chapter 2) series of workshops called a 3P. This is an acronym for people plus process plus product. BIDMC started by collecting data on their current state—volumes, utilization, staffing—and used this data to develop the strategic program. One of the first challenges that came out of the strategic programming was that the new facility BIDMC had leased had less space than the required square footage in light of the medical center's current operating practices and expected growth projections. With concepts from an Exam Room of the Future model, the user groups began to define the exam room. In this presentation, the potential of a larger exam room that would actually net less or equal space usage in the overall medical office building (MOB) was discussed. The exam rooms were also designed to accommodate a larger population, for example, an elderly patient with multiple family members

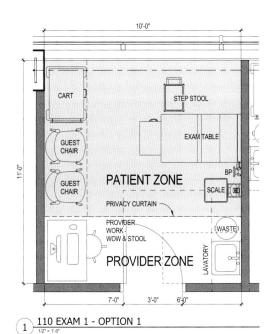

1 **110 EXAM 1 - OPTION 1**
   1/2" = 1'-0"

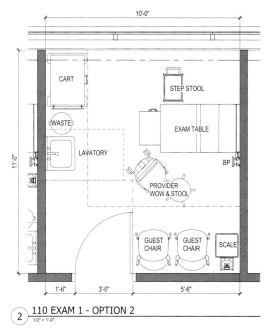

2 **110 EXAM 1 - OPTION 2**
   1/2" = 1'-0"

FIGURE 6-22: 110-square-foot Exam Room 1—Option 1 and 110-square-foot Exam Room 1—Option 2. These are the 110-square-foot exam rooms approved by the team. Option 1 has the sink right inside the door, with the provider workstation across from it. A cubicle curtain separates the consult zone from the exam zone, so that a family member or interpreter can be present during the exam. Option 2 relies on a workstation on wheels (WOW) for documentation. The guest chairs are right inside the door, and the sink is at the foot of the exam table. Image courtesy of Hammel, Green and Abrahamson, Inc.

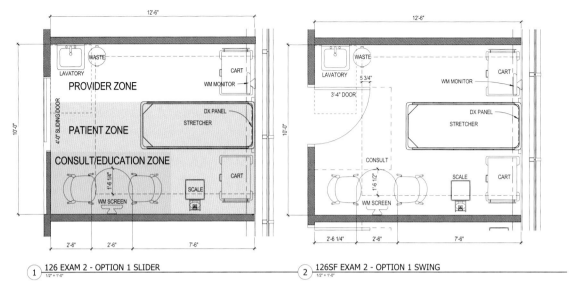

FIGURE 6-23: 126-square-foot Exam Room 2 Option 1 Slider and 126-square-foot Exam Room 2—Option 1 Swing. These are the 126-square-foot exam rooms approved by the team. One version of this exam room has a sliding door, and the other has a swing door. The sink is close to the door, although with the swing door it is more difficult to access as you enter the room. The consult space is arranged for face-to-face interaction between patient and provider.   Image courtesy of Hammel, Green and Abrahamson, Inc.

attending the visit. It also has space for consultation and a private exam through the use of a curtain. More activities are occurring in the exam room, which also increases utilization of the department gross square footage (DGSF). The groups (by department) assessed the traditional exam room versus the larger universal option. They mocked up each exam room concept with all the equipment, doors, chairs, etc. (see chapter 3, "Visualization Tools and Mock-ups"), to physically see and feel the difference in each of the room sizes. After each user group had had an opportunity to tour all of the prototypes, a Plus/Delta session was conducted. This session listed the pros (plus) and cons (deltas—areas to improve) of each room. The results were recorded, and the mock-ups were modified accordingly, taking the best ideas from each (figs. 6-22, 6-23).

◼ HENNEPIN COUNTY MEDICAL CENTER
Minneapolis, Minnesota

The design team toured several clinics and reviewed prototypical exam rooms and clinic module features to arrive at the specific exam room design that this public healthcare organization will use in one of its clinics. The design features a work surface in the shape of a semicircle that is large enough to accommodate a laptop computer, bench seating for patients and partners-in-care, sufficient space for multiple care team members to treat a patient on the exam table or participate in a group consult, and a reverse door-swing to eliminate the need for a privacy curtain.

Depending on how a specific exam room will be used, supplies can either be provided via a

TABLE 7-1: EXAM ROOM COMPARISON

Exam Prototype	sq ft	Patient Zone	Exam Table	Sink Location	Privacy Curtain	Door Swing
Exam Room A	98	Front	Front, Left Side	Back		Reverse
Exam Room B	110	Back	Back, Right Side	Front	Divide Room	
Exam Room C	110	Back	Front, Right Side	Back		
Exam Room D	110	Front	Front, Right Side	Back	Divide Room	
Exam Room E	110	Middle	Back, Right Side	Back	Divide Room	
Exam Room F	110	Back	Back, Right Side	Front	Around Door	
Exam Room G	90	Back	Front, Left Side	Back		Reverse
Exam Room H	110	Back	Front, Left Side	Back		Reverse
Exam Room I	114	Middle	Back, Left Side	Front		Reverse
Exam Room J	110	Back	Front, Left Side	Middle		Reverse
Exam Room K	110	Back	Back, Right Side	Front		
Exam Room L	120	Front	Back, Right Side	Back		Sliding
Exam Room M (Split)	130	Front	Separate (Back), Left Side	Back	N/A (Wall)	
Exam Room N (Three Part)	290	Front	Separate (Back), Right Side	Back	N/A (Wall)	
Exam Room O (ADA Bariatric)	132	Front	Back, Right Side	Back	Divide Room	
Exam Room P (Universally-Accessible)	132	Back	Middle, Left Side	Back		
Exam Room Q (Group)	480	Front	Back, Right Side	Back	N/A (Wall)	
Exam Room R (Group)	623	Front	Back, Left Side	Front	N/A (Wall)	
Exam Room S (Group)	240	N/A	N/A	Back Entry		

Courtesy of Hammel, Green and Abrahamson, Inc.

mobile procedure cart or stored in the room in wall-mounted containers and cabinetry. The door width accommodates wheelchair and scooter traffic.

Summary

Increasingly, exam rooms are becoming the place where the majority of tasks are completed in a clinic. A broader range of professional and support staff are using improved, more mobile technology to bring an expanded range of care services to patients in exam rooms rather than requiring that patients move to multiple locations. At the same time, tasks such as triage, registration, basic assessments and prescriptions, self-care recommendations, and scheduling are being completed outside of the clinic to allow more time for and improve the quality of consults.

The increase in the size and diversity of the patient population in the United States, shifts in provider mix and staffing strategies, and legislation that mandates the level of privacy (HIPAA) and accessibility (ADA) that health-care facilities must achieve have all led to a need for more intensely utilized, multipurpose exam rooms that can be used by a wide range of healthcare professionals and allied staffs (table 7-1). On average, design professionals have responded by creating exam rooms that are larger, more standardized, more flexible, and more comfortable.

As the exam room continues to be redefined and the options for its location expanded beyond the walls of the traditional clinic to include retail settings, schools, workplaces, and other sites, design professionals will be called upon to develop more prototypes to meet the ever-changing needs of clinics and the patients they serve.

GARY NYBERG

Notes

1. Thomas G. Pickering, William Gerin, and Amy R. Schwartz, "What Is the White-Coat Effect and How Should It Be Measured?" *Blood Pressure Monitoring* 7, no. 6 (2002): 293–300.

2. Armstrong, "High CAC Ceilings," http://www.armstrong.com/common/c2002/content/files/38240.pdf.

3. SPARC, Mayo Clinic, *From Foamcore to Function: 30 Days Of Prototyping Concepts for the Outpatient Practice. In Real Time. In Real Space. With Real People* (Rochester, MN: Mayo Clinic, n.d.), available at http://nexus.som.yale.edu/design-mayo/sites/nexus.som.yale.edu.design-mayo/files/imce_imagepool/Outpatient%20Lab%20Brochure.pdf.

4. http://www.criindex.com/home.

5. http://www.fullspectromsolutions.com/natural.

6. U.S. Department of Health and Human Services, "Access to Medical Care for Individuals with Mobility Disabilities" (July 2010), http://www.ada.gov/medcare_mobility_ta/medcare_ta.htm.

7. Ward R. Mann and Joanne Sloboch, "Computers in the Exam Room–Friend or Foe?" *Permanente Journal* 8, no. 4 (2004): 49–51.

8. Mark Isken, "Outpatient Clinics: HCM 540—Healthcare Operations Management" (presentation, Oakland University School of Business, 2006), http://www.sba.oakland.edu/faculty/isken/hcm540/Session09_ClinicOperations/HCM540_OPClinics.ppt.

9. Julka R. Almquist, Caroline Kelly, Joyce Bromberg, et al., "Consultation Room Design and the Clinical Encounter," *Health Environments Research & Design Journal* 3 (2009): 41–78.

10. SPARC, Mayo Clinic.

11. "leeroy1981," "What is Anti-Ligature?" (slideshare presentation, posted October 14, 2012), http://www.slideshare.net/leeroy1981/what-is-anti-ligature.

12. Kara Freihoefer, Gary Nyberg, and Christine Vickery, "Clinic Exam Room Design: Present and Future, Abstract," *Health Environments Research & Design Journal* 6 (2013): pp. 138–56.

Select Bibliography

Almquist, Julka R., Caroline Kelly, Joyce Bromberg, Sandra C. Bryant, Teresa J. H. Christianso, and Victor M. Montori. "Consultation Room Design and the Clinical Encounter." *Health Environments Research & Design Journal* 3 (2009): 41–78.

Freihoefer, Kara, Gary Nyberg, and Christine Vickery. "Clinic Exam Room Design: Present and Future, Abstract." *Health Environments Research & Design Journal* 6 (2013): 138–56.

Malone, Eileen, Julie R. Mann-Dooks, and Joseph Strauss. *Evidence-Based Design: Application in the MHS*. Falls Church, VA: U.S. Army Health Facility Planning Agency, Planning & Programming Division, 2007.

Shortliffe, Edward H., and Marsden S. Blois. *The Computer Meets Medicine and Biology: Emergence of a Discipline*. Bethesda, Maryland: American Medical Informatics Association, 2006.

Overview

Political decisions and other factors will shape the design of clinics in the future. Looking backward long enough to learn from the past, architects, interior designers, and other building industry professionals can develop a deep understanding of the history of care and how the need for environmental awareness can shape the future. Medical buildings today must meet immediate and long-term future needs.

This is an especially opportune moment for reviewing the historic interplay between politics and healthcare because healthcare reform is still in the early phases of implementation in the United States, and it is substantially altering the way that medical services are being delivered.

As has been the case in the past, politics and healthcare are clearly influencing each other, with the relationship ranging from synergistic to symbiotic or adversarial, depending on the specific issue at hand.

1600s–1700s

The first form of government healthcare starts in 1636 when the Pilgrims of the Plymouth colony vote to provide care for disabled soldiers, supported by the colony. During the Revolutionary War, the Continental Congress provides pensions to disabled veterans. By 1811 the first domiciliary is authorized by the federal government, providing care for wounded soldiers and veterans.

1800s

Abraham Lincoln in his second inaugural pronounces: "To care for him who shall have borne the battle and for his widow and his orphan," President Lincoln makes a commitment that all the veterans will be cared for.[1] During his term these benefits are extended to widows and their dependents. After the Civil War, the states provide care through domiciliaries.

During this century the prevailing belief is that the sick should be treated at home and paupers treated in hospitals. Public policy reinforces this belief. The post–Civil War era brought advances in medicine and the treatment of diseases. During the late 1800s a more central and organized medicine takes shape in urban areas of the United States.

Politics

Throughout the 1800s, the U.S. government takes no action to subsidize voluntary funds or make insurance for the sick compulsory. Instead, it leaves these decisions to the states, and the states leave these to private and voluntary programs.

The Roman Catholic Communities of Nuns is a key group that provides healthcare services for those who lack the means to pay for it. These sisters believe it is their mission to care for the poor and sick. By 1875, there are 75 Catholic hospitals in the United States. By the beginning of the 20th century this number nears 400. Over time, the Roman Catholic Church becomes one of the largest non-government providers of healthcare services in the world.[2]

Healthcare

By the latter part of the 19th century, advances made by medical professionals and improvements in hospital facilities lead more members of the general populace to seek care at inpatient facilities. The field of medicine is increasingly viewed as scientific and those who want to practice it are required to obtain a standard level of education. Thus, from the late 1800s onward, the education of healthcare professionals blends firsthand experience with scientific research.

In the 1870s, for example, the State University of New York's (SUNY) medical school becomes the first in the nation to be founded within a hospital so bedside training can be integrated into the medical students' curriculum. In 1893, Johns Hopkins University's Medical School revolutionizes physicians' formal training by stressing scientific methods and combining laboratory research with professional practice.

San Francisco sees several healthcare facilities open in the 1800s. The California Pacific Medical Center has its start through the efforts of leaders of the German immigrant community. The German General Benevolent Society leads in constructing a hospital between 1856 and 1858. In 1871 the Episcopal Diocese of California opens St. Luke's Hospital. In 1875 the Pacific Dispensary for Women and Children is founded, in large part through the efforts of Charlotte Amanda Blake Brown. It is a facility for women and children run by women.

Florence Nightingale (1820–1910)

The spread of infection is also a major focus in the work of nurse Florence Nightingale, who believes that disease arises spontaneously in dirty and poorly ventilated places.[3] Although these beliefs prove to be only partially accurate, they make sense because hospital wards at the time have more than 100 beds with multiple patients in each ward. They lack sufficient light, are poorly ventilated, and are unsanitary. Infectious patients are not properly isolated.

Nightingale's work leads to improvements in hygiene and healthier interior environments. She also advises on the development of district nursing and the establishment of a training program in Liverpool, England.

Nightingale and her nephew, Sir Douglas Galton of the Royal Engineers, test some of her theories by developing the pavilion design that Galton then uses in the design of the Royal Herbert Hospital. Each ward in this hospital connects to a central corridor to optimize access to natural light and ventilation. Each ward also has a large window at its end to provide patients with exterior views. St. Thomas Hospital in London and Johns Hopkins Hospital in Baltimore also use this plan.

1900s

Two other women help frame healthcare in the San Francisco area. Alta Bates opens the Alta Bates Sanatorium, now the Alta Bates Summit Medical Center, in 1905. She does so with credit from local merchants and $100 cash. Plans for the facility come from her father. Elizabeth Mills Reid, a prominent Millbrae community member, opens a six-bed facility in 1908.

By 1900 several rural areas begin to organize and construct hospitals.

The first decade of the 20th century is considered by many historians to mark the beginning of organized medicine. This is a time when people, typically more affluent, donated time and money to develop hospitals.

Theda Clark is the daughter of Charles Clark, who helps found Kimberly-Clark Corporation. Charles Clark is also a town mayor and later a member of Congress for Wisconsin. Theda is also a community activist who helps build the Neenah, Wisconsin, public library. She dies just after childbirth, leaving a $96,000 bequest. Her family uses this money and an additional $30,000 to build the Theda Clark Memorial Hospital that opens in Neenah in 1909.[4]

In 1917 a new system that includes insurance, disability compensation, and rehabilitation comes into being. These services are administered by three different agencies. In 1930 Congress authorizes the president to consolidate these services, and the Veterans Administration (VA) is created. The VA currently has more than 152 hospitals, 800 clinics, 126 nursing homes, and 35 domiciliaries.[5] In 1918, just after a devastating flu epidemic, Sacramento doctors and a civic leader come together to build a new hospital to meet the needs of the city. The hospital, one of California's finest, opens in 1923. Another first comes in 1937, when Sutter Health opens a satellite hospital, the first institution in California and the second west of the Mississippi River to operate more than one facility.

During the first few decades of the 20th century, there is a shift in the design of hospitals from a sanatorium design to a hospital design. Most sanatoriums are not built for medical care. Many of them are converted from large homes, old schools, or public buildings into facilities where patients with communicable diseases like tuberculosis are treated. In some cases, small sanatoriums of four to eight beds are constructed and become the first hospitals in the community. Over the next 40 years, the older buildings will be surrounded by newer wings to form what we recognize as modern hospitals.

Politics

The 20th century opens with the rise of the Progressive Era, during which reformers strive to improve social conditions for the working class. President Theodore Roosevelt supports "social insurance" on a personal basis because he believes that a country cannot be strong if its citizens are sick and poor. However, most of the reform that occurs is outside of the public realm. For example, railroad companies develop extensive employee medical programs.[6]

Healthcare

The American Medical Association (AMA) becomes a national force after consolidating the support of state and local associations into a single national organization. Between 1900 and 1910, its membership grows from 8,000 to 70,000 physicians—approximately half of the doctors then practicing medicine in the United States.

Surgery becomes common for removing tumors, infected tonsils, and inflamed appendixes, as well as for addressing issues of gynecological health. Public health nursing is now widespread after Lillian Wald pioneers the idea of stationing nurses in public schools to help increase school attendance.

Although the charitable missions of most hospitals survive, doctors are no longer expected to provide free services for all hospital patients. Like other buildings, healthcare facilities are transformed by the use of electric lights, elevators, central heating and ventilation, and new processes for cleaning and deodorizing interior spaces.

Doctors identify the first case of a healthy disease carrier in Irish immigrant and cook Mary Mallon, who is later labeled Typhoid Mary because she spreads this disease to dozens of other people who live in the households where she has worked.

George Soper, an engineer for the New York City Department of Health, identifies Mallon as the disease carrier and has her committed to an isolation center in the Bronx. She is released in 1910, with the proviso that she will never accept employment that involves handling food. She breaks this promise and is thought to cause typhoid outbreaks at a sanatorium in Newfoundland, New Jersey; and at Sloane Maternity Hospital in New York City. She had worked as a cook at both of these locations. She is returned to North Brother Island, where she spends the rest of her life.[7]

How a person can infect others without succumbing to a disease remains a mystery for decades. In 2013, however, scientists determine that the *Salmonella* bacteria that causes typhoid fever can hide in immune cells known as macrophages and "hack" into their metabolism to survive without the infected person developing symptoms.[8]

1910s

Once Woodrow Wilson is elected president (1912) and the United States is drawn into the First World War (1917), momentum for providing sickness insurance for those in need wavers and, ultimately, dies. Germany has compulsory sickness insurance and, thus, "German socialist insurance" is denounced as inconsistent with American values.[9]

Politics

In 1913, the American Association for Labor Legislation (AALL) holds its first national conference to address the issue of "social insurance." Its leaders draft a model bill in 1915 that limits health insurance coverage to the working class and the poor. This coverage includes paying for the services of care providers and other hospital-related expenses as well as sick pay, maternity benefits, and a death benefit of up to $50 to cover funeral expenses. Costs for this program are to be shared by workers, employers, and the states.

Initially, members of the AMA support this bill. In 1916, the AMA's board appoints a committee to work with the AALL to promote this legislation. However, when a number of state medical societies express opposition and disagreements arise over how to pay physicians, the AMA's leadership withdraws its support.

At the same time, Samuel Gompers, the president of the American Federation of Labor (AFL), criticizes compulsory health insurance "as an unnecessary paternalistic reform that would create a system of state supervision over people's health." AFL leaders are concerned that a government-based insurance system could weaken unions by taking over their role of providing social benefits to workers.[10]

The commercial insurance industry adds its opposition to the discussion. In response to a general fear among working-class people that they will "suffer a pauper's burial," insurance companies have already been offering policies that pay death benefits and cover funeral expenses. The AALL's health insurance plan also covers funeral expenses, and this creates unwanted competition for the association. The national debate over compulsory health insurance is suspended and does not resume until the 1930s.[11]

Healthcare

U.S. hospitals are now considered modern scientific institutions where cleanliness is highly valued. The need for private rooms begins to increase, although wards with many beds are still commonplace. The prevalent cause of death remains contagious diseases. The 1918 flu outbreak kills more than 600,000 people. It does not completely subside until the 1950s.

After Italian researchers discover and demonstrate how malaria parasites are transmitted to humans by infected mosquitoes (1899), a medical team led by Dr. William Crawford Gorgas, the chief sanitary officer for the Panama Canal project, applies this knowledge to develop a mosquito control program in Panama. Standing water is drained or has insecticide and oil added to it, adult mosquitoes are collected, and government buildings and workers' quarters are screened-in to keep mosquitoes out. As a prophylactic measure, quinine is given to workers.

This multipronged disease-control strategy substantially reduces malaria-related illnesses and deaths among canal workers. In 1906, there are more than 26,000 workers assigned to this project, and more than 21,000 of them are hospitalized for malaria at some point. By 1912, approximately 5,600 of the 50,000 canal workers fall sick with this disease.

In 1914, Congress approves funds for the Public Health Service (USPHS) to control malaria in the

United States. The USPHS establishes malaria control activities around military bases in the South, where this disease is a significant health threat.[12]

1920s

During this decade, there is limited government or citizen attention to the matter of health insurance. The fact that the relative cost of medical care begins to rise, however, does shift the emphasis of the public discourse to creating a social insurance program that would cover the cost of medical care rather than the loss of wages to sickness. The medical profession gains prestige, and a rise in physicians' salaries accompanies this increase in influence. The decade ends with the onset of the Great Depression.

Politics

The general attitude of complacency toward politics means that there is no strong, broad effort to reform health insurance during this period. There is some progress toward improving access for portions of the population with specific needs.

For example, in 1921, Congress passes the Sheppard-Towner Maternity and Infancy Protection Act, marking the first federal program specifically created to serve women and children. At this time, the vast majority of women (80 percent) receive no prenatal advice or professional care. This, combined with poverty, leads to high rates of infant and maternal mortality. The act expires after eight years but is not renewed. During the time the act is in force, infant and maternal death rates fall by 16 percent and 12 percent, respectively.[13]

Healthcare

Although scientists and others had experimented with the phenomenon of "anti-biosis"[14] ("against life") in the 19th century and some folk traditions used fungi and mosses for wound treatment earlier than that, no progress is made in developing a substance that can be used for medical treatment until 1928, when Alexander Fleming accidentally discovers penicillin. Although this is one of the most important discoveries for the fight against infectious diseases, 20 years pass until penicillin is commonly used. During World War II, penicillin will save many lives on the battlefield and in the hospital. This success prompts scientists to search for other microorganisms that can be used to combat infections.

In 1926, the Committee on the Cost of Medical Care (CCMC) meets to address concerns over the cost and distribution of medical care. This private group includes 50 economists, physicians, and public health specialists, as well as major interest groups. The CCMC's research reveals that a general need for more medical care exists. Its findings are published in 26 research volumes and 15 reports over a period of five years. It recommends that more national resources be allocated for medical care and that premiums from voluntary health insurance be used as the primary means for covering these costs.

In 1929, a group of teachers arranges for Baylor Hospital in Dallas, Texas, to provide room, board, and specific medical services for a predetermined monthly cost. This agreement becomes the forerunner for Blue Cross health plans.

1930s

In the 1930s, the public's focus shifts to expanding access because for most workers, the cost of medical care is now higher than the wages lost due to illness.

Politics

The Great Depression begins, and this further limits people's ability to afford medical care.

After being sworn into office in early 1933, President Franklin Roosevelt begins to draft social security legislation. Initially, this includes publicly funded healthcare programs, but he later removes these in response to organized opposition from groups such as the AMA. The Committee on Economic Security also fears that including public health insurance in the bill will weaken its chances of passing.

In 1935, President Roosevelt signs the Social Security Act into law. It includes programs for old-age assistance and retirement benefits, unemployment compensation, aid for dependent children and the disabled, and maternal and child welfare. The monthly benefit ranges from $10 to $85, remaining in this range until the 1950s.

Although some view the Social Security programs as necessary humanitarian measures, others worry that the programs will discourage people from working, because they can collect unemployment insurance, or from saving, because of the old-age and survivors benefits. The act also disregards sickness, which is the main cause of joblessness at this time.

A second push for national health insurance (NHI) comes from the Tactical Committee on Medical Care. This time, progress is stonewalled by southern Democrats, who align with Republicans to oppose the government expansion that passing any additional New Deal social reforms would require. The Wagner Bill, or National Health Act of 1939, which supports a national health program funded by federal grants to states, is introduced in the Senate. It dies in committee.

During World War II, government-mandated wage freezes prevent employers from using monetary compensation to woo workers during a labor shortage. The Internal Revenue Service addresses this with Section 104 of the Revenue Act of 1939, which allows companies to count benefits of up to 5 percent of the value of an employee's wages as nontaxable compensation. These include workers' compensation, as well as accident and health insurance. This ruling later becomes permanent (1954) and helps lay the foundation for the present-day insurance system in the United States.[15]

Healthcare

Individual hospitals begin to offer their own insurance programs. The first of these is Blue Cross, which offers private health insurance in locations across the United States. Groups of hospitals and physicians' groups, such as Blue Shield, also begin to sell health insurance policies to employers, who offer these to their staff and collect the premiums.

During the 1930s and continuing through World War II, tens of thousands of workers are hired by Kaiser Shipyards in Richmond, California, to meet the demand for Liberty ships and aircraft carriers. Henry Kaiser, owner of the shipyards, faces the challenge of providing healthcare for an enormous workforce, which ultimately peaks at 90,000 employees (many of whom were in poor health prior to starting work for Kaiser).

In 1945, he forms an association with Dr. Sidney Garfield, founder of the prepayment form of compensation for medical services, to develop a contract under which physicians agree to bypass the traditional fee-for-service system. Instead, they are paid a regular fee to meet all the medical needs of Kaiser's employees. After the war ends, Kaiser opens up this program to the public by forming a nonprofit organization called Kaiser Permanente. Within the first decade of its existence, enrollment surpasses 300,000 members in Northern California.

In 1935 and 1936, the U.S. Public Health Service conducts the first national survey designed to assess the health of the U.S. population and identify some of the underlying social and economic factors affecting health status. The survey shows that the health status of Americans is poor, despite declining mortality rates. It also demonstrates a strong link between poverty and illness.

Residency and specialized training are on the rise for healthcare professionals. Within a decade, 12 of the 15 specialty-certifying boards require at least three years of residency training. This helps to establish the basic components of the medical educational system in the United States. Students attend four years of college, then four years of medical school, followed by completion of an internship and a residency program. They take board exams as they progress through these steps.

1940s

Politics

In 1943, U.S. senators Wagner, Murray, and Dingell introduce a bill that proposes changes to Social Security and includes provisions for universal, compulsory health insurance that would be funded by a payroll tax. There is tremendous opposition to this bill. It generates extensive national debates and is never passed by Congress—even though it is reintroduced during every session for the next 14 years.

Harry Truman begins his first term as president in 1945 by proposing a broad restructuring of the healthcare industry that would include mandatory coverage and more hospitals. It would also double the number of nurses and doctors. This plan differs from President Roosevelt's plan of advocating for universal health insurance that serves all classes of society. FDR's plan separately addressed the provision of medical services for the needy. Truman's plan also drops the funeral benefit.

The AMA criticizes Truman's plan as "socialized medicine" at the onset of the Cold War, when the American people are especially afraid that communism will take hold and spread across the United States as it had in Eastern Europe. The chairman of the House committee refuses to hold hearings. Senior Senator Robert Taft says he thinks the plan came right out of the Soviet constitution, and he walks out of hearings in the Senate. The American Hospital Association also opposes Truman's plan.[16]

In 1946, the Communicable Disease Center (CDC) is established based on the success that the Malaria Control in War Areas efforts have had in keeping the southeastern United States free of this disease during World War II. Initially, the CDC focuses on preventing malaria from spreading by spraying areas with the pesticide dichlorodiphenyltrichloroethane (DDT), which first becomes available in 1943. By 1949, malaria no longer poses a significant health problem in the United States. However, improper use of DDT will later be found to pose health risks for humans.

Based on evidence of the pesticide's declining benefits and its environmental and toxicological effects, the U.S. Department of Agriculture takes regulatory action to prohibit many of DDT's uses in the late 1950s and early 1960s. In 1972, the Environmental Protection Agency issues a cancellation order for DDT based on adverse environmental and health effects of its use.

CDC founder Dr. Joseph Mountain extends the center's responsibilities to include other communicable diseases. By 1980, this agency evolves into the Centers for Disease Control and becomes one of the major operating divisions of the U.S. Department of Health and Human Services.

The 1946 Hospital Survey and Construction Act (also known as the Hill-Burton Act), provides states with grants to support the construction of new hospitals. From July 1947 through mid-1971, over $33 billion in funds are distributed for the construction and modernization of healthcare facilities.[17]

In 1949, after winning an upset victory over New York governor Thomas Dewey and being reelected president, Harry Truman includes national health insurance in his "Fair Deal" plan. Polls show that 74 percent of the public favors Truman's plan. More than half of those surveyed support some form of national health insurance. However, no progress is made on this issue because of continued Congressional opposition to expansion of the social welfare state.[18]

Instead, the U.S. healthcare system evolves into one with private insurance available for those who can afford it (which includes those whose costs are partially covered by their employers) and public welfare services for the poor, elderly, and disabled. Prepaid group healthcare begins.

In 1948, the United Nations establishes the World Health Organization (WHO) as a special agency with authority for international health matters. Its priorities are to prevent and control disease, develop equitable health systems based on primary care, and promote health for individuals and communities. WHO also publishes practical manuals, handbooks, and training materials for specific categories of health workers.

Healthcare

In this decade, the number of Americans with private health insurance increases from 20.6 million to 142.3 million based on a combination of increased competition, growing demand (the baby boom), and governmental policies.[19]

In 1945, water fluoridation is tested in four communities in the United States and Canada. The success of these tests in reducing tooth decay leads to broader implementation of fluoridation for drinking water. Over the next few decades, fluoride-containing products, such as gels, solutions, and pastes, are developed for topical use.

After World War II ends, the Supreme Court upholds a ruling that employee benefits can be included in collective bargaining negotiations. Labor unions focus on expanding health coverage as well as on increasing wages. Nonunion employers realize that they must offer health insurance as a benefit to remain competitive in a tight labor market. Thus, when health insurance first becomes available on a mass basis across the nation, it is driven by private-sector business decisions that are supported by public policies.

1950s

By the beginning of this decade, the employment-based health insurance system is firmly in place, and it continues to expand rapidly for the next several decades. While both supply and demand for healthcare services increase, providers continue to be paid on a fee-for-service basis. This enables them to retain substantial control over pricing and to strongly influence regulatory decisions.

Costs and aggregate expenditures for healthcare escalate rapidly, but are not of widespread concern because production, employment levels, and real wages are also increasing. These concurrent trends make it easy to attribute the increase in healthcare costs to investments in scientific research that are yielding medical advances as well as to economic prosperity.

The design of hospitals during this time is in transformation. While there are new hospitals being built, more often it is additions to existing hospitals that are being constructed. Also, mergers are taking place and creating medical centers or multiple campuses. Until this time, it is common for a hospital to provide inpatient (admitted) and outpatient services. This is noted by Theda Clark Memorial Hospital's annual report for 1957. It states that the hospital had 6,307 admitted patients, 1,082 births, 6,234 outpatients, and 5,342 operations.[20] Once two hospitals merge, it is typical that one becomes an outpatient facility while the other remains a hospital. After World

War II, this leads to the emergence of the medical office building (MOB).

Politics

In 1958, Rhode Island congressman Aime Forand introduces a proposal to cover hospital costs for people who receive Social Security benefits. Although the AMA launches a massive campaign to oppose this plan by presenting it as a threat to the patient-doctor relationship, the terms of this public debate begin to shift because of a strong focus on the needs of the elderly.

Senior citizens provide major grassroots support and force the issue of creating a national health insurance program back onto the national agenda. The AMA counters this by introducing an "eldercare plan," a voluntary insurance plan with broader benefits and physician services. The government responds by expanding its proposed legislation to include the provision that doctors will be paid "usual and customary fees" for the services they provide and hospitals will be compensated on a "cost plus reimbursement" basis. These compromises and concessions later help lead to the Medicare and Medicaid programs being passed into law in the mid-1960s.

Healthcare

In 1952, the U.S. Surgeon General Dr. Leonard A. Scheele reports that the Communicable Disease Center is ready to combat possible biological warfare. While researching how to shorten the time it takes to identify organisms that could be used for this purpose, Dr. William Cherry develops the first practical uses for the fluorescent antibody technique.[21] He identifies the pathogens for salmonellosis, plague, and anthrax. This technique is later applied to research related to rabies, as well as to streptococcal and staphylococcus infections.

Staff members from the CDC investigate an outbreak of polio in Paulding County, Ohio. This leads to the development of the first effective polio vaccine, which is initially used to inoculate children against polio in Pittsburgh, Pennsylvania. Mass immunization follows and this ultimately eradicates polio from the Americas.

Research for the birth control pill begins, but its impact on society is not fully felt until a decade later, when it helps to catalyze the sexual revolution.

Staph infections are a leading cause of healthcare associated infections (HAI). Some strains of this bacterium are of particular concern because they are evolving into superbugs that are resistant to antibiotics. HAI staph infections typically include surgical wound infections, urinary tract infections, bloodstream infections, and pneumonia.[22]

1960s

Since the price of care doubles in the 1950s, people outside of the workforce, particularly the elderly, find it hard to afford health insurance. This leads to the establishment of Medicare and Medicaid programs. The Vietnam War also has a long-term impact on the provision of care, as an especially large percentage of veterans of this conflict (30 percent or more) suffer from what comes to be known as posttraumatic stress disorder.[23] The use of chemical herbicides to defoliate areas or kill enemy crops during this war is later determined to cause chronic illnesses and deadly diseases.

A concern that a shortage of doctors and other medical professionals will arise by the end of the 20th century leads to measures by federal and state governments to expand medical education. The number of doctors who are full-time specialists grows from 55 percent to 69 percent during this period.[24]

Politics

After winning reelection by a landslide, President Lyndon B. Johnson pushes through Congress the legislation that establishes the Medicare and Medicaid programs and signs the bill into law on July 30, 1965. This action further expands the U.S. healthcare market because it makes insurance coverage accessible for millions of Americans who do not have it. These programs also shift the composition of aggregate spending for healthcare services from people paying out of pocket to the government's covering a larger portion of healthcare expenses.

Medicare and Medicaid

Medicare and Medicaid use the fee-for-service compensation model that has become prevalent as a basis for reimbursing care providers. Under this structure, third-party payments become one of the driving forces behind medical inflation because they incentivize medical professionals and healthcare organizations to maximize the quantity rather than optimize the quality of the services they provide.

Part A of the Medicare program covers hospitalization costs for people ages 65 years and older. It is funded by taxes collected from workers in the same way that the federal government does this for the Social Security program. Medicare Part B is designed to win the support of physicians by ensuring that they will receive the "usual and customary fees" for the medical services they provide. The third part of this legislation creates Medicaid, a federal–state program to expand healthcare for the poor.

Fears about the ability of Medicare and Medicaid to succeed persist long after this legislation passed. People wonder if doctors will refuse to see Medicare patients if the "usual and customary fees" are lower than those paid by others or by private health insurance plans.

Other Significant Legislation

Federal support for the creation of health centers begins in 1962 with passage of the Migrant Health Act. This legislation provides funds to cover healthcare services for migrant and seasonal farm workers and their families. Two years later, this effort is expanded to assist other families when the federal Office of Economic Opportunity (OEO) uses its demonstration authority to create the first Neighborhood Health Centers.[25]

In 1963, the Health Professions Educational Assistance Act provides $175 million over a three-year period to match funds that institutions raise to construct facilities for educating physicians, dentists, nurses, and other health professionals.

Social Security amendments passed in 1967 add optional Medicaid categories to provide healthcare for people who are not receiving cash assistance. Medicaid benefits are expanded to cover early and periodic screening as well as diagnostic testing services.

Healthcare

In 1964, the first surgeon general's report that links smoking to lung cancer is released. It states that "cigarette smoking is a health hazard of sufficient importance in the United States to warrant appropriate remedial action."[26] Over the next 50-plus years, periodic reports from the surgeon general move from presenting smoking as an issue of individual and consumer choice to one of epidemiology and public health.

In 1965, Jack Geiger and Count Gibson, physicians at Tufts University in Boston, open the first two community health centers funded by the Economic Opportunity Act of 1964. They establish an innovative care model for community-based primary care that blends social services with medical care and focuses on prevention and patient education. The community health center gradually becomes the dominant model for providing federally funded primary care as part of the U.S. healthcare safety net.

One aspect of community health centers (CHC) that make them unique is that at least 51 percent of all governing board members must be patients who have been treated at the CHC. A sliding-fee scale based on income is used to determine what each patient will be required to pay. By the early 21st century, CHCs provide primary and preventative care to more than 20 million people in the United States and its territories.[27]

Measles Eradication

The CDC announces a national measles eradication campaign in 1967, and within two years this program reduces the incidence of measles by more than 90 percent compared with prevaccine levels.

The Medical Home

In 1967, the American Academy of Pediatrics (AAP) introduces the phrase "medical home" in its *Standard of Child Health Care Manual* and advocates for the creation of a central location for all medical information related to children, especially those with chronic conditions or special needs. The definition of what constitutes a medical home will expand over the next 40 or so years until it evolves into a healthcare delivery model that emphasizes continuity of care and focuses on optimizing health and wellness through all life stages.

1970s

Healthcare costs escalate rapidly, due in part to unexpectedly high Medicare expenditures, "stagflation," rising hospital expenses and profits, and changes in medical care that include greater use of technology, medications, and more

conservative approaches to treatment. American medicine reaches a state of crisis.

The major healthcare-related legislation that passes during this period focuses on containing costs through better operational and management practices. Two major examples of this are the federal Health Maintenance Organization (HMO) Act of 1973 and the National Health Planning and Resources Development Act of 1974.

From the 1970s to the present, the design of medical facilities has been influenced by health and seismic standards set by individual state agencies. California, for example, enacts the Hospital Facilities Seismic Safety Act (HSSA) in 1971 with the intention of ensuring that hospitals are reasonably capable of providing services to the public after a disaster.

Politics

Major political events of this decade, including the end of the Vietnam War, the energy crisis, the Watergate scandal, and the Iran hostage crisis, distract political leaders from efforts to address the escalating costs of healthcare and the burgeoning number of uninsured people in the United States. By the middle of the decade, the country is mired in a deep economic recession.

In 1971, President Nixon imposes a price and wage freeze that includes specific annual limits for physicians' fees and hospital charges. The initial 90-day period for this freeze is extended three times until it reaches a total of 1,000 days. The medical limits are not lifted until 1974, more than a year after the other controls have expired.

Passage of the National Health Planning and Resources Development Act in 1974 requires states to develop plans that prevent the duplication of healthcare services. This leads to the widespread adoption of Certificate of Need (CON) programs because all 50 state health agencies must have a structure for reviewing and approving proposals for major capital projects or for investing in high-tech devices and equipment. Although the federal mandate is repealed in 1987, three dozen states still have some kind of CON program.

The Employment Retiree Income Security Act (ERISA) is also enacted in 1974. It permits employers to design their own coverage packages and allows them to refuse to cover services like in-vitro fertilization or to satisfy state requirements for minimal mental health coverage.

The Recession

In the midst of a major recession in 1975, President Gerald Ford says he will veto any health insurance reform. In January 1976, however, he proposes adding catastrophic coverage to Medicare that will be offset by increased cost-sharing.

By 1977, when President Jimmy Carter takes office, the need for a national health insurance program resurfaces, with cost containment being the top priority. However, his proposals are weighed down by debates in Congress that compare the merits of competition to regulation. Presidents and lawmakers try and fail to overhaul the healthcare system over the next few decades.

Healthcare

Attempts to combat the rising cost of healthcare services range from the wage and price controls imposed by President Nixon in 1971 prompt the creation of the Professional Standards Review Organization (PSRO). The PSRO requires regional groups of physicians to review the services provided under the Medicare, Medicaid, and Maternal Child Health programs, to verify the need for such programs, and to ensure that they comply with specific criteria, norms, and standards.

The HMO Act that President Nixon signs into law in 1973 leads to managed care being the prevalent healthcare delivery model for some four decades. An HMO is an organization that provides healthcare to people who make regular payments to it and who agree to use the care providers and facilities that belong to or have a contractual agreement with the organization. Care providers agree to comply with the HMO's requirements in exchange for a steady supply of patients.

The HMO Act provides federal endorsement, certification, and assistance for these types of healthcare organizations. It represents the first major step by the federal government to effect structural change in the delivery of medical services. Although it establishes standards for HMOs that operate under federal law, it leaves almost all other regulatory authority in the hands of individual states. Thus, the regulation of managed care continues to vary significantly across the nation.

President Nixon's plan for national health insurance is rejected by liberal politicians and labor unions, but his War on Cancer centralizes research at the National Institutes of Health (NIH).

Although the health risks associated with using asbestos as a building material have been observed and documented for many years, by the end of this decade a number of studies document the extent to which asbestos workers have been affected. One study shows that asbestosis is present in 10 percent of asbestos workers who had been employed in the industry for 10 to 19 years, in 73 percent of workers who had been employed in the industry for 20 to 29 years, and in 92 percent of workers who had been employed in the industry for more than 40 years. Thus, the EPA and OSHA begin regulating the use and safe removal of asbestos.[28]

The shift from surgery taking place only in hospitals to having it done in ambulatory surgery centers (ASCs) begins in the 1970s. The first ASC opens in Phoenix in 1970. The two physicians wanted to provide a more timely and comfortable setting for patients in their community.

1980s

By 1982, Americans have experienced 17 consecutive years of double-digit increases in healthcare spending, with healthcare inflation outpacing growth in gross domestic product (GDP). Wages can no longer keep pace with the sustained escalation of healthcare costs. Slow economic growth, a recession, and erosion of middle-class incomes intensify the public's general dissatisfaction with the state of the healthcare system.

These factors combine to fuel the managed-care revolution of the 1980s and 1990s. Federal aid that had helped to support nonprofit operations of nearly all of the nation's HMOs is eliminated, and many of these organizations transform themselves into for-profit ventures. By 1987 the Census Bureau reports that 31 million Americans do not have health insurance coverage.[29]

Politics

The Reagan era is characterized by deregulation and a strong faith that letting the market take its course will iron out inefficiencies and bring costs down in many areas of the economy, including healthcare. Corporations enter numerous healthcare-related businesses, and there is a general shift toward privatization.

When President Reagan takes office in 1981, the nation is in the midst of a two-year recession, with double-digit inflation and unemployment. Several trends and events of the 1970s have contributed to this period of "stagflation," including the reduction in industrial production in the Rust Belt and the energy crisis.

The OBRAs

The Omnibus Budget Reconciliation Act of 1981 (OBRA 81) requires states to restrict Medicaid eligibility and gives them more flexibility for using cost-containment strategies. In 1982, states are allowed to provide Medicaid to children with disabilities who require intensive care but can be cared for at home.

The Federal Budget Reconciliation Act of 1986 (OBRA 86) gives states the option of offering Medicaid coverage to infants, young children, and pregnant women up to 100 percent of the poverty level regardless of whether they receive public assistance. This is raised to 185 percent of the poverty level in the following year. OBRA 89, signed into law in 1989, mandates coverage for pregnant women and children under the age of six who are living at 133 percent of the poverty level.[30]

COBRA

In 1985, the Consolidated Omnibus Budget Reconciliation Act (COBRA) amends the Employee Retirement Income Security Act of 1974 to provide some employees with the ability to continue health insurance coverage for 18 to 36 months once they leave a job.

Emergency Medical Treatment

Passage of the Emergency Medical Treatment and Active Labor Act (EMTALA) in 1986 requires all hospitals that are part of the Medicare system to screen and stabilize all patients who use their emergency rooms, regardless of their ability to pay for healthcare services. The Consolidated Omnibus Budget Reconciliation Act (COBRA) is enacted in the same year to regulate how employees who lose their jobs can extend their healthcare coverage for 18 months.

Healthcare

After being elected president in 1980, Ronald Reagan declares that the U.S. healthcare system relies too heavily on federal funding, and he tries to shift this responsibility into the marketplace. HMOs grow in popularity as huge numbers of employers choose this option. By 1993, 67 percent of people with employer-provided coverage are enrolled in managed-care plans.[31]

In 1984, Roger Ulrich publishes his seminal study "View through a Window," which finds that patients with a view of trees have shorter post-operative hospital stays, need less pain medication, and have slightly lower rates of postsurgical complications.[32]

HMOs

The managed-care model changes the fee-for-service reimbursement structure by compensating providers according to fee schedules rather than in relation to the cost incurred. This helps to rein in healthcare costs from 1982 to 1986. By the end of the decade, however, healthcare inflation reaches 16 percent annually.[33] This is due, in part, to the fact that HMOs serves as intermediaries between the patient and the care provider, adding a layer of management costs.

Medicare shifts to a payment-by-diagnosis compensation structure instead of payment-for-treatment. Many private health insurance providers quickly shift to this model. There is growing concern by insurance companies that the traditional fee-for-service method of payment can be exploited by care providers and healthcare organizations. This leads to "capitated" payments becoming more common.[34] Under this system, care providers are compensated on a per-capita basis instead of being paid a fee for each service and procedure provided along the continuum of care. This is one of the first steps toward shifting the U.S. healthcare industry from a "pay for production" to a "pay for performance" compensation structure.

1990s

Healthcare costs rise at double the rate of inflation, which helps to bring the goal of reforming the U.S. healthcare delivery system back to the top of the political agenda. When Bill Clinton runs for president, he makes this issue a cornerstone of his campaign. Shortly after he takes office in 1993, he announces that his wife, First Lady Hillary Rodham-Clinton, will lead a task force charged with developing a plan for national healthcare reform. The Clinton policies in the 1990s stop all construction for a time, until healthcare systems can understand how they will be funded. Once this is ironed out, design and construction resum.

Since senior citizens have had a national health insurance plan for nearly three decades, Democrats resuscitate the long-standing, progressive goal of extending national health insurance to everyone in the country. Hundreds of experts are called in to help draft a plan. Congress feels excluded from this process, and the plan is never brought to a vote in the House or Senate. Although the dot.com bubble and baby boomer spending habits fuel rapid economic expansion, by the end of the decade 44 million Americans (16 percent of the nation's population) have no health insurance whatsoever.

Retirees begin to lose access to affordable healthcare during this decade because a 1990 ruling by the Financial Accounting Standards Board (FASB) requires businesses that offer health benefits to their retirees to include the future healthcare expenses for this group in their current financial reports. The implementation of this regulation reduces the market valuation of these firms. As a result, the percentage of midsize and large firms that offer healthcare to retirees falls by almost 50 percent of what it was in 1980.[35]

Steady advances in communications technology (most notably the Internet) not only facilitate collaboration among healthcare professionals and researchers but also increase patients' access to health information. These changes in technology and the delivery of care services are then extended into design of the built environment.

Politics

In 1990, Congress passes the Ryan White Care Act and President George H.W. Bush signs the American with Disabilities Act (ADA) into law. The Ryan White Care Act provides access to healthcare services for people living with HIV/AIDS who have no health insurance, have insufficient health coverage, or lack the financial resources they need. The ADA prohibits private employers, government agencies, and other organizations with 15 or more employees from discriminating against people with disabilities. Under Titles II and III of this legislation, public places, such as restaurants, stores, and modes of transportation or communication, are required to make "reasonable modifications" to remove physical barriers to access unless this creates an "undue hardship."

The Clinton healthcare plan is introduced as the Health Security Act on November 20, 1993. It includes universal healthcare for all Americans by way of "managed competition," which strives to maximize value for consumers and employers. Under this model, the entity purchasing the healthcare insurance for a group of subscribers (for example, an employer or a government agency) selects the participating plans, manages enrollment, and makes other decisions aimed at obtaining competitive prices while maintaining quality of care services.

During the latter half of this decade, the political will for overhauling the U.S. healthcare industry is lost as the U.S. economy experiences the strongest expansion it has had in decades and employers become more focused on recruiting and retaining staff than on controlling costs. However, some significant healthcare-related legislation is passed.

The Health Insurance Portability and Accountability Act of 1996 (HIPAA) establishes standards for achieving and preserving the privacy of patients' healthcare information. This leads healthcare organizations and design professionals to develop and refine strategies for maintaining visual and acoustical privacy in all locations where a patient's health information is exchanged.

Healthcare

Passage of the ADA during the same year plays a major role in the design of medical facilities. The ADA includes tax deductions for businesses of any size to remove barriers for people with disabilities. This includes providing accessible parking spaces, ramps, and curb cuts as well as making all interior areas of a facility wheelchair accessible. Accessibility is now a part of every a project. Meeting the requirements is a part of the design of all facilities and becomes a part of the Architect's licensing exam and the continuing education programs of several states'.

In 1993, a group of healthcare and design professionals found the Center for Health Design to collaborate on research and advocate for the ways that design can be used to improve patient outcomes in healthcare environments.

Evidence-Based Design

Roger Ulrich coins the phrase "evidence-based design" in 1999, and his research helps to build interest in the relationship between design of the built environment, health, and wellness.[36] Later in that year, the Institute of Medicine (IOM) publishes *To Err is Human: Building a Safer Health System,* a report that asserts that preventable medical errors may contribute to between 44,000 and 98,000 deaths. It defines "medical error" as "the failure of a planned action to be completed as intended or the use of the wrong plan to achieve an aim."[37]

The Healthcare Research and Quality Act of 1999 requires the Agency for Healthcare Research and Quality (AHRQ) to "conduct and support research and build public partnerships to: identify the causes of preventable health care errors and patient injury in health care delivery;

develop, demonstrate, and evaluate strategies for reducing errors and improving patient safety; and disseminate such effective strategies throughout the health care industry."

2000–Present

Interest in and knowledge about the relationship between the design of healthcare facilities and health outcomes steadily increases. For example, the Pebble Project is launched to "identify built environment solutions that measurably improve patient and worker safety, clinical outcomes, environmental performance and operating efficiency."[38]

Politics

The United States has been fighting terrorist movements for more than a decade. This increases and alters the demand for healthcare services in ways that will likely shape how care is provided for veterans well into the future. For example, improvements in military technology, such as body armor and vehicle shielding, improve survival rates from injuries that would have proved to be fatal in earlier wars. As a result military and civilian care providers must learn how to treat new types of traumatic injuries, such as those affecting the brain.

A Rand Corporation report calls for more research to improve knowledge about "invisible wounds," the psychiatric and mental health consequences of combat trauma and repeated deployments.[39] This report indicates that more than one-quarter of military personnel who have served in Iraq and Afghanistan may suffer from some type of mental disorder.

In 2002, President George W. Bush launches the Health Center Growth Initiative in order to increase access to primary care services by expanding the health center program. This initiative adds or expands health centers in the most underserved areas of the United States.

Over the course of five years, federal spending on the health center program nearly doubles.

In 2003, President Bush signs the Medicare Modernization Act into law. The act mandates a prescription drug plan for elderly and disabled Americans.

During their 2004 presidential campaigns, President Bush and Senator John Kerry present proposals for expanding healthcare coverage in the United States. Bush's proposals are more modest, and a variety of experts judge them to be less expensive to implement than Kerry's more comprehensive plan.

State Models for Reform

In 2006, Massachusetts and Vermont pass reform laws that strive to provide universal or near-universal healthcare coverage for their residents. The legislation in Massachusetts requires residents to obtain coverage and calls for the responsibility for financing expanded coverage to be shared by individuals, employers, and the state. Within two years, the number of uninsured residents in Massachusetts is cut in half.

Vermont's law creates the Catamount Health Plan for uninsured residents. By 2014, Vermont has developed Vermont Health Connect, an online healthcare marketplace where people can enroll in public healthcare programs such as Medicaid or Dr. Dynasaur, buy insurance from a private company, and determine if they are eligible for subsidies.

In 2007 the CDC reports that more people in the United States die from the staph infection "methicillin-resistant *Staphylococcus aureus*" (MRSA) than from AIDS.[40] This statistic helps to bring the issue of healthcare-associated infections (HAIs) into the national spotlight.

Behavioral Health

The Mental Health Parity Act is amended in 2008 to require insurance companies to treat behavioral health conditions the same as physical conditions when their policies provide coverage for both. During this election year, the two leading presidential candidates, President Barack Obama and John McCain, present proposals for healthcare reform. McCain's proposal focuses on providing tax credits for people who do have healthcare through their employers. He includes a guaranteed access plan in his proposal to help people who are denied coverage by insurance companies. In contrast, Obama advocates for universal healthcare coverage based on his belief that everyone living in the United States should have affordable access to quality care. His plan calls for the creation of a national health insurance exchange that would include private insurance plans and a "public option." The prime concern for voters of all political allegiances is affordability.

ARRA

In 2009, the American Reinvestment and Recovery Act (ARRA) makes a substantial investment in healthcare. For example, it does the following:

- Extends the transitional medical assistance program so that low-income parents can be eligible for Medicaid coverage for up to six months after their earnings have increased above the maximum allowed.

- Provides subsidies to enable some individuals to afford COBRA coverage if they were terminated between September 1, 2008, and December 31, 2009.

- Offers $17 billion in Medicare and Medicaid incentives to encourage providers to invest in electronic health record systems and to strengthen the measures they are using to protect patient privacy. The Congressional Budget Office (CBO) estimates that the health information technology (HIT) investments resulting from these incentives will generate

$12 billion in savings from improved care coordination and reduced medical errors and duplications.

- Allocates $2 billion for construction and operation of community health centers ($1.5 billion for construction projects, the remainder for operations).

ADA Updates

In 2010, the Department of Justice issues updates regulations for Titles II and III of the ADA and makes them effective as of March 15, 2011. These revisions include an "element by element safe harbor" that allows facilities built or altered in compliance with the 1991 ADA standards to remain as they are until they are "subject to a planned alteration." This safe harbor protection also applies to elements within the "path of travel" to an altered area.[41]

Affordable Care Act

On March 23, 2010, President Obama signs the Patient Protection and Affordable Care Act (ACA) into law. This is the first time in American history that a comprehensive healthcare bill is passed. Its primary goal is to provide affordable, quality healthcare services to all Americans. Some of the significant changes it makes include the following:

- The law calls for the creation of a website, www.healthcare.gov, which is to be designed to help consumers learn about the insurance options available to them, compare plans, and pick the best option for them and their families.

- Beginning in 2010, insurance companies are no longer permitted to deny coverage to children under the age of 19 with preexisting conditions. This requirement gradually expands to include people of all ages.

- Insurance companies are prohibited from cancelling a person's health insurance coverage (unless that person completes a fraudulent application) and from imposing lifetime dollar limits on essential benefits. During the drafting of the ACA, insurance companies have successfully lobbied to have an "individual mandate" also included in this legislation. This mandate requires everyone to buy into the system so that the costs of providing healthcare for those who are ill and injured are spread across a large patient population.

- Medicaid and the Children's Health Insurance Plan (CHIP) are expanded to cover 15 million men, women, and children who fell through the cracks in the past. However, some states choose to opt out of this expanded coverage.

- For new health insurance plans, essential health benefits and preventative services are covered, with no out-of-pocket costs for the patient.

- Young adults can remain covered under their parents' health insurance plans through the age of 26.

- Senior citizens and others enrolled in Medicare now receive free preventive services, such as annual wellness visits. In addition, people who have Medicare Part D prescription drug plans and who fall into the "donut hole" will receive discounts and other savings until this coverage gap is closed in 2020.[42]

- The 2015 employer mandate requires that full-time employees of large firms have access to health benefits. Small firms are exempted from this mandate. Large firms are those with 50 or more employees.

- For plans sold to individuals and small employers, the premium must be spent on health services and quality improvement. If insurance companies do not meet these goals because their administrative costs or profits are too high, they must provide rebates to consumers.

- The law creates an affordable, voluntary long-term-care insurance program (CLASS) that provides benefits to adults who become disabled.

- In the individual and small-group market, insurance companies are prohibited from charging higher rates based on gender or health status.

- Tax credits and reduced cost–sharing are provided to make health insurance coverage affordable for most Americans.

- Beginning in 2014, people who do not have coverage under an employer-based health plan will be able to purchase health insurance directly by way of an exchange. This online marketplace offers a choice of health plans that meet the benefit and cost standards established by the ACA.

- Members of Congress and federal employees will be purchasing health insurance through exchanges.

- When the second phase of the small-business tax credit is implemented, qualified small businesses will receive available credit for up to 50 percent of the employer's contribution so that they can afford to provide health insurance for their employees. There will also be a credit for small nonprofit organizations, whose employees will be eligible for a credit worth up to 35 percent of the employer's contribution.

- People earning less than 133 percent of the poverty level will be able to enroll in Medicaid. States will receive 100 percent federal funding for the first three years to support this expanded coverage. After that, they will receive 90 percent.

- Most people who can afford basic health insurance will be required to purchase coverage or pay a fine to help offset the costs of caring for uninsured people.

- As of 2015, physicians' compensation will be tied to patient health outcomes rather than being based on fees charged per service rendered.[43]

On October 1, 2013, however, the much-anticipated launch of healthcare.gov, the website designed to make comparison-shopping for health insurance easy, becomes one of the largest, most public software failures in recent history. Delays related to making sure that the website can keep up with demand and function well in other ways initially have a negative impact, and the actual number of people who sign up for coverage using the exchanges falls short of projections.

Healthcare

Healthcare spending in the United States continues to grow, and in 2008 reaches an average annual cost of $7,538 per person. This is substantially higher than spending in the next-highest countries of Norway and Switzerland, which spend $5,003 and $4,627 per capita on healthcare services, respectively.[44] According to a 2007 report by the National Coalition on Healthcare, someone in the U.S. files for bankruptcy every 30 seconds as a consequence of a serious health problem.[45]

Regardless of the fact that the U.S. spends more money on healthcare than its main international competitors, it ranks far behind other developed countries in terms of health outcomes such as longevity and child mortality rates.

The number of people living without health insurance in the United States continues to climb. By 2007, the Census Bureau places this number at 45.6 million. This number exceeds 48 million by 2011 but begins to decline in 2012,

fueling hopes that the Patient Protection and Affordable Care Act will, in fact, provide access to health insurance for millions of people who could afford it prior to the time that phased implementation of this law begins.

More Integration

The delivery of healthcare services is more holistic, integrated, and team-based. Services that were once considered "nontraditional" or "alternative" in the United States (acupuncture, for example) are now considered "complementary." As the baby boom generation ages, the rate of chronic illnesses rises. But information about health and wellness becomes more easily available and more widely discussed, and healthcare organizations shift their emphasis from treating diseases and injuries to preventing them.

Consolidation

Colocation and consolidation become more common. Generally, this occurs in two ways: various healthcare practices choose to locate near each other (primary, dental, and behavioral health practices, for example), or medical care is paired with community services such as housing assistance. Some private practices or organizations choose to open a clinic on hospital campuses so that they can share lab, diagnostic, and treatment facilities. This strategy can make care more convenient for patients when they can complete tests, physical exams, consultations, and follow-up care at a single location. It also allows clinics and hospitals to optimize utilization of expensive high-tech equipment such as magnetic resonance imaging (MRI) or x-ray machines.

EDAC Certification

In 2009, the Center for Health Design launches a specialized accreditation program for "evidence based design" (EDAC). To achieve EDAC certification, design professionals must pass an exam demonstrating that they not only understand how to apply the evidence-based process to designing healthcare facilities but also know how to measure and report the impact that design decisions have on the patients' safety, perceptions, and health outcomes.

Green Design

Awareness of and interest in green design grows. As more building owners, property managers, and developers use certification programs such as Leadership in Energy and Environmental Design (LEED), industry-specific guidelines are created for healthcare facilities, such as *The Green Guide for Healthcare* (2002), LEED for Healthcare (2011), and the Green Globes CIEB Healthcare (2011) programs.

Man-made and Natural Disasters

The attacks on September 11, 2001, shake the confidence of citizens from coast to coast. Within a month, anthrax-contaminated letters are mailed to several media outlets and to two U.S. senators (Daschle and Leahy). Twenty three people contract anthrax, and five of them die.

In 2002, a severe acute respiratory syndrome (SARS) appears in China. Since China suppresses news of the outbreak, it spreads to neighboring countries and then to more distant lands by way of international travelers.

Hurricane Katrina hits the U.S. Gulf Coast in 2005, and massive flooding destroys much of New Orleans. The resulting contamination of water from decaying bodies, chemicals, and other matter creates the largest public health disaster in American history.

These and other major events cause public health officials to more thoroughly analyze how major cities can prepare for and respond to man-made and natural disasters, which include various forms of terrorism. "Resilient design" becomes a common phrase. It is defined by the Resilient Design Institute as "the intentional design of buildings, landscapes, communities, and regions in response to vulnerabilities to disaster and disruption of normal life."[46]

Present Time Onward

Driven by the Affordable Care Act, the U.S. healthcare system keeps evolving into a decentralized, tiered system of clinic-based care with the outmigration of services extending into the workplace and home. However, today and well into the future, political factors beyond this historic piece of legislation will continue to influence where and how health and wellness are promoted and achieved across the United States.

Healthcare

As more healthcare organizations form accountable care organizations (ACOs) and medical homes, hospitals acquire or form partnerships with local clinics. These new alliances are expected to improve utilization as healthcare organizations determine how to use excess capacity on hospital campuses more flexibly.

For example, the University of Michigan's Trauma and Burn Center has developed a strategy for making its intensive care unit more flexible by moving patients down to a lower acuity of care as they recover. The patients remain in the ICU, but payers are charged fees commensurate with the actual care provided. This has improved the continuity of care and patient satisfaction levels while putting a department with high fixed costs to better use.

The increased recognition of the mind/body connection is expected to continue to transform the way care services are provided, with more emphasis being placed on keeping people well in both of these realms. Since research completed by the CDC has demonstrated that four modifiable behaviors increase the risk of developing chronic diseases, public agencies, nonprofit organizations, and private companies have all developed programs to encourage people to be more physically active, to improve their access to and knowledge about nutrition, to quit smoking, and to limit alcohol consumption.

As electronic health record systems become the norm, the coordination of care between providers will improve. The emphasis of how technology is employed has begun to shift from diagnosis to prevention and health maintenance. Only the sickest patients and those recovering from major surgery or injuries will be treated in hospitals.

Politics

Several states' decisions to legalize same-sex marriage have begun to make healthcare benefits that were once limited to heterosexual married couples available to gay spouses.

U.S. involvement in wars in Iraq and Afghanistan during the first decade of this century has increased the number of patients requiring long-term care. This is one of the factors fueling the trend toward outmigration of care. It has helped spur innovations in telehealth and in-home healthcare services as well as the addition of infusion, dialysis, and other specialized services at convenient care clinics and other community-based locations.

Operationalized

While understanding that the historical interplay between healthcare and politics provides important context for design professionals, clients value action over rumination. The healthcare industry has for decades felt pressure to simultaneously lower costs and improve quality. Thus, the most highly valued design professionals quickly determine how much analysis is merited, effectively communicate the value of research and

planning, and know how to efficiently progress from schematic design through construction. They also consult and collaborate with clients on an ongoing basis to make sure that healthcare facilities continue to adapt to changes in operational and care delivery processes.

For this reason, some of the major questions explored throughout this textbook include:

- How have design professionals addressed the constantly changing challenges presented by political forces and other factors?

- How have they acted on new opportunities?

- What can design professionals do to maintain and enhance their valued position as trusted advisors for their clients?

Research has shown that over the course of a 30-year period, there is a 1:10:200 relationship between the costs of designing and operating a healthcare facility and the costs of attracting and retaining the highly skilled and professionally trained staff who deliver health and wellness services with in it.[47] This means that for every dollar spent on construction costs, $10 are spent on the ongoing operational expenses (energy costs and maintenance, for example) and $200 on employee compensation. The potential for design decisions to have a positive, exponential impact on the healthcare industry is clear.

Technology in healthcare has pushed the boundaries of culture, morality, and politics. Gene therapy has become a political agenda in the United States. Questions are being asked such as "if a heart can be grown for a transplant, should it be?" Or "is a child worse off without altering the genes to avoid illness or lifelong disabilities?"

The outcome of these political decisions will influence not only the building architecture but the type of service and facilities altogether.

The baby boomer's need for healthcare and facilities will mean more ASC and MOB facilities.

The chapters of this book outline some of the design considerations for these facilities. We will likely see advances in the design of infusion centers, along with full cancer centers, diabetic treatment, obesity, and small hospitals and larger ASCs. The design will be centered on patient's experience while visiting. The design will also focus on overall health and planning to prevent visits to the emergency room.

Globalization is another trend in healthcare. While the United States is not seeing as many large hospital projects, other countries are developing large medical campuses that include complete medical centers combined with hotels and recreation facilities. This is called destination healthcare. These campuses are often designed entirely in the United States and Europe, are typically run by American and European healthcare executives, and are staffed with physicians from around the world.

New overseas facilities are providing services more cost effectively, with some on a cash-only basis. We will see an increase in destination healthcare and likely political agendas to help keep some of this employment in the United States.

Douglas Whiteaker

Notes

1. "Abraham Lincoln's Classroom," http:// abrahamlincolnsclassroom.org.

2. "Catholicism," http://www.worldreligions. com/index.php/Christianity/Christianity.

3. "Public Health History Timeline," Southeast Public Health Training Center, http://www .sphtc.org/timeline/timeline.html.

4. "Our History," ThedaCare, http://www .thedacare.org/Getting-Involved/Foundations/ Theda-Clark-Medical-Center-Foundation/ Our-Community.aspx.

5. "Public Health History Timeline."

6. *Encyclopedia Brittanica,* "Typhoid Mary," http://www.britannica.com/EBchecked/ topic/611790/Typhoid-Mary.

7. "Typhoid Mary Mystery May Have Been Solved at Last, Scientists Say," *Huffington Post*, August 17, 2013, http://www.huffingtonpost. com/2013/08/17/typhoid-mary-mystery- solved_n_3762822.html.

8. Karen Palmer, "A Brief History: Universal Health Care Efforts in the U.S.," Physicians for a National Health Program, 1999, http:// www.pnhp.org/facts/a-brief-history- universal-health-care-efforts-in-the-us.

9. Ibid.

10. Ibid.

11. Centers for Disease Control and Prevention, "The History of Malaria, an Ancient Disease," 2010, http://www.cdc.gov/malaria/about/ history.

12. Stanley J. Lemons, "The Sheppard-Towner Act: Progressivism in the 1920s," *Journal of American History* 55 (1969): 776–86.

13. "Public Health History Timeline."

14. "Timeline: History of Health Reform in the U.S.," n.d., Kaiser Family Foundation, http:// kaiserfamilyfoundation.files.wordpress. com/2011/03/5-02-13-history-of-health- reform.pdf.

15. Karen Palmer, "A Brief History: Universal Health Care Efforts in the U.S.," 1999. http:// pnhp.org/facts/a-brief-history-universal- health-care-efforts-in-the-us.

16. Ibid.

17. Truman Scholars Association, "Harry and Health Care," 2010, http://trumanscholars. org/for-scholars/harry-and-health-care.

18. David Blumenthal, "Health Policy Report: Employer-Sponsored Health Insurance in the

United States—Origins and Implications," *New England Journal of Medicine* 355 (2006): 82–88.

19. "Theda Clark Memorial Hospital," http://images.library.wisc.edu/WI/EFacs/NeenahLocHist/NHHistSFS/reference/wi.nhhistsfs.i0039.pdf. As accessed by the author on 29 August 2014.

20. Centers for Disease Control and Prevention, "The History of Malaria, an Ancient Disease."

21. Superbug, Super-Fast Evolution," University of California, Berkeley, 2008, http://evolution.berkeley.edu/evolibrary/news/080401_mrsa.

22. Randall B. Williamson, "VA Health Care: Progress and Challenges in Conducting the National Vietnam Veterans Longitudinal Study," United States Government Accountability Office, May 5, 2010.

23. "Healthcare Crisis: Healthcare Timeline," n.d., Public Broadcasting Service, http://www.pbs.org/healthcarecrisis/history.htm.

24. "Migrant Health Center Legislation," n.d., National Center for Farmworker Health, http://www.ncfh.org/?pid=186.

25. "The Reports of the Surgeon General," U.S. National Library of Medicine, n.d., http://profiles.nlm.nih.gov/ps/retrieve/Narrative/NN/p-nid/60. \

26. "Community Health Centers in the United States," Wikipedia, http://en.wikipedia.org/wiki/Community_health_centers_in_the_United_States.

27. Roberta C. Barbalace, "Asbestos: A Manufacturing Health Hazard Dating to Prehistoric Times," 2004, http://environmentalchemistry.com/yogi/environmental/asbestoshealthhazards.html.

28. Uwe Reinhardt, "The Managed-Care Industry in Perspective," Public Broadcasting Service, 1998, http://www.pbs.org/wgbh/pages/frontline/shows/hmo/procon/hmoperspective.html.

29. "1981 Omnibus Budget Reconciliation Act," University of California, Berkeley, n.d., http://bancroft.berkeley.edu/ROHO/projects/debt/1981reconciliationact.html.

30. Jonathan Gruber, "Health Insurance and the Labor Market," National Bureau of Economic Research, October 1998, http://economics.mit.edu/files/69.

31. Roger S. Ulrich, "View Through a Window May Influence Recovery from Surgery," *Science* 224 (1984): 420–22.

32. "The Effect of Health Care Cost Growth on the U.S. Economy," U.S. Department of Health and Human Services, http://aspe.hhs.gov/health/reports/08/healthcarecost/report.pdf.

33. "Healthcare Crisis: Healthcare Timeline," Public Broadcasting Service.

34. Stephanie Kelton, "An Introduction to the Health Care Crisis in America: How Did We Get Here?" Center for Full Employment and Price Stability, 2007, http://www.cfeps.org/health/chapters/html/ch1.htm.

35. Sara O. Marberry, "A Conversation with Roger Ulrich," *Healthcare Design*, October 31, 2010, http://www.healthcaredesignmagazine.com/article/conversation-roger-ulrich?page=sho.

36. Linda T. Kohn, Janet M. Corrigan, and Molla S. Donaldson, eds., *To Err Is Human: Building a Safer Health System* (Washington, DC: National Academy Press, 2000), http://iom.edu/Reports/1999/To-Err-is-Human-Building-A-Safer-Health-System.aspx.

37. "The Pebble Project," Center for Health Design, https://www.healthdesign.org/pebble.

38. "Invisible Wounds: Mental Health and Cognitive Care Needs of America's Returning Veterans," RAND Corporation, 2008, http://www.rand.org/pubs/research_briefs/RB9336/index1.html. BOOK?

39. "Skin Problems and Treatments Health Center," Web MD, n.d., http://www.webmd.com/skin-problems-and-treatments/news/20071016/more-us-deaths-from-mrsa-than-aids.

40. "Highlights of the Final Rule to Amend the Department of Justice's Regulation Implementing Title III of the ADA," http://www.ada.gov/regs2010/factsheets/title3_factsheet.html.

41. "Costs in the Coverage Gap," http://www.medicare.gov/part-d/costs/coverage-gap/part-d-coverage-gap.html.

42. "Key Features of the Affordable Care Act," http://www.hhs.gov/healthcare/facts/timeline.

43. David A. Squires, "The U.S. Health System in Perspective: A Comparison of Twelve Industrialized Nations," Commonwealth Fund, July 2011.

44. Kelton, "An Introduction to the Health Care Crisis in America.

45. "Resilient Design Institute," http://www.resilientdesign.org.

46. Cynthia S. McCullough, ed., *Evidence-Based Design for Healthcare Facilities*" (Indianapolis, IN: Sigma Theta Tau International, 2009), 154.

Select Bibliography

Annenberg Classroom. "Health Care Timeline." n.d. http://www.annenbergclassroom.org/Files/Documents/Timelines/HealthCare.pdf.

Durbin, Senator Dick. "Health Care Reform Implementation Timeline." n.d. http://www.durbin.senate.gov/public/index.cfm/health-care-reform-implementation-timeline.

The Green Guide for Health Care. "Who We Are." n.d., http://www.gghc.org/about.whoweare.overview.php.

"Typhoid Mary Mystery May Have Been Solved at Last, Scientists Say." *Huffington Post*, August 17, 2013. http://www.huffingtonpost.com/2013/08/17/typhoid-mary-mystery-solved_n_3762822.html.

Palmer, Karen. "A Brief History: Universal Health Care Efforts in the U.S." Physicians for a National Health Program. 1999.http://www.pnhp.org/facts/a-brief-history-universal-health-care-efforts-in-the-us.

"Timeline: History of Health Reform in the U.S." *Kaiser Family Foundation*. n.d. http://kaiserfamilyfoundation.files.wordpress.com/2011/03/5-02-13-history-of-health-reform.pdf.

Overview

The image that often comes to mind when people hear the phrase "retail clinics" is that of a convenient care clinic (CCC) located in a mass-merchandise, drug, or grocery store. While these are the most common retail clinic facilities in the United States, design professionals and healthcare industry leaders also use this phrase to refer to all clinics located in retail settings, including those that are conversions of former big box stores or that occupy tenant spaces in malls.

Although retail clinics run the gamut from simple, one-room facilities to health and wellness destinations, they are unified by their focus on making it easier, more convenient, and more affordable for patients to gain access to healthcare services. Their use of electronic health records is especially critical for ensuring continuity and coordination of care as retail clinics have increasingly formed alliances with local primary care clinics, health systems, and insurers.

The most recent surge in construction of convenient care clinics has helped to address the shortage of primary care physicians by employing nurse practitioners and various midlevel professionals who welcome the opportunity to work to the top of their licensure and can refer patients on to doctors as needed.

History

Some key dates in the evolution of this healthcare facility type include the following.

2000   MinuteClinic opens the first convenient care clinic in the Twin Cities Metro Area (Minnesota).[1,2] During the first decade of its existence, this clinic operator grows to establish more than 750 convenient care clinics across the nation.

2006   The Convenient Care Association (CCA) is founded to advocate for the development of industry-wide standards for this type of retail clinic.[3] This leads to all CCA members being required to comply with OSHA, CLIA, HIPAA, ADA, and CDC standards.

2009   In June of this year, Walgreens and CVS Caremark announce the expansion of their retail clinic services to include treatment of minor skin conditions as well as injections for chronic conditions. Some convenient care clinics launch pilot programs to test the feasibility of offering breathing treatments and special infusion treatments.

2013   Ambulatory infusion centers begin to appear in retail settings, including Walgreens and Schnuck's grocery stores. Walgreens begins a free home delivery service for prescription medications.

Convenient Care Clinics (CCCs)

This care model and related facility type arose because of the difficulty people faced when trying to schedule clinic appointments at times that were convenient for them. For many years, patients who needed both low- and high-acuity care during off-hours had to seek it at an urgent-care clinic or in the emergency room. The wait times at these facilities were typically long, and costs for healthcare services were substantially higher than those provided in a primary care clinic.

Most CCCs are open during the evenings and on weekends. They are typically located in places that are already destinations for patients, such as discount retailers, pharmacies, or grocery stores, with services provided on a fee-for-service, walk-in basis.

By offering convenient, easily accessible, and affordable healthcare services, CCCs addressed a clear market need. Passage of the Patient Protection and Affordable Care Act (ACA) and an aging population have combined with other factors to

Previous page: HealthEast Spine Clinic, Maplewood, Minneosta; Hammel, Green and Abrahamson, Inc. Photography by Steve Henke

spur rapid growth in the number of CCCs and the range of services they offer because the size of the patient population and the need for ongoing care have increased concurrently.

According to the Convenient Care Association, CCCs typically feature a streamlined check-in area and efficient layout that minimizes staffing and rental costs while maximizing throughput. Some are compact enough to occupy as little as 100 square feet of space.[4] They typically offer a limited range of services, such as the diagnosis and treatment of the following medical conditions:

- Cold and flu symptoms.
- Sinus, urinary tract, and ear infections.
- Allergies/allergic reactions.
- Minor injuries and rashes.
- Headaches and stomachaches.

Some CCCs also offer health screenings, immunizations, and physicals and serve as collection locations for blood, urine, and other samples that are then sent to an external lab for analysis. Although nurse practitioners who work in CCCs are qualified to diagnose common medical conditions, order basic tests, and prescribe some medications, any patient with an emergent condition must be referred to an appropriate care provider. In this way, CCCs not only handle some triage decisions that were formerly addressed by staff in larger clinics but also serve as "feeder locations" for larger healthcare systems.

Clinics in Retail Settings

Near the end of the first decade of this century, healthcare organizations across the United States began to take advantage of the glut in vacant retail properties to convert these into clinics. Retail stores and tenant spaces in malls or shopping centers offered good visibility, easy access, proximity to expanding patient populations, and convenient parking. At the same time, the recession drove purchase prices and lease rates down into the range that made constructing clinics in retail settings a viable option.[5,6,7,8]

Although the strategies for providing healthcare in specific retail settings vary by geographic location, the qualities of the sites available, the care model of the medical practice, characteristics of the patient population served, and the type of services offered, clinics constructed in former stores or in retail centers have several distinct characteristics, including the following:

- Time is a major factor driving the decision to locate a clinic in a retail setting. On average, it takes about half the time to adapt an existing store or space for medical functions as it does to build new. This is an especially important consideration for healthcare organizations that want to expand rapidly into new areas.

- Going into existing retail structures can also save on construction costs when there is little to no demolition required because of this building type's basic design characteristics. Retail structures are typically designed to make it easy for owners or tenants to reconfigure space in response to new market demands.

- The open layout and large areas of free-span space found in some vacant big box retail stores can make them more easily adaptable for medical functions.

- More spacious retail settings can also present opportunities to colocate complementary services or related income-generating amenities (such as a café) with a clinic to make it a health and wellness destination.

- Retail stores tend to have ample parking nearby.

Trends

Early expansion in number of retail clinics occurred at a very fast pace for convenient care facilities, with visits quadrupling from 2007 to 2009.[9] According to Rand Health, approximately six million visits were completed at CCCs in 2009. Experts predict this growth to continue across the United States before leveling off in 2015.[10]

Key aspects of the Affordable Care Act (ACA) and major cultural, economic, and demographic trends have converged to make retail settings more available and desirable for healthcare organizations that need to expand or relocate clinic facilities.

Healthcare Reform

Passage of the ACA has added millions of people to the insured patient population in the United States. This has increased the demand for healthcare services—especially routine and preventative care. Since many newly insured people do not have an established relationship with a clinic or a care provider, healthcare organizations have opened retail clinics to meet this demand and provide additional access points in places that are convenient and familiar.

The fact that the ACA bases reimbursement on the quality of health outcomes for a specific patient population has also motivated retail clinics to use electronic health records and regular follow-up procedures to coordinate patient care effectively with local clinics, hospitals, and other medical facilities.

Cultural Shifts

Until recently, real estate developers and property owners neither pursued nor welcomed medical clinics as tenants because the possibility of seeing people who were ill or in pain did not seem to mix well with retail stores and restaurants that wanted an upbeat, energetic environment for selling products and services. Some retail malls and shopping centers even had agreements that prohibited healthcare organizations from leasing space for medical facilities.

Wellness versus Disease Treatment

The shift in cultural beliefs from clinics being viewed as places for disease treatment to being hubs for health management and wellness has not only helped to alleviate concerns about sick people mixing with shoppers but has also led to retail clinics being colocated with fitness centers, spas, pharmacies, and other complementary services or products.

For example, the tenant mix for the Calhoun Village Shopping Center in Minneapolis, Minnesota, includes a FastCare Urgent Care Clinic, Calhoun Vision Center, Orange Theory Fitness Center, a Modo Yoga studio, a Massage Envy Spa, and a Walgreens pharmacy store, along with other retail stores and various restaurants. A Whole Foods store, Jamba Juice bar, and Vitamin Shoppe are located in another mall across the street. Calhoun Village is also located along the Midtown Greenway and near this city's chain of lakes, which provide a wealth of sports and recreation opportunities for athletes and sports enthusiasts.

Landlord Attitudes

Designing and constructing a clinic in a retail setting requires finding the right landlord as well as the right building or space. The Great Recession helped make it easier for healthcare organizations to achieve both of these goals. Landlords facing high vacancy rates became more flexible and willing to invest in the tenant improvements needed to make the numbers work. Since medical facilities can be more systems-intensive than an average retail store requires, healthcare organizations have been able, in some instances, to negotiate improvements to the mechanical and electrical systems being part of the landlord's responsibilities.

The lease period for medical tenants appeals to landlords, too. Medical tenants typically sign longer leases (10 years) than most retail stores (5 years). With the demand for healthcare services strong and growing, mall owners can expect a lower-risk, steady income stream for retail clinics. The costs associated with marketing and fitting out the space are reduced because these activities are required less frequently.

Consumerism

Thanks to the Internet, patients are better educated about their options than they have been in the past and they can easily shop for what they consider to be the best value for their healthcare dollars. Those who prefer a quick, affordable, easily accessible healthcare experience often choose a CCC because they are able to combine seeing a care provider with the completion of other tasks when they are already at a routine destination.

The 2013 launch of the Clinician and Group CAHPS (CG-CAHPS) Survey and website has strengthened the influence of consumerism on clinic design by giving patients a chance to comparison shop for care based on area of specialization, type of professional, location, and other criteria—all via the Internet before they leave home or work. The Agency for Healthcare Research and Quality (AHRQ) developed this standardized research tool to measure patients' perceptions of the care they receive in a clinic setting.[11]

Economics

The recession that began in 2008 helped make retail spaces and facilities cost-competitive at the same time that healthcare organizations were determining how to best expand their outpatient services to meet growing demand.

According to Len Kaiser, director of network development for HealthEast Care System, standard rental rates in the Twin Cities, Minnesota, metro area had formerly been $35 to $40 per square foot. Mall owners recognized that these rates were no longer achievable and that having more space that is occupied than vacant is better for attracting additional tenants and retaining existing ones. By 2013, lease rates had dropped as low as $22 to $25 per square foot for clinics in retail settings.

Reimbursement Structures

Although for many years CCCs only accepted cash payments, the major operators now accept reimbursement from large insurance companies. Generally, "episodes of care" initiated at retail clinics cost substantially less than those completed in physicians' offices, urgent-care clinics, and emergency departments. Thus, insurers that tested the market by covering most or all of the cost of flu shots, for example, have gradually expanded the range of services that qualify for reimbursement.

As patient numbers have increased, deductible amounts to keep their health insurance premiums affordable, the lower up-front costs associated with obtaining routine, and low-acuity care in retail clinics have made this option more appealing. A study featured on the consumer-focused Health Harbor website found that diagnosing an earache cost $59 at a retail clinic, $95 in a conventional clinic, $135 at an urgent-care center, and $184 in a hospital's emergency room. The cost differential was even greater for treating a sore throat, which was "$74 at a retail clinic, $133 in a doctor's office, and $496 in an emergency room."[12]

Return on Investment

The rise of retail clinics occurred at the same time that healthcare organizations began applying the Lean Methodology to the design of outpatient facilities. The efficiencies associated with Lean have not only driven down operational costs but have also made it possible for retail clinics to meet the increased demand for health and wellness services.

Generally, these trends have improved the return on investment for healthcare organizations that have needed to relocate clinics or open new locations in retail settings. The HealthEast project examples included later in this chapter illustrate how this has been the case for three retail clinics that serve different patient populations and are in distinctly different locations within the Twin Cities.

Demographics

The aging population, an increase in the number of young adults who have health insurance coverage because they can now stay on their parents' policy until age 26, and the long-lasting wars in Iraq and Afghanistan have led to a need for more clinics in the United States that can provide basic preventative and routine care services as well as health management and maintenance for patients with chronic conditions.[13]

A 2013 poll by Harris Interactive/HealthDay revealed that 27 percent of all adults in the United States have used either walk-in retail or work-based clinics to obtain medical care in the two years leading up to the survey. This compares with 7 percent in 2008. A survey of healthcare consumers completed by the Deloitte Center for Health Solutions found the following:

- Baby boomers showed an especially high level of interest in using retail clinics (38 percent).

- Senior citizens were the least likely to seek care at a retail clinic. Millennials were the most likely to do this.

- Patients treated at retail clinics were in better-than-average health.

- They were also more likely to be suspicious of medications that hospitals and doctors prescribe.[14]

Ownership

Initially, growth in the CCC sector of the healthcare industry was driven by established pharmacy chains—such as CVS, Rite Aid, and Walgreens—that acquired clinic operators and then expanded the number of stores that featured these facilities. For example, in 2006 CVS Caremark acquired 83 MinuteClinics.[15] At that time, MinuteClinic was the largest provider of retail-based healthcare services in the United States. It continues to hold this market position. As a wholly owned subsidiary of CVS Caremark, MinuteClinic now has over 650 locations across the United States. A year later, Walgreens acquired TakeCare Health Systems and more than doubled the operations of TakeCare Clinics, from 60 to 130, by the end of 2007.[16]

Today, most convenient care clinics have formed relationships with physicians, groups and healthcare organizations, have been built as a satellite location for a health system, or are owned by private companies that blend retail and healthcare. CVS, Walgreens, and Target, for example, house approximately three-quarters of the convenient care clinics in the United States. CCCs that have partnered with or are a satellite location of integrated delivery systems such as Allina Health, Sutter Health, and Geisinger Health System are able to compete on a regional basis with major operators because of their strong brand recognition.[17]

Design Considerations and Challenges

Much of what works well for retail facilities makes them attractive for clinics: optimal locations with ample parking, an interesting and/

or flexible architectural design, good visibility, strong brand recognition, and other qualities that can make the consumer (patient) experience a pleasant one (figs. 8-1, 8-2).

Since the design goals for most retail clinics are similar to those for conventional care settings, adapting retail stores and tenant spaces for medical functions addresses many of the same issues. Technology and staffing are particularly key considerations because of the heavy reliance of this care model on the use of electronic health records and midlevel healthcare professionals.

Location

Important location factors that design professionals review -in analyzing the costs and benefits associated with each retail setting under consideration include the following:

- **Population served.** The ideal clinic location is one that is most convenient and easily accessible for the largest number of patients a clinic serves. Constructing a clinic in a retail setting that is already a destination adds familiarity and comfort to this equation. Some health systems open retail clinics near the epicenter of where growth is occurring in a particular community because a vacant store or mall tenant space is the best property available to bring services closer to patients.

- **Availability of suitable space.** Design professionals ask questions such as:

  - Does the building or tenant space have the proper size, visibility, infrastructure, and other characteristics needed to meet the typically more rigorous demand of a healthcare facility?

  - If expansion is desired, is there adjacent space available?

- **Convenience.** Is the site on the way to a destination or already the destination itself, and

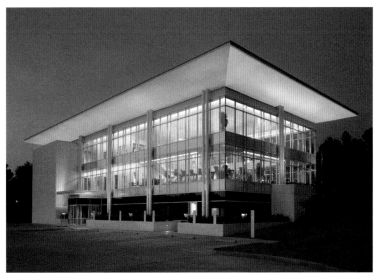

FIGURES 8-1, 8-2: ETMC Lake Palestine Clinic and Olympic Center, Lake Palestine, Texas. Located on a prominent retail corridor, the Lake Palestine Clinic and Olympic Center was strategically designed as a transparent glass box. This retail solution for health and wellness was meant to encourage passersby to see others exercising and to inspire others to get fit. One of 20 centers owned by ETMC, this facility houses a primary care clinic on the ground level, with a fitness center on the second and third floors. Photography by © Gary Zvonkovic easily accessible by car (for suburban and rural areas) or multimodal forms of transportation (in urban areas)? In more densely populated locations, this includes assessing the extent to which a site is connected to busy pedestrian pathways, bike routes, and mass transit lines.

- **Adjacencies.** Is the building or tenant space located near complementary businesses and amenities? For example, there is a trend toward retail clinics being located near pharmacies within big box stores or in community hubs near businesses that offer complementary services or products (such as massage studios or vitamin stores).

- **Geographic distribution.** In many instances, health systems select retail settings for clinics because these enable them to locate their clinics strategically in ways that support other facilities. For example, a hospital can serve as the hub for these systems, and the retail clinics can be positioned at the end of the spokes to draw patients toward the hub as needed.

- **Parking.** In addition to quantity of spaces, it is important to consider the proximity of parking and peak hours of use. For example, it is important to consider when the parking demand for neighboring businesses will also be high in relation to the hours a retail clinic will be open.

- **Distance from collaborating physicians.** Some states mandate a maximum distance from a convenient care clinic at which a collaborating physician can practice (for example, 30 to 50 miles).

Architecture

To a great extent, the architecture of retail clinics is shaped by the original use of a store or tenant space. Generally, however, design professionals:

- Create layouts that provide clear sightlines between the check-in area and surrounding store (or mall) environment as well as to the exam room areas.

- Strive to create an open, comfortable, and welcoming environment to enhance the patient experience.

- Confirm that the retrofitted building or tenant space complies with all applicable local, state, and federal codes.

- Address privacy concerns of patients and providers (e.g., HIPAA requirements).

- Apply Lean Design principles to optimize functional efficiency.

- Select furniture and finishes that meet the durability, safety, and maintenance requirements of healthcare facilities and spaces.

- Collaborate with lighting designers and health information technology staff to minimize glare.

- Relate design quality of the retail clinic to its surroundings so that it blends with or complements them through the use of color, signage, lighting, and architectural forms.

- Design clinics within mass merchandisers, supermarkets, or drugstores as destinations and locate these near main public entries and checkout lanes or next to the pharmacy in order to make it easy for patients to gain access.

Visibility and Brand Recognition

High visibility from major thoroughfares, highways, crossroads, and mass transit stations or hubs is especially important for retail clinics because consumers (prospective patients) are accustomed to shopping for products, not medical services, in these nonconventional care settings.

Attractive architecture and well-designed signage not only help patients find a clinic easily but also can make it memorable and help to establish or bolster brand recognition in communities where a health system is expanding its operations or range of services. Design professionals consider how the architectural and interior design palette, typography, and other details of a healthcare organization's brand program can be appropriately extended into a retail setting.

Although convenient care clinics are often quite small and built on a shoestring budget, creatively integrating the logo/logotype, color palette, and general aesthetic of a healthcare organization into the design can help to establish comfort through familiarity for a reasonable cost. A subset of the healthcare organization's larger corporate identity system can also be developed for its retail clinics so that there is a consistent look across this facility type that makes them easily identifiable in their new contexts.

The Patient Experience

Locating clinics in retail settings can enhance the patient experience in several ways, including the following:

- Having other retail options available nearby may make the patient experience seem less institutional.

- Positioning a retail clinic adjacent to cafés or similar commercial partners can help to reduce the stress patients often feel by providing a relaxing place to read, eat, or work while waiting for an appointment to begin.

- Using finishes, furnishings, and other design elements that match the quality standards established by the store or mall in which the clinic is located. This makes the transition between these spaces more comfortable.

- Clear signage, distinct architectural forms, or patterns on the wall or floor can make a clinic easier to find within a larger store.

- Strategically placed windows provide access to daylight and exterior views and increase a clinic's visibility from the outside.

The Clinician and Group CAHPS (CG-CAHPS) survey developed by the Agency for Healthcare Research and Quality (AHRQ) measures patients' perceptions of care in clinics.[18] It can be a useful tool for design professionals because it includes a number of questions that can be influenced by design.

Survey Questions:

- How well did staff protect your safety?

  Related design question: Is there enough room for a staff member to comfortably and safely accompany a patient who is ill or injured to an exam room?

- How well did staff express concern for your privacy?

  Related design question: Are areas where patient information is viewed or exchanged designed to provide visual and acoustical privacy?

- How was the cleanliness of the practice?

  Related design question: Was proper space allocated for storing cleaning supplies and equipment? Where should this storage space be located? Have the maintenance and repair requirements of finishes and furnishings been considered?

- What was the extent to which staff washed or sanitized their hands before providing care services?

  Related design question: What is the best location for the sink or hand-sanitizing station in the check-in area and in the exam room?

- How well did the staff work together to care for you?

  Related design question: What is the proper sizing and layout of staff areas? Do staff members have easy access to equipment and supplies they need in order to efficiently and effectively provide care services? Should these be neatly, safely, and efficiently stored near the point of care?

- In the last 12 months, how often did you see a provider within 15 minutes of your appointment time?

  Related design question: How can Lean Design principles be applied to keep wait times to less than 15 minutes?

- During your visit, did the provider give you easy to understand information about health questions?

  Related design question: What educational materials need to be stored on-site and where? How should the computer be positioned to make it easy for the care provider and patient to view information together? Where should a printer be located so that health education information can be printed on demand?

- During your most recent, visit did the provider seem to know important information about your health history?

  Related design questions: In what ways does this clinic use electronic health records (EHRs)? For check-in and checkout? During the exam or consultation? To provide telehealth services? How can privacy of this information be maintained?

- On a scale of one to five, with one being "very poor" and five being "very good," please rate the following:

  - Ease of getting through to the clinic on the telephone.

  Related design questions: Will there be a separate telehealth or telephone triage station? If so, how can visual and acoustical privacy be achieved? How large should a triage station be? How should it be furnished and equipped?

  - Convenience of office hours.

  Related design questions: How do the clinic 's hours relate to those of adjacent mall tenants or the retail store in which a clinic is located? Is a separate entry or exit needed from the public one?

  - Ease of scheduling appointment.

  Related design questions: How can the reception/checkout areas be designed to feel welcoming for patients as well as efficient for staff and equipment? Will a kiosk be used?

Care Philosophy

While the majority of convenient care clinics focus on maximizing throughput, clinics in other retail settings provide a variety of services, from primary care to highly specialized, concierge-style services. Thus, the design of a specific retail clinic is strongly influenced by the mission, vision, and values of its owners.

Technology

The ability to gather, store, and share patients' health information electronically has contributed to the growth of retail clinics by making it easier for patients to be diagnosed and treated in a variety of locations without losing the continuity of their care. This makes integrating health information technology into retail clinics in ways that preserve patient privacy a critical design consideration—one that is especially challenging for convenient care clinics that are often adjacent to high-traffic public areas and shoehorned into tightly constrained spaces.

Bricks versus Clicks

As mobile digital technology has improved patients' ability to monitor their health status and the Internet has made access to telehealth services easier, many healthcare organizations have faced a bricks versus clicks decision similar to the ones retailers confronted in the late 1990s. They have had to determine the ideal blend of mobile, online, telephonic, and in-person care, factoring in their geographic location and characteristics of the patient population they serve.

Some of the questions design professionals ask about patients in order to help establish how health information and other medically related technology will be used at a retail clinic include the following:

- How comfortable are patients with using technology?

- Do patients have easy and affordable access to the Internet or mobile technology when they are away from the clinic?

- If so, how likely are they to use telehealth services rather than to be present in person?

- How easy is it for them to take time off from work or away from other activities to visit a clinic in person?

Electronic Health Records

The advent and expanded use of electronic health records has helped fuel the growth of retail clinics because these allow clinic staff to diagnose and treat low-acuity medical conditions in the context of a patient's health history.

Since EHRs have eliminated the need to keep paper health records, retail clinics need less on-site storage space. Instead, staff inputs information directly into the patient's EHR so that care providers located at clinics where patients typically receive care—primary and specialized—can gain access to this new data.

Telehealth

Telehealth options offered by some healthcare organizations may slow the growth of clinics in retail settings by providing patients with the option of an even more convenient location for basis assessment and diagnostic services. In general, virtual visits are expected to evolve from online chats to interactive video-visits and consults via Skype and similar services. Some examples include:

- VirtuWell: This care model is completely electronic. Patients answer a series of questions, and nurse practitioners review this information. The cost for receiving a diagnosis within 30 minutes of completing the online interview is $40.00. Since some health plans cover part of this fee, patients also have the option of filling in their insurance information.

- Care Anywhere (BCBS): This web-based service, which is owned by Blue Cross Blue Shield, allows patients to answer questions and chat online rather than waiting for an e-mail to arrive with a diagnosis. It promises to provide patients with access to "real doctors, real care, real quick."

- Care Anywhere Mobile App (HealthPartners): This free software application can be used on mobile digital devices, such as smartphones, to help patients find the nearest care locations, schedule appointments, and view lab results. With the help of global positioning satellite (GPS) technology, it can also detect where patients are and help them locate the nearest pharmacy where they can obtain or refill prescriptions. This feature is especially valuable when people are traveling away from home.

- HealthEast Care Connection: Patients can connect with the online healthcare service round-the-clock to chat with a nurse practitioner or registered nurse by phone or the Internet. Translators are available for speakers of Hmong, Somali, and Spanish. The demand for this remote care option was so strong that HealthEast built a centralized call center. Patients' calls or online questions are acknowledged in 25 seconds or less. Care Connection staff can gain access to electronic health record information for HealthEast patients and, if necessary, also connect patients directly with a clinic if they have complex symptoms or a complicated condition.

Standards of Operation and Regulations

In response to concerns expressed by the American Medical Association (AMA) about the quality of care and professional oversight associated with convenient care clinics in particular, the AMA and other professional organizations, such as the American Academy of Family Physicians (AAFP), developed basic standards for this evolving clinic type.[19,20] Design professionals keep current with and review these standards and other relevant laws or guidelines as a routine part of planning and designing retail clinics. Examples include rules and regulations of:

- The Americans with Disabilities Act (ADA).
- The Occupational Safety and Health Administration (OSHA).
- The Clinical Laboratory Improvement Amendments (CLIA).
- The Health Insurance Portability and Accountability Act (HIPAA).
- The Centers for Disease Control and Prevention (CDC).

Specialized organizations, such as the Convenient Care Association, have also sprung up to make sure that clinic operators and health systems "provide consumers with accessible, affordable, quality healthcare in retail-based locations."[21] Based on best practices information shared by its members, the CCA established 10 operational and care standards for this type of retail clinic.

Type of Services

Some clinics are better suited for being located in specific retail settings. For example, the degree of privacy patients seek often relates to the kind of medical services they are obtaining. If they need routine or preventative care, they are typically healthy when they arrive at a clinic and less likely to be self-conscious if they are seen seeking medical services in more public places such as a big box retail store or mall.

In contrast to this, patients undergoing chemotherapy or receiving infusions may be feeling weak or ill when they arrive at and leave a clinic. Thus, design professionals pay close attention to eliminating physical barriers and including features such as handrails and chairs with arms to provide extra support. Since chemotherapy and infusion treatments can cause pallor and other alterations in patients' physical appearance, those receiving such care may desire more privacy than patients stopping at a retail clinic merely to get a flu shot or check on a common ailment. In a conventional infusion clinic, patients typically prefer to exit the clinic without having to cross back through the main entry and waiting area.

Building Systems

It is ideal for a retail clinic located within a larger store or in a tenant space within a mall to have its own heating and cooling system. In these instances, it is also important to have entry doors that provide some ability for the clinic's interior climatic conditions to be controlled independently from its retail home.

When a clinic includes a laboratory, imaging equipment, or numerous exam rooms that each require a sink, design professionals pay especially close attention to how the existing mechanical, electrical, and low-voltage electronic (voice and data, in particular) infrastructure will need to be modified to serve a medical rather than a retail function. Since the costs of achieving proper ventilation or sizing and configuring electrical and plumbing system components can be especially high, it is recommended that the engineers on a design team complete a feasibility study as part of the initial project planning phase so that they can provide their clients with this cost information prior to the beginning of lease negotiations.

Feasibility Study Tasks

Key tasks design professionals complete to determine the feasibility of adapting a retail facility for use as a clinic include the following:

- Conducting a walk-through to review and document existing conditions.

- Meeting with building maintenance and facility management personnel to obtain information about the existing building systems, ask about any areas of concern, and understand how these systems have been operated and maintained in the past.

- Assessing the following aspects and components of the mechanical systems:

  - Chillers

  - Boilers

  - Fans and air distribution

  - Plumbing

  - Fire protection

  - Controls and automation

- Evaluating the following aspects and components of the electrical systems:

  - Primary power

  - Power distribution

  - Emergency power

  - Lighting

  - Security

  - Fire alarm

Report

The report resulting from completion of the preceding tasks typically:

- Summarizes key issues, applicable codes, and proposed recommendations.

- Identifies any areas of concern.

- Addresses the potential for future expansion.

- Estimates the remaining useful service life for the major mechanical and electrical systems.

- Identifies any repairs or deferred maintenance projects that need to be completed.

- Presents information about the extent to which existing systems can be used for the new medical function, as well as the costs of replacing, extending, or otherwise adapting these systems.

Safety

Some special safety measures that design professionals consider when designing retail clinics include providing:

- An entry to the clinic that is separate from the high-traffic main public entry of a retail store or mall.

- Adequate outdoor lighting to secure parking areas as well as for the travel path to the front door.

- Clear sightlines between the check-in desk and the route patients seeking care will take to reach the clinic as well as between check-in and the exam room area so that staff can monitor who is approaching, waiting, and being seen by a care provider.

- Specified parking close to the clinic's entry.

- A staffed registration/information desk or a person located near the front door to answer questions and guide patients.

- As short a distance as possible between parking and the clinic entry.

- The design should also make it easy to keep the clinic clean and to maintain the proper hygiene of equipment and supplies along the paths these travel to, through, and out of the clinic.

Staffing

Shortages of physicians and other healthcare professionals have led to the creation of a tiered delivery of care system, with health institutions using a variety of new strategies to extend services into the community, control costs, and provide opportunities for nurse practitioners, complementary care professionals, and midlevel staff to work to the top of their licensure. Retail clinics are increasingly part of this tiered system and, in many instances, serve as the initial entry point for healthcare networks that can connect patients with higher-acuity medical conditions to specialists or hospitals.

Due to concern expressed by professional organizations, such as the American Medical Association, about the quality and consistency of care provided in retail clinics, some states have set physician to physician-extender ratios for this care model. How healthcare organizations are required to work out the details of collaborative relationships among physicians, nurse practitioners, and physician's assistants varies. A 2009 analysis by the National Academy for State Health Policy cited the following examples:[22]

- **California:** The nurse practitioner to physician ratio is 4:1, with physician supervision required for prescriptions. Retail clinics are also required to formalize the physician collaboration and practice protocol in writing.
- **Florida:** The nurse practitioner to physician ratio is also 4:1, and physicians are not allowed to supervise the work of staff at more than four offices beyond their primary practice location.
- **Illinois:** A written physician collaboration and practice protocol are required. Physicians must be on-site once a month. They can delegate the authority for writing prescriptions to nurse practitioners.
- **Massachusetts:** A written physician collaboration and practice protocol are required. The supervising physician must review charts at least once every three months.
- **New Jersey:** Physician collaboration is required for prescriptions. Physicians are also required to review charts, but the frequency of these reviews is not specified.
- **Texas:** The nurse practitioner to physician ratio is 3:1. A written physician collaboration and practice protocol are also required, with physician delegation required for prescriptions. A physician must be on-site 20 percent of the time and must review 10 percent of all charts, although these requirements can be adjusted downward for underserved areas.

Design professionals keep current with requirements such as these to confirm that staff areas in retail clinics are properly sized, configured, equipped, and furnished. Knowing staffing requirements in advance also makes it easier during the site analysis and selection phases of a design project to determine if a particular retail store or tenant space can accommodate these.

Project Examples: Convenient Care

The following case studies introduce a range of ways clinics are being integrated into retail settings. Since this segment of the healthcare industry is evolving quite rapidly, the challenges addressed by each example in this section are meant to catalyze discussion and spark innovative design strategies.

■ CVS CAREMARK: MINUTE CLINICS

In 2000, Minneapolis-based MinuteClinic became the first company to open a convenient care clinic in the United States, and it later became the first to be accredited by the Joint Commission. CVS Caremark acquired Minute-Clinic in 2006, and by 2012 had expanded the number of clinics operating in pharmacies, grocery stores, and big box chain stores to 650, with plans to add another 350 by the year 2016.[23] CVS Caremark is now the largest pharmacy healthcare provider in the nation. The initial acquisition and rapid growth can be attributed, in part, to CVS Caremark's established relationships with physicians through its pharmaceutical offerings.

MinuteClinics are staffed by certified nurse practitioners and physician's assistants who provide preventative and routine healthcare services that are intended to supplement rather than replace those provided by the patient's primary care physician. The design of these retail clinics facilitates and expresses CVS Caremark's goals of providing convenient, timely, and cost-effective healthcare services by:

- Operating according to guidelines established by the American Medical Association and published by the American Academy of Family Physicians.

- Ensuring that the size, layout, equipment, finishes, and furnishings of each clinic efficiently support and enhance a clearly defined, limited scope of care services. Continuity and quality of care are of paramount importance.

- Posting its prices on the web, at the check-in point, and in pamphlets.

- Effectively using electronic health records and electronic prescribing.

■ SUTTER HEALTH EXPRESS CARE CLINICS

In 2006, Sutter Health opened several retail health clinics inside stores of a national drug store chain in the greater Sacramento area. Although prevalent in other states, retail health clinics were a new option for patients in California at that time. Sutter Health's Sutter Express Care clinics provide convenient, affordable access to medical care for common health conditions.

The design team faced several challenges when constructing the clinic locations, including how to maximize the experience for patients, fit all the necessary functions of a medical clinic into a 140- to 150-square-foot room, and represent Sutter Health's brand and organizational values in a retail setting.

The design team addressed these challenges by:

- Locating the medical clinics near the store's pharmacy. The two functions share a single waiting space and patients can conveniently fill any prescriptions ordered during their visit.

- Providing all registration paperwork and instructions at the patient check-in window.

- Allowing patients to provide a cell phone or pager number so that they can shop rather than sit in the nearby waiting room until their appointment begins.

- Using electronic health records and electronic prescribing in order to eliminate the storage space that would be needed for paper forms and files.

- Limiting furnishings in the exam room to an exam table, two guest chairs, and a computer workstation for the nurse practitioner.

- Fitting additional casework into the exam/consult space because all supplies, equipment, and educational materials are stored in this room.

- Ensuring that all clinic-related signage meets Sutter Health's graphic standards. Using Sutter Health's brand colors and typography helps patients to easily find the medical clinic in the drugstore.

A flat fee is charged for most services, with most health plans reimbursing patients for all or part of this amount. No insurance is necessary for a patient to be treated, however. Certified nurse practitioners in each clinic diagnose common illnesses, prescribe medication for conditions such as strep throat or eye, ear, or sinus infections, perform physicals, and provide immunizations. Their work is overseen by a physician/medical director.

◼ WALGREENS HEALTHCARE CLINICS

Healthcare Clinics, a wholly owned subsidiary of Walgreens, is the second largest convenient care operator in the United States, with nearly 400 clinics open nationwide. These facilities are staffed by nurse practitioners and physician's assistants who treat patients 18 months and older for common illnesses. The nurse practitioners are also qualified to provide diagnostic screenings, physicals, basic health evaluations, and vaccinations and to write prescriptions that can usually be filled at a pharmacy located in the same store as the clinic.[24]

In 2013, Walgreens stores in Knoxville, Tennessee, began offering free home delivery for prescriptions in order to improve adherence to medication therapy regimes by patients, particularly those with mobility issues.

To emphasize the importance of access, convenience, cost, and quality, the basic design for one of these convenient care clinics features:

- Patient registration via a kiosk.
- Two exam rooms with sinks.

- Use of an electronic health records system to document each visit and coordinate care with patients' primary clinics.
- Durable furniture and finishes that are easy to clean and repair.
- Soothing colors and textures that blend well with the overall design of the stores.
- An atmosphere that is comfortable for a broad variety of patients across all age groups and of all sizes.

The finished clinics create a "health corner" in each store that makes patients feel as though they are walking into a doctor's office at a conventional clinic.

In addition to preventative care, some Walgreens Healthcare Clinics provide infusion services and other services required by patients with chronic conditions, such as asthma and diabetes. The decision to provide infusion services was not a difficult one for Walgreens, which for decades had been a leading provider of home infusion therapies.

The company has also developed clinical affiliations with large hospital systems and primary care clinics across the country and formed accountable care organizations with major providers such as CIGNA and Aetna to "transform the role of the community pharmacy."

Project Examples: Clinics in Retail Settings

While a major goal of locating clinics in retail settings is to provide convenience for patients, converting former stores or retail tenant spaces to accommodate specific clinic functions presents some significant challenges.

The first critical step toward developing a framework for objectively evaluating vacant retail stores is to complete a program document. This defines the type of services a clinic will offer, lists staffing, equipment, and resource requirements, provides hours of operation, and describes plans to include any specialized imaging, lab, treatment, or procedure areas.

Design professionals use information from the program document to calculate preliminary space needs for a clinic based on industry standards, such as the provider/exam room ratio. They also use a number of key physical criteria to analyze the feasibility and identify the costs associated with locating a clinic in a particular tenant space. Some examples include the following:

- The structural-bay size must be large enough to achieve the clinic's programmatic requirements. If the structural-bay size is too small or oddly shaped, this can lead to an inefficient use of space.

- The above-ceiling space must also be sufficient in order to route heating, ventilation, air conditioning, electric, voice/data, and lighting systems as well as to accommodate materials used to reduce noise from mechanical systems or to achieve acoustical separation between spaces. These are especially salient issues for clinics with labs, diagnostic equipment, or procedure rooms, as these present unique ventilation, cooling, and electrical system requirements.

- Certain exterior wall systems may compromise acoustic separation between exam rooms.

- The location of windows can be an issue for on-grade clinic facilities.

See chapter 5 for further details on clinic planning concepts.

While programmatic requirements and preferences vary greatly among clinics, criteria commonly used to review shell-space options include:

- Convenient access to and optimal visibility from elevators and stairs.

- Ability to negotiate for exterior signage.

- Proximity to parking areas or ramps.

- Existence of a separate elevator to serve back-of-house functions.

- Flexible design standards for the entry leading into the clinic.

- Opportunities for future expansion or contraction.

■ HEALTHEAST SPINE CENTER
Maplewood, Minnesota

This clinic occupies 16,600 square feet of space in a former Gander Mountain retail facility that has high visibility and ample parking and is approximately one block away from St. John's Hospital, where ancillary support is available (full surgical capabilities, for example). This location is also ideal because it is where a large number of patients who suffer from spinal pain live or work.

The Spine Center began as a start-up program within the HealthEast Pain Clinic, but it outgrew this space. Its clinicians provide nonsurgical treatments to reduce back and neck pain, decrease medications, and restore patients' functional capabilities. Examples of specific services include the following:

- Specialized spine treatment.

- Innovative, minimally invasive surgical procedures.

- Physical therapy and rehabilitation.

- Lifestyle management counseling.

- Interventional pain management.

- Discography.

- Spinal cord stimulation.

- Conservative medication management.

- Behavioral health counseling.

The existing building had open shell space with few columns, which made it flexible enough for conversion to medical functions. HealthEast calls consultation and exam rooms at this facility "care rooms."

The design team developed an on-stage/off-stage layout for staff space that includes a core where clinicians can collaborate and complete tasks that do not require interaction with patients. This layout also allows patients to focus on their "journey" while they are in the care rooms and not be distracted by supply deliveries, equipment, and the staff's back-of-house activities.

The clinic's design employs Lean strategies and expresses HealthEast's vision for a state-of-the-art, evidence-driven spinal care model with:

- A single point of entry rotunda for common entry to care areas.
- Dedicated individual, seated registration areas for each patient.
- Ample room for queuing at registration desk without blocking circulation paths.

- Direct sightlines from the main entry door to registration desk.
- Skylights in the patient walkway areas.
- Heated sidewalks.
- Ergonomic chairs.
- iPads for viewing educational videos.
- Touch screens in exam/consult rooms to project x-rays and MRI images.
- A warm-hued color palette.
- Lighting and music that can be adjusted to suit the preferences of individual patients.
- A checkout area located and configured for inflow from procedure zone only.[25]

While staff satisfaction levels stayed the same between the old and new location (4.25 on a 5-point scale), the patient experience scores rose from 37 percent of those interviewed saying they would recommend the clinic to others, to 95 percent being willing to do this for the new facility and the services it provides. The new layout enabled care providers to double the number of patients they saw from 22 patients a day in

FIGURES 8-3, 8-4: HealthEast Spine Clinic, Maplewood, Minnesota. The Spine Center is a 16,000-square-foot renovation of a former Gander Mountain store surrounded by adjacent retail, services, and office spaces in a highly visible "city-center" location that reaches out to the surrounding community. HealthEast realized the advantage of converting retail spaces into clinics when the glut in vacant retail properties presented itself. With the recession driving purchase prices and lease rates down, constructing clinics in retail settings became a viable option. Photography by Steve Henke

September 2012 to 59 patients a day in August, 2013. During this same period total revenues climbed from $139,000 to $357,000. The construction cost for the Spine Center was $1,400,000, with a total project cost of $2,062,000 (figs. 8-3, 8-4).[26]

■ MIDWAY CLINIC
St. Paul, Minnesota

The prime geographic location, tall ceilings, and ample free-span space of a vacant Borders bookstore prompted HealthEast to relocate and expand one of its internal medicine clinics into this building. HealthEast had searched for four years to find a site that met its criteria and was, at first, hesitant to consider retail properties. Its goals for this project included:

* Staying south of Interstate 694 to avoid disconnecting the new clinic from its established patient base, which was older, required ongoing treatment for chronic conditions, and had strong physician loyalty.

* Preserving and expanding this clinic's role as a destination for health and wellness.

* Being close to a major freeway.

While this site was at the far edge of the catchment area that HealthEast was targeting, it had a number of advantages over other properties, including the fact that Optimum Rehabilitation was an adjacent tenant and the existing building was flexible enough to apply the Lean Methodology to design of this clinic.

One of the unique recommendations that the Lean Design team made was for the creation of separate intake, exam, and checkout rooms in order to improve the patient experience and efficiency. This made it possible for the "right person at the right time to do the right job."

Patients register in "intake rooms" on the ground level of the building. The combination of repeat patients and the use of electronic health records helps streamline the check-in process occurring in these. Patients then move to the second level or to another area on the ground floor, depending on the type of care they require.

After leaving an exam room, patients stop in one of the private checkout offices where they are connected with a specialist who reviews the self-care and other actions they should take. This gives the patient a little time to think about questions or concerns as he or she moves from the exam/consult room to the checkout space. Since a discharge plan is printed for every patient, each checkout space needs a printer and access to HealthEast's electronic health record system.

The intake process in the original clinic lasted seven minutes. However, the Lean Design team's research revealed this was too short a period because clinicians were not able to collect all of the information needed. This meant that a lot of vaccines that should have been given were missed.

The clinic's new 15-minute check-in period reduces the time physicians formerly spent filling in missing information during exam periods and enables them to spend more time diagnosing, treating, and consulting with patients. Vaccine administrations also increased by 5 percent. More efficient use of exam time also meant the exam room ratio could be reduced to 11 providers working out of 18 rooms.

Lean principles also influenced the design of staff areas. Physicians have small offices at the end of a shared provider and staff work area. Skylights boost the natural light level to make this a pleasant area in which to work. This is the first HealthEast clinic to use white noise to eliminate sound transfer between patient spaces.

Although staff satisfaction levels between the original and replacement clinic remained the same (4.25 on a 5-point scale), the patient experience scores soared. At the original clinic,

FIGURES 8-5, 8-6: HealthEast Midway Clinic, St. Paul, Minnesota. When a former retail location in St. Paul's Midway area became available, HealthEast's Midway Internal Medicine Clinic decided to relocate to this former Borders bookstore. There are advantages to having this location: parking, visibility, access to the light rail and freeway, plus the convenience of having amenities like shopping and fitness facilities nearby. Photography by Steve Henke

37 percent of the patients who were interviewed said they would recommend the clinic to family and friends. This percentage jumped to 95 percent at the new location. Gross revenues also increased significantly, from $7,400,000 at the original location to $8,200,000 at the new one. The new 23,000-square-foot Midway Clinic opened in April 2011. Its construction cost was $1,415,000, with a total project cost of $2,606,000 (figs. 8-5, 8-6).[27]

Retail Mall Tenant Spaces

Some healthcare organizations are providing commercial amenities within retail clinics or selecting tenant spaces in malls near complementary businesses.

■ HEALTHEAST GRAND AVENUE CLINIC
St. Paul, Minnesota

In 2009, HealthEast moved a primary care clinic from a residential neighborhood into the former EQ Life store on a busy commercial corner in St. Paul. In addition to community-based family medicine, the clinic specializes in integrative care, obstetrics, gynecology, midwifery services, and diabetes education. Weekend hours are available on a walk-in basis.

The 12,000-square-foot storefront location selected for this clinic offered several key benefits:

- High visibility in an upscale historic district.
- Proximity to the affluent, highly educated patient population it had served since 1996.
- Access to mass transit and free on-street parking.

At the time, locating clinics in retail centers such as this one was still a novel idea. This meant that HealthEast had to invest extra time to meet with community organizations, such as the Summit Hill Association, to demonstrate how healthcare functions could blend with retail. The quality of design established by neighboring stores, such as Pottery Barn and J. Crew, led the project team to create a design that was warm, comfortable, and inviting.

The design team achieved HealthEast's goal of making this clinic a "medi-spa" by integrating decorative backlit nature panels along the corridor leading to the exam rooms, selecting earth-tone finishes and comfortable furnishings, blending soft pendant lighting in the entry and waiting areas, and using rich walnut wood paneling to highlight the exam room entries. Interior lighting levels are bright enough to make the areas without windows appear as though there is daylight present. (figs. 8-7–8-10).

FIGURE 8-7: HealthEast Grand Avenue, St. Paul, Minnesota. The interior design of the HealthEast Grand Avenue Clinic was influenced by neighboring retail shops. Photography by Steve Henke

FIGURE 8-9: HealthEast Grand Avenue. Spa-like details such as walnut veneer, wooden screens, and pendant lighting soften the space and help give a warm and welcoming feeling. Photography by Steve Henke

FIGURE 8-8: HealthEast Grand Avenue. Backlit nature images help to bring a feeling of natural daylight in back areas of the clinic. Photography by Steve Henke

FIGURE 8-10: HealthEast Grand Avenue. Entries to the exam rooms are clearly identified by a wood panel and sconce. Photography by Steve Henke

Since the footprint for this clinic space was small and the downstairs portion of it could be used only for storage, laying out the clinic and meeting programmatic requirements proved especially challenging.

The existing narrow public frontage minimized the street presence of the clinic, which meant that patients had to look for it. However, the majority of people parking at the shopping area must walk past the clinic as they exit the parking ramp. Public access is on the first floor.

The website for this clinic has a patients portal that allows them to leave secure messages with their care provider and request appointments online. Notebook computers are used throughout the clinic to access patient health records and input new medical information. This eliminates the need for personal computers in exam rooms. Printing is done in a central location.

Since this was HealthEast's first significant foray into locating clinics in retail settings, a number of lessons learned from this project helped inform this healthcare organization's decisions and priorities for this facility type. These lessons included the following:

- The reception area was too small to accommodate the substantial increase in patient load that occurred once the clinic moved to its new location. Since this created a bottleneck at the main entry desk, more queuing space was needed, and this had to be moved out of the main circulation route.

- The checkout process was challenging, too, because check-in and checkout are completed at the same desk. Ideally, the checkout desk should be directed back toward the corridor that connects it with the exam rooms.

- Dividers were used to create a physical separation between the registration and waiting areas. The waiting area proved to be adequately sized for the increased number of patients served by the relocated clinic.

- Exam rooms used a conventional layout, with recessed charting stations provided along the corridor.

- HealthEast has remodeled this relatively new clinic to accommodate a significant staff increase. The number of care providers has doubled from 5 to 10 in the first few years of operation.

- The staff work area was compartmentalized, with physicians and administrative staff having separate areas within this space.

Patient referral scores, staff satisfaction levels, and gross revenues all increased after the new clinic opened. Staff satisfaction improved from a score of 3.25 on a 5-point scale to 4.06. At the old location, only 45 percent of the patients surveyed said they would recommend the clinic to family and friends. This increased to 85 percent for the new clinic. Gross revenues grew from $3,917,000 at the original clinic location to $ 6,906,000 for the Grand Avenue retail clinic. The construction cost for this project was $935,000, with a total project cost of $1,330,000. These figures do not include tenant improvement amounts covered by the landlord.[28]

Project Examples: Emerging Models

At first, the lines between convenient care clinics and clinics in retail settings were clear. Convenient care clinics were typically located within a retail store instead of occupying a former retail tenant space or building. They offered the most basic of primary care services on a fee-for-service basis, and no appointment was needed.

On the other hand, clinics in retail settings offered a broader range of primary care services provided by physicians and other staff, or they specialized in a discipline to serve the needs of a specific patient population (for example, HealthEast's Spine Center). Patients needed to schedule appointments in advance.

In recent years, as the outmigration of care has continued to extend the reach of healthcare organizations so that they can provide services closer to where people live and work, convenient care clinics have begun to grow in size and offer services such as infusion that require scheduling in advance and specialized furnishings and equipment as well as staff with specific training and skills.

■ SCHNUCK'S INFUSION SOLUTIONS
St. Louis, Missouri

These clinics represent a relatively recent trend in the range of healthcare services that are offered in retail settings. In November 2013, Midwest-based Schnuck's Markets opened a 6,500-square-foot infusion center in one of its grocery stores in St. Louis, Missouri. Since Schnuck's stores also have pharmacies, the infusion therapy treatments can be administered by pharmacists or by certified registered nurses with proper infusion accreditations from the Infusion Nurses Certification Corp. The design of this facility features:

- Access to patients' online health records.

- Three infusion chairs per room.

- Provision of positive distractions, such as no-cost Internet, cable television, and snacks during infusion sessions (which can take up to eight hours).

- The option of making evening or weekend appointments in addition to visiting the clinic during regular workday hours.

According to industry experts, this business model makes sense because infusion treatments can be provided at a lower cost than at most hospitals while expanding the range of services used to attract patients to clinics and shoppers to the grocery store.

■ WALMART PRIMARY CARE CLINICS
Nationwide

In 2008, Walmart's leaders began looking into ways to integrate healthcare into this retail giant's marketing mix by first opening in-store clinics and then, in 2011, developing a private health insurance program for its employees.

These strategies make sense for a big box retail chain that appeals to frugal shoppers in an aging America. Walmart is already a shopping destination for the increasing number of people who are on Medicare and Medicaid. It has also shown strong support for the U.S. military, and the veteran's population has grown significantly in the wake of the wars in Iraq and Afghanistan.

Walmart offers its employees two Blue Cross/Blue Shield–managed options: a health reimbursement account and an HRA High, which has a higher deductible requirement but lower premiums. Walmart employees can also set up and contribute to health savings accounts. They can obtain medical services from several of the nation's highest-ranking healthcare institutions, including the Mayo Clinic, Geisinger Medical Center, and the Cleveland Clinic.

"The Clinic at Walmart," as the in-store clinics are called, offers primary, diagnostic, and preventative care services on a walk-in basis seven days a week. Since each clinic is independently owned and operated, their design uses a standardized format that enables them to cobrand with local hospitals, medical groups, or organizations—such as RediClinics —that specialize in the provision of convenient care. Walmart decided to use this collaborative approach once research indicated that its customers preferred to have medical services delivered by a trusted local practice or healthcare organization.

In January 2013, Walmart announced a plan to offer full primary care services in its convenient care clinics within five to seven years. Walmart now hopes to become "the largest provider of primary healthcare services in the nation."[29,30]

Summary

The growth in the number of clinics located in retail settings reflects increased consumer demand for convenient and affordable healthcare services. Patients not only want "the right care, at the right time, at the right place" but also want it at the "right price." Insurance companies and healthcare organizations agree with consumers now that the Affordable Care Act has increased the number of people who have health insurance coverage and shifted the industry toward an outcomes-based reimbursement structure.

An aging U.S. population and large number of veterans who need ongoing care services are also putting pressure on the healthcare industry to provide more access points and better utilize the full training and skills of midlevel care providers, such as nurse practitioners and physician's assistants. Retail clinics are helping to achieve these goals, too.

Growth in this care model and related facility types is expected to remain strong as the range of services provided at clinics in retail settings continues to extend beyond routine and preventative care to include spa services (e.g., manicures and podiatry), ongoing treatment for chronic conditions, and other amenities. Design professionals will have ample opportunities to apply knowledge they have acquired from working on traditional clinics projects to the design of retail clinics.

CHRISTINE GUZZO VICKERY

Notes

1. John Goodman, "Lessons from MinuteClinic," The Health Care Blog, August 6, 2012, http://healthbolg.ncpa.org/lessons-from-minuteclinic.

2. Dean Deale, "Retail Clinics: The Evolution of CVS' Minute Clinic," Retailnet Group, May 9, 2012, http://www.instoretrends.com/index.php/2012/05/09/retail-clinics-the-evolution-of-cvs-minute-clinic/.

3. Website of Convenient Care Association, http://www.ccaclinics.org.

4. Tara Kulash, "Schnucks Moves into Health Care," St. Louis Post-Dispatch, November 5, 2013.

5. Advisory Board Company, "Report: Number of Retail Clinics to Double by 2015," June 13, 2013.

6. Margaret Laws, "The Emergence of Retail-Based Clinics in the United States: Early Observations," Health Affairs 27 (2008): 1293–98.

7. Frank Jossi, "Health Clinics See Success Setting up Shop in Former Stores," Finance & Commerce, December 18, 2012.

8. Burl Gilyard, "As Medical Space Tightens, Clinics are Drawn to Former Retail Stores," Finance & Commerce, May 2, 2012.

9. Rand Health, "Health Care on Aisle 7: The Growing Phenomenon of Retail Clinics," Rand Corporation, 2010, http://www.rand.org/content/dam/rand/pubs/research_briefs/2010/RAND_RB9491-1.pdf.

10. Laws, "The Emergence of Retail-Based Clinics."

11. HealthStream, "CG-CAHPS Is Coming...Are You Prepared?" http://info.healthstream.com/cg-cahps-sem?component=701300000 00lEvY&product=CG-CAHPS&gclid=CN7n-9PF_roCFYNaMgodTlcA4w.

12. HealthHarbor, "Retail & Walk-In Healthcare: Comparing Costs," 2011, http://www.healthharbor.com/saving-on-retail-healthcare/retail-health-comparing-costs.

13. Phil Galewitz, "Census: Uninsured Numbers Decline as More Young Adults Gain Coverage," *Kaiser Health News,* September 12, 2012.

14. Paul H. Keckley, Howard R. Underwood, and Malay Gandhi, "Retail Clinics: Facts, Trends, and Implications," Deloitte Center for Health Solutions, 2008, http://www.deloitte.com/assets/Dcom-UnitedStates/Local%20Assets/Documents/us_chs_RetailClinics_230708(1).pdf.

15. Ibid.

16. CVS Caremark Corporation, "About MinuteClinic," http://www.minuteclinic.com/about.

17. Molly Gamble, "17 Largest Retail Clinic Operators in the United States," *Becker's Hospital Review,* April 6, 2012, http://www.beckershospitalreview.com/lists/17-largest-retail-clinic-operators-in-the-united-states.html.

18. HealthStream, "CG-CAHPS Is Coming..."

19. Laws, "The Emergence of Retail-Based Clinics."

20. "AAFP Operational Standards for Retail Clinics," as accessed by the author on 3 September 3, 2014, http://www.aafp.org/about/policies/all/retail-clinics.html.

21. Convenient Care Association, http://www.ccaclinics.org.

22. Mary Takach and Kathy Witgert, *Analysis of State Regulations and Policies Governing the Operation and Licensure of Retail Clinics* (Washington, DC: National Academy of State Health Policy, 2009), http://nashp.org/sites/default/files/RetailClinics.pdf?q=files/RetailClinics.pdf

23. CVS Caremark Corporation, "About MinuteClinic."

24. Walgreens Healthcare Clinics, http:www.walgreens.com/topic/pharmacy/healthcare-clinic.jsp.

25 "HealthEast Will Open Spine Clinic Near Maplewood Mall." *Star Tribune* (Minneapolis, MN). May 19, 2012, http://www.startribune.com/local/east/152160855.html.

26. Tony Thomas, Len Kaiser, Dennis Vonasek, and Christine Guzzo Vickery, "Converting Retail Spaces into Clinics—The Challenges and Opportunities," *Healthcare Design* Conference, November 18, 2013.

27. Ibid.

28. Ibid.

29. Advisory Board Company, "Walmart's New Plan: 'Full Primary Care Services' within Seven Years," January 14, 2013.

30. Julie Appleby and Sarah Varney. "Walmart Wants to Be Nation's Biggest Primary Care Provider, November 9, 2011, " http://www.kaiserhealthnews.org/stories/2011/november/09/walmart-primary-care-medical-services.aspx.Kaiser Health News.

Select Bibliography

Advisory Board Company. "Walmart's New Plan: 'Full Primary Care Services' within Seven Years." January 14, 2013.

Convenient Care Association. http://www.ccaclinics.org.

CVS Caremark Corporation. "About MinuteClinic." n.d. http://www.minuteclinic.com/about.

Deloitte Center for Health Solutions. "Health Care Retail Clinics Continue Gradual Expansion

Through 2012: Deloitte Center for Health Solutions Report." November 16, 2009. http://www.deloitte.com/view/en_US/us/Industries/US-federal-government/center-for-health-solutions/6fa41d3b16de4210VgnVCM100000ba42f00aRCRD.htm.

———. "Center for Health Solutions." As accessed by the author on 9/4/2014 http://www.deloitte.com/view/en_US/us/Insights/centers/center-for-health-solutions.

Dolan, Pamela Lewis. "AMA Meeting: Delegates Seek More Oversight of Retail Clinics." American Medical Association. July 16, 2007. http://www.amednews.com/article/20070716/profession/307169973/2.

HealthStream. "CG-CAHPS is coming...Are you prepared?" http://info.healthstream.com/cg-cahps-sem?component=70130000000lEvY&product=CG-CAHPS&gclid=CN7n-9PF_roCFYNaMgodTlcA4w.

Herrick, Devon. "Retail Clinics: Convenient and Affordable Care." National Center for Policy Analysis. January 14, 2010. http://www.ncpa.org/pdfs/ba686.pdf.

Keckley, Paul H., Howard R. Underwood, and Malay Gandhi. "Retail Clinics: Facts, Trends, and Implications." Deloitte Center for Health Solutions. 2008. http://www.deloitte.com/assets/Dcom-UnitedStates/Local%20Assets/Documents/us_chs_RetailClinics_230708(1).pdf.

Laws, Margaret. "The Emergence of Retail-Based Clinics in the United States: Early Observations." *Health Affairs* 27 (2008): 1293–98.

Maryland State Medical Society. "Retail Clinics." House of Delegates CL Report 2-09, 2009. http://www.medchi.org/sites/default/files/CL%20Report%202-09%20-%20Retail%20Clinics%20FINAL.pdf.

Rand Health, "Health Care on Aisle 7: The Growing Phenomenon of Retail Clinics." Rand Corporation, 2010. http://www.rand.org/content/dam/rand/pubs/research_briefs/2010/RAND_RB9491-1.pdf.

Sutter Express Care Clinics. http://www.sutterexpresscare.com.

Takach, Mary, and Kathy Witgert. *Analysis of State Regulations and Policies Governing the Operation and Licensure of Retail Clinics.* Washington, DC: National Academy of State Health Policy, 2009. http://nashp.org/sites/default/files/RetailClinics.pdf?q=files/RetailClinics.pdf.

Walgreen's Healthcare Clinics. http://www.walgreen's.com/topic/pharmacy/healthcare-clinic.jsp.

Overview

A major challenge of designing a clinic that best serves the needs of a "medical home" is that even after nearly half a century of growth and development, this healthcare delivery model is still a work in progress. The definition and key characteristics of the medical home model continue to be broadly interpreted, tested, recontextualized, and refined.

There are hundreds of demonstration projects underway across the United States. Details for reforming payment structures to better align with this new care model, incentives for upgrading and improving the health information technology needed to help it work well, and the role that community service organizations can play in complementing and augmenting care provided by medical homes are still being resolved. The approaches for addressing these challenges also vary greatly at the state, local, and institutional levels.

The good news is that this degree of complexity and fluidity makes the role of design professionals especially valuable as they collaborate with clinic owners, public agencies, community service organizations, foundations, and others to determine how the built environment can facilitate and enhance the services provided by medical practices that choose to implement this team-based, tech-savvy, patient-centric care model.

History

The definition of the medical home model has evolved significantly from its initial focus on centralizing the health records of children to today, when it is also known as the "patient-centered medical home model (PCMH)" because its definition, key attributes, and objectives have been broadened to address the preventative, acute, chronic, and end-of-life care for all patients throughout all life stages. The following chronology highlights key points in this evolution:

1967 The phrase "medical home" is introduced by the American Academy of Pediatrics (AAP) in its *Standards of Child Health Care Manual* as a way to describe its vision for creating a "home"—a central location, for all medical information related to children, particularly those with chronic conditions or other special needs.

1978 The World Health Organization meets to establish the basic tenets of the medical home while affirming the importance primary care in implementing and sustaining this model. The Alma Ata Declaration asserts that health is "a state of complete physical, mental, and social well-being, and not merely the absence of disease or infirmity" and that primary care should be delivered as close as possible to where people live and work.[2]

1980s Through his efforts to find new approaches for improving early childhood development in Hawaii, pediatrician Dr. Calvin Sia lays the groundwork for a 1992 statement by the AAP that further defines the medical home as a care delivery strategy.

1990s In 1992, the AAP issues a policy statement that outlines the seven attributes a healthcare practice—or, more specifically, a "regular source of care"—must have to be considered a medical home.[3] According to the AAP, care provided by a medical home must be accessible, continuous, comprehensive, family-centered, coordinated, compassionate, and culturally effective. These tenets are embraced by the Institute of Medicine. By the end of this decade, the phrase "medical home" also begins to appear in family medicine literature.

2000 The Family Practice Working Party (WP) and the Academic Family Medicine Organization (AFMO) conceive of the Future of Family Medicine Project as a joint effort aimed at transforming and renewing this medical specialty to meet patient needs in a changing healthcare environment. Key questions to be addressed by this research effort are: "What do patients want and expect from health care professionals...and what is the role that family physicians could or should play?"

2002 The Future of Family Medicine Project is officially launched in January 2002. The findings and recommendations of this project are presented to the WP and AFMO in August 2003, with a final report published as a supplement to the March/April 2004 issue of *Annals of Family Medicine*.

2004 The American Academy of Pediatrics issues an updated policy statement that addresses two major challenges physicians using the medical home model continue to encounter: this concept is still open to a broad variety of interpretations, and many of the services medical homes need to provide for this model to succeed are inadequately reimbursed.

The Future of Family Medicine Project's report states that all Americans should have a "personal medical home" to meet their preventative, acute, and chronic care needs.[4] It also recommends that this "new care model" should:

- Use a patient-centered team approach.
- Eliminate barriers to access.
- Use advanced information systems, including the creation and use of electronic health records.
- Feature redesigned, more functional offices.
- Focus on the quality of health outcomes.

It concludes that the care services provided by patient-centered medical homes should be "accessible, accountable, comprehensive, integrated, patient-centered, safe, scientifically valid, and satisfying to both patients and their physicians."[5] This report catalyzes national conversations that lead to the more comprehensive care model now referred to as the "patient-centered medical home" (PCMH).

2006 The Patient-Centered Primary Care Collaborative is formed to promote the medical home model. Within the next few years its membership grows to include approximately 500 large employers, insurers, consumer groups, and doctors.

The American Academy of Family Physicians launches a National Demonstration Project (NDP) to test and refine the emerging consensus principles of the PCMH.

The American College of Physicians (ACP) develops an "advanced medical home model" that expands the medical home concept first presented by the American Academy of Pediatrics in 1967 and builds on the description of the medical home formulated and presented as part of the Future of Family Medicine Project. In 2006, the ACP publishes the results of its research in a document titled "The Advanced Medical Home: A Patient-Centered, Physician Guided Model of Healthcare."[6] The extended name of the medical home model reflects the ACP's emphasis on the importance of a medical home being led by a primary care physician. The ACP's report also states that physicians and practices adopting its advanced medical home model will:

- Use evidence-based medicine and clinical decision support tools to guide recommendations made at the point of care regarding the condition and needs of specific patients.

- Base care delivery for all patients on the Chronic Care Model (CCM) because nearly half the population in the United States has a chronic illness or condition and 75 percent of our nation's healthcare dollars go to treatment of chronic diseases.[7]

- Create integrated, coherent plans for partnering with patients and their families to provide continuous care.

- Provide convenient access by telephone, e-mail, and other modes of communication as well as in person in face-to-face visits.

Use health information technology to provide safe, quality, affordable care and promote the exchange of health information while protecting the privacy of individual patients.

The ACP's report also underscores that payment reform will be essential to the successful implementation of this advanced vision for medical homes.

The organization for Improving Chronic Illness Care (ICIC) asserts that since "improved functional and clinical outcomes are the product of an informed, activated patient and a prepared, proactive practice team," basic elements of its model can be applied to provide enhanced care for all patients with or without a chronic condition.[8]

2007 In March of this year, four major primary care physician associations release the Joint Principles of the Patient-Centered Medical Home: the American Academy of Family Physicians (AAFP), the American Academy of Pediatrics (AAP), the American College of Physicians (ACP), and the American Osteopathic Association (AOA).

Within a few years, 19 additional physician organizations endorse the core principles and definition presented in the Joint Principles document.

During this year, the National Academy for State Health Policy (NASHP) also provides its first round of financial assistance to eight states (Colorado, Idaho, Louisiana, Minnesota, New Hampshire, Oklahoma, Oregon, and Washington) that are working to create medical homes for patients participating in Medicaid programs for adults and children.

2009 The National Committee for Quality Assurance releases a set of voluntary standards for the recognition of physician practices as medical homes in a document titled Physician Practice Connections–Patient-Centered Medical Home (PPC-PCMH).

The Accreditation Association for Ambulatory Health Care (AAAHC) adds the medical home to the types of organizations that it accredits. Its program includes on-site surveys conducted by qualified professionals who directly observe the quality of patient care and the facilities in which it is delivered.

The National Academy for State Health Policy (NASHP) supports the efforts of a second set of states to develop new medical home programs: Alabama, Iowa, Kansas, Maryland, Montana, Nebraska, Texas, and Virginia. Some of the common themes that emerge as these (and earlier) states test the medical home model with the support of the NASHP include:

- The definition and priorities of the medical home model vary according to the specific needs and characteristics of individual states. For example, in Montana, the definition of medical home addresses the importance of cultural context and community-based care.

- Payment policies can foster collaboration and reward performance. Iowa compensates primary care providers when they conduct remote consultations with hospital-based specialists. Alabama pays more to practices that collaborate with their local networks. Some states provide higher medical home payments to practices that meet more demanding standards, such as effectively using a registry, and some share the savings realized by practices that perform well.

- Some states are explicitly directing participating practices to use part of their medical home payments to hire staff to coordinate care, while others are focusing on connecting practices with public and community organizations that can provide support services that complement and augment the medical care that patients are receiving.

2010   The final report on the National Demonstration Project that the American Academy of Family Physicians initiated in 2006 is published. It concludes that the PCMH model offers "significant promise" for improving the patient experience and reducing healthcare costs. It also identifies some barriers to adoption of this model, such as:

- Insufficient information technology capabilities among primary care physicians.

- The fact that hospitals do not yet have a defined role in the creation of PCMHs—although some integrated service networks, or ISNs, are developing hospital-based PCMH models. [9]

In an article titled "The Future of Health Information Technology in the Patient-Centered Medical Home," David W. Bates and Asaf Bitton identify seven key health information technology domains that are necessary for the success of the PCMH model: telehealth, measurement of quality and efficiency, care transitions, personal health records, registries,

team care, and clinical decision support for chronic diseases. [10]

2011   On January 31, 2011, the National Committee for Quality Assurance (NCQA) releases new standards for patient-centered medical homes that practices must meet to become NCQA-certified. The standards call on all medical practices to be more patient-centered and reinforce the federal "meaningful use" incentives that can help primary care practices purchase the health information technology they need in order to become a medical home. Many PCMH demonstration projects use these standards as a measurement tool, and some health plans require NCQA certification before making incentive payments to practices. [11]

In July 2011, the Joint Commission launches the Primary Care Medical Home Certification program for ambulatory care organizations. This certification program dovetails with the Affordable Care Act's efforts to improve health outcomes by achieving continuity, quality, and efficiency in the delivery of care. The Joint Commission's PCMH certification program also stresses education and self-management by the patient.

2014 and beyond   Healthcare industry experts predict that thousands of primary care practices will attempt to convert to the PCMH model. Demonstration projects that are underway garner support from a diverse range of constituencies—from professional organizations and governmental agencies to insurers, major employers, and foundations.

Definition

The Joint Principles of the Patient-Centered Medical Home (2007)[12] defines the patient-centered medical home (PC-MH or Medical Home) as "a healthcare setting that facilitates partnerships between individual patients...their personal physicians, and...the patient's family." In 2011, the National Committee for Quality Assurance further clarified this definition by stating that medical homes "strengthen the clinician-patient relationship by "replacing episodic care with coordinated care and a long-term healing relationship."[13]

Over the years, a number of states and professional organizations have developed their own definitions of what constitutes a medical home. However, they all use a team-based approach to delivering healthcare services with the goal of providing the "right care, by the right person, at the right time."

Key Characteristics

The Joint Principles document identified seven key characteristics that medical homes have in common: continuity, team-based care, whole-person orientation, coordination, quality and safety, and enhanced access. It also addressed the need for a new payment structure that recognizes and rewards the added value provided to patients who have a patient-centered medical home.

Continuity

In a medical home, each patient has an ongoing, personal relationship with a physician who is trained to be the first point of contact and to provide continuous and comprehensive care. The practice provides patients with the tools and information they need to manage their health on a daily basis and throughout their lives.

Team-Based Care

Medical homes are committed to collaboratively providing care for patients. A physician typically leads a care team that collectively takes responsibility for providing the full spectrum of care—preventative, acute, chronic, and end-of-life—for patients throughout all life stages.

Most medical home collaborative teams are led by primary care physicians who are accustomed to addressing a wide variety of medical conditions, coordinating care with other health professionals, and providing care to individuals within the context of their family, culture, and community. The care team also provides patients with resources, information, and tools for monitoring and managing their own health and wellness over time.

Whole-Person Orientation

The medical home ensures that all patient needs are met, whether or not specific services are offered by a particular practice. This means that the patient's personal physician will make referrals to other health professionals as needed and coordinate the care that he/she provides with educational programs and materials, out-of-home care, family support, and other public or private community services.

Coordination

The medical home team coordinates care for patients across all settings, leveraging nonmedical support and services when needed. The coordination of care is facilitated by the use of information technology and health information exchanges.

Quality and Safety

Healthcare organizations and practices using the medical home model emphasize delivering high-quality, safe care. They measure their success based on the level of health and wellness that they help patients attain and sustain. Care teams use evidence-based medicine and clinical decision-support tools, such as computerized alerts and reminders, online collection of information, electronic health records, and patient data reports to enhance the quality of their decisions and related care recommendations. They also actively seek feedback from patients and their family members to ensure that expectations are being met. Patients (and their families) are responsible for providing the care team with feedback about the quality of care they are receiving so that continuous improvements can be made.

Enhanced Access

If medical homes truly want to provide the right care, by the right person, at the right time, they need to make care easily accessible for patients. This means that patients must be able to obtain quality healthcare services, including triage, when and where they need it. Accessible care is also financially affordable and conveniently located.

Medical homes use a variety of strategies for enhancing patients' access to care, including open scheduling; expanded hours; web-based assessment, registration, and follow-up tools; e-visits and remote consults; and the option of exchanging information (or obtaining reminders) by phone, e-mail, or text messaging.

Payment Reform

Over time, the structure of the healthcare system in the United States has led to care services being spread across multiple providers and locations for the majority of patients. A fee-for-service payment system reinforced these care (and data) siloes and rewarded the quantity of services provided rather than the quality of care. The reformed payment structure associated with the medical home model rewards doctors to keep their patients healthy—rather than limiting reimbursement to the treatment of sick patients at clinics.

Thus, healthcare professionals who have attempted to implement the medical home model stress the importance of payment reform for shifting healthcare from a reactive mode of operation to a proactive approach of preventing illnesses and injuries whenever possible.

While a wide variety of strategies and tactics have been discussed for accomplishing this reform, they generally share these principles:

- All members of the collaborative care team should be compensated based on their contributions to achieving desired health outcomes. This includes compensating clinicians who provide direct care, ancillary specialists brought in to consult on individual cases, and clinic staff members who assist with care coordination and health management tasks that fall outside of the traditional face-to-face clinic visit.

- Payment reform should support the adoption and use of information technology for improving the quality of care, improving communications, and increasing access for patients via telephone, e-mail, the web, other interactive or digital media. This includes e-visits, remote visits and consults, and web-based registration and health-risk assessments, and the like.

- Payment for fee-for-service visits should be separated from payment for care services that are not provided face-to-face in the clinic.

- Practices should be able to share in the savings that result from improved efficiency and effectiveness of care.

- The payment structure should recognize the case-mix differences within the patient population being treated by a particular practice.

- Physicians and nonphysician staff members should be paid for time they spend using technology to optimize patient care, measure performance, improve communication, share knowledge and information, and better collect, store, and monitor health data.

In the future, a clinic will have to comply with PCMH recognition/certification requirements to be reimbursed according to the reformed payment structure.

Trends

While many of the factors that have contributed to the evolution of the medical home model have been mentioned in the preceding chronology, healthcare reform, reimbursement methods, staffing, and the use of health information and communications technology are having the greatest impact on decisions about the design of clinics using this care delivery method.

Healthcare Reform

It is clear that the evolution of the medical home model started long before the Patient Protection and Affordable Care Act (ACA) was signed into law on March 23, 2010. In fact, research conducted over the 40-plus years that passed after the AAP first coined the phrase "medical home" helped to shape key aspects of this legislation, such as linking reimbursement to the achievement of optimal health outcomes, advocacy of a team-based approach to providing care, and using technology to collect, store, and synthesize health data, both for individuals and for patient populations.

The patient-centered medical home is specifically cited in several sections of the ACA, including those addressing the quality of care, health plan choices, and the development of new patient care models. Section 3502 of the ACA directs the Secretary of Health and Human Services to either provide grants to or enter into contractual agreements with "entities" eligible for establishing the "interdisciplinary,

interprofessional health teams" needed to create medical homes.[14] This has prompted more healthcare organizations, including integrated service networks, to undertake demonstration projects to test the medical home model.

ACOs versus Medical Homes

The Affordable Care Act encourages the formation of accountable care organizations (ACOs) and patient-centered medical homes. Both of these care models strive to provide safe, cost-effective, quality healthcare services through improved access, better coordination, more preventative care, and optimized use of technology.

The collaborative care teams of a medical home include primary care physicians, nurses, medical specialists, health coaches, some licensed complementary care practitioners (acupuncturists, for example), medical assistants, and support staff. The primary care practice is held accountable for the outcomes of the patients it serves.

In contrast, ACOs connect hospitals, group practices, individual practices (which can include medical homes), and specialized care professionals. There is joint accountability by all providers involved, and compensation blends fee-for-service payments with shared savings achieved across the entire care continuum. This includes care provided within and outside of medical homes and other clinical practices—so care provided at hospitals or other ACO member locations is bundled together for reimbursement as part of an episode of care.

Clinics that are part of an ACO do not have to be medical homes. However, the shared characteristics of team-based care, outcomes-based compensation, and integration of health information technology to improve care quality make medical homes a natural fit with the ACO. This has led some healthcare industry leaders to refer to ACOs that include medical homes as "medical home neighborhoods."[15]

Reimbursement

The majority of medical home demonstration projects sponsored by health plans use a hybrid compensation structure that reimburses physicians for the extra care coordination expenses associated with each patient and still compensates them for the fee-for-service clinical work they do.

A major challenge, however, is that there is currently no agreement about how high the care coordination fees should be. Those in favor of using the medical home model assert that cost savings from reducing emergency room visits and hospitalizations will help payers to cover the costs of investments in technology, additional staff, research, and ongoing training that medical practices must make to transform themselves into medical homes. Thus, shared savings is being discussed as part of the reformed payment structure for medical homes.

In the meantime, medical homes continue to experiment with various staffing strategies in an attempt to achieve a structure that is economically sustainable and that will enable them to achieve their targeted health outcome goals. The ongoing reform of reimbursement structures will continue to have a major effect on the design of medical home facilities because these will determine the ratio of "other staff" per physician that is needed to optimize patients' health outcomes, and these emerging staff roles have unique space needs.

For example, clinicians who have telehealth responsibilities require spaces with high levels of acoustical privacy, yet typically need to be located in or near the central work core of a medical home in case a patient needs to speak with a physician or specialist (e.g., a behavioral health counselor) during an e-consult or phone triage session.

Staffing Changes

Research conducted by the Medical Group Management Association (MGMA) indicates that the majority of medical homes are addressing a shortage of primary care physicians by shifting some tasks that were once performed by doctors to other staff members. This strategy enables primary care physicians to work to the top of their licensure and lead integrated care teams.

Results of a survey conducted by MGMA in 2012 indicate that the major increases accredited and recognized PCMHs are noting are in the categories of licensed practical nurses (LPNs) and medical assistants (MAs). The substantial increase in administrative staff also revealed by this survey relates to the emphasis medical homes place on care coordination. Specifically:

- 49 percent of survey respondents said they had seen a considerable increase in administrative staff, such as medical records technicians.

- 42 percent had experienced a considerable increase in "other clinical staffing," such as LPNs and medical assistants (43 percent).

- 55.1 percent indicated they had experienced a considerable increase in registered nursing staff and in nonphysician provider staffing (54.3 percent).

- 78.2 percent saw neither an increase nor a decrease in physician staffing as a result of implementing the PCMH care model.[16]

Other studies reinforce these findings. For example, a 2013 study conducted by researchers at the University of Pennsylvania titled "Estimating the Staffing Infrastructure for a Patient-Centered Medical Home," found that the "care manager" is the most consistent staff position added at medical homes. Registered nurses typically fill this role at a rate of 1:1 for each physician.

This study also found that medical homes used health coaches or educators (0–0.25 per physician FTE) and behavioral health providers (0–0.83) to address the importance of self-management and to provide emotional support and added pharmacists (0–0.53) to assist with medication management, chronic disease care, and consultations. Several practices also employed nutritionists (0–0.20) to address dietary issues.

Generally, it is clear that physicians are collaborating with other clinicians and support staff to provide care and that an increasing number of nurses and physician extenders are being included on integrated care teams in medical homes. Since these healthcare professionals often need to consult with physicians, private and convenient consultation space is needed where they can present and discuss the patient's symptoms, medical history, and other essential information.[17]

Although the precise staffing levels and mix of personnel will continue to vary according to the needs of individual practices, researchers agree that medical homes will require new staff with specialized training, such as care managers, data analysts, pharmacists, and behavioral health providers.

These trends underscore how critical it is for design professionals to keep pace with changes in the roles and responsibilities of all clinic staff working at medical homes.

Operational Changes

The most formidable challenge most practices face when implementing the medical home model is the need to overhaul clinic operations as medical home workflows focused on receiving fees for services provided in a clinic must be redesigned to provide a new range of preventative and care management services. This transformation, in turn, significantly alters who provides which services at what time and where (that is, via phone or the Internet).

This transformation in the processes of medical practices translates into changes in the sizing, allocation, and features of clinic spaces. Design professionals addressing these issues for medical homes thus pay especially careful attention to how the workflows of individual practices are changing to make better use of technology, expand or introduce new staff roles, and improve the quality of health outcomes for specific patient populations.

For example, the need to add specialized expertise can be handled by clinics through either dedicated or shared exam or consult rooms. If the degree to which a clinic uses telehealth processes increases the need for work areas to serve these employees, it may decrease space needs in other clinic areas. The delegation of tasks once completed by physicians will likely alter exam room ratios.

Community Connections

The design of clinics for some medical homes is beginning to be influenced by the innovative alliances they are establishing with public agencies and other community organizations to control costs while enhancing health outcomes for the patient populations they serve. An example of this is Hennepin Health.

■ HENNEPIN HEALTH
Minneapolis, Minnesota

In 2012, Hennepin County Medical Center partnered with NorthPoint Health and Wellness Center, Metropolitan Health Plan, and Hennepin County's Human Services and Public Health Department to form an accountable care organization called Hennepin Health that provides a combination of social, behavioral, dental, and medical services for a certain number of its adult patients who do not have dependent children and whose income is at or below 75 percent of federal poverty guidelines.[18]

Hennepin Health's goals are to improve health outcomes for this patient population while decreasing the average care costs per patient through better coordination and by avoiding duplication of services that are being (or can be) provided by community organizations. It uses data sharing across systems to help achieve these goals.

The first step Hennepin Health took was to set up a coordinated care clinic in its downtown Minneapolis medical center, where teams of social workers and case managers could collaborate to connect patients with the services they need (such as housing, transportation, and behavioral health care) in order to better manage their health outside of the clinic. Examples of how this approach decreased costs while improving health outcomes include:

- After staying sober for several months, a patient was able to reduce the amount of blood pressure medication he needed to take. Care providers were then able to focus their attention on his other ailments, such as shortness of breath and other problems related to his lungs.

- A caseworker learned that a diabetes patient who kept showing up at the hospital with an upset stomach had not been able to take his medication with food because his refrigerator was broken. She helped him to secure the financial assistance he needed to remedy this situation.

- A patient with congestive heart failure was admitted to the HCMC hospital five times in two months. Caseworkers arranged for the nurse at the homeless shelter where he lived to weigh him daily so that a sudden change in weight could be detected. They also gave

him a pill box that helped him keep track of when to take his medications and bus tokens for transportation. These preventative steps enabled him to go several months without a return to the hospital for care.

- A homeless man suffering from chemical addiction and mental health issues had an average of six hospital admissions each year. He is now able to manage his asthma with routine clinic visits and by routinely taking his outpatient medications.

- The three case managers, a social worker, and health plan coordinator who were working with one patient were unable to share health information under the old system. Once Hennepin Health made this possible, they were able to work together to improve health outcomes, reduce redundancies, and reduce the cost of care.

Thus, front-loading care by augmenting it with the services provided by other agencies and organizations has proven to be a cost-effective way to keep patients healthier and out of the emergency room. During the first year Hennepin Health tried this approach, emergency room visits were cut in half for the 150 patients who were in its test group.

Based on these results, Hennepin Health established a formal demonstration project that can include up to 12,000 low-income adults who use a disproportionate share of the county's healthcare and social services. More than two dozen clinics will be set up as hubs, and staff will work with the patients to connect them with public housing, food banks, addiction treatment and recovery programs, and services related to immigration, domestic violence, and corrections.

The cost savings related to using this coordinated care model are expected to be substantial. Prior to the launch of this project, 10 percent of Hennepin County Medical Center's care costs were accumulated by 60 patients treated in intensive care units—which roughly equaled the cost of 25,000 outpatient visits or 16,000 emergency room visits.

Medicaid dollars go directly to HCMC for this project in order to give the county the flexibility to channel funds where they are most needed, whether this entails hiring more crisis outreach workers or making addiction treatment available for more patients. By February 2013, Hennepin Health had an enrollment of about 6,000 people (fig. 9-1).[19,20]

Home-Based Care

In the future, it is likely that the medical home will actually *be* people's homes because this is where most of the preventative and health management activities will occur. Home-based care is also likely to increase because a major goal of the medical home model is to keep patients as healthy as possible and, thus, out of the hospital and away from the clinic.

Technology Considerations

The medical home model's emphasis on using technology to coordinate care and improve health outcomes, its focus on sharing health information, and the unique combinations of healthcare services clinics must devise to address the specific needs of their patients are all major factors that design professionals consider when addressing the physical facility needs of medical homes (fig. 9-2).

Impact of Technology

The type and degree of technology a medical home uses to streamline and improve the quality of care strongly influence space planning and

FIGURE 9-1: Hennepin County Medical Center Whittier Clinic, Minneapolis, Minnesota. Hennepin County Medical Center, a large urban safety-net health system, envisioned a "flagship" clinic to enhance its image and broaden its target market. In addition, the medical center desired a unique planning model focusing on staff efficiency and communication. The project features a unique clinic module in which exam rooms are clustered around a central work area serving both nurses and physicians. This layout provides visibility to each exam room from the central work area. It also positions providers and nurses in close proximity for efficient communication, ideal for supporting the medical home model.
Photography by Paul Crosby

other design decisions. For example, if care providers expect to have access to electronic health records during exams and consultations, the decision to use desktop, laptop, or tablet computers will have an impact on the space needs of these rooms as well as those related to them, such as registration and checkout areas or collaborative work cores.

The simultaneous emphasis medical homes place on team-based and patient-centric care also presents design professionals with the challenge of identifying all of the locations within a clinic where health information will be exchanged and understanding the systems and spatial requirements of the technology to be used in each location. For example, while all medical homes need a central work core, other factors such as clinic size, services provided, and care delivery processes may result in a decision to combine this feature with team huddle spaces located near clusters of exam rooms or to the need for multiple centralized work cores within a clinic, with each serving a different care team.

Some medical homes also locate consult rooms near exam rooms so that clinicians can use these to discuss more complex cases or to provide telehealth services between physical exams. Consult rooms tend to use different technology than exam rooms in order to serve an expanded range of communication functions.

Health IT in the Medical Home

Medical homes not only use technology to achieve this care model's fundamental goal of creating a single location where all patient-related health information resides but also to

FIGURE 9-2: Froedtert Hospital & Medical College of Wisconsin–Moorland Reserve Health Center, New Berlin, Wisconsin. Developing a program and operational concept that dovetails with medical home care was a goal for Froedtert Hospital & Medical College of Wisconsin–Moorland Reserve Health Center. Decentralized work pods that include space for medical assistants, registered nurses, and physicians provide a collaborative work space for the care team. Additionally, consultative spaces and offices for nurse navigators are logically distributed throughout the clinical plan to support patient education efforts. Photography © 2013 by Darris Lee Harris

pool knowledge and information about various patient populations and provide enhanced access.

The Agency for Healthcare Research and Quality, which has invested more than $4 million to study the transformation of primary care clinics into patient-centered medical homes, found that medical homes need health IT tools that help them to efficiently and effectively:[21]

- Identify subpopulations of patients.

- Review and analyze detailed characteristics of these subpopulations.

- Generate care reminders for patients and care providers.

- Track and report on quality performance measures.

- Make data available in multiple forms, including health summaries for individual patients and subpopulations.

Electronic Health Records (EHRs)

Instituting an electronic health record system (EHR) is usually the first step medical homes take toward integrating technology into their clinical practice—especially since medical home certification programs, such as the one administered by the National Committee for Quality Assurance (NCQA), require the use of EHRs.

However, the up-front costs of investing in the hardware, software, and building improvements needed to implement an EHR system can present a major barrier for clinics that want to become medical homes. To address this issue, Title IV, Division B of the HITECH Act of 2009 authorized the Centers for Medicare and Medicaid Services to provide incentive payments to care providers that meet the federal government's thresholds for the meaningful use of EHRs.

Converting from a printed, paper file system to electronic health records enables a medical

home to coordinate care across all settings and provides a number of other benefits for patients and care providers. EHRs:

- Can be sent and shared electronically between healthcare professionals. This is especially important for medical homes because the team-based approach they use for providing care means that they rely on multiple perspectives to holistically treat patients. If specialists joining a care team can review electronic health records, they can avoid asking patients to duplicate entry of basic health information. Instead, specialists will only need to add details related to their areas of expertise.

- Can be provided to patients in portable forms. They can also be stored online and shared via secure websites, such as MyChart.com.

- Can be updated and kept current so that patients do not have to fill out a full set of forms with the same basic information (home address, for example) each time they visit a clinic. This also means that less information should "fall through the cracks" or be lost in transit. Missing information can be identified electronically and need only be provided by the patient and entered into the EHR system once.

- Provide physicians and other care providers with immediate access to patient health information (versus retrieving and rifling through paper files) in advance of an exam from a variety of locations within a clinic. These healthcare professionals can then focus on caring for the patient during a clinic visit instead of searching for and collecting missing patient information.

- Can be designed to consolidate all the known information about a patient—from lab results and imaging reports to correspondence from specialists, and medication lists, dosages, and refill histories, to chart notes added by all members of an integrated care team.

- Are expected to improve the accuracy of health information, since in many instances patients can enter information directly by completing digital forms. Errors need only be corrected once. When patients have access to EHRs, they can also verify information and call attention to inaccuracies.

If desktop computers are used for viewing and updating EHRs in the exam room, they should be positioned on a desk or other work surface located away from the sink. If tablet computers are used, these can be placed on a rolling, adjustable height stand to maximize flexibility of use and ensure that care providers are able to maintain eye contact with the patient while reviewing and entering information into the EHR system.

There are penalties for not implementing EHR systems in a timely and meaningful manner. Medicare eligible professionals who cannot successfully demonstrate meaningful use of a certified EHR system by 2015 will have their fee schedule amounts for covered services adjusted downward each year by 1 percent. Some medical practices will be able to secure a hardship exception, but that will need to be renewed each year and will not be granted for more than five years.[22]

Disease Registries

Increasingly, medical homes are using external, web-based registries that compile information about specific categories of patients who need preventative or long-term care. These public health surveillance systems are used to collect and maintain information about new developments related to specific diseases or conditions. Information provided by these registries can give context and information about new methods for treating the patient population that a clinic serves.

These registries are continuously updated with information from various sources, ranging from EHRs to practice management systems, labs, and pharmacies. Members of the integrated care team can select topics of specific interest and receive alerts when related information becomes available via a registry. When a registry is linked to an outbound messaging system, patients can be notified via a phone, e-mail, or text message that new information is available.

A registry should include all of a medical home's patients to optimize its use as a population health management tool. Search filters can then be based on specific information the clinic needs to improve care. For example, being able to identify all of the patients who have diabetes could enable a clinic to determine if there are care gaps or deficiencies that should be addressed in relation to how a medical home is treating patients with this chronic disease.

Health Information Exchanges

The Affordable Care Act includes incentives for state and local healthcare systems to establish health information exchanges that enable healthcare professionals to share electronic health records across different care settings and locations. These exchanges are intended to connect facilities and healthcare professionals in ways that facilitate collaborative care and reduce the redundancies, inaccuracies, and gaps in information that have arisen from patients' health records being kept in different locations.

These can help reduce healthcare costs and improve the patient experience in a number of ways, including by eliminating needless duplication of tests. Health information exchanges should also aid in the implementation of bundled payment programs by enabling care providers to avoid other redundancies for which they will no longer be reimbursed.

Health Risk Assessments (HRAs)

HRAs can help medical homes effectively manage care by serving as the basis for interventions. They enable practices to sort the patients they treat into three categories: healthy, in the early stages of a chronic disease or condition, or in the advanced stage of a chronic disease. These groups change constantly because people who are well can become sick, and chronic diseases and conditions can progress. Regular use of HRAs as a reference tool can help keep medical home clinicians aware of which patients need the most care and which may require additional care in the future.

Automated Education Materials

A major premise underlying the medical home model is that making lifestyle changes can improve health and wellness. Annually, approximately 7 out of 10 deaths among Americans are a result of chronic conditions. Modifying four behaviors could help reduce the suffering and early deaths associated with these conditions and also lower the cost of healthcare in the United States. Positive changes would include increasing physical activity, improving nutrition, smoking cessation, and avoiding excessive consumption of alcohol.[23]

To reinforce the value of positive lifestyle decisions, medical homes can use information technology to tailor communications and interventions so that they address the specific health challenges and wellness goals of patients. For example, electronic educational materials and online resources can be linked to health risk assessments so that patients can access or request additional information as they complete these interactive forms. Automated reminders can be sent to patients via phone, e-mail, or text message.

Open-Access Scheduling

This is also known as advanced, same-day, or walk-in access, which has become increasingly difficult for primary care clinics to provide as shortages of physicians have arisen. Routine appointments often must be booked well in advance, and urgent appointments are squeezed into schedules that are already too full. When patients have to seek urgent care from physicians other than their primary care providers, this can disrupt the continuity of care they receive. In extreme instances, patients present at emergency rooms because they have not been able to be seen by their primary care provider in time.

To address these problems, medical homes are devising technological and staffing strategies that enable them to provide open-access scheduling and improve the quality of care they provide. Open-access scheduling allows patients to call a practice and be assured of securing a same-day or next-day appointment.

Telehealth

The use of "health" in this word demonstrates the shift in focus from treating diseases to promoting health. This is a cornerstone of the medical home care philosophy. Since the success of this model depends on keeping patients informed, equipped, and "activated" so that they can maintain an optimal level of health throughout their lives, medical homes use the telephone and Internet to complete tasks that extend beyond scheduling clinic visits. For example, medical homes are using a variety of telehealth strategies to provide triage, health coaching, and e-consult services as well as to simply check in with patients to make sure they are complying with their healthcare plans.

E-Conferences and E-Consults

Medical homes that share specialists or that are located in remote areas have begun using video conferencing to conduct patient-panel review sessions, host webinars to share information between care providers based in different locations, and provide cross-disciplinary remote consults with patients and their families that include health professionals who have the unique expertise needed to properly diagnose and treat complex conditions.

These telehealth activities can help to build relationships between primary care clinicians and specialists that promote and facilitate the sharing of information on an ongoing basis. They can also be especially valuable for connecting the separate components of an accountable care organization that must effectively co-manage care.

Telephonic and E-Visits

These healthcare visits are conducted either by phone or online instead of in person. Patients either speak with a nurse practitioner or physician via telephone or complete online forms themselves to answer questions that give care providers basic assessment information. A care provider then uses this information to determine if a patient's condition can be addressed by e-mail or if a patient needs to be seen at the clinic. Some websites also provide self-care recommendations for patients based on the answers they provide via online forms. In some instances, a care provider can issue prescriptions electronically.

Telephonic and e-visits can help both patients and care providers save time and reduce the cost of care. They are especially helpful to clinics serving large geographic areas with remote or rural patient populations or to patients who do not have easy access to transportation.

Digital Health

Digital health is just beginning to explode. Corporations such as Google, Apple, and Samsung are advancing technologies in the area of digital health. This will have a profound impact on the ways in which healthcare data is transmitted in the future.

■ PROJECT ECHO
University of New Mexico, Albuquerque

The Extension for Community Health Outcomes launched a telehealth program called Project ECHO more than a decade ago as an integral part of a healthcare program serving rural and underserved populations in New Mexico. Project ECHO uses videoconferencing to connect specialists with primary care providers (PCP) who practice in rural areas with the goal of training the PCPs to provide proper, continuous care for patients with chronic and complex conditions.

Project ECHO also hosts weekly "tele-ECHO clinics," during which clinicians from different areas present patient cases for collaborative review. Other universities and healthcare institutions, such as the University of Chicago, the University of Washington, and Harvard University through the Beth Israel Deaconess Medical Center, have replicated and adapted this model to serve specialized areas of medicine such as diabetes and cardiovascular care, women's health, psychiatry, and HIV/AIDS.[24]

■ SOUTH CENTRAL FOUNDATION PRIMARY CARE CENTER
Anchorage, Alaska

Located at the southern edge of the Alaska Native Health Campus in Anchorage, this clinic houses a primary care practice that serves patients from 55 villages throughout a 107,000-square-mile geographic area. Integrated care teams are assembled based on the whole-person, "mind and body" needs of patients. In addition to primary care clinicians, these teams include specialists such as behaviorists, tribal doctors, and acupuncturists.

In 2000, South Central Foundation became the first major care provider in Alaska to provide same-day access in most of its departments for patients seeking care for any reason. To maintain its commitment to keeping 70 to 80 percent of its appointment slots open on any day, clinicians provide as much care as possible via the telephone. If a face-to-face visit is needed, it can be scheduled for the same day with any members of a patient's care team. This optimizes the provision of care by shifting it to where and when it is needed most.

Multiuse "talking rooms" can be used for these telehealth functions or to provide a less clinical setting for the 60 percent of total patient visits that do not require an exam table. Patients, family members, and the care team are able to sit next to each other in these rooms to promote interaction and ease stress. Talking rooms can also be used by staff, patients, or visitors for phone calls, as waiting areas for families, or for a variety of private interactions.[25]

Biometric Home Monitoring (BHM)

Although biometric home monitoring (BHM) technology has been available for well over a decade, health plans have begun to recognize its value and provide some financial support for its use. In the future, it is likely that medical homes will use BHM for patients with chronic or high-risk conditions, such as those in danger of heart failure. When something irregular occurs in the constant stream of data these devices provide, a patient will know to seek immediate care or a care provider may be notified automatically. Healthcare technology experts predict that new technologies that instantly read blood pressure and body temperature will be followed by other noninvasive capabilities, such as monitoring specific substances in the blood, and by quick and accurate lab tests or imaging techniques.

Design Features and Challenges

The component that is common to all medical home clinics is a central work core (or area), which is needed to facilitate and enhance collaboration by integrated care teams. The size, configuration, and features of these shared work areas vary greatly because these design decisions are based on the type of services provided, staffing strategies, and degree of technology employed by each medical home.

Generally, central work cores serving medical homes are larger than those in other clinics because medical homes' staffs can include physician extenders, care coordinators, and community health workers, as well as specialized members of integrated care teams, such as nutritionists, social workers, and pharmacists.

Type of Services

Decisions about space needs and qualities of a clinic that uses the medical home model are strongly shaped by the type and range of services it must provide to meet the needs of a particular patient population.

When a medical home does not have the in-house ability to provide certain specialized healthcare services for a patient, the care team is still responsible for ensuring that the patient receives the necessary care—and that this care is effectively coordinated across all settings.

Some smaller medical home practices network in order to develop partnerships with specialists that they need to provide the full range of services their patients require. Others align themselves with ACOs in order to share resources and staff. For example, a medical home neighborhood formed through either of these strategies could collaboratively hire one full-time dietician to provide health education and consulting services at each individual clinic. In this instance, it might make sense to provide a flexible consult room or (depending on the size of the patient subpopulation) a group visit/meeting room that can be used for other purposes when the dietician is not at a particular clinic.

Privacy

As part of the space needs analysis for medical home clinics, design professionals pay especially close attention to the privacy needs associated with this care model's increased focus on sharing health information between patient and physician, between members of integrated care teams, and across various settings.

Since patients want to know that the confidentiality of their medical history and current health details will be ensured and that phone conversations or team discussions about their health will not be overheard, all clinic spaces where this information is exchanged must achieve the visual and acoustical privacy standards included in the Health Insurance Portability and Accountability Act of 1996 (HIPAA).

■ FAIRVIEW CLINIC
Maple Grove, Minnesota

This clinic addresses the need for a variety of clinicians to complete portions of their work in private by providing enclosed consult rooms that can be used for telephone triage or consultation with specialists such as pharmacists, dieticians, behavioral health experts, or radiologists. These rooms are designed to be more comfortable than exam rooms and are located near the front entrance to this clinic to provide easy access for patients and collaborative care team members (fig. 9-3).

Central Work Core

Central work cores of medical homes are designed to promote the collaborative, team-based approach to providing care that is the hallmark of this model. They typically:

- Are surrounded by single-door exam rooms and individual physician workstations or private offices are nearby.

Or

- Use an on-stage/off-stage layout that places the work core in the center of exam rooms that have two doors: one used by the patient to enter from an outer, public circulation loop and one used by clinic staff to enter from the collaborative work area. The on-stage/off-stage clinic module is very effective for clinics that use a self-rooming process.

Exam Rooms

Most medical homes frequently use large, universally designed exam rooms that are equipped to serve a variety of activities, ranging from routine physicals and basic exams through team consults and minor procedures. Space is provided for family members, social workers, translators, and other partners in care.

Determining the proper number of exam rooms that a particular medical home needs is especially challenging for design professionals. For many years, the industry standard has been to provide three exam rooms per physician. However, the wide variations in the way that the medical home model is being implemented make understanding the provider mix and healthcare delivery processes of a clinic especially critical for optimizing the use of exam rooms.

As more tasks are completed in the exam room, the 3:1 ratio may stay the same, but the exam rooms may either be used by more than a single physician or the physician may use exam rooms differently (for example, to provide telemedicine/e-visits on some days or during some hours).

In the past, exam rooms used by specialists and primary care physicians could have markedly different equipment, furniture, and space needs. Today, design professionals are determining how to simultaneously address the needs of these care providers in ways that will allow them to share exam rooms.

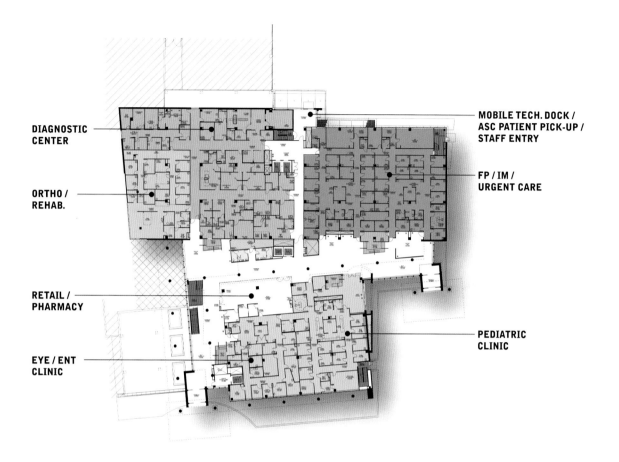

DIAGNOSTIC CENTER

ORTHO / REHAB.

RETAIL / PHARMACY

EYE / ENT CLINIC

MOBILE TECH. DOCK / ASC PATIENT PICK-UP / STAFF ENTRY

FP / IM / URGENT CARE

PEDIATRIC CLINIC

FIRST FLOOR

FIGURE 9-3: The clinic plan at Fairview Maple Grove places enclosed consult rooms near the department entries. These private rooms allow space for the provider to talk privately with a patient while also allowing space for the collaborative care team to gather as required. Image courtesy of Hammel, Green and Abrahamson, Inc.

In addition to this, as nurse practitioners continue to complete basic exams that do not require a physician, standard exam ratios may change. The current exam room per nurse practitioner ratio is 1:1. By maximizing utilization, medical homes may thus decrease the total number of exam rooms needed per physician to as low as 2:1. It is also possible that the exam room ratio could go down if a clinic uses technology to complete tasks that were formerly done in exam rooms or to conduct e-visits.

Education Space

Not only can care providers benefit from sharing knowledge across patient populations, but patients can also better care for themselves and manage their health and wellness when information is provided for them in culturally appropriate ways, from a variety of sources, and in language they can understand.

Since self-care and preventative care are top priorities for medical homes, most include spaces dedicated to patient education. These range from displays in lobbies and exam rooms to resource centers and computer workstations where patients (and staff) can gain access to online health-related information. Medical homes also frequently include group meeting rooms.

Administrative Work Areas

The fact that the largest growth in staffing for medical homes is in the area of administrative and other staff means that there is also a growing need to provide properly designed space for these employees.

Project Examples

The following examples demonstrate the wide range of ways that design professionals have designed clinics to facilitate and enhance the delivery of care services by medical home practices.

■ HEALTHEAST SPINE CLINIC

Although this clinic specializes in providing patients with health and complementary care services that focus on strengthening specific regions of the back and neck, it has many features that medical homes require: a centralized work core where integrated teams of physicians, chiropractors, physical therapists, behavioral health and lifestyle management counselors, nurses, medical technicians, and other staff can collaborate; a rehabilitation zone where patients can receive ongoing care to recover from an injury or manage chronic pain; and a triage station where a nurse practitioner assesses the severity of patients' pain

and determines if there are integrated care strategies that can help them avoid the need for surgery.

■ HENNEPIN COUNTY MEDICAL CENTER (HCMC)

HCMC is the largest public safety net and academic medical center in Minnesota. It serves more than 140,000 patients from throughout the state and trains the majority of healthcare professionals who care for them. It has begun to implement medical home care models in several of its clinics to serve as hubs for Hennepin Health, the accountable care organization (ACO) it formed in 2012. The following three examples illustrate different approaches to creation of the medical homes for this ACO.

The payer mix is slightly different for these medical homes, with Whittier being located in a densely populated, low-income urban neighborhood. Whittier also serves a larger patient population than HCMC's Golden Valley and St. Anthony Clinics, which are located in first-ring suburbs of the Twin Cities.

■ WHITTIER CLINIC

This clinic was not initially designed to serve as a medical home, but its conversion to this care model was straightforward because its layout featured a large central work area and ample space for support staff. The central work core is enclosed to provide acoustical separation from patient areas. Workstations for physicians and medical assistants are clustered together to make it easy for them to collaborate on the care of individual patients.

■ ST. ANTHONY CLINIC

The original 5,000-square-foot clinic is designed with six exam rooms, a full lab, imaging capabilities, and a pharmacy (with a drive-through service). The layout colocates workspace for providers and medical assistants. Plans call for the addition of 1,400 square feet of space to accommodate two additional providers as demand for services offered by this medical home continues to grow.

■ GOLDEN VALLEY CLINIC

Two lines of nurse triage stations bookend the centralized work core in this 9,200 -square-foot clinic. Two enclosed care coordinator offices can also be used by other clinicians when they need to complete tasks that require full visual and acoustical privacy, such as discussing confidential information with patients during phone triage or for team consult sessions.

Mayo Clinic Health System

Mayo Clinic has a number of medical home demonstration projects underway at various locations in Minnesota and Wisconsin.

■ ALBERT LEA, MINNESOTA

This clinic was not designed as a medical home, but it could be transformed to serve this care model because it has a centralized staff work area. The triage area is located near the physician workstations to make it easier for nurses to consult informally with doctors before providing medical advice to patients. This layout also facilitates collaboration among all clinicians. Although staff does not have direct views of all exam rooms because these are located down the corridor from the centralized work core, this feature is not essential for the implementation of the patient-centered medical home (PCMH) model of care. The exam room layout is universal, with the physician's work zone located close to the door.

■ OSSEO, MINNESOTA

The central work core for this clinic is open, larger than that of the Whittier Clinic, and has a combination of open and enclosed offices. Physicians' offices located in the work core have higher walls and doors to provide privacy. Nurse triage stations are located near physicians' offices in the central work core in case a patient requires a doctor's opinion during a phone conversation. The medical assistants' work areas are on the corners of the central work area so that they can observe exam rooms. Since the exam rooms are located directly across from staff work areas, they have reverse door-swings to provide patients with visual privacy. Individual, fully enclosed physicians' offices are also provided along a corridor that is separate from the exam and collaborative work areas.

Employee and Community Health

To fully implement its "Health Care Home Model of Patient Care," in the winter and spring of 2011–2012 Mayo collaborated with a team of design professionals to identify space needs for a five-year period and develop a strategic plan for meeting them. The study also explored other scenarios for the distribution of space for primary care services provided via a medical home model.

The goals of transforming Employee and Community Health into a patient-centered medical home include reducing:

- The number of days that patients spend in the hospital.
- The number of emergency room visits made by patients.
- The number of specialty visits.
- The cost per patient per month.

The design team recommended testing a number of design concepts resulting from this study wherever Mayo had the flexibility to do so. It reviewed several prototypical clinic modules, such as the following, which have features conducive to implementation of the medical home model.

Academic Clinics

These layouts illustrate alternatives for academic clinics with variations in the placement of academic offices and teaching spaces. The collaborative staff work or teaching areas are centralized and surrounded by exam rooms.

Clinic Modules A and B

Module A has standard, same-handed exam rooms that improve acoustic separation of patient-physician discussions. All exam rooms are visible from the central work core (fig. 9-4).

Module B features a large, centrally located teaching zone that could also be used for group education sessions. Exam rooms are visible from four nurse stations located on the corners of the centralized work/teaching zone (fig. 9-5).

FIGURE 9-4: Module A includes universal exam rooms used to improve acoustic separation. Image courtesy of Hammel, Green and Abrahamson, Inc.

CLINIC MODULE

CLINIC MODULE

CLINIC
RESIDENCY
MODULE

RESIDENCY WORK /
CLASSROOM /
INTERPRETERS

LAB

DIABETES
EDUCATION

WAITING /
PUBLIC

OPEN TO
BELOW

ADMINISTRATION

FIGURE 9-5: Module B's centrally located teaching zone to be used for group education.   Image courtesy of Hammel, Green and Abrahamson, Inc.

Clinic Modules C and D

The layouts for these modules accommodate patient self-rooming. They feature a public corridor that provides patient access to exam rooms. Care providers enter through a second door in each exam room that connects it to a centralized staff work core.

Module C arranges exam rooms in a doughnut shape around a central work core. A public corridor runs along the outside rim of the exam rooms. Patients enter the exam rooms from this corridor, which gives them access to daylight and exterior views (fig. 9-6).

Staff workstations for Module D are located between two rows of exam rooms. It also includes a separate, shared office area for physicians and a private space for telehealth activities (fig. 9-7).

Members of the Employee and Community Health planning and design team also toured three facilities that have similar features. Design professionals on the team then developed bubble diagrams to relate aspects of the prototypical clinic modules and benchmarking facilities to the specific operations and space needs.

This led to the development of four options that feature centralized team huddle space and cluster individual and shared staff work areas together.

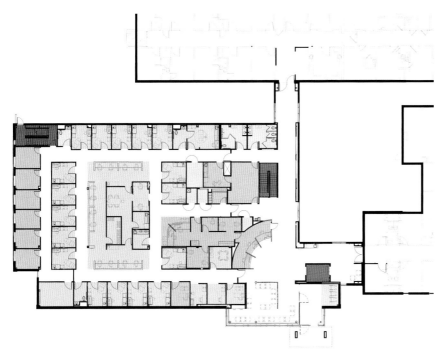

FIGURE 9-6: Module C utilizes a central work core that promotes staff interaction, which is critical to a medical home model. Image courtesy of Hammel, Green and Abrahamson, Inc.

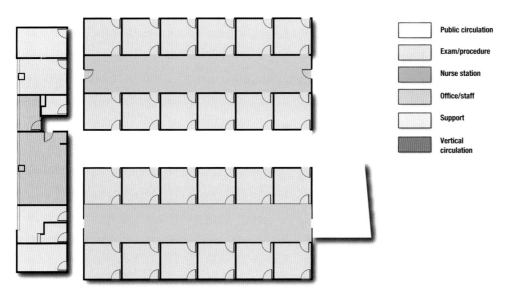

☐	**Public circulation**
☐	**Exam/procedure**
☐	**Nurse station**
☐	**Office/staff**
☐	**Support**
☐	**Vertical circulation**

FIGURE 9-7: Module D's public corridor is used for circulation and waiting, which can compromise visual and acoustic privacy. Image courtesy of Hammel, Green and Abrahamson, Inc.

Options 1A, 1B, and 2 feature exam rooms with one door that is utilized for entry by both patients and clinic staff. Option 3 provides a separate entry door for staff that connects each exam room to the central work core. It also has group visit or education rooms. All options have work spaces for newly emerging positions that are needed by medical homes, such as care managers (figs. 9-8 htrough 9-11).

Summary

The medical home model was initially conceived of by the American Academy of Pediatrics in 1967 as a method for centralizing the health information of children. This basic concept was further developed by primary care medical societies over the course of four decades, until it emerged as the patient-centered medical home model, which strives to provide personalized, team-based,

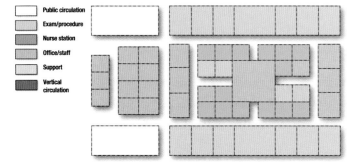

Public circulation
Exam/procedure
Nurse station
Office/staff
Support
Vertical circulation

FIGURE 9-8: Option 1A locates clinical assistants close to the entry of the module. Image courtesy of Hammel, Green and Abrahamson, Inc.

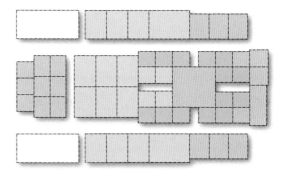

FIGURE 9-10: Option 2 locates more exam rooms close to the patient waiting area. Image courtesy of Hammel, Green and Abrahamson, Inc.

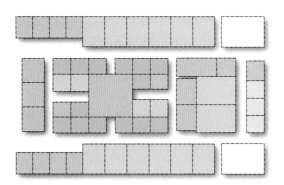

FIGURE 9-9: Option 1B locates clinical assistants close to the office at the back of the module. Image courtesy of Hammel, Green and Abrahamson, Inc.

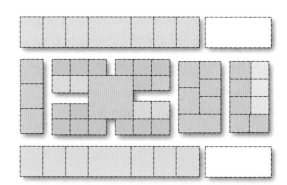

FIGURE 9-11: Option 3 has dual access exam rooms. Patients enter from one side, and caregivers enter from central work core. Image courtesy of Hammel, Green and Abrahamson, Inc.

well-coordinated, easily accessible, high-quality, safe healthcare for patients throughout all stages of their lives.

Despite the high level of interest and support for the medical home model, there is no consensus about which of its components are most likely to yield the desired results—both for the new hybrid practices that have emerged to test this model and for primary care clinics that are attempting to become medical homes. This is due largely to the fact that implementing a medical home model significantly alters how primary and specialized care providers deliver services. There is also a wide range of ways that this model can be interpreted and applied.

For now, all medical home facilities have a collaborative work space for physicians and staff. Most have larger, universally designed exam rooms, educational and group meeting space, and private rooms that can be used for consults, telehealth tasks, and other purposes.

As research results accumulate from the hundreds of demonstration models underway, challenges that healthcare organizations adopting the medical home model have experienced include:

- Managing noncompliant patients. This was the top response (60.9 percent) given by representatives of accredited or recognized PCMHs to a 2012 survey conducted by the Medical Group Management Association (MGMA).[26]

- Coordinating care for high-risk patients. According to results of the same MGMA survey, 47.3 percent of respondents said this is a "considerable" or "extreme" challenge.[27]

- Inadequate payment for care coordination.[28] Decisions about how to resolve this challenge are expected to have a major impact on clinic design in the future because they will directly affect the staffing levels and personnel mix of medical homes and their ability to improve health outcomes for their respective patient populations. This, in turn, shapes the basic space programming information upon which design professionals base their recommendations.

- The high cost of implementing EHR systems.[29] In order to be accredited or recognized as a medical home—or to receive proper payment from Medicare and Medicaid—practices must demonstrate meaningful use of electronic health records. This has made instituting EHR systems a top priority. The degree to which medical homes use EHRs and other technology (e.g., telehealth) to coordinate care and improve access directly influences the quantity and qualities of space within a clinic (for example, less or different space needed for records storage; private spaces for telehealth).

- Physician resistance to the fundamental shift in roles, responsibilities, and workflows required for a clinic to be transformed into a medical home.[30] For example, physicians are used to having control over three exam rooms each under design standards that have been in place for decades. The shortage of primary care physicians combined with the need to serve a larger number of patients means that doctors now often must share more universally designed exam rooms with other team members (specialists and nurse practitioners, for example) and that spaces once used solely for exams and consultations are now utilized for a broader range of tasks.

Regardless of these challenges and the wide range of ways that the medical home model can be implemented, all medical homes are committed to providing the "right care, by the right person, at the right time." Design professionals who continue to find creative, innovative ways to help clinic owners achieve this goal through the design of the built environment will remain highly valued advisors.

JENNIFER KLUND

Notes

1. Raymond A. Christy, "Improving the Manual on Standards of Child Health Care," *American Academy of Pediatrics* 41 (1968): 1143, http://pediatrics.aappublications.org/content/41/6/1143.1.abstract.

2. "Declaration of Alma-Ata," presented at the International Conference on Primary Health Care, USSR, September 6–12, 1978, http://www.who.int/publications/almaata_declaration_en.pdf.

3. Institute of Medicine, http://www.iom.edu.

4. "Future of Family Medicine Project," *Annals of Family Medicine* 2, no. 1 (2004): n.p., http://www.ncbi.nlm.nih.gov/pubmed/15080220.

5. Ibid.

6. American College of Physicians, *The Advanced Medical Home: A Patient-Centered, Physician-Guided Model of Healthcare* (Philadelphia: American College of Physicians, 2005), http://www.acponline.org/advocacy/current_policy_papers/assets/adv_med.pdf.

7. "Chronic Diseases: The Leading Causes of Death and Disability in the United States," Centers for Disease Control and Prevention, http://www.cdc.gov/chronicdisease/overview/index.htm.

8. "The Chronic Care Model," Improving Chronic Illness Care, http://www.improvingchroniccare.org/?p=The_Chronic_Care_Model&s=2.

9. American Hospital Association, 2010 Committee on Research, *AHA Research Synthesis Report: Patient-Centered Medical Home (PCMH)* (Chicago: American Hospital Association, 2010).

10. David W. Bates and Asaf Bitton, "The Future of Health Information Technology in the Patient-Centered Medical Home," *Health Affairs* 29 (2010): 614–21.

11. NCQA PCMH Expert Certification Program, http:www.ncqa.org/Educational Events/Seminars and Webinars PCMH content Expert Certification.aspz?gclid=CNHQ94;JyMACFaY-mgodz10AJg.

12. "Joint Principles of the Patient-Centered Medical Home," Patient Centered Primary Care Collaborative, February 2007.

13. National Committee for Quality Assurance, *NCQA Patient Centered Medical Home 2011: Health Care that Revolves Around You: An Established Model of Care Coordination*, 2011, http://www.ncqa.org/Portals/0/Programs/Recognition/2011PCMHbrochure_web.pdf.

14. Colorado Medical Home Initiative, "The Affordable Care Act (ACA): Medical Homes," http://coloradomedicalhome.org/wp-content/ACA_Medical_Home_Fact_Sheet.pdf.

15. "Patient Centered Medical Home: Secure Telehealth Face-to-Face Video Conferencing Can Be Used to Build a Functional Medical Neighborhood for the Patient-Centered Medical Home," Secure Telehealth, 2013. http://www.securetelehealth.com/telehealth-uses/for-medical-homes.html

16. "The Patient-Centered Medical Home," Medical Management Association Survey, 2012.

17. Mitesh Patel et al., "Estimating the Staffing Infrastructure for a Patient-Centered Medical Home," *American Journal of Managed Care* 19 (2013): 509–16.

18. Hennepin Health, http://www.hennepin.us/residents/health-medical/hennepin-health.

19. Hennepin Health Infographic, http://www.hennepin.us./=/media/hennepinus/your-government/leadership/documents/hennepin-health-infographic.pdf.

20. Hennepin County Minnesota, County Administration, *2011 Hennepin County Highlights,* 2011.

21. U.S. Department of Health and Human Resources, Agency for Healthcare Research and Quality, "Patient Centered Medical Home," http://www.ahrq.gov/professionals/systems/primary-care/pcmh.

22. Health IT.gov, "Are There Penalties for Providers Who Don't Switch to Electronic Health Records (EHR)?", http://www.healthit.gov/providers-professionals/faqs/are-there-penalties-providers-who-don%E2%80%99t-switch-electronic-health-record.

23. Centers for Disease Control and Prevention, "Chronic Disease Prevention and Health Promotion," last modified May 21, 2014, http://www.cdc.gov/gov/chronicdisease/index.htm

24. Jessica Zigmond, "Project ECHO Expands, Spreads Telehealth Model," *Modern Healthcare,* June 26, 2013.

25. NBBJ. "A Village Leads a Nation: Southcentral Foundation Primary Care Center," http://www.nbbj.com/work/southcentral-foundation-primary-care-center.

26. "The Patient-Centered Medical Home," Medical Management Association Survey 2012.

27. Patel et al., "Estimating the Staffing Infrastructure."

28. "The Patient-Centered Medical Home: Moving to a New Level of Performance Through Automation," Phytel White Paper, 2011, http://www3.phytel.com/pcmh/pdf/patient_centered_final.pdf.

29. Ibid.

30. Ibid.

Select Bibliography

American College of Physicians. *The Advanced Medical Home: A Patient-Centered, Physician-Guided Model of Healthcare.* Philadelphia: American College of Physicians, 2005. http://www.acponline.org/advocacy/current_policy_papers/assets/adv_med.pdf.

American Hospital Association. "AHA Research Synthesis Report: Patient-Centered Medical Home." 2010. http://www.aha.org/research/cor/content/patient-centered-medical-home.pdf.

Future of Family Medicine Project Leadership Committee, "Future of Family Medicine Project." *Annals of Family Medicine* 2, suppl. 1 (2004): s3–s32. http://www.ncbi.nlm.nih.gov/pubmed/15080220.

"Joint Principles of the Patient-Centered Medical Home." Patient Centered Primary Care Collaborative. February 2007. http://www.aafp.org/dam/AAFP/documents/practice_management/pcmh/initiatives/PCMHJoint.pdf.

Kaye, Neva, Jason Buxbaum, and Mary Takach. *Building Medical Homes: Lessons from Eight States with Emerging Programs.* New York: Commonwealth Fund, 2011. http://www.commonwealthfund.org/~/media/Files/Publications/Fund%20Report/2011/Dec/1569_Kaye_building_medical_homes_v2.pdf.

"Medical Home Recognition & Accreditation Programs." National Center for Medical Home Implementation. n.d. http://www.medicalhomeinfo.org/national/recognition_programs.aspx.

National Committee for Quality Assurance. "NCQA's Physician Practice Connection: Patient-Centered Medical Home Program." National Committee for Quality Assurance, http://www.ncqa.org/portals/0/public%20policy/PCMH_Policy_Fact_Sheet.pdf.

———. NCQA PCMH Expert Certification Program. http://www.ncqa.org/Educational Events/SeminarsandWebinars/PCMHContentExpert Certification. aspx?gclid=CNHQ94;JyMACFaY-Mgodz10AJg.

"The Patient-Centered Medical Home: Moving to a New Level of Performance Through Automation." Phytel White Paper, 2011.

U.S. Department of Health and Human Resources, Agency for Healthcare Research and Quality. "Patient Centered Medical Home." n.d. http://www.ahrq.gov/professionals/systems/primary-care/pcmh.

"What Is the Difference Between a Medical Home and an ACO?" Accountable Care Facts. n.d. http://www.accountablecarefacts.org/topten/what-is-the-difference-between-a-medical-home-and-an-aco-1.

Overview

In recent years, the phrase "point of care" has taken on a new, expanded meaning in the United States as healthcare services have increasingly flowed beyond the walls of conventional clinic facilities toward locations that are part of patients' daily lives: their homes, schools, workplaces, and community hubs.

This outmigration of care continues to gain momentum as healthcare professionals' and researchers' knowledge of how to keep people well and out of the clinic has grown and new technologies and therapies have made it easier for patients to manage their own health and wellness better than in the past.

This major shift in the delivery of care is expected to impact design decisions for many years as healthcare organizations work to improve access, affordability, and health outcomes by seeing patients in a greater variety of settings.

Trends and Driving Forces

Key trends and forces that are driving the outmigration of care include the pressure for healthcare organizations to reduce costs while maintaining quality. Additional changes such as demographic shifts, shortages of key healthcare professionals, high levels of chronic disease, and technological advances have made mobile and remote care more desirable, easier, and more affordable.

Economics

Since most people who have health insurance in the United States are covered by employer-based plans, a major trend has been for private companies and other organizations to open clinics in their workplaces.[1] For example, information reported by the American College of Occupational and Environmental Medicine indicates that "for every dollar spent on wellness, employers get a return on investment (ROI) ranging from $2 to $5."[2] These returns result from reduction in absenteeism, medical costs, and insurance premiums, as well as increased productivity.

Demographics

The aging population, longer life expectancies, the prevalence of patients with chronic illnesses or conditions, and an increase in the number of veterans who require ongoing or long-term care are key demographic trends that have spurred the outmigration of care. These trends have also led to the advancement of technologies that help patients more actively monitor and manage their health.

Aging Population

By the year 2050, the number of senior citizens living in the United States is expected to reach 88.5 million, with 19 million being 85 years of age and older.[3] These numbers could climb higher depending on the results of efforts to develop medications that can slow or reverse the effects of aging.

For example, the body of knowledge about how diseases can be prevented and treated includes new and emerging fields of research, such as pharmacogenomics[4] (which examines how patients' genes influence the effectiveness of drugs) and regenerative medicine, which helps the body "to repair, replace, restore, and regenerate damaged or diseased cells, tissues, and organs."[5] Combined with improvements in vaccines and other preventative measures, medical discoveries in these new areas of scientific exploration are expected to further extend life expectancies.

Already, members of the "Silver Tsunami" have begun to delay retirement, and many are doing as much as possible to avoid nursing home care.[6] However, more than 60 percent of patients in this demographic group will likely develop chronic conditions as they continue to advance in years.[7] This means that they eventually will require assistance with daily activities and increased contact with their care providers to maintain a desired quality of life.

Chronic Conditions

According to the Centers for Disease Control and Prevention, about 133 million people in the United States have at least one chronic condition. The realization that 75 percent of the dollars spent on healthcare in the United States currently goes to the treatment of chronic illnesses has helped shift the industry's focus toward preventing disease rather than treating people after they have become sick, debilitated, or permanently disabled.[8]

Insurance companies, public and community health organizations, employers, and care providers are all investing more time and resources into activating patients by providing the information and support they need to modify the four modifiable health risk behaviors that are responsible for most of the suffering and early death related to chronic illness. These are: lack of sufficient physical activity, poor nutrition, tobacco use, and excessive alcohol consumption.

The reach of health education and wellness programs that have been based in clinics or on medical campuses is rapidly extending into the places where people live, work, attend school, or congregate. This outreach is being accomplished through the use of incentive programs, new technologies, and bricks-and-mortar strategies.

Veterans

During the 1990s, the U.S. Department of Veterans Affairs (VA) recognized the need to shift the majority of care being provided for veterans from hospitals and other long-term care facilities to clinics, community-based health centers, and the home. The 1998 report titled *VA Long Term Care at the Crossroads* advocated making this change, and a year later, the Veterans Millennium Healthcare and Benefits Act of 1999 (which was finalized in March 2002) established the basic benefits of home- and community-based, long-term care.

Since then, the VA has focused on implementing recommendations made in the *Crossroads* report, as well as carrying out requirements of the Millennium Act. The VA has not only expanded its community-based healthcare programs; it has also increased the skilled nursing and primary care services it provides to veterans in their homes.

Every medical center in the VA's health system is now required to provide noninstitutional services, which include:

- A care coordination program.
- Home health aides.
- Skilled home care.
- Home-based primary, respite, hospice, and/or palliative care.
- Community and VA-operated adult daycare.

The VA has also launched a medical foster home program for veterans who do not want to live in an institutional setting but cannot live independently at home. Technological advances have made home telehealth available for veterans, too. This option is particularly important for veterans who live in rural areas, where time and distance limit access to care services.

My HealtheVet.Com

This interactive digital tool provides veterans, their caregivers and dependents, and active duty service members who have access to the Internet with a method for viewing their electronic health records from home or another remote location.[9] Examples of information that can be accessed electronically include notes by members of a patient's care team, immunization and prescription records, detailed lab reports, and a list of the patient's specific medical issues.

Psychographics

The fitness craze that swept across the United States in the 1980s evolved into a more holistic view of wellness over the ensuing decades. Some healthcare organizations have capitalized on the "health is the new wealth" mantra that aptly expresses this trend by transforming their medical campuses into wellness destinations for healthy living. Services provided at these locations extend beyond diagnosis, treatment, and recovery to include fitness training and complementary care.

Self-Service Healthcare

In many instances, patients can evaluate the degree and type of healthcare they require before they spend time and money traveling to a clinic.

Self-Assessment

Healthcare organizations, medical schools, insurers, and others have developed a variety of web-based tools designed to improve the assessment phase of the patient's journey. Patients use these tools to self-assess from remote locations at a time that is convenient for them or when a decision about where to seek care must be well-informed, yet expeditious (for example, when a patient is traveling and away from home).

HowsYourHealth.Org

This website was developed by community and family medicine professionals at Dartmouth Medical School to help patients assess their confidence in managing and understanding their disease.[10] Patients complete an online health assessment, then receive a summary of findings and a list of more information about their specific condition prior to meeting with their physician or

integrated care team at a clinic. This information helps patients to be better prepared for the consultation portion of a clinic visit and can also help to ease their anxiety about the physical exam.

More than 100,000 patients have completed the health assessment survey and approximately 100 clinics are using data that has been aggregated from this website. The goal is to achieve participation by patients as close to 100 percent as possible so that their care providers can better understand the characteristics, anticipate the needs, and optimize health outcomes. The site is free and used by care providers, public officials, employers, and others.

"Get Care Now"

To reduce the number of calls it was receiving while improving responsiveness to patients, HealthPartners, an integrated healthcare system based in Minneapolis, introduced this web portal (www.healthpartners.com/public/care/get-care-now/) that enables patients to determine if they need healthcare services, decide what level of care they need, and obtain this care in a variety of ways (nurse call line, phone or e-mail visits, telemedicine visits, and standard or urgent care visits, for example).[11]

Zipnosis

For a fee of $25.00 per e-visit, Fairview Health Services provides a convenient diagnosis and treatment option for patients living in Minnesota who have minor health conditions, such as colds or the flu, urinary tract or yeast infections, sinus infections, and allergies.[12]

It takes patients approximately five minutes to complete an online survey and enter payment information. Then a Fairview clinician will respond electronically in less than an hour. For privacy purposes, the patient receives an e-mail notification that diagnosis and treatment information has been posted to his or her account, which is password-protected. If a prescription needs to be filled, patients can request this electronically, too, and select where they would like to pick up the medication.

By limiting the range of conditions covered by Zipnosis to those that generally do not require a physical exam, this interactive web-based tool is able to connect patients with board-certified care providers promptly and affordably.

Kiosks

Interactive kiosks located in retail settings are helping to meet the increased demand for health assessments. For example, SoloHealth stations, which are installed in stores such as Walmart, allow patients to check their blood pressure or body mass index, test their vision, assess their risk of heart disease, and obtain advice about diet and exercise habits.[13]

People answer on-screen questions about their age, gender, allergies, and health symptoms. The software that runs the kiosks tailors its recommendations to information included in individuals' completed profiles. It can even provide a list of local physicians and help patients to schedule an appointment. Customers typically spend less than five minutes at these kiosks, and once they have set up their private accounts they can retrieve health data in the future free of charge.

Some healthcare experts have expressed concerns that patients might be unnecessarily alarmed by test results they receive from a kiosk if no medical professional is nearby to interpret these. The potential for having a positive impact on people's health also rests on the decisions individuals make about what to do with the information they receive. Ideally, they will be motivated to take care of their health or to seek services from a healthcare professional earlier than they typically would have done this.

Remote Health Monitoring and Management

In addition to the wide variety of software applications described earlier in this book that enable patients with digital devices to monitor and manage their health, wireless and wired biosensor devices that automate the monitoring of chronic conditions, such as diabetes and heart disease, are being used more often. Such technological innovations can help preempt a hospital visit by detecting a change in patients' physical conditions earlier than they (or their care providers) have previously been able to do.

TeleHealth

Telehealth technology is increasingly being used to care for patients in their home or workplace as well as at community health centers. As reimbursement for telehealth services becomes more common, experts predict that remote care services will increasingly be provided through direct video connections, web interfaces (Skype, for example), or the telephone.

Providing virtual care via a telehealth program provides benefits for patients and healthcare organizations alike. Some healthcare organizations, such as the Cleveland Clinic, have observed that home telehealth monitoring can produce better health outcomes than occasional checkups can. Since patients in rural areas often lack access to specialists and must travel substantial distances to be seen by them, telehealth exams and consults typically saves them time and money (on travel expenses, for example).

The increased use of telehealth services, however, has led to a need for hubs or centralized facilities where data can be received from patients, transmitted to the appropriate members of patients' care teams, and securely stored.

Researchers also point out that types of monitoring systems and devices vary in effectiveness and note that obtaining daily reports from patients at home requires a cultural adjustment to this new care model. Healthcare professionals are also still determining how to best interact with patients remotely.

Mayo Clinic's Center for Connected Care

The Telestroke program at Mayo Clinic and Cleveland Clinic provides audio, video, and digital connections between Mayo specialists and patients in emergency rooms so that the specialists can see and be seen by patients, talk with them, monitor their vital signs, and recommend action by other healthcare professionals who are at the same location as the patient. Specialists can respond in a matter of minutes.[14,15]

Healthcare Reform

Implementation of the Patient Protection and Affordable Care Act (ACA) has spurred the out-migration of care by changing reimbursement structures and by providing funding for the creation or expansion of community-, school-, and employer-based health centers. It has also provided incentives for healthcare organizations to explore ways to integrate home-based (domiciliary) healthcare into their delivery models.

Capitation

The ACA's shift toward compensation being calculated on a per-capita basis rather than per procedure performed is one of the major forces motivating healthcare organizations to keep patients well and out of the clinic. This has presented new challenges and opportunities for design professionals.

Not only are clinics being integrated into locations that are part of the everyday lives of patients, such as workplaces, community centers, and schools, there are new types of facilities and destinations arising from attempts to achieve the blend of fitness, wellness, and medical care best suited to the needs of a particular patient population or community.

Community Health Centers

The ACA established the Community Health Center Fund that has provided $11 billion in funding for the new construction, renovation, and expansion of these medical facilities as well as financial support for implementation of electronic health record systems and other health information technology. The new (or expanded) community health center access points are expected to extend the care to an additional 860,000 patients.

School-Based Health Centers

From 2010 to 2013, the ACA appropriated $200 million in funding for capital projects aimed at improving and supporting the care services delivered by school-based health centers. The U.S. Department of Health and Human Services' Health Resources and Services Administration (HRSA) awarded these funds under the "School-Based Health Center Capital (SBHCC) Program" to 470 school-based health programs that enabled them to create new centers or to upgrade and expand the services they already provided in existing facilities. Public leaders estimate that this program will provide preventative and primary care services to an additional 875,000 patients.[16]

Workplace Wellness and Incentive Programs

The ACA also includes new federal rules that limit the extent to which health plans can charge higher premiums based on factors such as an individual's health status, age, gender, and tobacco use. In the past, the states regulated this practice, and there were wide variations in how much insurers could adjust their rates.

Wellness programs that are part of an employer-sponsored health plan must comply with federal rules barring workplace discrimination. Although the Health Insurance Portability and Accountability Act of 1996 (HIPAA) generally prohibits group health plans from charging employees different premiums based on their health status, it includes an exception that allows employers to provide financial incentives for employees who achieve certain health goals or participate in certain health promotion programs. The ACA expanded this exemption so that employers can offer employees enrolled in their group plans incentives of up to 30 percent of the cost of their coverage if they meet employer-defined health targets.[17]

Home-Based Healthcare

Some measures contained in the ACA support the provision of healthcare services in the home. For example, Section 3024 of the ACA established the Independence at Home Medical Practice Demonstration Program to test, refine, and, ultimately, implement the objectives of the Independence at Home Act (IHA), which focuses on creating a new model for physician-led, home-based primary care. In addition, some of the accountable care organization (ACO) pilot programs are experimenting with ways to integrate home-based health and wellness services into their care delivery models.[18]

Improvements in Communication

Today, information about health and wellness is not only far easier to find than it has been in the past but is also flowing toward people from all directions. Insurance companies, healthcare organizations, private businesses, nonprofit and community groups, public agencies, and many other sources regularly announce new research findings and medical discoveries, distribute newsletters, send e-mail updates to targeted patient groups, host seminars and webinars, and use a broad range of other communications strategies to inform patients about how they can take charge of their own health and wellness.

In addition, widespread use of and access to the Internet has led to the development of online peer groups that provide patients with the opportunity to learn from one another's' experiences. Online communities can also deepen patients' connections to groups they join in person by enabling them to better articulate concerns and empowering them to share what they have learned from their online peers.

Peer-to-Peer Communication

A study conducted by the Pew Research Center in 2011 found that peer-to-peer communication plays a significant role in patients' decisions about healthcare inside and outside of the clinic. The survey data, gathered from 3,001 adults by telephone and from 2,156 adults over the Internet, revealed that patients in the United States find that information from peers is more useful than that provided by healthcare professionals in such areas as practical knowledge, coping methods, quick remedies for everyday health issues, and assistance finding other resources.

Healthcare professionals remain the central source of information, care, and support for diagnoses and disease management. Other key findings of this study include:

- Approximately one in five Internet users (18 percent) said they have sought to connect online with others who might have health concerns that are similar to theirs.

- These ratios increase to one in four for people living with chronic conditions, such as high blood pressure, diabetes, heart or lung conditions, or cancer.

- Other groups of Internet users who are likely to seek peers online who share their concerns about certain health issues include patients' family members, friends, and other partners-in-care, as well as people who have experienced a health crisis within the past year or who are experiencing a significant change in their physical health (e.g., pregnancy or quitting smoking).

- People living with a rare disease outpaced all others for "tapping into the wisdom of their peer network." More than half of this respondent subgroup indicated that they turned to family, friends, or others who have the same health condition.

- Internet users who are 65 years of age or older are less likely than younger Internet users to seek health information from peers online.[19]

Technology

In general, healthcare organizations have been using technology more and more to transport data instead of transporting people. Numerous pilot programs have shown how this can improve health outcomes while reducing costs.

Veterans Health Administration Care Coordination/Home Telehealth Program

Between 2003 and 2007, the Veterans Health Administration (VHA) introduced a national home telehealth program, referred to as Care Coordination/Home Telehealth (CCHT), which was designed to improve the coordination of care for veterans who have chronic conditions and to reduce the need to admit them to long-term care facilities. Implementing this program required the VHA to institute health informatics, home telehealth, and disease management technologies. During the introductory period for this program, the number of veterans using CCHT increased from 2,000 to 31,570. The VHA's analysis of data gathered from 17,025 CCHT patients revealed a 25 percent reduction in the number of bed days spent in a care facility and a 19 percent reduction in the number of hospital admissions. The annual per-patient cost of CCHT in 2008 was $1,600, which was substantially less than other noninstitutional care (NIC) programs and nursing home care. Based on these early results, the VHA set a goal of having 92,000 patients on home monitoring by 2012.[20]

CCHT has now become a standard NIC service that provides care for veterans with chronic conditions in their homes as they age. After patients enroll in this program, they work with a care coordinator to determine what home telehealth technology is required. A technology algorithm is used to relate a patient's health status, unique needs, and ability to use technology to the most appropriate, affordable CCHT devices, such as:

- Videophones to make audio-video consultations possible.

- Messaging machines.

- Biometric devices that record and monitor vital signs.

- Digital cameras.

- Telemonitoring equipment.[21]

In recent years, the convergence of medical, communications, and information technologies have made it possible for some veterans to use a single device that serves multiple health monitoring and management functions (for example, smartphones with customized software applications that can gather and transmit information from biometric devices and sensors).

The patients and their caregivers are then provided with training to learn how to use this technology, and the coordinator shifts his or her focus to providing active case management services and continuing to coordinate care with other members of a patient's health team.

Project Examples

As the project examples in the following section will illustrate, some of the key factors that design professionals consider when designing for the outmigration of care include geographic location, characteristics of the patient population served, the type of services provided, and staffing strategies.

Wellness Centers

The shift from treating illnesses and injuries to trying to prevent their occurrence has not only motivated healthcare organizations to create healing environments but has also generated a demand for wellness centers and destinations that are designed to achieve mind, body, and spiritual health.

■ MAYO CLINIC DAN ABRAHAM HEALTHY LIVING CENTER

This health and wellness center, which is located at Mayo Clinic Hospital–Saint Marys Campus, was designed to meet an increased demand for fitness services while creating an atmosphere that is welcoming for avid athletes as well as casual users. The facility occupies two levels below grade and encompasses a total of 10,000 square feet.

The upper level includes fitness testing rooms and office space. The lower level houses a fitness floor, an activity classroom, an indoor track, a lap pool, a separate pool for water-based exercises, a mind/body studio, a large fitness floor with high-quality equipment, and locker rooms. Special features include a sound system and cardiotheater with eight televisions that are positioned for viewing from the cardiovascular exercise equipment. The center is staffed by health and wellness specialists and group fitness instructors.

There are also locations on the Mayo Campus that serve Mayo Clinic employees, students, volunteers, retirees, and spouses. In aggregate, these centers occupy 127,000 square feet. They offer wellness and nutrition services as well as group fitness, health coaching, and work-site wellness and relaxation programs.

■ EAST TEXAS MEDICAL CENTER, OLYMPIC/ REHABILITATION CENTERS
Various Locations, Texas

These post-acute-care centers are designed to help patients recover function and independence after they have been ill or injured. In addition to outpatient physical therapy and cardiopulmonary rehabilitation programs, these centers offer an array of health-enhancing fitness services to help members improve the quality of their lives.

Amenities include rehabilitation saltwater pools, running tracks, cardiovascular and strength-training equipment, aerobic and yoga studios, and weight training and massage therapy facilities. Outpatient rehabilitation services range from physical, occupational, and speech therapies, sports medicine, and hydrotherapy to functional capacity evaluations, impairment ratings, work conditioning, and personal training.

■ THE MARSH
Minnetonka, Minnesota

This 67,000-square-foot wellness destination is located on a gently sloping site overlooking a scenic marshland that inspires a healthy approach to life. Since construction is prohibited on the marshland, this tranquil setting will remain undisturbed.

The Marsh's founder, Ruth Strickler, was diagnosed with lupus in 1975, and this helped to fuel her lifelong passion for helping others by presenting a balanced approach to living with a chronic illness. The center's architecture and art reflect Strickler's study and appreciation of Chinese culture.

When it opened in 1985, the Marsh was on the forefront of what is now called "integrative care." It began with an acupuncturist and cardiologist working together to blend Western medical treatment with complementary care. Today, health and wellness speakers from around the world present classes and seminars at the Marsh.

The three-level, universally accessible complex houses a medically based fitness center, lap swimming and warm water therapy pools, group exercise and Pilates studios, a full-service spa, a restaurant and boutique, a running track, outdoor walking paths, six overnight guest rooms, and several meditative spaces.

■ VIRTUA HEALTH AND WELLNESS CENTER
Washington Township, New Jersey

The major goal for this $31 million ambulatory care center was to provide integrated, concierge-level health services for patients in a state-of-the-art facility. The 39-acre total health destination is also the keystone development in a city master plan that includes the new Washington Township Town Center.

Patients, staff, and members of the community can use the following facilities, which are staffed by board-certified medical professionals as well as experts in fitness training, rehabilitation, and complementary care therapies:

- An ambulatory surgery center.
- Cardiac rehabilitation.
- A nutrition and diabetes care center.
- A high-risk pregnancy center.
- Virtua Express Urgent Care.
- Outpatient lab and preadmission testing services.

- Physician offices.
- A radiation oncology suite.
- A SleepCare Center.
- Sports Medicine.
- The Virtua Center for HealthFitness.
- Virtua in Motion (physical therapy and rehabilitation).
- A 14,000-square-foot spa.
- Wound care.
- A 3,000-square-foot café/restaurant.

The HealthFitness Center houses:

- Three pools, ranging from a 25-meter lap pool to individual pools for group exercise and warm-water therapy.
- A 9,000-square-foot fitness floor for strength and cardio training.
- A running track.
- A 2,500-square-foot group exercise studio.
- A 1,000-square-foot spinning studio.

Strategies that the design team employed to deliver the world-class ambulatory care center at a cost that was affordable to Virtua Health and its physician partners included (figs. 10-1, 10-2):

- Reducing the overall roof and exterior wall ratios.
- Specifying alternative exterior cladding materials—such as cast stone products and burnished block—that maintained a high-quality appearance at an appropriate budget level.
- Reducing the amount of glass surfaces through the use of translucent polycarbonate panels.
- Limiting the use of more expensive materials, such as natural wood, to the most visible high-use areas, such as the main lobbies.
- Using a two-story masonry wall to act as a fire separation wall between the medical office

building and the wellness center. This wall allowed the building to be compartmentalized, thereby reducing the fireproofing scope of the project and resulted in significant savings.

Employee Health Centers

Employers are partnering with their health insurance providers to establish employee health centers so that their employees have convenient access to medical services. In some instances, these workplace-based clinics also provide space and equipment for on-site wellness programs.

The range of incentives employers and insurers are offering is also expanding to include everything from workday walking and fitness groups, health club credits or rebates, and weekly grocery store discounts for the purchase of healthy foods, to cash or gift card rewards that are given to employees for completing

health-risk assessments. More recently, programs have begun to relate incentives to specific biometric outcomes, such as body weight or cholesterol levels.

■ BRAC 133 AT MARK CENTER HEALTH AND FITNESS CENTERS
Alexandria, Virginia

These facilities are located in one of the most visible built landmarks on the west side of Alexandria, Mark Center. BRAC stands for Base Realignment and Closure, which is the official process that the U.S. Department of Defense (DoD) uses to periodically reorganize its military base structure. In 2005, Congress mandated that many DoD offices be moved into secure sites to meet this agency's high antiterrorism security standards. As a result, more than 6,000 DoD employees were relocated to the BRAC 133 at Mark Center location.

FIGURES 10-1, 10-2: Virtua Health and Wellness Center. The project goal was to provide "concierge-level service" to ambulatory patients in a state-of-the-art facility. Designed around a program based on the concept of "one-stop shopping," the facility offers an expansive health fitness center, an ambulatory surgery center with four operating rooms, a radiation oncology center, retail functions, med-spa, conference center, day care, café, diagnostic and testing services, and ample room for multiple private physician practices. Photography by Don Pearse Photographers

Since many of the DoD employees were transferred from locations on Washington D.C.'s Metro system, providing key amenities on-site was especially important for smoothing this transition. This included making health and wellness services available so that employees could easily integrate these into their workday schedule.

The building includes a 4,400-square-foot occupational health and wellness center where a range of medical and employee assistance services are provided. This center is located adjacent to a fitness facility that offers DoD employees a full complement of cardio and strength equipment, an indoor track, and lap swimming pools.

■ GENERAL MILLS WORKPLACE CLINIC
Minneapolis, Minnesota

This Minnesota-based corporation has advocated for healthy workplaces for more than a quarter century. In 2004, its in-house health services staff developed the General Mills Health Number screening tool that employees can use to assess health risks and learn about healthy lifestyle choices. In addition to a fitness center, General Mills's corporate headquarters has an on-site preventative health clinic where patients can obtain medical and dental services. It includes exam and consult rooms, offices for care providers, and a basic lab (fig. 10-3).

■ HEALTH PARTNERS WELL AT WORK CLINICS
North St. Paul and Stillwater, Minnesota

After experiencing strong demand for its workplace-based clinics on corporate campuses, HealthPartners Inc. opened clinics in the Stillwater High School and in the North St. Paul Independent School District's headquarters.

Each clinic has two exam rooms, a basic laboratory, and a toilet room with a pass-through window. While there is no reception desk, a medical staff member circulates throughout the space to keep people flowing through the exam rooms. Staff includes a nurse practitioner or physician's assistant. Appointments can be made in advance, but walk-ins are also welcome.

The clinics are located near a vestibule or main entry so that they can be open before and after work hours. The clinic in the Stillwater High School was placed in a formerly occupied classroom.

The primary goal for the school districts is to keep teachers and other staff members on-site by making healthcare services easy for them to obtain. This reduces the amount of time they need to take off to seek care elsewhere and makes monitoring and managing chronic conditions a more integral part of patients' typical daily activities. When teachers have to take time off, for example, the school district has to hire a substitute teacher for a full day rather than the two hours it would typically take for an employee to drive to a clinic, be treated, and return to work.

In addition, because of tenure in teaching positions and other factors, school districts generally retain staff longer than many private businesses. Thus, it is in the districts' (and taxpayers') best interest for employees to keep on top of their health from the time they start their career. Moreover, the Stillwater District has added incentive to reduce healthcare costs for its employees because it recently instituted a self-funded plan, which means it pays for healthcare services out of its budget.

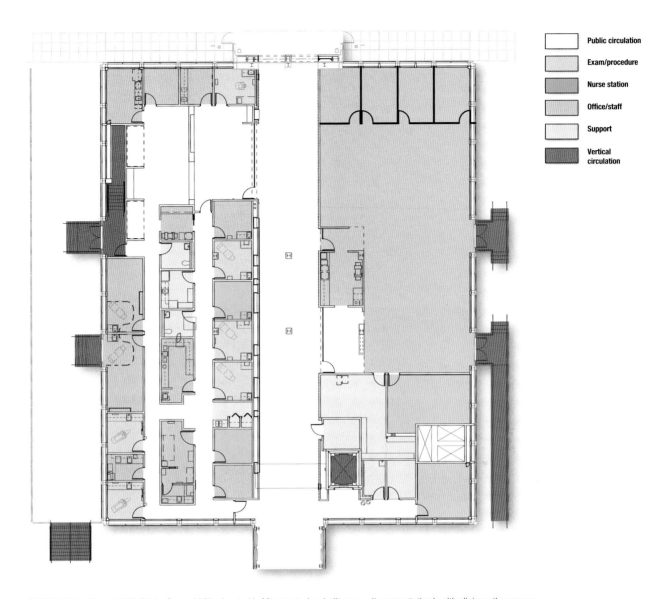

	Public circulation
	Exam/procedure
	Nurse station
	Office/staff
	Support
	Vertical circulation

FIGURE 10-3: General Mills Clinic. General Mills, located in Minnesota, has built an on-site preventative health clinic on the campus of its corporate headquarters to give employees convenient access to medical services. Image courtesy of Hammel, Green and Abrahamson, Inc.

MAYO EMPLOYEE AND COMMUNITY HEALTH EXPRESS CARE CLINICS
Rochester, Minnesota

Patients with minor medical conditions, such as a sore throat, ear pain, urinary tract infection, or nausea, can schedule an appointment online or at an Express Care kiosk. All appointment types are allotted 15 minutes. Since no preparatory or follow-up interactions are scheduled there, the exam room utilization rate is higher than at other ECH clinics.

These clinics are staffed by certified nurse practitioners and physician's assistants who are supported by primary care physicians. Information from each visit is entered into Mayo's electronic health record system so that it can be retrieved and reviewed by members of the patient's collaborative care team as needed.

NPR'S HEALTH CLINIC
Washington, DC

In 2013, National Public Radio (NPR) partnered with Cigna Insurance Company to open an employer-based health clinic in its new 330,000-square-foot headquarters building. The center is staffed by a nurse practitioner and medical assistant. It is available for use by approximately 800 full- and part-time NPR employees on an appointment or walk-in basis (without a copay or other fee required).

The decision to include an employer-based clinic in the building's program supports NPR's efforts to help its staff improve their overall health and productivity. Services offered at the clinic range from routine physicals and flu shots to immunizations for journalists who are assigned to work abroad. Health management coaching is also available for employees who have chronic conditions such as heart disease, asthma, or diabetes. Classes and workshops for weight loss, smoking cessation, and other behavioral health issues are also offered on-site.

NPR's leaders expect the investment they have made in this clinic to save the organization money in the long run. Cigna projects that NPR could save as much as $390,000 during the first three years of the wellness center's operation through lower insurance costs, less lost work time, and employees' use of generic drugs. NPR estimates that providing on-site wellness services could translate into a 25 percent decrease in the amount employees pay for primary care, a 32 percent reduction in specialist visits, and a 38 percent reduction in trips to the emergency room.[22]

School-Based Health Centers

School-based health centers often operate as a partnership between a K–12 school and a community health organization to make basic services affordable and easily accessible for students, their families, faculty, staff, and, at times, other members of the surrounding community. These services typically include:

- Primary, behavioral, and oral health care.
- Health screening for dental, vision, and hearing problems.
- Health education programs and resources.
- Substance abuse counseling.
- Case management.

A major benefit of school-based clinics is that they enable care providers to intervene at the earliest moment possible and to treat patients where many of them spend the majority of their weekdays. They also help to create a culture of health. This is especially important because obesity, dental disease, uncontrolled asthma, and many behavioral health conditions that begin in childhood and adolescence can most successfully be addressed with a blend of clinical and preventative strategies.

The number of patients seen in a school-based health center or clinic is often limited by the fact that they are typically much smaller than a more comprehensive Federally-Qualified Community Health Center (FQHC) and their hours of operation usually coincide with the school day schedule.

■ JORDAN WELLNESS CENTER
Los Angeles, California

The Jordan Wellness Center is located on the campus of the Jordan High School in the Watts neighborhood of South Los Angeles. It is also near the Jordan Downs Housing Development and will serve students attending the high school as well as nearby elementary and middle schools, while also allowing local residents and business owners to obtain healthcare services near where they live, work, and attend school.

The center, which opened in 2013, is operated by Watts Healthcare Corporation (WHCC), a private, nonprofit Federally-Qualified Community Health Center that provides clinical, preventive, behavioral, and restorative healthcare services to underserved communities throughout South Los Angeles.

The new Jordan Wellness Center replaced an outdated two-room facility that had been operating in the Jordan High School since the 1970s. WHCC leaders decided to invest in improving this facility's appearance and capabilities based on their belief that when students and local residents take pride in a community clinic, they are more likely to take advantage of the affordable services it offers.

The new clinic building houses five exam rooms and offers basic medical and behavioral healthcare services as well as family planning guidance (teen pregnancy is a significant concern for this patient population) and preventative care, such as immunizations.

■ SUNSET HEALTH CENTER
Airway Heights, Washington

This school-based health center was launched as a pilot project to provide on-site healthcare for students enrolled in the Cheney School District and their siblings. It is run by the Community Health Association of Spokane and is funded by the School Health Care Association of Spokane County, a nonprofit organization that was founded to establish school-based health centers in this area of Washington State.

The Sunset Health Center is staffed by a physician's assistant and a medical assistant, who are available on a part-time basis during school hours. A licensed clinical social worker counsels students at the center one day per week. Approximately one in five of the patients seen at the clinic have a behavioral health condition or concern.

The center occupies 900 square feet or half of a classroom module located behind Sunset Elementary School. It has a waiting area, three exam rooms, office space, and a bathroom, as well as the capabilities to run blood and urine tests. Since the center is closed during school breaks, families must seek care at other clinics during these times. However, some area clinics use the same electronic health record system, which can make coordination and continuity of care easier to achieve.

Sunset Elementary School was chosen as the location for the pilot health center because the nearest clinic was nine miles away. The health center supplements the role of the school's nurse, who remains the first point of contact for most students.

■ SCHOOL HEALTH CONNECTION
New Orleans, Louisiana

This affiliated program of the Louisiana Public Health Institute (LPHI) was established in 2006 to help rebuild and expand the School-Based Health Centers (SBHCs) in and around New Orleans in the aftermath of Hurricane Katrina, as well as to help schools to develop and implement comprehensive wellness programs.

The School Health Connection is largely funded by the W.K. Kellogg, Robert Wood Johnson, and the GE foundations. It is also supported by Louisiana State University Public Hospital, LSUHSC Pediatrics, and Tulane Medical Center. For example, a physician who is also the director of community medicine and disease management at LSU Public Hospital oversees the operations of two of the SBHCs.

The SBHCs supported by this organization are located and designed to increase access that students and their families have to preventative, primary, and behavioral health services—particularly patients who are uninsured, underinsured, or may not have access to other healthcare facilities or care services.

Typical services include comprehensive physicals and immunizations, behavioral health screenings and treatment; and diagnosis and treatment of clinical symptoms and conditions, such as hypertension, diabetes, or asthma. The school wellness programs are designed to provide increased physical activity, enhanced health curricula, staff health and wellness screenings, and better nutritional guidance for students and staff.

Based on the financial and technical support provided by the School Health Connection, there are now 12 SBHCs operating in the Orleans, Jefferson, and St. Bernard parishes, with more planned for the future.

Community Health Centers

One of the key rationales for providing better access to affordable care in underserved communities is that healthcare industry experts and public leaders believe this can improve public health in general. Once more people in these communities have health insurance, they will be able to take advantage of preventative and routine care services rather than only seek care when they have a health emergency.

Insurance can only go so far, however. The top consideration for most clients who are constructing a community health center is to pick a location that is easily accessible and, ideally, familiar and already a destination for all members of the patient population being served.

■ MARTIN LUTHER KING MEDICAL CENTER CAMPUS AND WELLNESS COMMUNITY (MLKMCC)
Los Angeles, California

The master plan for this medical campus and wellness community, which is located in South Los Angeles, addresses the need for health and wellness facilities in this sector of the city, which has been neglected and underserved for decades.

The City of Los Angeles decided to reopen the hospital as the first step toward revitalization of this neighborhood. The completed medical campus and wellness community will include full-service inpatient and outpatient facilities, a behavioral health center, assisted care housing, and a mix of transit-oriented development, and community-serving uses.

There will be plenty of open space for new parks, outdoor recreation areas, community gardens, and urban agriculture because a key project goal is to address health epidemics such as diabetes and obesity by increasing opportunities for physical activity in the community and providing easy access to healthy food.

A defining element of the master plan is the Wellness Spine, which makes multimodal transportation preferable in a city that is well known for its car-dependent culture. This is possible because the MLKMCC is adjacent to the second-busiest public transit station in Los Angeles County.

The Wellness Spine is composed of a system of bike and pedestrian pathways that connect different areas of the campus to each other and the campus to its urban environs. The vehicular circulation system is designed to minimize potential conflicts between city traffic and emergency vehicles. It includes a helipad and dedicated emergency vehicle routes.

YMCA Clinics

A key aspect of this organization's mission is to help people to achieve a healthy spirit, mind, and body. In some instances, this has prompted YMCAs to open medical and/or dental clinics in their facilities to support the organization's focus on "improving the nation's health and well-being…and foster[ing] connections through fitness, sports, fun, and shared interests." [23]

■ LEGACY FOUNDATION CHRIS-TOWN YMCA MEDICAL AND DENTAL CLINIC
Phoenix, Arizona

In response to the closings of underfunded school-based clinics in Arizona during a period of economic decline, this YMCA partnered with Phoenix Baptist Hospital Family Medical Center to open an on-site health center in 2011.

Initially, the Legacy Foundation Chris-Town YMCA Medical and Dental Clinic provided medical and oral health services to approximately 2,000 children per year who would not otherwise have access to them. It later began offering services every other Wednesday night to adults in need.

Abrazo Health Care provides an on-site coordinator to help families determine their eligibility for treatment. Other medical and dental professionals from throughout the Phoenix area volunteer their time to see patients at the clinic. Although the clinic is not located in a school building, it uses the school-based clinic care model at a location (the YMCA) that is familiar and convenient for the surrounding community.

■ TOM TAYLOR FAMILY YMCA MULTICARE HEALTH CLINIC
Gig Harbor, Washington

Based on their shared commitment to improving community health and wellness, MultiCare Health Systems and the YMCA of Pierce and Kitsap Counties formed a 10-year partnership in 2005 to provide nutrition and physical activity programs that help patients "get healthy" and then stay well. This led to the inclusion of a MultiCare clinic on the second floor of the 74,756-square-foot Tom Taylor Family YMCA building.

MultiCare's professional staff members provide hand therapy (massage), physical therapy, and nutritional services in the clinic, which is located on the building's second floor. Physical therapists also offer aquatic therapy in the YMCA pool. Programs based in the YMCA's Women's Fitness Center include cardio and strength training as well as yoga for female YMCA members aged 15 years or older.

Key design goals for the YMCA facility were to provide amenities for people of all ages and for the building to have a prominent presence in the community.

■ PROJECT OASIS
South Wichita, Kansas

In 2013, GraceMed, Via Christi Health, and the Greater Wichita YMCA announced plans to build a $7.5 million clinic at the Richard A. DeVore South YMCA to provide oral health and medical services to people living in the middle of a "healthcare desert." This motivated project organizers to name the proposed clinic "Project Oasis." The YMCA was willing to donate three acres of land as long as it would be used for construction of a clinic facility.

The facility is designed to serve an estimated 17,000 people per year in an area where 8 in 10 people live at or below 200 percent of the federal poverty level. The new clinic is expected to strengthen the YMCA's role as a community destination for a variety of services.

Via Christi's role is to make sure the building is properly constructed. It will serve as the "landlord" for the clinic, in concert with GraceMed. Six of Via Christi's Family Medicine residents will work as a team once the new 30,000-square-foot clinic is constructed. It will have 36 medical exam rooms and 12 dental operatories as well as 2 optometric lanes. Services at this clinic are expected to include prenatal and pediatric care, geriatrics, and optometry. It will house a pharmacy, an urgent-care center, and a basic lab. Behavioral health consultants will be integrated with the primary care providers.

Project Oasis will also serve as a hub for four of GraceMed's school-based clinics and will complement the primary care services provided in these satellite locations.

Mobile Care

Mobile health clinics typically serve patients where people congregate or live: at homeless shelters, nursing homes, or community centers. The majority schedule visits to particular sites on a regular basis, although some also conduct roving outreach activities.

Most patients served by mobile healthcare programs lack the insurance coverage, time, and/or transportation needed to gain access to care at a clinic or other medical facility. Often, community service or public agencies collaborate with mobile healthcare providers to bring medical, dental, behavioral, and specialized care services to those in need. In some rural communities mobile clinics are the sole source of medical and dental care. Mobile clinics can also serve areas recovering from natural disasters.

The majority of mobile healthcare organizations provide care services to patients inside their mobile units, with the remaining programs transporting clinicians and equipment to remote sites where they set up temporary operations in an existing building.

Mobile clinics use a variety of remodeled or custom-designed vans, trucks, and buses. The type of services provided, characteristics of the patient population, environment, and cost are key factors that influence the size and type of vehicles that are used. Major design considerations include location, visibility, staffing, care delivery model, type of services provided, and technology.

Location

Since mobile units are often parked in unsafe areas, design professionals often employ safety and security strategies that are customary for use in stationary clinics, such as achieving proper illumination levels and providing clear sightlines between work areas as well as to the outside.

For practical purposes, shorter vehicles are used more commonly to serve urban populations because of the limited navigational and parking space.

Visibility

Graphic design and exterior finishes on mobile units are especially important for announcing the presence of mobile healthcare programs in a community and establishing brand recognition for a healthcare organization. Decisions about the colors, graphics, and typography used on the exterior of their vehicles can help boost a program's visibility, communicate the type of services offered, and build comfort and familiarity for patients. Thus, design professionals focus on making mobile units both attractive and easily identifiable.

Staffing

Most often, one to two staff members ride in each mobile health vehicle, with some larger accommodating six to seven clinicians and other staff (driver, social workers, and case managers, for example).

The staff who provide healthcare services as part of a mobile healthcare program face unique challenges. They have limited opportunities to collaborate with their professional peers and often work in dangerous or remote areas with patients who may not feel at ease in any clinical setting. Thus, the more comfortable, safe, and welcoming a mobile clinic is, the more likely it will be able to attract and retain qualified, committed staff.

Types of Services and Vehicles

The types and designs of mobile clinics are as diverse as the services they offer and the patient populations they serve. Mobile health practices that transport clinicians and equipment to remote sites frequently use converted or custom-made passenger vans. Larger mobile units can serve more patients, but they are heavier, more difficult to maneuver, and more expensive to drive long distances. Their drivers must also have a commercial license.

Since space is at a premium, design professionals carefully review medical equipment specifications, select furnishings, and review care delivery processes to make sure that space inside a mobile clinic is efficiently configured, functions well, and is comfortable. Sufficient space must be provided for storage of medications and supplies that are dispensed and distributed to patients at remote sites.

■ HEALTH ON WHEELS
Norwalk, California

This school-based mobile pediatric clinic opened in 1996 as a partnership between Kaiser Permanente, California State University in Long Beach, the City of Norwalk, and Norwalk–La Mirada Unified School District. It provides free healthcare services to uninsured and underinsured children throughout the school district. The care providers are bilingual and include three pediatric nurse practitioners and a medical assistant.

The clinic is housed in a large truck that visits 10 schools on a weekly rotating schedule throughout the school year.

■ KLEINBANK
Multiple locations, Minnesota

Stroke Detection Plus, a stroke detection service based in Des Moines, Iowa, is offered in multiple KleinBank locations in Minnesota. This convenient, cost-effective program is not covered by Medicare and is not covered by insurance, yet it offers low-cost stroke screening by evaluating the buildup of fatty blockage in the carotid arteries. Stroke Detection Plus estimates that the patient cost for this mobile screening service ranges from 20 to 50 percent below the cost of testing within a hospital setting.

Technology

Since health information is often collected on-site as part of a clinic visit, using an electronic health record system conserves space and enhances efficiency in mobile clinics, which usually require wireless Internet systems and backup generators for computers as well as specialized medical or dental equipment. As is the case with all clinic design, noise from generators and other equipment should be dampened or masked, and the need for any vibration control should be reviewed and addressed during the planning phase of a project.

■ MAMMO-A-GO-GO
Multiple locations, Minnesota

Determined to raise awareness about the importance of early detection of breast cancer and to make screening mammograms convenient for women to fit into their busy schedules, Park Nicollet's Jane Brattain Breast Center launched a mobile mammography program by investing in a custom designed truck that proudly displays the name Mammo-a-go-go on its side.

FIGURE 10-4: Mammo-a-go-go. Mobile screening vehicles such as this custom designed truck are used to bring women's health awareness and screening services beyond the walls of the clinic. Park Nicollet proudly displays the name "Mammo-a-go-go" on the side of its mobile mammography screening clinic.   Image courtesy of HealthPartners.

The exterior of the truck is covered with a large, predominantly pink floral pattern that makes it highly visible when it is driving between locations or parked near one of 13 clinics where Park Nicollet offers these mobile medical services. Its interior finishes relate to the spa-like design that women throughout the Twin Cities associate with the stationary Jane Brattain clinic (fig. 10-4).

■ APPLE TREE DENTAL
Multiple locations, Minnesota, Fergus Falls, North Dakota, and San Mateo, California

This nonprofit dental practice's mission is to make state-of-the-art oral healthcare accessible for everyone, and, especially, for people in underserved communities who lack insurance coverage or the time, financial resources, physical ability, or means of transportation needed to be treated in a clinic. Some individuals also lack access to care because they live in locations where there is a shortage of dentists.

Instead of opening a stationary clinic, Apple Tree launched its practice in 1985 with a mobile dental care delivery program aimed at treating patients who faced these barriers to access. Although it began by providing services to patients in nursing homes, over the years Apple Tree's practice has evolved to become a "Community Collaborative Practice" as its dental care professionals work with a range of community partners to treat patients in a variety of places— from where they live and work to where they attend school or receive other health or social services.

From 1999 to 2001, Apple Tree teamed up with a leading dental equipment manufacturer to design an innovative mobile dental office. The need to move these mobile offices efficiently, as well as to set up multiple dental chairs at larger locations, prompted the design of a new, "multi-site delivery vehicle" that Apple Tree now uses to haul up to three complete mobile offices at one time.

Apple Tree also employs truck drivers to move the equipment during the evening so that it is ready for use the next morning. This frees Apple Tree's dental teams to focus on providing oral healthcare services.

Each day, a team of one dentist and two assistants travels to a satellite site. A truck delivers the portable dental equipment needed to set up a complete dental office within minutes. The dental teams provide checkups, cleanings, fillings, root canals, and extractions. Dental team members can also take digital x-rays and use intra-oral cameras to facilitate diagnosis and treatment or make impressions for new dentures, relines, and repairs. At the end of each day, the equipment is picked up by the truck drivers and delivered to other sites.

Challenges addressed by design professionals include providing a garage at Apple Tree's main stationary clinic facility, where the delivery vehicles and mobile dental equipment can be properly cleaned, maintained, repaired, and stored.

As programs such as this continue to grow and become more common, the community partner organizations will likely need design professionals' services to ensure that the spaces where dental care services are provided on-site are comfortable, meet the needs of the professionals providing services and the patients receiving them, and are flexible enough to be used for other purposes to maximize their utilization.

Home-Based Healthcare

Physicians' house calls used to play a major role in the delivery of healthcare services across the United States. For example, according to *American Family Physician* in 1930, approximately 40 percent of patient interactions occurred when doctors conducted house calls. By 1980, this number had plummeted to 1 percent.[24]

In recent years, that downward trend has not only ended but has been reversed. For example, a 2011 article published by the American Academy of Home Care Physicians noted an increase from 1.4 million home visits in 1999 to 2.3 million home visits in 2009 for patients covered by Medicare Part B plans. This growth was largely due to a 50 percent increase in reimbursement for home-based care services.[25]

Public leaders and healthcare industry experts predict the demand for home-based healthcare will continue growing for the following reasons:

- As the U.S. population ages, a steadily and rapidly increasing number of people will live at home with conditions or disabilities that make travel to a clinic or other healthcare facility difficult.

- Studies, such as the ones mentioned in a 2013 report by the Advisory Board Company, indicate that at-home healthcare visits had the potential to decrease hospitalization rates by more than 60 percent, thereby reducing total care costs by 25 percent.[26]

- Providing care in a familiar place makes it less stressful for patients.

- New mobile diagnostic and information technologies make it possible to deliver care in the home in ways that were not previously feasible.

As home healthcare providers become a more common and essential part of integrated care teams, there will be an increased need to provide ongoing training and in-clinic support for them. They will likely become more involved in discharge planning activities at hospitals and in follow-up strategy sessions with patients and their families at clinics.

In addition, the provision of home-based healthcare services typically requires specialized training for care providers and patients. This may lead to a need for additional education space in clinics or higher utilization of existing spaces, such as group exam and health education rooms.

Since healthcare professionals often work alone or in small groups, there may also be a need for a respite area or place where they can meet, get support and additional information, and exchange knowledge in the clinic.

■ NORTH MEMORIAL COMMUNITY PARAMEDIC PROGRAM
Robbinsdale, Minnesota

Based on the recognition that providing home-based care can be a cost-effective way to monitor the health of complex patients, North Memorial Healthcare set up a community paramedic program that uses certified community paramedics (CPs) to monitor and provide nonemergent care for patients in their homes.

This pilot project operates 12 hours a day, six days a week. The emergency paramedic/community paramedics (EMT/CPs) primarily respond to emergency calls. However, for approximately one shift per week they change uniforms and drive their own cars to visit patients as CPs.

There are no restrictions related to insurance coverage or age. To avoid duplication of services, the CPs do not call on patients who are eligible for home health nurses. The typical patient they visit is elderly and does not have a good family or social support system.

The services provided by CPs have ranged from helping patients to set up their medication schedules and connecting them with Meals on Wheels or other community services to drawing blood for a variety of purposes. They also conduct health screenings, treat wounds, and give immunizations. Each visit ranges from 30 minutes to two hours as CPs discuss the health concerns each patient has. Care providers have

found that the time spent in patients' homes can prove to be invaluable because they are better able to assess the challenges that their patients confront outside of the clinic. The goal of this program is to shift the location of care from emergency rooms to the home, where serious illness and injuries can, ideally, be prevented and chronic conditions managed effectively. The Minnesota legislature implemented a fee schedule for community paramedicine services two years ago.

■ RADIOLOGIST'S HOME OFFICE
Confidential Location

Internet access and advances in digital technology have made it possible for physicians to review diagnostic imaging and lab results, answer health-related questions, provide medical advice, and otherwise respond to patient needs and concerns from the comfort of their own home or from other locations outside of the clinic.

The client for this comfortable, functional, at-home physician's office is a radiologist who wanted a space where he could view multiple x-ray images simultaneously during telehealth consultations with other members of his collaborative care team. Since the need for the radiologist's expertise could arise at any time, day or night, and he often had to review information quickly to recommend an appropriate medical response, having the ability to work from home not only enables him to spend more time with his family and friends, but also can improve response time for patients.

The at-home office features multiple workstations and large-screen monitors so that he can view digital images (x-rays), review online information, and interact with other care team members. These equipment requirements made providing proper power and electrical distribution (with surge protection) especially important. The space is also versatile enough to be updated as work needs and technology change.

Finishes and furnishings, such as the custom built-in wood cabinetry and work surfaces, area rug, upholstered occasional chair, and wood floors, make the office feel like a natural extension of the physician's home, rather than a "clinic in a house." Large windows bring natural daylight into the office while providing views of nature and the surrounding area.

The office is connected to the master bedroom for middle-of-the-night consults, but separated from the sleeping area by a small television room/library so that there is sufficient acoustical separation between these spaces, allowing the radiologist to work at all hours without disturbing others (fig. 10-5).

FIGURE 10-5: Radiologist Home Office. This comfortable, at-home physician's office belongs to a radiologist who wanted a space where he could view multiple x-ray images simultaneously during telehealth consultations with other members of his collaborative care team. Since the need for the radiologist's expertise could arise at any time, day or night, and he often had to review information quickly to recommend an appropriate medical response, having the ability to work from home has improved response time for his patients. Reproduced by permission of Vujovich

■ SINCLAIR HOME CARE TIGERPLACE AIP PROJECT
Columbia, Missouri

This licensed home care agency was created as a department within the University of Missouri's Sinclair School of Nursing (MUSSON) to provide community-based in-home care to residents of two apartment-style senior residences: TigerPlace and Lenoir Woods.

TigerPlace residents are all 55 years of age or older and must be able to function independently. They receive basic care from the Sinclair Home Care Aging in Place (AIP) program, including routine assessments. They can pay privately for additional services they need or desire, such as personal care or medication management.

The Centers for Medicare and Medicaid (CMS) gave the university a $2 million grant to start this agency and use it to evaluate clinical outcomes for the school's AIP program. The MUSSON team developed and tested sensor networks that were installed in TigerPlace homes in 2005. This equipment included motion sensors, chair pads, a stove sensor, and a bed sensor, which were used to monitor residents' restlessness, pulse rates, and respiration rates. An integrated intelligent monitoring system developed by the MUSSON team then collected data about the residents and their home environments in a noninvasive way.

A registered nurse/care coordinator served as a primary contact for residents participating in this program. Personal care attendants and nursing staff assisted patients with daily care, as needed. The RN was also responsible for coordinating the efforts of all care team members for each patient, which can include social workers, physical therapists, and other medical specialists.

TigerPlace residents received a comprehensive health assessment by an RN at least every six months, with ongoing care coordination provided five days a week at the Wellness Center that is part of this residential development. Each patient's care plan and the services they received were entered into an electronic health record (EHR) system.

Design and healthcare professionals collaborated on the planning and creation of TigerPlace to ensure that it would be comfortable as well as functional for its residents. Faculty members from the university's Computer Engineering department also participated during the planning phase to ensure that TigerPlace's infrastructure would support the technology that was envisioned and ultimately implemented.

Challenges design professionals addressed included the following:

- Incorporating technology in a way that was transparent for residents. People generally do not like to have wires, sensors, monitors, or electrical cords cluttering up their living space. So using wireless technology and designing storage spaces in which equipment could be concealed was especially important.

- Balancing the researchers' tendency to want to put sensors everywhere with practical considerations, such as installing them in locations where they functioned properly and were easy to repair and maintain.

- Creating custom configurations to accommodate the sensing technology because the residential units at TigerPlace are not all the same size and larger apartments required more sensors.

- Determining where to locate the computer that monitors the data in each apartment. These computers were first placed on the floor behind a large piece of furniture. However, this created problems when some residents unplugged the computer to use the power outlet to which it had been connected for

other purposes. This problem was resolved by installing a storage cabinet for the computer above the refrigerator in each apartment. The cabinet had proper ventilation as well as its own power outlet and network port so that all wires and cables could be neatly concealed.

Since changes in activity patterns can indicate a potential change in a patient's health status, algorithms were set to e-mail real-time alerts to the RN care coordinator, social worker, and research team members if changes occurred that could be of concern. The care team could then use sensor data and information from the patient's EHR to determine if medical treatment was necessary.

To evaluate the impact of this program, the MUSSON team compared a group of patients living with sensors to a group of patients who were not equipped with this technology. The two patient groups had identical care coordination and care services. A statistical analysis revealed that patients with sensors functioned better than those without, when comparing metrics such as the number of ED visits, hospitalizations, and falls, as well as activity levels associated with daily living.

Summary

As technological advances have made it possible to bring care to patients when they need it most in settings that are comfortable and familiar to them, homes, schools, workplaces, and other locations where people congregate are rapidly becoming extensions of the healthcare delivery system in the United States. This outmigration of care is helping to reduce the per-capita cost of healthcare services by making preventative care more easily accessible and a part of people's everyday lives. It is also maintaining, and in many instances improving, health outcomes, the quality of care, and the overall health of formerly underserved, elderly, frail, disabled, chronically ill, or high-risk patient populations.

Although this chapter has provided an overview and examples to illustrate the design of workplace-, school-, community-, and home-based health facilities, in addition to wellness centers and destinations, the outmigration of care is also expected to have an impact on the design of some clinic facilities. Since the patient population in the United States is expected to increase substantially, it is unlikely that the number of exam rooms in conventional clinics will decrease. Rather, as mentioned in previous chapters, their utilization will likely increase and be diversified. Or, some may be retrofitted to serve as technology-equipped consult rooms. Group exam and consult rooms will likely also be used to meet a growing need to train healthcare professionals who extend the care provided by base clinics into the community, workplace, schools, or individual homes.

Jennifer Klund

Notes

1. U.S. Department of Health and Human Services, Agency for Healthcare Research and Quality, "Employer-Sponsored Health Insurance: Trends in Cost and Access," September, 2004.

2. American College of Occupational and Environmental Medicine, "The Value of Occupational and Environmental Medicine," http://www.acoem.org/ValueofOEM.aspx.

3. United States Census Bureau, "An Older and More Diverse Nation by Midcentury," August 14, 2008. http://www.census.gov/newsroom/releases/archives/population/cb08-123.html.

4. Genetics Home Reference, "What Is Pharmacogenomics?", http://ghr.hlm.nih.gov/handbook/genomicresearch/pharmacogenomics.

5. Pall Corporation, "Frequently Asked Questions: Cell Therapy and Regenerative Medicine," http://www.pall.com/main/medical/frequently-asked-questions-cell-therapy-38848.page#38850.

6. Central Indiana Community Foundation, "Baby Boom Becomes Silver Tsunami," October 9, 2012, http://www.cicf.org/cicf-news/2012/October/baby-boom-becomes-silver-tsunami.

7. Centers for Disease Control and Prevention, *The State of Aging and Health in America 2013* (Atlanta, GA: Centers for Disease Control and Prevention, U.S. Department of Health and Human Services, 2013), http://www.cdc.gov/features/agingandhealth/state_of_aging_and_health_in_america_2013.pdf.

8. Centers for Disease Control and Prevention, "Chronic Disease Prevention and Health Promotion," ast modified May 21, 2014, http://www.cdc.gov/chronicdisease

9. United States Department of Veterans Affairs, "My HealtheVet," January 25, 2013, https://www.myhealth.va.gov/index.html.

10. How's Your Health, 2014, http://www.howsyourhealth.org/.

11. "Get care the way you want it, when you need it," https:www.healthpartners.com/public/care/get-care-now.

12. "Zipnosis," https://zipnosis.com.

13. SoloHealth, "Solohealth Station," https://solohealth.com/products/solohealth-station/.

14. "Telestroke," ClevelandClinic.org.

15. "Stroke Telemedicine," Mayo Clinic.org.

16. U.S. Department of Health and Human Services, "School-Based Health Centers," http://www.hrsa.gov/ourstories/schoolhealthcenters/.

17. American Cancer Society Action Network, "New Federal Rating Rules," http://www.acscan.org/pdf/healthcare/implementation/background/NewFederalRatingRules.pdf.

18. Independence at Home, "What Is the Independence at Home Act?" http://www.iahnow.com/IAHlegislation.htm.

19. Susannah Fox, "Peer-to-Peer Health Care" Pew Research Internet Project, February 28, 2011.

20. Adam Darkins, "Care Coordination/Home Telehealth: The Systematic Implementation of Health Informatics, Home Telehealth, and Disease Management to Support the Care of Veteran Patients with Chronic Conditions," *Telemedicine Journal and e-Health* 14 (2008): 1118–26.

21. Ibid.

22. Kathryn Mayer, "Is the Workplace Health Clinic the New Health Care Fix?" *BenefitsPro*, April 26, 2013.

23. "YMCA Mission," YMCA.org.

24. Brian K. Unwin and Paul E. Tatum, "House Calls," *American Family Physician* 83 (2011): 925–31.

25. Ibid.

26. The Advisory Board Company, "The House Call Is Making a Comeback," September 10, 2013.

Select Bibliography

Burris, James F. "VA Responds to the Needs of Aging Veterans." Health Services Research & Development Service, April 2008.

Centers for Disease Control and Prevention. *The State of Aging and Health in America 2013*. Atlanta, GA: Centers for Disease Control and Prevention, U.S. Dept of Health and Human Services, 2013.

Darkins, Adam. "Care Coordination/Home Telehealth: The Systematic Implementation of Health Informatics, Home Telehealth, and Disease Management to Support the Care of Veteran Patients with Chronic Conditions." *Telemedicine Journal and e-Health* 14 (2008): 1118–26.

Davies, Stephen. "10 Sensor Innovations Driving the Digital Health Revolution." *Bionicly*, March 6, 2013.

"Employer-Sponsored Health Insurance: Trends in Cost and Access." Agency for Healthcare Research and Quality (Sept. 2004): 1–12.

Fox, Susannah. "Peer-to-Peer Health Care." Pew Research Internet Project, February 28, 2011.

U.S. Department of Health and Human Services, n.d. "The Affordable Care Act and Health Centers."

U.S. Department of Health and Human Services. Agency for Healthcare Research and Quality. "Employer-Sponsored Health Insurance: Trends in Cost and Access." September 2004. http://archive.ahrq.gov/research/findings/factsheets/costs/empspria/empfig1.html.

Afterword
Planning for a Flexible Future

Clinics likely will not disappear, but the basic concept of clinics will evolve as technology, reimbursements, and patient needs evolve.

Healthcare providers will continue to find innovative ways to provide services for patients at home, work, on vacation, or at other convenient locations remote from the clinic.

Communications technology certainly is paving the way with tablets, apps, and other wireless devices yet to be imagined. Online video sessions with caregivers will become the norm, eliminating the need for most in-person visits. Workplaces, pharmacies, retail stores, malls, and libraries will become community "ports," where vitals can be taken and then digitally transmitted via mobile device. This is already happening, but newer and better software applications will make it even easier and more common.

Technology will not completely replace the need for human interaction, of course, but it will be a driving force behind positive change in the healthcare industry.

The Clinic Visit in the Future

Clinics will be flexible and adaptable, enabling the exam, procedure, treatment, and diagnostic modules to be reconfigured within a universal care platform. Procedures will be less invasive and primarily conducted on an outpatient basis, thanks to constantly advancing medical technology.

When patients arrive at a clinic, they will swipe an identification card carrying their insurance, health history, and other pertinent information to expedite their visit.

The movement toward wellness and preventative care certainly will accelerate as incentives to lower healthcare costs increase. The checkout process will include information about self-care, follow-up appointments and tests, and ongoing monitoring. Care providers may then suggest a home remedy, recommend additional monitoring, or advise patients to travel to a specialty clinic. When an anomaly occurs, patients will be asked to obtain further diagnostic tests and transmit the results before their next visit.

Minimizing Future Shock

With flexibility and adaptability as key design considerations, the most successful clinics will address the increasing cycles of change. Alvin Toffler wrote *Future Shock* in 1970 to describe the psychological impact of absorbing too much change too quickly. We live in future shock every day. The role of the healthcare designer is to partner with healthcare providers to lessen the shock so that the future manifests a better healthcare delivery process.

CHRISTINE GUZZO VICKERY, GARY NYBERG, AND DOUGLAS WHITEAKER

Select Bibliography

Advisory Board Company. "Walmart's New Plan: 'Full Primary Care Services' Within Seven Years." January 14, 2013.

Almquist, Julka R., Caroline Kelly, Joyce Bromberg, Sandra C. Bryant, Teresa J. H. Christianson, and Victor M. Montori. "Consultation Room Design and the Clinical Encounter." *Health Environments Research & Design Journal* 3 (2009): 41–78.

American College of Physicians. *The Advanced Medical Home: A Patient-Centered, Physician-Guided Model of Healthcare.* Philadelphia: American College of Physicians, 2005. http://www.acponline.org/advocacy/current_policy_papers/assets/adv_med.pdf.

American Hospital Association, Committee on Research. *Patient-Centered Medical Home: AHA Research Synthesis Report.* Chicago: American Hospital Association, 2010. http://www.aha.org/research/cor/content/patient-centered-medical-home.pdf.

Americans with Disabilities Act of 1990. P.L. 110-325. http://www.ada.gov/pubs/ada.htm.

Annenberg Classroom. "Health Care Timeline." n.d. http://www.annenbergclassroom.org/Files/Documents/Timelines/HealthCare.pdf.

Beryl Institute. "Defining Patient Experience." http://www.theberylinstitute.org/?page=DefiningPatientExp.

Brown, Jack, Fred Doloresco III, and Joseph M. Mylotte. "Never Events: Not Every Hospital-Acquired Infection Is Preventable." *Clinical Infectious Diseases* 49 (2009): 743–46.

Burris, James F. "VA Responds to the Needs of Aging Veterans." Health Services Research & Development Service, April 2008.

Buxbaum, Jason, Neva Kaye, and Mary Takach. *Building Medical Homes: Lessons from Eight States with Emerging Programs.* New York: Commonwealth Fund, 2011. http://www.commonwealthfund.org/~/media/Files/Publications/Fund%20Report/2011/Dec/1569_Kaye_building_medical_homes_v2.pdf.

Center for Health Design. "Pebble Project." https://www.healthdesign.org/pebble.

Centers for Disease Control and Prevention. *The State of Aging and Health in America 2013.* Atlanta, GA: Centers for Disease Control and Prevention, U.S. Dept of Health and Human Services, 2013.

Centers for Medicare & Medicaid Services. "HCAHPS: Patients' Perspectives of Care Survey." 2013. http://www.cms.gov/Medicare/Quality-Initiatives-Patient-Assessment-Instruments/HospitalQualityInits/HospitalHCAHPS.html.

Committee on Quality of Health Care in America. *Crossing the Quality Chasm: New Health System for the 21st Century.* Washington, DC: National Academies Press: 2001. http://www.iom.edu/~/media/Files/Report%20Files/2001/Crossing-the-Quality-Chasm/Quality%20Chasm%202001%20%20report%20brief.pdf.

Convenient Care Association. http://www.ccaclinics.org.

CVS Caremark Corporation. "About MinuteClinic." n.d. http://www.minuteclinic.com/about.

Cwiek, Katherine, Jennifer Etkin, Craig Holm, George Karageorgiou, and Elisabeth Meinert. *Primary Care in an Era of Health Care Reform: Strategies for Reorienting the Health Care Delivery System Toward Primary Care.* Philadelphia: Health Strategies and Solutions, Inc., 2012.

Darkins, Adam. "Care Coordination/Home Telehealth: The Systematic Implementation of Health Informatics, Home Telehealth, and Disease Management to Support the Care of Veteran Patients with Chronic Conditions." *Telemedicine Journal and e-Health* 14 (2008): 1118–26.

Davies, Stephen. "10 Sensor Innovations Driving the Digital Health Revolution." *Bionicly,* March 6, 2013.

Deloitte Center for Health Solutions. "Center for Health Solutions." http://www.deloitte.com/view/en_US/us/Insights/centers/center-for-health-solutions.

———. "Health Care Retail Clinics Continue Gradual Expansion Through 2012: Deloitte Center for Health Solutions Report." November 16, 2009. http://www.deloitte.com/view/en_US/us/Industries/US-federal-government/center-for-health-solutions/6fa41d3b16de4210VgnVCM100000ba42f00aRCRD.htm.

Dolan, Pamela Lewis. "AMA Meeting: Delegates Seek More Oversight of Retail Clinics." *American Medical Association.* July 16, 2007. http://www.amednews.com/article/20070716/profession/307169973/2.

Durbin, Dick. "Health Care Reform Implementation Timeline." n.d. http://www.durbin.senate.gov/public/index.cfm/health-care-reform-implementation-timeline.

Facility Guidelines Institute. *Guidelines for Design and Construction of Health Care Facilities.* Chicago: ASHE, 2010.

Fox, Susannah. "Peer-to-Peer Health Care." Pew Research Internet Project, February 28, 2011.

Freihoefer, Kara, Gary Nyberg, and Christine Vickery. "Clinic Exam Room Design: Present and Future, Abstract." *Health Environments Research & Design Journal* 6 (2013): 138–56.

"Future of Family Medicine Project." *Annals of Family Medicine* 2, no. 1 (2004). http://www.ncbi.nlm.nih.gov/pubmed/15080220.

Green Guide for Health Care. "Who We Are." n.d. http://www.gghc.org/about.whoweare.overview.php

HealthStream. "CG-CAHPS Is Coming...Are You Prepared?" http://info.healthstream.com/cg-cahps-sem?component=70130000000lEvY&product=CG-CAHPS&gclid=CN7n-9PF_roCFYNaMgodTlcA4w.

Herrick, Devon. "Retail Clinics: Convenient and Affordable Care." National Center for Policy Analysis. January 14, 2010. http://www.ncpa.org/pdfs/ba686.pdf.

"Joint Principles of the Patient-Centered Medical Home." Patient Centered Primary Care Collaborative. February 2007. http://www.aafp.org/dam/AAFP/documents/practice_management/pcmh/initiatives/PCMHJoint.pdf.

Keckley, Paul H., Howard R. Underwood, and Malay Gandhi. "Retail Clinics: Facts, Trends, and Implications." Deloitte Center for Health Solutions, 2008. http://www.deloitte.com/assets/Dcom-UnitedStates/Local%20Assets/Documents/us_chs_RetailClinics_230708(1).pdf.

Keller, Amy, Anjali Joseph, Ellen Taylor, Xiaobo Quan, and Callie Unruh. *Promising Practices in Safety-Net Clinic Design: An Overview.* Oakland, CA: California HeathCare Foundation, 2011.

Laws, Margaret. "The Emergence of Retail-Based Clinics in the United States: Early Observations." *Health Affairs* 27 (2008): 1293–98.

Liker, Jeffrey. *The Toyota Way: 14 Management Principles from the World's Greatest Manufacturer.* New York: McGraw-Hill, 2004.

Malone, Eileen, Julie R. Mann-Dooks, and Joseph Strauss. *Evidence-Based Design: Application in the MHS.* Falls Church, VA: U.S. Army Health Facility Planning Agency, Planning & Programming Division, 2007.

Maryland State Medical Society. "Retail Clinics." House of Delegates CL Report 2-09. 2009. http://www.medchi.org/sites/default/files/CL%20Report%202-09%20-%20Retail%20Clinics%20FINAL.pdf.

"Medical Home Recognition & Accreditation Programs." National Center for Medical Home Implementation, n.d. http://www.medicalhomeinfo.org/national/recognition_programs.aspx

National Committee for Quality Assurance. "NCQA's Physician Practice Connection: Patient-Centered Medical Home Program." National Committee for Quality Assurance. http://www.ncqa.org/portals/0/public%20policy/PCMH_Policy_Fact_Sheet.pdf.

———. NCQA PCMH Expert Certification Program. http://www.ncqa.org/Educational Events/SeminarsandWebinars/PCMHContentExpert Certification.aspx?gclid=CNHQ94;JyMACFaY-Mgodz10AJg .

Page, Ann, ed. *Keeping Patients Safe: Transforming the Work Environment of Nurses.* Washington, DC: National Academies Press, 2004.

Palmer, Karen. "A Brief History: Universal Health Care Efforts in the U.S." Physicians for a National Health Program. 1999. http://www.pnhp.org/facts/a-brief-history-universal-health-care-efforts-in-the-us.

"The Patient-Centered Medical Home: Moving to a New Level of Performance Through Automation." Phytel White Paper, 2011.

Rand Health. "Health Care on Aisle 7: The Growing Phenomenon of Retail Clinics." Rand Corporation, 2010. http://www.rand.org/content/dam/rand/pubs/research_briefs/2010/RAND_RB9491-1.pdf.

Schmidt III, Robert, Toru Eguchi, Simon Austin, and Alistair Gibb. "What Is the Meaning of Adaptability in the Building Industry?" Paper presented at the CIB 16th International Conference, Bilbao, Spain, May 17–19, 2010.

Shojania, Keveh G., Bradford W. Duncan, Kathryn M. McDonald, and Robert M. Wachter. *Making Health Care Safer: A Critical Analysis of Patient Safety Practices.* Rockville, MD: Agency for Healthcare Research and Quality, 2001.

Shortliffe, Edward H., and Marsden S. Blois. *The Computer Meets Medicine and Biology: Emergence of a Discipline.* Bethesda, MD: American Medical Informatics Association, 2006.

Sutter Express Care Clinics. http://www.sutterexpresscare.com.

Takach, Mary, and Kathy Witgert. *Analysis of State Regulations and Policies Governing the Operation and Licensure of Retail Clinics.* Washington, DC: National Academy of State Health Policy, 2009. http://nashp.org/sites/default/files/RetailClinics.pdf?q=files/RetailClinics.pdf.

"Timeline: History of Health Reform in the U.S." Kaiser Family Foundation. n.d. http://
  kaiserfamilyfoundation.files.wordpress.com/2011/03/5-02-13-history-of-health-reform.pdf.

"Typhoid Mary Mystery May Have Been Solved at Last, Scientists Say." *Huffington Post,* August 17, 2013.
  http://www.huffingtonpost.com/2013/08/17/typhoid-mary-mystery-solved_n_3762822.html.

Ulrich, Roger S. "View Through a Window May Influence Recovery from Surgery." *Science* 224 (1984):
  420–22.

U.S. Department of Health and Human Services. n.d. "The Affordable Care Act and Health Centers."

U.S. Department of Health and Human Services, Agency for Healthcare Research and Quality.
  "Employer-Sponsored Health Insurance: Trends in Cost and Access." September, 2004.

———. "Patient Centered Medical Home." http://www.ahrq.gov/professionals/systems/primary-care/
  pcmh.

Walgreen's Healthcare Clinics. http://www.walgreen's.com/topic/pharmacy/healthcare-clinic.jsp.

"What Is the Difference Between a Medical Home and an ACO?" Accountable Care Facts. n.d. http://www
  .accountablecarefacts.org/topten/what-is-the-difference-between-a-medical-home-and-an-aco-1.

Worth, Judy. *Perfecting Patient Journeys.* Cambridge, MA: Lean Enterprise Institute, 2012.

Contributors

Editors

Christine Guzzo Vickery, CID, EDAC

Christine is Vice President and Senior Interior Designer with HGA Architects and Engineers, where she partners with national healthcare systems to design thoughtful, research-based interiors that promote operational efficiencies and patient well-being. She leads HGA's Healthcare Research Collaborative, an interdisciplinary, firm-wide initiative that promotes and publishes evidence-based design research. She additionally speaks at national healthcare conferences, contributes regularly to industry journals, and writes a monthly blog for *Healthcare Design* magazine. She has a bachelor of arts from the University of Iowa.

Gary Nyberg, RA

Gary is a retired Healthcare Principal of HGA Architects and Engineers, where he specialized in medical planning, master planning, and design for more than 30 years. Throughout his career, he served as an informed advisor to healthcare clients on demographic, financial, and technological changes impacting the healthcare industry. He continues to research evolving changes in healthcare delivery processes. He has a bachelor of architecture from the University of Minnesota.

Douglas Whiteaker, AIA

Douglas is a Healthcare Principal and Project Manager with HGA Architects and Engineers, where he focuses on healthcare planning and sustainable design. He additionally taught sustainable design at Cosumnes River College in Sacramento, California, and has led Architect Registration Exam (ARE) prep seminars. He has a master of architecture from the University of Nebraska–Lincoln, and a bachelor of science in advanced technical science in architecture from Southern Illinois University–Carbondale.

Contributing Author

Heather Beal, MA

Heather has written about the built environment for 25 years. She earned a bachelor of arts (economics) from Carleton College and a master of arts (journalism) from the University of Minnesota. In addition to writing magazine articles and columns, she was a contributing author for *100 Places+1* and *Works of ART* and the contributing editor for *Design and Dignity*. She is a member of Kappa Tau Alpha and Phi Kappa Phi.

Content Contributors

Amy Douma, AIA, LEED AP

An award-winning designer, Amy brings an innovative approach to the complex needs of healthcare facilities. Her work has received over two dozen national and regional design awards, including honors from AIA/Modern Healthcare, *Healthcare Design* magazine, and *Contract* magazine. An advocate for design innovation, Amy speaks and writes frequently on emerging technologies and their role in healthcare design. She has a bachelor of architecture from Iowa State University and a master's from Harvard University's Graduate School of Design.

Len Kaiser

Len Kaiser is the Director of Network Management for HealthEast Care System, located in St. Paul, Minnesota. He has 25 years of experience working with healthcare systems in roles ranging from operations leadership and business development to healthcare reform. He has led the development of over 15 ambulatory facilities that incorporate Lean concepts into the design process. As a liaison between users and developers, designers, and contractors, he facilitates spaces that create an optimal patient, staff, and provider experience. Len attended the University of Wisconsin–River Falls.

Jennifer Klund, AIA, ACHA

Jennifer Klund, AIA, ACHA, is a healthcare principal specializing in medical planning and design. As principal, she leads multidisciplinary design teams to research and plan sustainable, operationally efficient healthcare facilities, both locally and nationally. She is currently serving on the board of the American College of Healthcare Architects and the Health Care Institute Midwest Chapter. Jennifer has a bachelor of architecture from North Dakota State University and a master of architecture from Notre Dame.

Brent Peterson, PE

Brent applies Lean product development and production principles to the design of healthcare, manufacturing, and service facilities. He leads multidisciplinary teams to define and evaluate the customer needs of today with a predictive eye toward the future. He uses the tools of the production preparation process (3P), including value-stream mapping, Gemba walks, mock-ups, and simulation, connecting people with process, technology, and the physical environment to achieve high-performing solutions. He received his bachelor of science in industrial engineering from the University of Iowa.

Jennifer Romer

Jennifer is a Senior Project Manager for Medical Planning at Stanford Health Care with experience working with users and employing Lean principles to create buildings with an environmental focus and guiding principles of patient safety, family-centered care and operational efficiency. Her experience includes the new 824,000-square-foot Stanford Hospital and the 521,000-square-foot expansion of the Lucile Packard Children's Hospital, Palo Alto, California. Jennifer received her bachelor of science in nursing from the University of Florida.

Index

in exam rooms, 167–169
healthcare reform, 230
and medical home model, 260–264
and need for flexible, adaptable building design, 93–99
and outmigration of care, 284–290
ownership, 232
and patient experience, 22–28
and retail clinics, 230–232
Triage, 2, 131–132
Truman, Harry, 208, 209
Two-dimensional representations, 74–76

U

Ulrich, Roger, 2, 215, 216
Unevenness (mura), 56–67
United Health District Winnebago Treatment Center (Winnebago, Minnesota), 25, 26
U.S. Public Health Service (USPHS), 205–208
Universal accessibility, 139–141
    bariatric-ready/universally accessible exam rooms, 189, 190
    of exam rooms, 177–178
Universal building layouts, 112, 113, 117, 118
Universal exam rooms, 114, 184
University of Michigan Trauma and Burn Center, 221
University of Minnesota, 13
University of Minnesota Physicians (UMP), 13
University of Minnesota Physicians (UMP) Mill City Clinic (Minneapolis, Minnesota), 35, 177, 178
University of Missouri Sinclair School of Nursing (MUSSON), 305
Unnecessary transportation, 59
UPlan Medical Program, 2
Uplighting, 10
Urology Clinic (Lean project), 63
Utilization, 94, 180

V

Value, 53, 54, 63
Value-stream mapping, 62–63
Verde Valley Medical Center (VVMC, Sedona and Cottonwood, Arizona), 86–88

Vermont reform laws, 217
Vestibules, 37–39
Veteran care, 285–286
Veterans Administration (VA), 203, 285
Veterans Health Administration (VHA), 290
Veterans Millennium Healthcare and Benefits Act of 1999, 285
Via Christi Health, 300
Views, 29, 41
Virtua Health and Wellness Center (Washington Township, New Jersey), 292–293
Virtual mock-ups, 81–84
Virtual Reality Design Lab, University of Minnesota, 81, 82
VirtuWell, 237
Visibility:
    assessing, 7–12
    of retail clinics, 234–236
Visualization tools, 73–90
    computer-based models/simulations, 85–86
    mock-ups, 75, 77–85
    project examples, 86–89
    three-dimensional representations, 75–77
    two-dimensional representations, 74–76
Visual privacy, 173–176
Voice of the customer, 61–62

W

Waiting, 57–58
Wald, Lillian, 204
Walgreens, 228, 232
Walgreens Healthcare Clinics, 242
Wall finishes, 138
Walmart Primary Care Clinics (nationwide), 249–250
Warren Medical Office Campus (Tulsa, Oklahoma), 3–4, 149–151
Waste (Lean Design), 56–60
Water features, 41–42
Watts Healthcare Corporation (WHCC), 297
Wayfinding, 31–33, 141–150
    and architecture, 32, 33, 145–147
    and comfort of patients/visitors, 31–33
    connection to other structures, 149–150
    and demographics, 141–142